Bayesian Nets and Causality

Bayesian Nets and Causality

Philosophical and Computational Foundations

Jon Williamson

OXFORD
UNIVERSITY PRESS

OXFORD
UNIVERSITY PRESS

Great Clarendon Street, Oxford OX2 6DP

Oxford University Press is a department of the University of Oxford.
It furthers the University's objective of excellence in research, scholarship,
and education by publishing worldwide in

Oxford New York

Auckland Bangkok Buenos Aires Cape Town Chennai
Dar es Salaam Delhi Hong Kong Istanbul Karachi Kolkata
Kuala Lumpur Madrid Melbourne Mexico City Mumbai
Nairobi São Paulo Shanghai Taipei Tokyo Toronto

Oxford is a registered trade mark of Oxford University Press
in the UK and in certain other countries

Published in the United States
by Oxford University Press Inc., New York

First published 2005

A catalogue record for this title is available from the British Library

Library of Congress Cataloging in Publication Data
(Data available)

ISBN 0 19 853079 X

1 3 5 7 9 10 8 6 4 2

Typeset by Author using LaTeX
Printed in Great Britain
on acid-free paper by
Biddles Ltd., Kings Lynn, Norfolk

PREFACE

How should we reason with causal relationships? Much recent work on this question has been devoted to the theses (i) that Bayesian nets provide a calculus for causal reasoning and (ii) that we can learn causal relationships by the automated learning of Bayesian nets from observational data. The aim of this book is to present coherent foundations for such work.

After an overview of the book in Chapter 1, Chapter 2 provides an introduction to probability and its interpretations. Chapter 3 introduces Bayesian nets and Chapter 4 discusses the problems that beset current proposals for their use in causal reasoning. This book presents new foundations for Bayesian nets based on the objective Bayesian interpretation of probability, according to which probabilities represent the degrees of belief that an agent ought to adopt (Chapter 5). This interpretation leads naturally to a two-stage methodology for constructing Bayesian nets, where one first appeals to causal knowledge to generate a Bayesian net and then refines this net in the light of new information (Chapter 6).

At this point, the book turns to the nature of causality and the problem of discovering causal relationships. Chapter 7 introduces current theories of causality. A range of proposals for discovering causal relationships are presented in Chapter 8. Then Chapter 9 develops epistemic causality, the view that causal relationships are purely a mental device to aid reasoning about the world, and do not exist as physical relations in the world. Such a view fits well with the objective Bayesian interpretation of probability, and forms the basis of a new approach to learning causal relationships using Bayesian nets.

The resulting framework for causal reasoning admits a number of extensions. Reasoning about nested causal relationships requires an extension to recursive Bayesian nets (Chapter 10). Logical relationships can be treated analogously to causal relationships and a general framework can be produced for reasoning about both (Chapter 11). Finally the framework is extended in Chapter 12 to cope with changes in the language an agent uses to speak about causality.

ACKNOWLEDGEMENTS

I am hugely indebted to Donald Gillies, whose constructive criticism has helped hone my ideas over the course of the last decade, and whose insights no doubt permeate this book.

I am also very grateful to the following for comments and fruitful discussions: David Corfield, Dov Gabbay, Stephan Hartmann, Colin Howson, and Jeff Paris.

I would like to thank Nancy Cartwright, Julian Reiss, Elliott Sober, John Worrall and all participants of the Causality Seminar at the London School of Economics from 2000 to 2004 for providing a very stimulating environment in which to discuss Bayesian nets and causality. Thanks too to the Philosophy Department at King's College London who were guinea pigs for material in this book, to the British Academy and the UK Arts and Humanities Research Board for partly funding this research, and to Alison Jones and Carol Bestley at Oxford University Press for their help and expertise in publishing this book.

Material in §§3.7 and 3.8 appeared in Williamson (2000*a*,*b*). Many thanks to Dr. Rana Conway for the nutrition and pregnancy database described in §3.8. Some of the material in Chapters 3 and 4 was originally presented in Williamson (2001*b*) and is reproduced with kind permission of Kluwer Academic Publishers. Techniques in Chapter 5 for maximising entropy efficiently appeared in Williamson (2002*a*). Chapter 10 is based on a paper with Dov Gabbay, Williamson and Gabbay (2004), and appears with kind permission of King's College Publications. Chapter 11 is based on Williamson (2001*a*, 2002*b*); the latter appears with kind permission of Elsevier. Chapter 12 is a development of Williamson (2003*b*); material from that paper appears with kind permission of Kluwer Academic Publishers.

Last but most, I thank Kika Williamson for shrewd audience and boundless support.

CONTENTS

1

INTRODUCTION

Before diving into the computational and philosophical details, I shall describe the central claims of the book from a broad perspective. Jargon will be explained in due course.

1.1 Philosophical Claims

From a philosophical point of view, this book explores the ontology and epistemology of two concepts central to science: probability and causality.

I argue in favour of a particular interpretation of probability, objective Bayesianism, in Chapter 5. This interpretation holds that probabilities are an agent's rational degrees of belief (and so are mental entities) and these degrees of belief are fixed as a function of the agent's background knowledge (and so are objective). The main tenets of objective Bayesianism—calibration of degrees of belief with objective chances and the application of the Maximum Entropy Principle—are introduced and defended and I present some responses to criticisms of objective Bayesianism. In particular I discuss criticism of the computational complexity of objective Bayesianism, criticism of its ability to handle causal knowledge, and (in Chapter 12) criticism of its lack of language invariance. In Chapter 11 I show that objective Bayesianism can be used to provide a practical semantics for probabilistic logic and, in Chapter 12, that it offers a natural means of handling changes in degrees of belief as an agent's language changes.

The book offers a critique of notions of causality that appeal to the Causal Markov Condition. I argue in Chapter 4 that the condition fails under most interpretations of probability and causality. However, under the objective Bayesian interpretation of probability the Causal Markov Condition does hold as a default rule (§6.1). In Chapter 9, I develop an epistemic view of causality, whereby causal relations, though objective, are part of an agent's epistemic state. This view fits well with the objective Bayesian interpretation of probability and can be used as a foundation for a new account of discovering causal relationships, a synthesis of a Popperian hypothetico-deductive approach and the Baconian inductive approaches currently popular in artificial intelligence. In Chapter 10 I argue that causal models need to be extended to handle recursive causal relationships and offer a framework for doing so. I stress an analogy between causal and logical influence in Chapter 11 to argue that logical knowledge can be handled in parallel with causal knowledge using the techniques presented in this book.

The philosophical positions advocated in this book, objective Bayesianism and epistemic causality, are part of a coherent scientific outlook: one in which the entities of science (probability and causality in this case) are neither physical, mind-independent features of the world, nor arbitrary, subjective entities, varying from individual to individual. By treating probability and causality as mental notions we avoid problems that arise when we try to project them onto the physical world, escaping what Edwin Jaynes called the mind projection fallacy:

> Common language—or, a least, the English language—has an almost universal tendency to disguise epistemological statements by putting them into a grammatical form which suggests to the unwary an ontological statement. A major source of error in current probability theory arises from an unthinking failure to perceive this. To interpret the first kind of statement in the ontological sense is to assert that one's own private thoughts and sensations are realities existing externally in Nature. We call this the 'mind projection fallacy', and note the trouble it causes many times in what follows. But this trouble is hardly confined to probability theory; as soon as it is pointed out, it becomes evident that much of the discourse of philosophers and Gestalt psychologists, and the attempt of physicists to explain quantum theory, are reduced to nonsense by the author falling repeatedly into the mind projection fallacy.[1]

1.2 Computational Claims

From a computational point of view, this book investigates the relationship between Bayesian nets and maximum entropy methods.

In Chapter 3, I argue that the problem of constructing Bayesian nets can be construed as the most basic computational problem connected with Bayesian nets. I present three techniques for constructing Bayesian nets. One that performs well in practice and is easy to justify simply involves repeatedly adding arrows to construct the graph in the net (Chapter 3). While this adding-arrows algorithm fits a machine learning methodology, the second technique is based on knowledge elicitation: a Bayesian net is constructed around a causal graph provided by an expert (Chapter 4). This strategy is harder to justify but can be viewed as a special case of a third technique, namely an algorithm for constructing a Bayesian net from a maximum entropy probability function (Chapter 5). Under this approach a Bayesian net is constructed to represent the degrees of belief that an agent ought to adopt on the basis of given causal and probabilistic background knowledge. A technique for updating these nets is given in §12.11, and an extension of the technique to cope with dynamic domains is advocated in §12.13.

The maximum entropy approach justifies the creation of a Bayesian net around a causal graph as the first step of a two-stage methodology (Chapter 6). The second step involves improving the fit between the causal net and a target probability function by applying the adding-arrows algorithm.

There are a number of computational techniques for inducing a causal model from a database (Chapter 8), many of which output a minimal Bayesian net that best represents the distribution of the data. While this approach is flawed as a

[1](Jaynes, 2003, p. 22)

general strategy, in Chapter 9 I put forward a procedure for generating a causal graph representing the causal beliefs that an agent ought to adopt on the basis of the knowledge embodied in the database, and show that in certain circumstances this general approach will yield minimal Bayesian nets.

In Chapter 10, I show how Bayesian nets can be extended to cope with recursive causal relationships. These recursive Bayesian nets may be applied in the automation of logical reasoning, as shown in Chapter 11, where we also see that Bayesian nets can be used to decide entailment in probabilistic logic.

While the subject matter of this book can look radically different from the computational and philosophical points of view, the subject matter is the same. I hope the book demonstrates the benefits that can accrue from pursuing an integrated investigation.

2

PROBABILITY

For a treatment of Bayesian nets and causality we will not require the full apparatus of the mathematical theory of probability—we can stick to the simple framework of probability functions as defined over finite domains of variables. This chapter begins with an introduction to this framework (§§2.1 and 2.2), followed by a brief survey of the major philosophical interpretations of probability.

2.1 Variables

A probability function will be defined relative to a set V of variables. V will always be assumed to be finite, and we shall use upper-case letters for variables. Each variable $A \in V$ is capable of taking any of a finite number $||A||$ of values. An assignment of a particular value to a variable is denoted by the corresponding lower-case letter. We shall write $a@A$ to assert that a is an assignment to A.

For example $V = \{A, B\}$ is a domain of variables, where A signifies *age of vehicle* taking possible values *less than 3 years*, *3–10 years*, and *greater than 10 years*, and B signifies *breakdown in the last year* taking possible values *yes* and *no*. Here $||A|| = 3$ and $||B|| = 2$. An assignment $b@B$ is of the form $B = yes$ or $B = no$. The assignments $a@A$ are most naturally written $A < 3, 3 \leq A \leq 10$, and $A > 10$.

An assignment u to a subset $U \subseteq V$ of variables is a conjunction of assignments to each of the variables in U. For example, if $U = \{A, B, C\} \subseteq V$ then an assignment $u@U$ is of the form abc where $a@A, b@B$, and $c@C$. For a variable $A \in U \subseteq V$ and $u@U$, we shall denote by a^u the assignment to A induced by u. Likewise if $T \subseteq U \subseteq V$ then t^u is the assignment to T induced by u. Assignment $u@U$ is *consistent* with assignment $t@T$, written $u \sim t$, if u and t agree on $U \cap T$. We will use $|U|$ to refer to the number of variables in U and $||U||$ to refer to the number of assignments to U. Thus $||U|| = \prod_{A_i \in U} ||A_i||$.

Suppose, continuing our example, that $a@A$ is $A < 3$ and $b@B$ is $B = no$. Then ab, which may be written $A < 3 \cdot B = no$, is an assignment to V. On the other hand if $v@V$ is $A < 3 \cdot B = no$ then a^v is just the assignment $A < 3$.

To avoid a lot of superscripting we shall adopt the following convention. If an assignment occurring in an expression has not been explicitly defined, it is assumed to be induced by the nearest more general assignment to its left. Thus, e.g., 'for all $v@V, p(v) = p(a|bc)$' is short for 'for all $v@V, p(v) = p(a^v|b^v c^v)$'. Similarly if $A, B \in U \subseteq V$ then '$\sum_{v@V} p(u) \log p(a|b)$' is short for '$\sum_{v@V} p(u^v) \log p(a^{u^v} | b^{u^v})$'.

The set of variables in V but not in $U \subseteq V$ is written $V \backslash U$ or simply $\overline{U}$.

2.2 Probability Functions

A *probability function* on V is a function p that maps each assignment $v@V$ to a non-negative real number and which satisfies *additivity*:

$$\sum_{v@V} p(v) = 1.$$

This restriction forces each probability $p(v)$ to lie in the unit interval $[0,1]$.

The *marginal probability function* on $U \subseteq V$ induced by probability function p on V is a probability function q on U which satisfies:

$$q(u) = \sum_{v@V, v\sim u} p(v)$$

for each $u@U$. The marginal probability function q on U is uniquely determined by p. Marginal probability functions are usually thought of as extensions of p and denoted by the same letter p. Thus p can be construed as a function that maps each $u@U \subseteq V$ to a non-negative real number. p can be further extended to assign numbers to conjunctions tu of assignments where $t@T \subseteq V, u@U \subseteq V$: if $t \sim u$ then tu is an assignment to $T \cup U$ and $p(tu)$ is the marginal probability awarded to $tu@(T \cup U)$; if $t \not\sim u$ then $p(tu)$ is taken to be 0.

A *conditional probability function* induced by p is a function r from pairs of assignments of subsets of V to non-negative real numbers, which satisfies (for each $t@T \subseteq V, u@U \subseteq V$):

$$r(t|u)p(u) = p(tu),$$

$$\sum_{t@T} r(t|u) = 1,$$

Note that $r(t|u)$ is not uniquely determined by p when $p(u) = 0$. If $p(u) \neq 0$ and the first condition holds, then the second condition, $\sum_{t@T} r(t|u) = 1$, also holds. Again, r is often thought of as an extension of p and is usually denoted by the same letter p.

Thus p maps conjunctions of assignments to subsets of V, or pairs thereof, to non-negative real numbers. Given some fixed ordering of assignments $v@V$, each probability function p on V can be represented by a vector of parameters $x = (x^v)_{v@V}$ such that each $x^v \in [0,1]$ and $\sum_{v@V} x^v = 1$, by setting $p(v) = x^v$ for each v. The space of probability functions corresponds accordingly to the space

$$\mathbb{P} = \{x \in [0,1]^{||V||} : \sum_{v@V} x^v = 1\}.$$

Take the example $V = \{A, B\}$ of the last section. According to the above definition a probability function p on V assigns a non-negative real number to each assignment of the form ab where $a@A$ and $b@B$, and these numbers must sum to 1. For instance,

$$p(A < 3 \cdot B = yes) = 0.05$$

$$p(A < 3 \cdot B = no) = 0.1$$

$$p(3 \le A \le 10 \cdot B = yes) = 0.2$$

$$p(3 \le A \le 10 \cdot B = no) = 0.2$$

$$p(A > 10 \cdot B = yes) = 0.35$$

$$p(A > 10 \cdot B = no) = 0.1.$$

This function p is represented by the vector of parameters

$$x = (0.05, 0.1, 0.2, 0.2, 0.35, 0.1)$$

and can be extended to assignments of subsets of V, yielding $p(A > 10) = p(A > 10 \cdot B = yes) + p(A > 10 \cdot B = no) = 0.35 + 0.1 = 0.45$, e.g., and to conjunctions of assignments in which case inconsistent assignments are awarded probability 0, e.g. $p(B = yes \cdot B = no) = 0$. The function p can then be extended to yield conditional probabilities and in this example the probability of a breakdown conditional on age greater than 10 years, $p(B = yes|A > 10)$, is $p(A > 10 \cdot B = yes)/p(A > 10) = 0.35/0.45 \approx 0.78$.[2]

[2]Note that probability is often defined on domains other than assignments to variables. In the mathematical theory of probability, probability is defined over a field of subsets of an outcome space Ω and then probabilities over assignments to 'random' variables are developed from within this framework—see, e.g., Billingsley (1979). However, the full expressive power of the mathematical formalism is not required in many applications of probability, and it is often simplest to focus attention just on variables and their assignments. Logicians tend to define probability over logical languages (Paris, 1994); but as we shall see in §§11.2 and 11.9 it is often easiest to first define probability over assignments to two-valued 'propositional' variables, and then to extend such a function to the sentences of a logical language.

Many texts define probability over variables but there are notational differences to be wary of. In particular texts often denote the value that a variable can take by the same symbol as the assignment of the variable to that value. Thus $p(B = no)$ may be written $p(no)$. In such cases care must be taken when one variable can take the same value as another: $p(no)$ might be short for $p(B = no)$ or $p(C = no)$. Also, commas are often used to delineate assignments: $p(A > 10, B = no)$ means $p(A > 10 \cdot B = no)$ and does not imply that p is a function of two arguments.

A probability function on a domain of finitely many variables, each taking finitely many values, is often called a *distribution* or *probability distribution* (probability 1 is distributed among the assignments to the variables); this should not be confused with a *distribution function* or *cumulative distribution function*, which associates probabilities with a range of assignments or an interval of continuously varying assignments (Billingsley, 1979, p. 175). A probability function on V is sometimes called a *joint distribution* on V to distinguish it from a marginal distribution defined on a proper subset of V.

2.3 Interpretations and Distinctions

The definition of probability given in §2.2 is purely formal. In order to apply the formal concept of probability we need to know how probability is to be interpreted. The standard interpretations of probability will be presented in the next few sections.[3] These interpretations can be categorised according to the stances they take on three key distinctions:

Single-Case / Repeatable A variable is *single-case* (or *token-level*) if it can only be assigned a value once. It is *repeatable* (or *repeatably instantiatable* or *type-level*) if it can be assigned values more than once. For example, variable A standing for *age of car with registration AB01 CDE on 1 January 2005* is single-case because it can only ever take one value (assuming the car in question exists). If, however, A stands for *age of vehicles selected at random in London in 2005* then A is repeatable: it gets reassigned a value each time a new vehicle is selected.[4]

Mental / Physical Probabilities are *mental* (or *epistemological*[5] or *personalist*) if they are interpreted as features of an agent's mental state, otherwise they are *physical* (or *aleatory*[6]).

Subjective / Objective Probabilities are *subjective* (or *agent-relative*) if two agents with the same background knowledge can disagree as to a probability value and yet neither of them be wrong. Otherwise they are *objective*.[7]

There are four main interpretations of probability: the frequency theory (§2.4), the propensity theory (§2.5), chance (§2.6), and Bayesianism (§2.7).[8]

2.4 Frequency

The *frequency* interpretation of probability was propounded by Venn[9] and Reichenbach[10] and developed in detail by Richard von Mises.[11] Von Mises' theory can be formulated in our framework as follows. Given a set V of repeatable variables one can repeatedly determine the values of the variables in V and write

[3] For a more detailed exposition of the interpretations see Gillies (2000).

[4] 'Single-case variable' is clearly an oxymoron because the value of a single-case variable does not vary. The value of a single-case variable may not be known, however, and one can still think of the variable as taking a range of possible values.

[5] (Gillies, 2000)

[6] (Hacking, 1975)

[7] Warning: some authors, such as Popper (1983, §3.3) and Gillies (2000, p. 20), use the term 'objective' for what I call 'physical'. However their terminology has the awkward consequence that the interpretation of probability commonly known as 'objective Bayesianism' (described in Chapter 5) does not get classed as 'objective'.

[8] The logical interpretation of probability, which is no longer widely advocated, is discussed in §11.10.

[9] (Venn, 1866)

[10] (Reichenbach, 1935)

[11] (von Mises, 1928, 1964)

down the observations as assignments to V. For example, one could repeatedly select cars and determine their age and whether they broke down in the last year, writing down $A < 3 \cdot B = no, A < 3 \cdot B = yes, A > 10 \cdot B = yes$, and so on. Under the assumption that this process of measurement can be repeated ad infinitum, we generate an infinite sequence of assignments $\mathcal{V} = (v_1, v_2, v_3, \ldots)$ called a *collective*.

Let $|v|^n_{\mathcal{V}}$ be the number of times assignment v occurs in the first n places of $\mathcal{V}$, and let $freq^n_{\mathcal{V}}(v)$ be the frequency of v in the first n places of $\mathcal{V}$, i.e.

$$freq^n_{\mathcal{V}}(v) = \frac{|v|^n_{\mathcal{V}}}{n}.$$

Von Mises noted two things. First, these frequencies tend to stabilise as the number n of observations increases. Von Mises hypothesised that

Axiom of Convergence $freq^n_{\mathcal{V}}(v)$ tends to a fixed limit as $n \longrightarrow \infty$, denoted by $freq_{\mathcal{V}}(v)$.

Second, gambling systems tend to be ineffective. A gambling system can be thought of as function for selecting places in the sequence of observations on which to bet, on the basis of past observations. Thus a *place selection* is a function $f(v_1, \ldots, v_n) \in 0, 1$, such that if $f(v_1, \ldots, v_n) = 0$ then no bet is to be placed on the $n + 1$-st observation and if $f(v_1, \ldots, v_n) = 1$ then a bet is to be placed on the $n + 1$-st observation. So betting according to a place selection gives rise to a sub-collective $\mathcal{V}_f$ of $\mathcal{V}$ consisting of the places of $\mathcal{V}$ on which bets are placed. In practice we can only use a place selection function if it is simple enough for us to compute its values: if we cannot decide whether $f(v_1, \ldots, v_n)$ is 0 or 1 then it is of no use as a gambling system. According to Church's thesis a function is computable if it belongs to the class of functions known as *recursive* functions.[12] Accordingly we define a *gambling system* to be a recursive place selection. A gambling system is said to be effective if we are able to make money in the long run when we place bets according to the gambling system. Assuming that stakes are set according to frequencies of $\mathcal{V}$, a gambling system f can only be effective if the frequencies of $\mathcal{V}_f$ differ to those of $\mathcal{V}$: if $freq_{\mathcal{V}_f}(v) > freq_{\mathcal{V}}(v)$ then betting *on* v will be profitable in the long run; if $freq_{\mathcal{V}_f}(v) < freq_{\mathcal{V}}(v)$ then betting *against* v will be profitable. We can then explicate von Mises' second observation as follows:

Axiom of Randomness Gambling systems are ineffective: if $\mathcal{V}_f$ is determined by a recursive place selection f, then for each v, $freq_{\mathcal{V}_f}(v) = freq_{\mathcal{V}}(v)$.

Given a collective $\mathcal{V}$ we can then define—following von Mises—the probability of v to be the frequency of v in $\mathcal{V}$:

$$p(v) =_{df} freq_{\mathcal{V}}(v).$$

[12](Church, 1936)

Clearly $freq_{\mathcal{V}}(v) \geq 0$. Moreover $\sum_{v@V} |v|^n_{\mathcal{V}} = n$ so $\sum_{v@V} freq^n_{\mathcal{V}}(v) = 1$ and, taking limits, $\sum_{v@V} freq_{\mathcal{V}}(v) = 1$. Thus p is indeed a well-defined probability function.

Suppose we have a statement involving probability function p on V. If we also have a collective $\mathcal{V}$ on V then we can interpret the statement to be saying something about the frequencies of $\mathcal{V}$, and as being true or false according to whether the corresponding statement about frequencies is true or false respectively. This is the frequency interpretation of probability. The variables in question are repeatable, not single-case, and the interpretation is physical, relative to a collective of potential observations, not to the mental state of an agent. The interpretation is objective, not subjective, in the sense that once the collective is fixed then so too are the probabilities: if two agents disagree as to what the probabilities are, then at most one of the agents is right.

2.5 Propensity

Karl Popper initially adopted a version of von Mises' frequency interpretation,[13] but later, with the ultimate goal of formulating an interpretation of probability applicable to single-case variables, developed what is called the *propensity* interpretation of probability.[14] The propensity theory can be thought of as the frequency theory together with the following law:[15]

Axiom of Independence If collectives $\mathcal{V}_1$ and $\mathcal{V}_2$ on V are generated by the same repeatable experiment (or repeatable conditions) then for all assignments v to V, $freq_{\mathcal{V}_1}(v) = freq_{\mathcal{V}_2}(v)$.

In other words frequency, and hence probability, attaches to repeatable experiment rather than a collective, in the sense that frequencies do not vary with collectives generated by the same repeatable experiment. The repeatable experiment is said to have a propensity for generating the corresponding frequency distribution.

In fact, despite Popper's intentions, the propensity theory interprets probability defined over repeatable variables, not single-case variables. If, e.g., V consists of repeatable variables A and B, where A stands for *age of vehicles selected at random in London in 2005* and B stands for *breakdown in the last year of vehicles selected at random in London in 2005*, then V determines a repeatable experiment, namely the selection of vehicles at random in London in 2005, and thus there is a natural propensity interpretation. Suppose on the other hand that V contains single-case variables A and B, standing for *age of car with registration AB01 CDE on 1 January 2005* and *breakdown in last year of car*

[13](Popper, 1934, chapter VIII)

[14](Popper, 1959; Popper, 1983, part II)

[15]Popper (1983, pp. 290 and 355). It is important to stress that the axioms of this section and the last had a different status for Popper than they did for von Mises. Von Mises used the frequency axioms as part of an operationalist definition of probability, but Popper was not an operationalist. See Gillies (2000, chapter 7) on this point. Gillies also argues in favour of a propensity interpretation.

with registration AB01 CDE on 1 January 2005. Then V defines an experiment, namely the selection of car AB01 CDE on 1 January 2005, but this experiment is not repeatable and does not generate a collective—it is a single case. The car in question might be selected by several different repeatable experiments, but these repeatable experiments need not yield the same frequency for an assignment v, and thus the probability of v is not determined by V. (This is known as the *reference class problem*: we do not know from the specification of the single-case how to uniquely determine a repeatable experiment which will fix probabilities.) In sum the propensity theory is, like the frequency theory, an objective, physical interpretation of probability over repeatable variables.

2.6 Chance

The question remains as to whether one can develop a viable objective interpretation of probability over single-case variables—such a concept of probability is often called *chance*.[16] We saw that frequencies are defined relative to a collective and propensities are defined relative to a repeatable experiment; however, a single-case variable does not determine a unique collective or repeatable experiment and so neither approach allows us to attach probabilities directly to single-case variables. What then does fix the chances of a single-case variable? The view finally adopted by Popper was that the 'whole physical situation' determines probabilities.[17] The physical situation might be thought of as 'the complete situation of the universe (or the light-cone) at the time',[18] the complete history of the world up till the time in question,[19] or 'a complete set of (nomically and/or causally) relevant conditions ... which happens to be instantiated in that world at that time'.[20] Thus the chance, on 1 January 2005, of car with registration AB01 CDE breaking down in the subsequent year, is fixed by the state of the universe at that date, or its entire history up till that date, or all the relevant conditions instantiated at that date. However, the chance-fixing 'complete situation' is delineated, these three approaches associate a unique chance-fixer with a given single-case variable. (In contrast, the frequency / propensity theories do not associate a unique collective / repeatable experiment with a given single-case variable.) Hence we can interpret the probability of an assignment to the single-case variable as the chance of the assignment holding, as determined by its chance-fixer.

Further explanation is required as to how one can measure probabilities under the chance interpretation. Popper's line is this: if the chance-fixer is a set of relevant conditions, and these conditions are repeatable then the conditions

[16]Note that some authors use 'propensity' to cover a physical chance interpretation as well as the propensity interpretation discussed above.

[17](Popper, 1990, p. 17)

[18](Miller, 1994, p. 186)

[19](Lewis, 1980, p. 99); see also §2.8.

[20](Fetzer, 1982, p. 195)

determine a propensity and that can be used to measure the chance.[21] Thus if the set of conditions relevant to car AB01 CDE breaking down that hold on 1 January 2005 also hold for other cars at other times, then the chance of AB01 CDE breaking down in the next year can be equated with the frequency with which cars satisfying the same set of conditions break down in the subsequent year. The difficulty with this view is that it is hard to determine all the chance-fixing relevant conditions, and there is no guarantee that enough individuals will satisfy this set of conditions for the corresponding frequency to be estimable.

2.7 Bayesianism

The *Bayesian* interpretation of probability also deals with probability functions defined over single-case variables. But in this case the interpretation is mental rather than physical: probabilities are interpreted as an agent's rational degrees of belief.[22] Thus for an agent, $p(B = yes) = q$ if and only if the agent believes that $B = yes$ to degree q and this ascription of degree of belief is rational in the sense outlined below. An agent's degrees of belief are construed as a guide to her actions: she believes $B = yes$ to degree q if and only if she is prepared to place a bet of qS on $B = yes$, with return S if $B = yes$ turns out to be true. Here S is an unknown stake, which may be positive or negative, and q is called a *betting quotient*. An agent's *belief function* is the function that maps an assignment to the agent's degree of belief in that assignment.

An agent's betting quotients are called *coherent* if one cannot choose stakes for her bets that force her to lose money whatever happens. (Such a set of stakes is called a *Dutch book*.) It is not hard to see that a coherent belief function is a probability function. First $q \geq 0$, for otherwise one can set S to be negative and the agent will lose whatever happens: she will lose $qS > 0$ if the assignment on which she is betting turns out to be false and will lose $(q-1)S > 0$ if it turns out to be true. Moreover $\sum_{v@V} q_v = 1$, where q_v is the betting quotient on assignment v, for otherwise if $\sum_v q_v > 1$ we can set each $S_v = S > 0$ and the agent will lose $(\sum_v q_v - 1)S > 0$ (since exactly one of the v will turn out true), and if $\sum_v q_v < 1$ we can set each $S_v = S < 0$ to ensure positive loss.

Coherence is taken to be a necessary condition for rationality. For an agent's degrees of belief to be rational they must be coherent, and hence they must be probabilities. *Subjective Bayesianism* is the view that coherence is also sufficient for rationality, so that an agent's belief function is rational if and only if it is a probability function. This interpretation of probability is subjective because it depends on the agent as to whether $p(v) = q$. Different agents can choose different probabilities for v and their belief functions will be equally rational. *Objective Bayesianism*, discussed in detail in Chapter 5, imposes further rationality constraints on degrees of belief—not just coherence. The aim of objective

[21](Popper, 1990, p. 17)

[22]This interpretation was developed by Ramsey (1926) and de Finetti (1937). See Howson and Urbach (1989) and Earman (1992) for recent expositions.

Bayesianism is to constrain degrees of belief in such a way that only one value for $p(v)$ will be deemed rational on the basis of an agent's background knowledge. Thus objective Bayesian probability varies as background knowledge varies but two agents with the same background knowledge must adopt the same probabilities as their rational degrees of belief.

Note that many Bayesians claim that an agent should update her degrees of belief by *Bayesian conditionalisation*: her new degrees of belief should be her old degrees of belief conditional on new knowledge, $p_{t+1}(v) = p_t(v|u)$ where u represents the knowledge that the agent has learned between time t and time $t+1$. In cases where $p_t(v|u)$ is harder to quantify than $p_t(u|v)$ and $p_t(v)$ this conditional probability may be calculated using *Bayes' theorem*: $p(v|u) = p(u|v)p(v)/p(u)$, which holds for any probability function p. 'Bayesianism' is variously used to refer to the Bayesian interpretation of probability, the endorsement of Bayesian conditionalisation or the use of Bayes' theorem.

2.8 Chance as Ultimate Belief

The question still remains as to whether one can develop a viable notion of chance, i.e. an objective single-case interpretation of probability. While the Bayesian interpretations are single-case, they either define probability relative to the whimsy of an agent (subjective Bayesianism) or relative to an agent's background knowledge (objective Bayesianism). Is there a probability of my car breaking down in the next year, where this probability does not depend on me or my knowledge?

Bayesians typically have two ways of tackling this question.

Subjective Bayesians tend to argue that although degrees of belief may initially vary widely from agent to agent, if agents update their degrees of belief by Bayesian conditionalisation then their degrees of belief will converge in the long run: chances are these long run degrees of belief. Bruno de Finetti developed such an argument to explain the apparent existence of physical probabilities.[23] He showed that prior degrees of beliefs converge to frequencies under the assumption of *exchangeability*: given an infinite sequence of single-case variables $A_1, A_2, \ldots$ which take the same possible values, an agent's degrees of belief are *exchangeable* if the degree of belief $p(v)$ she gives to assignment v to a finite subset of variables depends only on the values in v and not the variables in v—for example, $p(a_1^1 a_2^0 a_3^1) = p(a_3^0 a_4^1 a_5^1)$ since both assignments assign two 1s and one 0. Suppose the actual observed assignments are $a_1, a_2, \ldots$ and let $\mathcal{V}$ be the collective of such values (which can be thought of as arising from a single repeatable variable A). De Finetti showed that $p(a_n|a_1 \cdots a_{n-1}) \longrightarrow \mathit{freq}_{\mathcal{V}}(a)$ as $n \longrightarrow \infty$, where a assigns A the value that occurs in a_n. The chance of a_n is then identified with $\mathit{freq}_{\mathcal{V}}(a)$. The trouble with de Finetti's account is that since degrees of belief are subjective there is no reason to suppose exchangeability holds. Moreover, a single-case variable A_n can occur in several sequences of variables, each with

[23](de Finetti, 1937; Gillies, 2000, pp. 69–83)

a different frequency distribution (the reference class problem again), in which case the chance distribution of A_n is ill-defined. Haim Gaifman and Marc Snir took a slightly different approach, showing that as long as agents give probability 0 to the same assignments and the evidence that they observe is unrestricted, then their degrees of belief must converge.[24] Again, the problem here is that there is no reason to suppose that agents will give probability 0 to the same assignments. One might try to provide such a guarantee by bolstering subjective Bayesianism with a rationality constraint that says that agents must be *undogmatic*, i.e. they must only give probability 0 to logically impossible assignments. But this is not a feasible strategy in general, since this constraint is inconsistent with the constraint that degrees of belief be probabilities: in very general frameworks for probability the laws of probability force some logical possibilities to be given probability 0.[25]

Objective Bayesians have another recourse open to them: objective Bayesian probability is fixed by an agent's background knowledge, and one can argue that chances are those degrees of belief fixed by some suitable all-encompassing background knowledge. This strategy is discussed in some detail by David Lewis.[26] Lewis suggests that the chance at time t of a single-case is the degree to which one ought to believe it were one to know (i.e. conditional on) the history of the world up to time t and any laws that govern the determination of chances. Thus the problem of producing a well-defined notion of chance is reducible to that of developing an objective Bayesian interpretation of probability (discussed in Chapter 5). I shall call this the *ultimate belief* notion of chance to distinguish it from physical notions such as Popper's (§2.6).

2.9 Applying Probability

In this book then, we focus on probability functions defined on assignments to sets of variables, and four key interpretations of probability: frequency and propensity interpret probability over repeatable variables while chance and Bayesianism deal with single-case variables; frequency and propensity are physical interpretations while Bayesianism is mental and chance can be either mental or physical; all the interpretations are objective apart from Bayesianism which can be subjective or objective.

Having chosen an interpretation of probability, one can use the probability calculus to draw conclusions about the world. Typically, having made an observation $u@U \subseteq V$, one determines the conditional probability $p(t|u)$ to tell us something about $t@T \subseteq (V \backslash U)$: a frequency, propensity, chance, or degree of belief.

In the next chapter, we will look at techniques for efficiently determining these conditional probabilities.

[24](Gaifman and Snir, 1982, §2)

[25]See, e.g. Gaifman and Snir (1982, Theorem 3.7).

[26](Lewis, 1980)

3

BAYESIAN NETS

In this chapter, I shall introduce the concept of a Bayesian network (§3.1). A Bayesian net offers a natural way of representing the probabilistic independencies satisfied by a probability function (§3.2) and, as we shall see in §3.3, can be used to efficiently represent a probability function. While inference using Bayesian nets is an important issue (§3.4), perhaps the key problem is that of constructing a Bayesian net to represent a target probability function (§3.5). I shall present one strategy in the remainder of this chapter. In the next chapter, we shall see how causal knowledge might be used to construct a Bayesian net.

3.1 Bayesian Networks

As before we will be concerned with a finite set V of variables, each of which can take finitely many values.[27]

A *Bayesian network* $\mathcal{B}$ on V consists of two components:

- A directed acyclic graph $\mathcal{G}$. $\mathcal{G} = (V, E)$, where V and E are respectively the sets of vertices and directed edges in the graph. Note that the set V of vertices is the set of variables on which the Bayesian network is defined. The directed edges are often called the *arrows* of $\mathcal{G}$. Fig. 3.1 gives an example of a directed acyclic graph. When discussing the relationships between variables that are induced by the directed acyclic graph $\mathcal{G}$, family notation is often used: for $A \in V$ the set Par_A of *parents* of A is the set of variables from which there is an arrow going to A in $\mathcal{G}$. The *children* Chi_A of A are the variables that are reached by an arrow from A. The *ancestors* Anc_A of A are its parents, their parents, and so on, while the *descendants* Des_A are its children, their children, etc. In Fig. 3.1, $Par_C = Anc_C = \{A\}$, $Chi_A = \{B, C\}$, and $Des_A = \{B, C, D, E\}$.
- A probability specification $\mathcal{S}$. For each variable $A \in V$, $\mathcal{S}$ specifies the probability distribution of A conditional on its parents, i.e. the probability of each assignment to A, conditional on each assignment to the parents of A. Thus $\mathcal{S}$ consists of statements of the form '$p(a|par_A) = y_A^{a,par_A}$' for each $A \in V, a@A, par_A@Par_A$, where $y_A^{a,par_A} \in [0,1]$ and $\sum_a y_A^{a,par_A} = 1$. The specifiers in $\mathcal{S}$ which determine the probability distribution of A conditional on its parents are often collectively known as the *probability table* for vertex

[27] It is possible to work with Bayesian networks involving (finitely many) variables, some or all of which have infinitely many possible values. For the development of Bayesian networks involving continuous variables subject to Gaussian distributions see chapter 7 of Cowell *et al.* (1999).

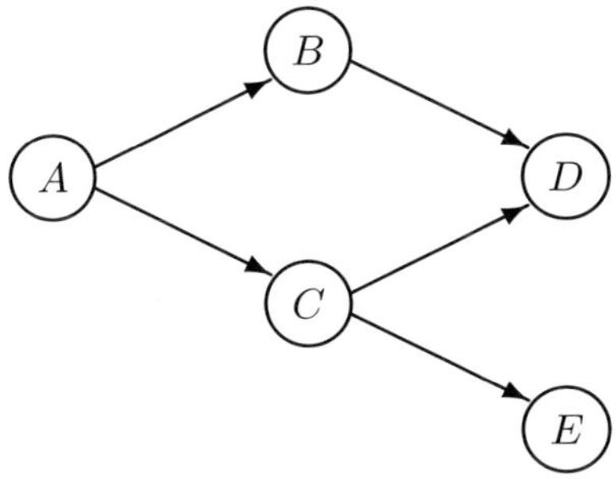

FIG. 3.1. An example of a directed acyclic graph.

Table 3.1 *An example of a probability table*

$p(d^0\|b^0c^0) = 0.7$	$p(d^1\|b^0c^0) = 0.3$
$p(d^0\|b^0c^1) = 0.9$	$p(d^1\|b^0c^1) = 0.1$
$p(d^0\|b^1c^0) = 0.2$	$p(d^1\|b^1c^0) = 0.8$
$p(d^0\|b^1c^1) = 0.4$	$p(d^1\|b^1c^1) = 0.6$

A. Table 3.1 gives an example probability table for D in Fig. 3.1, under the supposition that the variables involved each have two possible assignments, superscripted by 0 and 1.

The graph and probability specification of a Bayesian network are linked by a fundamental assumption known as the *Markov Condition*. This says that conditional on its parents, any variable is probabilistically independent of all other variables apart from its descendants. We write $R \perp\!\!\!\perp S \mid T$ to stand for 'R is probabilistically independent of S conditional on T',[28] which means in turn that $p(r|st) = p(r|t)$ for all consistent assignments $r@R, s@S, t@T$ such that $p(st) > 0$. There is no standard notation for probabilistic dependence, the negation of probabilistic independence; I shall adopt the notation $R \rightleftharpoons S \mid T$ to stand for 'R and S are probabilistically dependent conditional on T'. Unconditional independence is written $R \perp\!\!\!\perp S$, and $R \perp\!\!\!\perp S \mid \emptyset$ is taken to stand for the unconditional independence $R \perp\!\!\!\perp S$. Likewise $R \rightleftharpoons S \mid \emptyset$ is read as unconditional dependence $R \rightleftharpoons S$. Let $ND_A = V \backslash (\{A\} \cup Des_A)$ be the non-descendants of A. Then the Markov Condition may be written:

Markov Condition $A \perp\!\!\!\perp ND_A \mid Par_A$, for each $A \in V$.

By the definition of conditional probabilistic independence, the Markov Condition is equivalent to $A \perp\!\!\!\perp ND_A \backslash Par_A \mid Par_A$ for each $A \in V$.

For example, if the Bayesian network involves the graph of Fig. 3.1 then the Markov Condition determines the following independencies:

$$B \perp\!\!\!\perp C, E \mid A$$

[28]Conditional probabilistic independence is occasionally written $I(R, T, S)$ or $I(R, S|T)$.

$$C \perp\!\!\!\perp B \mid A$$

$$D \perp\!\!\!\perp A, E \mid B, C$$

$$E \perp\!\!\!\perp A, B, D \mid C.$$

In sum, then, a Bayesian network $\mathcal{B} = (\mathcal{G}, \mathcal{S})$ consists of two components, a directed acyclic graph $\mathcal{G}$ and a set $\mathcal{S}$ of corresponding probability specifiers, and is subject to the Markov Condition.[29] Bayesian networks are often called *Bayesian nets* for short.

3.2 Independence and D-Separation

The following properties follow easily from the definition of independence and are often useful:

Proposition 3.1. (Properties of Independence) *For $R, S, T, U \subseteq V$,*

Equivalencies *$R \perp\!\!\!\perp S|T$ is equivalent to each of*
(i) $p(rst)p(t) = p(rt)p(st)$ for all $r@R, s@S, t@T$.
(ii) $p(rs|t) = p(r|t)p(s|t)$ for all $r@R, s@S, t@T$ such that $p(t) > 0$.
(iii) $p(r|st) = p(r|s't)$ for all $r@R, s, s'@S, t@T$ such that $p(st), p(s't) > 0$.

Symmetry *$R \perp\!\!\!\perp S|T$ if and only if $S \perp\!\!\!\perp R|T$.*

Decomposition *$R \perp\!\!\!\perp S, U|T$ implies $R \perp\!\!\!\perp S|T$ and $R \perp\!\!\!\perp U|T$.*

Weak Union *$R \perp\!\!\!\perp S, U|T$ implies $R \perp\!\!\!\perp S|T, U$.*

Contraction *$R \perp\!\!\!\perp S|T$ and $R \perp\!\!\!\perp U|S, T$ imply $R \perp\!\!\!\perp S, U|T$.*

Intersection *If p is strictly positive then $R \perp\!\!\!\perp S|U, T$ and $R \perp\!\!\!\perp U|S, T$ imply $R \perp\!\!\!\perp S, U|T$.* ■

The Markov Condition implies a panoply of probabilistic independencies, and these can be determined from the graph $\mathcal{G}$ in the Bayesian network as follows. A *path* between two vertices A and B is a graph whose vertices can be enumerated $C_1, \ldots, C_k \in V$ such that C_1 is A and C_k is B, and whose arrows consist of an arrow linking C_i and C_{i+1} (the direction does not matter) for $i = 1, \ldots, k-1$. A *directed path* or *chain* $A \rightsquigarrow B$ from A to B is a path whose arrows go from C_i to C_{i+1}. A path or chain is *in* $\mathcal{G}$ if it is a subgraph of $\mathcal{G}$. $T \subseteq V$ *D-separates* or *blocks* a path in $\mathcal{G}$ if either

- the path contains some variable D in T and the arrows adjacent to D meet head-to-tail ($\longrightarrow D \longrightarrow$) or tail-to-tail ($\longleftarrow D \longrightarrow$), or
- the path contains some variable E whose adjacent arrows meet head-to-head ($\longrightarrow E \longleftarrow$) and neither E nor any of its descendants are in T.

[29] Note that some early writings include a minimality condition in the definition of Bayesian network, which says that the graph $\mathcal{G}$ must be the smallest graph for which the Markov Condition holds, in the sense that removing any arrows from $\mathcal{G}$ invalidates the Markov Condition. The minimality condition is not normally included in the definition of Bayesian network however, and will not be included here.

$T \subseteq V$ *D-separates* $R, S \subseteq V$ if each path between a variable in R and a variable in S is D-separated by T. D-separation is important because it determines all and only the probabilistic independencies implied by $\mathcal{G}$ under the Markov Condition:

Proposition 3.2. (Verma and Pearl, 1988) *Given a directed acyclic graph $\mathcal{G}$ and $R, S, T \subseteq V$, T D-separates R and S if and only if $R \perp\!\!\!\perp S \mid T$ for all probability functions that satisfy the Markov Condition with respect to $\mathcal{G}$.*

Thus by testing for D-separation one can 'read off' from a directed acyclic graph the probabilistic independencies implied by the graph via the Markov Condition.

3.3 Representing Probability Functions

Suppose $V = \{A_1, \ldots, A_n\}$ and $a_i@A_i$ for $i = 1, \ldots, n$. The *chain rule*, an elementary theorem of probability which follows by induction from the definition of conditional probability, says that

$$p(a_1 a_2 \cdots a_n) = p(a_n|a_1 \cdots a_{n-1}) \cdots p(a_2|a_1)p(a_1).$$

Suppose we are given a Bayesian net $\mathcal{B} = (\mathcal{G}, \mathcal{S})$. Ensure that the variables in V are ordered *ancestrally*, i.e. for each $A_i \in V$, all ancestors A_j of A_i have index $j < i$ in the order (and thus no descendant A_j of A_i has index $j < i$). This is always possible because of the directed acyclic structure of $\mathcal{G}$. The Markov Condition and the Decomposition property of independence imply that for each $i = 1, \ldots, n$, $A_i \perp\!\!\!\perp \{A_1, \ldots, A_{i-1}\} \mid Par_i$ (writing Par_i for Par_{A_i}). Thus if $p(a_1 \cdots a_{i-1}) > 0$, $p(a_i|a_1 \cdots a_{i-1}) = p(a_i|par_i)$, where par_i is the assignment to Par_i, which is consistent with $a_1 \cdots a_n$. So if $p(a_1 \cdots a_{i-1}) > 0$ for each i, then

$$p(a_1 a_2 \cdots a_n) = p(a_n|par_n) \cdots p(a_2|par_2)p(a_1). \tag{3.1}$$

Note that if $p(a_1 \cdots a_{i-1}) = 0$ for some i, then $p(a_1 \cdots a_n) = 0$ and moreover either $p(a_1) = 0$ or there is some $k \leq i$ for which $p(a_1 \cdots a_{k-1}) > 0$ and $p(a_1 \cdots a_k) = 0$, in which case $p(a_k|par_k) = p(a_k|a_1 \cdots a_{k-1}) = 0$. Thus both the left-hand side and the right-hand side of eqn (3.1) are zero and the condition that $p(a_1 \cdots a_{i-1}) > 0$ for each i is not required. Hence,[30]

Theorem 3.3 *A Bayesian network determines a probability function over its variable set V. For each assignment $v@V$, $p(v) = \prod_{A \in V} p(a|par_A)$.* ■

Conversely, given a probability function p over $V = \{A_1, \ldots, A_n\}$, define a Bayesian net as follows. For each variable A_i choose a set of parents $Par_i \subseteq \{A_1, \ldots, A_{i-1}\}$ such that $A_i \perp\!\!\!\perp \{A_1, \ldots, A_{i-1}\} \mid Par_i$, and construct graph $\mathcal{G}$ by

[30] Recall we adopt the convention that an assignment which is not explicitly defined is induced by the nearest more general assignment to its left, so $p(v) = \prod_{A \in V} p(a|par_A)$ is short for $p(v) = \prod_{A \in V} p(a^v|par_A^v)$.

including an arrow from each member of Par_i to A_i, for each $i = 1, \ldots n$. Specification $\mathcal{S}$ contains $p(a_i|par_i)$ for each $a_i@A_i, par_i@Par_i$ and each $i = 1, \ldots, n$. Then the function p' determined by the Bayesian net is the same as the original function p:

$$p'(v) = \prod_{i=1}^{n} p(a_i|par_i) = \prod_{i=1}^{n} p(a_i|a_1 \cdots a_{i-1}) = p(v)$$

by the chain rule. Hence,

Theorem 3.4 *Each probability function on V can be represented by a Bayesian network on V.* ■

Note that $A_1, \ldots, A_n$ is then an ancestral ordering so we have,

Corollary 3.5 *Suppose $V = \{A_1, \ldots, A_n\}$, where $A_1, \ldots, A_n$ are ordered ancestrally with respect to directed acyclic graph $\mathcal{G}$. Then the Markov Condition holds if and only if $A_i \perp\!\!\!\perp \{A_1, \ldots, A_{i-1}\} \mid Par_i$ for $i = 1, \ldots, n$.* ■

Theorem 3.3 and Theorem 3.4, simple as they are, provide the key properties of Bayesian nets. Every Bayesian net on V represents a probability function on V, and every probability function on V is represented by a Bayesian net on V. Thanks to these properties, Bayesian nets are primarily used to represent probability functions. Thus in a typical Bayesian net application a probability function p yields some observed data, and this data is used to construct a Bayesian net that represents p. The observed data will rarely determine p completely and the Bayesian net will at best represent an estimate of or approximation to p. For example, from observed data consisting of lists of symptoms and diagnoses of past patients one might construct a Bayesian net that represents (an approximation to) the frequency distribution of symptoms and diagnoses, and use this Bayesian net to calculate the probability of various diagnoses conditional on a new patient's symptoms, and thereby offer a diagnosis to the new patient. The underlying probability distribution that one is trying to represent is called the *target* probability function.

Bayesian nets are useful as a means of representing probability functions largely for computational reasons: in certain circumstances a Bayesian net can offer a compact representation of probability function from which one can calculate desired probabilities quickly. To help clarify this remark we shall compare Bayesian nets with the standard representation of probability functions.

We saw in §2.2 that a probability function on V is determined by a vector of parameters $x \in \mathbb{P} = \{x \in [0,1]^{||V||} : \sum_{v@V} x^v = 1\}$ by setting $p(v) = x^v$ for each $v@V$. By the results of this section, a probability function p on V is also determined by a Bayesian network on $V = \{A_1, \ldots, A_n\}$ by setting $p(v) = \prod_{i=1}^{n} y_i^{a_i par_i}$, where $y_i^{a_i par_i}$ is the numerical value given to $p(a_i|par_i)$ in the probability specification of the Bayesian net. These y-parameters are subject to the constraints $y_i^{a_i par_i} \in [0,1]$ and $\sum_{a_i@A_i} y_i^{a_i par_i} = 1$. Let y_i be the vector of parameters $(y_i^{a_i par_i})_{a_i @ A_i, par_i @ Par_i}$ corresponding to the probability table for A_i, and let y be the matrix of parameters $(y_i)_{1 \leq i \leq n}$, corresponding to the entire probability specification $\mathcal{S}$. Then given the ordering of variables in V, the information about parenthood expressed by $\mathcal{G}$ and a fixed ordering of assignments to parents of each variable, p can be reconstructed from y. p can be determined either from the standard x-parameterisation or from the Bayesian net y-parameterisation.

Note that there is some redundancy in these parameterisations. One of the x-parameters is determined by the others by the additivity constraint $\sum_{v @ V} x^v = 1$, and so $||V|| - 1 = (\prod_{i=1}^n ||A_i||) - 1$ x-parameters are in fact required to determine p. For each $A_i \in V$ and $par_i @ Par_i$ one of the y-parameters is determined from the others by the additivity constraint $\sum_{a_i @ A_i} y_i^{a_i par_i} = 1$, and so only $\sum_{i=1}^n (||A_i|| - 1)||Par_i|| = \sum_{i=1}^n (||A_i|| - 1) \prod_{A_j \in Par_i} ||A_j||$ y-parameters are required to determine p. For example, Table 3.1 contains 8 specifiers, but 4 of these can be determined from the other 4 by the additivity constraints $p(d^1|b^i c^j) = 1 - p(d^0|b^i c^j)$ for each $i, j \in \{0, 1\}$. The *size* of a representation of p is the number of parameters required in the representation to determine p. Thus the size of a standard representation of p is $||V|| - 1$ and the size of a Bayesian net representation of p is $\sum_{i=1}^n (||A_i|| - 1)||Par_i||$.

One key advantage of a Bayesian net representation of p over the standard representation of p is that it may be smaller: fewer y-parameters than x-parameters may be required to determine p. Consider a probability function p on $V = \{A, B, C, D, E\}$ represented by a Bayesian net involving the graph of Fig. 3.1, where each variable has two possible values. The Bayesian net representation of p has size $1+2+2+4+2 = 11$, but the standard representation requires $2^5 - 1 = 31$ parameters. In general, if $|V| = n$, the number of parents of a variable is bounded above by k and the number of values of a variable is bounded above by K then a Bayesian net has size bounded above by nK^{k+1}, a number linear in the number n of variables. In contrast the standard representation has size of the order K^n, which is exponential in n. Thus Bayesian nets have the potential to be *scalable*: their size need not get out of hand as the number n of variables in V increases.

From the point of view of size of representation, the construction used in the derivation of Theorem 3.4 is practically useless in the worst case. This worst case occurs when $Par_i = \{A_1, \ldots, A_{i-1}\}$ is chosen as the parent set of each A_i. Then the Bayesian net used to represent probability function p is based on the *complete graph* (every pair of variables is connected by an arrow) and thus the size of the network is $\sum_{i=1}^n (||A_i|| - 1) \prod_{j=1}^{i-1} ||A_j||$, which can be shown by induction to equal $\prod_{i=1}^n ||A_i|| - 1$, the size of the corresponding standard representation. Hence under this construction the Bayesian net representation is no smaller than the standard representation. A very important question for Bayesian net researchers is the *construction problem*: given probability function p, how can one find a Bayesian net of small size that represents p? This problem will be considered in some detail in §3.5 and subsequent sections.

We have seen that Bayesian nets can help with the *space complexity* of representing probability functions—but they can also help with the *time complexity* of probabilistic reasoning. Many problems require the calculation of conditional probabilities for their solution. A diagnosis problem, for instance, requires the calculation of the probability of a fault conditional on an assignment to observed symptoms; a prediction problem requires the calculation of future assignments to variables conditional on an observed current assignment to variables; decision-making requires the calculation of the probability of desired outcomes conditional on different possible assignments to the decision variables. One can determine conditional probabilities from specifiers in a standard representation via

$$p(a|u) = \frac{\sum_{v@V, v\sim ua} p(v)}{\sum_{v@V, v\sim u} p(v)},$$

where $a@A, u@U, A \in V, U \subseteq V$. However, such a calculation requires in general a very large number of additions, rendering the standard representation impractical from the time complexity as well as the space complexity point of view. Again, Bayesian nets can offer complexity savings here, via the techniques outlined in the next section. Parallel to the construction problem, Bayesian net researchers face an *inference problem*: how can desired probabilities be calculated quickly from a given Bayesian net?

3.4 Inference in Bayesian Nets

The general problem of determining conditional probabilities from Bayesian nets is NP-hard.[31] Hence (unless $P = NP$) any algorithm for determining conditional probabilities from Bayesian nets will in the worst case not be practical for large n.[32] This worst case will occur when the graph in the Bayesian net is very highly connected. On the other hand, it is known that if the graph is *singly connected* (i.e. there is at most one path between any pair of variables) then inference can be performed in time that increases linearly with the number n of variables.[33] If the graph is *directed-path singly connected* (i.e. there is at most one directed path from one variable to another), then the same is true for the case of *predictive inference*, where evidence variables (variables that are conditioned on) have no non-evidence parents.[34]

One strategy for probabilistic inference is to construct a Bayesian net that represents a target probability function p, and if this network turns out to be highly connected, to run an *approximate inference algorithm*, whose object is to determine approximations to required conditional probabilities.[35] However, even approximate inference in Bayesian nets is NP-hard,[36] and so this strategy is only

[31](Cooper, 1990)

[32]See Papadimitriou (1994) for an introduction to computational complexity concepts.

[33](Neapolitan, 1990, chapter 6)

[34](Shimony and Domshlak, 2003)

[35]See Dagum and Luby (1997) and Jordan (1998, part 1).

[36](Dagum and Luby, 1993)

useful in special cases.[37]

A second strategy is to perform exact inference in a net that approximates the target function. There are computational complexity difficulties with inference in arbitrary networks. On the other hand there are a plethora of special-case algorithms which perform very well on a limited domain—e.g. exact inference on singly connected networks. So a useful general methodology is to construct a Bayesian net that has properties known to admit efficient inference (such as single-connectedness) and that represents an approximation to the target probability function—then one can perform inference in this network using a suitable special-case algorithm. Under this approach the inference problem naturally ties in with the construction problem: the task of calculating an approximation to a required probability is reduced to that of constructing a Bayesian net that approximates the target probability function and allows efficient inference. The advantage of this approach is that while inference is normally performed a large number of times, an approximation net need only be constructed once, so it makes sense to keep inference quick and to spend the bulk of available computational resources on the construction task. This methodology will be developed further in the next section.

3.5 Constructing Bayesian Nets

Apart from inference in Bayesian nets, the other important problem is construction: how does one construct a Bayesian net of small size that represents a target probability function p^*?

Just as with the inference problem, this is an active area of current research,[38] and one which is strongly constrained by computational considerations. The general construction problem is NP-complete,[39] and constructing a Bayesian net may take more time than is available. Moreover, there is always a danger that a construction algorithm will yield a Bayesian net whose size is larger than available storage space or whose structure does not permit efficient inference. Given these considerations and the methodology pointed out in the last section, it is wise to limit the class of Bayesian nets that can be constructed to those within acceptable size and inferential-complexity bounds, and to look for a Bayesian net in this class that represents an approximation to the target function p^*.

A key task for the knowledge engineer, then, is to choose some *approximation subspace* $\mathbb{S}$ of the space $\mathbb{B}$ of Bayesian nets such that for nets in this subspace, computational complexities (such as size of the network and the time complexity of inference) are catered for by available resources. Consider, e.g., the subspace

[37] Approximation algorithms for inference in Bayesian nets is fast-moving area, but the latest results tend to be available at the online conference proceedings of the Association for Uncertainty in AI, www.auai.org. Exact inference in arbitrary (i.e. not necessarily singly connected) Bayesian nets uses the clique-tree algorithm put forward in Lauritzen and Spiegelhalter (1988)—see chapter 7 of Neapolitan (1990) and also Cowell *et al.* (1999).

[38] See parts III and IV of Jordan (1998), and www.auai.org.

[39] (Chickering, 1996)

of nets that are singly connected and whose vertices have no more than two parents; for such nets we can be assured that both the size of the network and the time complexity of inference will be linear in the number of variables n. The construction problem is that of producing a Bayesian net in a given subspace $\mathbb{S}$ of nets that approximates a target function p^* well.

How do we measure closeness of an approximation p to p^*? The standard way is to use the *cross entropy* measure of the distance of function p from p^*:

$$d(p^*, p) = \sum_{v@V} p^*(v) \log \frac{p^*(v)}{p(v)},$$

where continuity arguments dictate that $0 \log 0 = 0$ and $x \log x/0 = \infty$ for $x \neq 0$. Cross entropy is not a distance function in the usual mathematical sense, since it is not symmetric and does not satisfy the triangle inequality. However, we do have that $d(p^*, p) \geq 0$ and $d(p^*, p) = 0$ iff $p^* = p$,[40] which is enough for our purposes here. The distance to a Bayesian net from a target probability function p^* is then defined as the distance from p^* to the probability function p determined by the network.

The task of finding a network $\mathcal{B} = (\mathcal{G}, \mathcal{S})$ in an approximation subspace that is closest to target p^* can be divided into two sub-problems, namely that of determining the graph $\mathcal{G}$ in the network and the subsequent problem of determining the corresponding probability specifiers $\mathcal{S}$. The latter problem is a statistical one: we need to find accurate estimates $p(a_i|par_i)$ of the target probabilities $p^*(a_i|par_i)$, for $i = 1, \ldots, n$ and all $a_i@A_i$, $par_i@Par_i$. If p^* is a physically interpreted probability function then the most obvious strategy here is to observe frequencies generated by p^* by sampling individuals which satisfy par_i and determining the proportion of these individuals that satisfy a_i. Assuming that the statistical problem is relatively unproblematic, we shall focus on the determination of the graph $\mathcal{G}$. This can be achieved along the following lines.

First, given a Bayesian net $\mathcal{B} = (\mathcal{G}, \mathcal{S})$ on $V = \{A_1, \ldots, A_n\}$ that represents probability function p, we attach a weight to each arrow in $\mathcal{G}$. For each variable A_i, enumerate its parents Par_i as $B_1, \ldots, B_k$. Then the *arrow weight* attached to the arrow from B_j to A_i is the *conditional mutual information* of A_i and B_j conditional on $B_1, \ldots, B_{j-1}$,

$$I(A_i, B_j \mid B_1, \ldots, B_{j-1}) =$$

$$\sum_{a_i@A_i, b_1@B_1, \ldots, b_j@B_j} p^*(a_i b_1 \cdots b_j) \log \frac{p^*(a_i b_j | b_1 \cdots b_{j-1})}{p^*(a_i | b_1 \cdots b_{j-1}) p^*(b_j | b_1 \cdots b_{j-1})}.$$

We define the *network weight*, attached to the Bayesian net as a whole, to be the sum of its arrow weights.[41]

[40] See, e.g. Paris (1994, Proposition 8.5).

[41] While the weight of arrow $B_j \longrightarrow A_i$ depends on the ordering chosen for the parents of A_i, the network weight does not depend on parent orderings.

Under the assumption that the statistical problem is solvable, we need only consider networks whose probability specifiers are accurate estimates of target probabilities—i.e. we shall assume that $p(a_i|par_i) = p^*(a_i|par_i)$ for $i = 1, \ldots, n$ and all $a_i @ A_i, par_i @ Par_i$. Then:

Theorem 3.6 *The Bayesian net (within some subspace of all nets) which affords the closest approximation to p^* is the net (within the subspace) with maximum network weight.*

Proof: The distance from target function p^* to a Bayesian net determining probability function p is

$$\begin{aligned}
d(p^*, p) &= \sum_{v@V} p^*(v) \log \frac{p^*(v)}{p(v)} \\
&= \sum_{v@V} p^*(v) \log p^*(v) - \sum_{v@V} p^*(v) \log \prod_{i=1}^{n} p^*(a_i|par_i) \\
&= \sum_{v@V} p^*(v) \log p^*(v) - \sum_{v@V} p^*(v) \sum_{i=1}^{n} \log p^*(a_i|par_i) \\
&= \sum_{v@V} p^*(v) \log p^*(v) - \sum_{v@V} p^*(v) \sum_{i=1}^{n} \log \frac{p^*(a_i par_i)}{p^*(a_i)p^*(par_i)} \\
&\quad - \sum_{v@V} p^*(v) \sum_{i=1}^{n} \log p^*(a_i) \\
&= -H(p^*) - \sum_{i=1}^{n} I(A_i, Par_i) + \sum_{i=1}^{n} H(p^*_{\downharpoonright A_i}),
\end{aligned}$$

where $H(p^*)$ is called the entropy of function p^* (see §5.4), $I(A_i, Par_i)$ is the mutual information between A_i and its parents and $H(p^*_{\downharpoonright A_i})$ is the entropy of p^* restricted to node A_i. The entropies are independent of the choice of Bayesian net, so the distance from the target distribution to the net is minimised just when the total mutual information is maximised.[42]

Note that

$$\begin{aligned}
&I(R, S) + I(R, T|S) \\
&= \sum_{r@R, s@S, t@T} p^*(rst) \left[\log \frac{p^*(rs)}{p^*(r)p^*(s)} + \log \frac{p^*(rt|s)}{p^*(r|s)p^*(t|s)} \right] \\
&= \sum_{r,s,t} p^*(rst) \log \frac{p^*(rs)p^*(rst)p^*(s)p^*(s)}{p^*(r)p^*(s)p^*(s)p^*(rs)p^*(ts)}
\end{aligned}$$

[42]This much is a straightforward generalisation of the proof of Chow and Liu (1968) that the best tree-based approximation to p^* is the maximum weight spanning tree (i.e. the case in which the subspace of nets under consideration is the space of nets whose graphs are connected and contain no variable with more than one parent).

$$= \sum_{r,s,t} p^*(rst) \log \frac{p^*(rst)}{p^*(r)p^*(ts)} = I(R, \{S,T\}).$$

By enumerating the parents Par_i of A_i as $B_1, \ldots, B_k$, we can iterate the above relation to get

$$I(A_i, Par_i) = I(A_i, B_1) + I(A_i, B_2|B_1) +$$

$$I(A_i, B_3|\{B_1, B_2\}) + \cdots + I(A_i, B_j|\{B_1, \ldots, B_{j-1}\}).$$

Therefore,

$$\sum_{i=1}^{n} I(A_i, Par_i) = \sum_{i=1}^{n} \sum_{j} I(A_i, B_j|\{B_1, \ldots, B_{j-1}\}),$$

and the cross entropy distance between the network distribution and the target distribution is minimised just when the sum of the arrow weights is maximised. ∎

3.6 The Adding-Arrows Algorithm

There are various ways one might try to find a net (within an approximation subspace) with maximum or close to maximum weight, but perhaps the simplest is a greedy *adding-arrows* strategy: start off with the discrete net (whose graph contains no arrows) and at each stage find and weigh the arrows whose addition would ensure that the net remains within the chosen subspace (in particular the graph must remain acyclic), and add one with maximum weight. If more than one maximum weight arrow exists we can spawn several new nets by adding each maximum weight arrow to the previous graph, and we can constantly prune the nets under consideration by eliminating those which no longer have maximum total weight. We stop the process when no more arrows can be added and output the resulting Bayesian nets.

Note that if membership of $\mathbb{S}$ depends only on the structure of the graph, not the probability specification, then probability specifications only need to be ascertained when the final nets are output.[43]

The adding-arrows algorithm can be motivated by the following fact: adding an arrow will never yield a network that is further from the target distribution than the original network. It will yield a closer approximation only if the arrow corresponds to a probabilistic dependence relation:

Theorem 3.7 *Suppose Bayesian net $(\mathcal{G}, \mathcal{S}_{\mathcal{G}})$ determines probability function $p_{\mathcal{G}}$ and $\mathcal{G}$ contains no arrow from A_i to A_j. Bayesian net $(\mathcal{H}, \mathcal{S}_{\mathcal{H}})$, which determines $p_{\mathcal{H}}$, is constructed from $(\mathcal{G}, \mathcal{S}_{\mathcal{G}})$ by adding an arrow from A_i to A_j and corresponding probability specifiers. Then*
(i) $p_{\mathcal{H}}$ is no further from the target p^* than $p_{\mathcal{G}}$;

[43] See the example of §3.7.

(ii) $p_{\mathcal{H}}$ *is closer to* p^* *if and only if* $A_i \rightleftharpoons A_j \mid Par_j^{\mathcal{G}}$ *(i.e.* A_j *is probabilistically dependent on* A_i*, conditional on* A_j*'s other parents) if and only if* $I(A_i, A_j \mid Par_j^{\mathcal{G}}) > 0$ *(i.e. the arrow's weight is greater than* 0*).*

Proof: To begin with we shall assume that $p_{\mathcal{G}}$ and $p_{\mathcal{H}}$ are strictly positive over the assignments.

For (i) we need to show that $d(p^*, p_{\mathcal{H}}) - d(p^*, p_{\mathcal{G}}) \leq 0$, where d is cross entropy distance. So,

$$\begin{aligned} d(p^*, p_{\mathcal{H}}) - d(p^*, p_{\mathcal{G}}) &= \sum_{v @ V} p^*(v) \log \frac{p^*(v)}{p_{\mathcal{H}}(v)} - \sum_{v @ V} p^*(v) \log \frac{p^*(v)}{p_{\mathcal{G}}(v)} \\ &= \sum_{v @ V} p^*(v) \log \frac{p_{\mathcal{G}}(v)}{p_{\mathcal{H}}(v)}, \end{aligned}$$

bearing in mind that $p_{\mathcal{H}}(v) > 0$. Now for real $x > 0, \log(x) \leq x - 1$. By assumption $p_{\mathcal{G}}(v)/p_{\mathcal{H}}(v) > 0$, so

$$\sum_{v @ V} p^*(v) \log \frac{p_{\mathcal{G}}(v)}{p_{\mathcal{H}}(v)} \leq \sum_{v @ V} p^*(v) \left[\frac{p_{\mathcal{G}}(v)}{p_{\mathcal{H}}(v)} - 1\right] = \sum_{v @ V} p^*(v) \frac{p_{\mathcal{G}}(v)}{p_{\mathcal{H}}(v)} - 1,$$

and thus we need to show that

$$\sum_{v @ V} p^*(v) \frac{p_{\mathcal{G}}(v)}{p_{\mathcal{H}}(v)} \leq 1.$$

Now since we are dealing with Bayesian networks,

$$\frac{p_{\mathcal{G}}(v)}{p_{\mathcal{H}}(v)} = \frac{\prod p^*(a_k | par_k^{\mathcal{G}})}{\prod p^*(a_k | par_k^{\mathcal{H}})},$$

for each a_k consistent with v, where $par_k^{\mathcal{G}}$ is the state of the parents of A_k according to $\mathcal{G}$ which is consistent with v, and likewise for $par_k^{\mathcal{H}}$. $\mathcal{H}$ is just $\mathcal{G}$ but with an arrow from A_i to A_j, so the terms in each product are the same and cancel, except when it comes to assignments a_j to A_j. Thus

$$\frac{p_{\mathcal{G}}(v)}{p_{\mathcal{H}}(v)} = \frac{p^*(a_j | par_j^{\mathcal{G}})}{p^*(a_j | par_j^{\mathcal{H}})} = \frac{p^*(a_j | par_j^{\mathcal{G}})}{p^*(a_j | a_i par_j^{\mathcal{G}})}.$$

Substituting and simplifying,

$$\begin{aligned} \sum_{v @ V} p^*(v) \frac{p_{\mathcal{G}}(v)}{p_{\mathcal{H}}(v)} &= \sum p^*(a_i a_j par_j^{\mathcal{G}}) \frac{p^*(a_j | par_j^{\mathcal{G}})}{p^*(a_j | a_i par_j^{\mathcal{G}})} \\ &= \sum p^*(a_j | par_j^{\mathcal{G}}) p^*(par_j^{\mathcal{G}} | a_i) p^*(a_i). \end{aligned}$$

Consider the new set of variables $\{A_i, A_j, B\}$, where A_i and A_j are as before and B takes as values the assignments to the parents of A_j according to $\mathcal{G}$. Form a

Bayesian network T incorporating the graph $A_i \longrightarrow B \longrightarrow A_j$ (with specifying probabilities determined as usual from the probability function p^*). Then since T is a Bayesian network, $\sum p^*(a_j|b)p^*(b|a_i)p^*(a_i) = \sum p_T(a_i a_j b) = 1$ by the additivity of probability, and $\sum_v p^*(v)p_{\mathcal{G}}(v)/p_{\mathcal{H}}(v) = 1$ so $d(p^*, p_{\mathcal{H}}) - d(p^*, p_{\mathcal{G}}) \leq 0$, as required.

Let us now turn to (ii). From the above reasoning we see that

$$d(p^*, p_{\mathcal{H}}) - d(p^*, p_{\mathcal{G}}) < 0 \Leftrightarrow \log \frac{p_{\mathcal{G}}(v)}{p_{\mathcal{H}}(v)} < \frac{p_{\mathcal{G}}(v)}{p_{\mathcal{H}}(v)} - 1$$

for some assignment v. But $\log x < x - 1 \Leftrightarrow x \neq 1$, and

$$\frac{p_{\mathcal{G}}(v)}{p_{\mathcal{H}}(v)} \neq 1 \Leftrightarrow \frac{p^*(a_j|a_i)}{p^*(a_j|a_i par_j^{\mathcal{G}})} \neq 1 \Leftrightarrow p^*(a_j|a_i par_j^{\mathcal{G}}) - p^*(a_j|par_j^{\mathcal{G}}) \neq 0,$$

where the $a_i, a_j, par_j^{\mathcal{G}}$ are consistent with v. Therefore, $d(p^*, p_{\mathcal{H}}) - d(p^*, p_{\mathcal{G}}) < 0$ if and only if there is some $a_i, a_j, par_j^{\mathcal{G}}$ for which the conditional dependence holds. (That $A_i \rightleftharpoons A_j \mid Par_j^{\mathcal{G}}$ if and only if $I(A_i, A_j \mid Par_j^{\mathcal{G}}) > 0$ is straightforward: independence implies the log term in the mutual information is zero; conversely if the mutual information is zero then its log term must be zero in which implies independence.)

The assumption that $p_{\mathcal{G}}$ and $p_{\mathcal{H}}$ are positive over atomic states is not essential. Suppose $p_{\mathcal{H}}$ is zero over some atomic states. Then in the above,

$$\sum_{v@V} p^*(v) \log \frac{p_{\mathcal{G}}(v)}{p_{\mathcal{H}}(v)} =$$

$$\sum_{v:p_{\mathcal{H}}(v)>0} p^*(v) \log \frac{p_{\mathcal{G}}(v)}{p_{\mathcal{H}}(v)} + \sum_{v:p_{\mathcal{H}}(v)=0} p^*(v) \log \frac{p_{\mathcal{G}}(v)}{p_{\mathcal{H}}(v)}.$$

The first sum on the right-hand side is ≤ 0 as above. The second sum is zero because each component is, as we shall see now. Suppose $p_{\mathcal{H}}(v) = 0$. Then $\prod_{k=1}^n p^*(a_k|par_k^{\mathcal{H}}) = 0$ so $p^*(a_k par_k^{\mathcal{H}}) = 0$ for at least one such k, in which case $p^*(v) = 0$ since for any probability function p, $p(u) = 0$ implies $p(uv) = 0$. Now in the sum read $p^*(v) \log p_{\mathcal{G}}(v)/p_{\mathcal{H}}(v)$ to be $p^*(v) \log p_{\mathcal{G}}(v) - p^*(v) \log p_{\mathcal{H}}(v)$. In dealing with cross entropy by convention $0 \log 0$ is taken to be 0. Therefore $p^*(v) \log p_{\mathcal{G}}(v)/p_{\mathcal{H}}(v) = 0 \log p_{\mathcal{G}}(v) - 0 = 0$. The same reasoning applies if $p_{\mathcal{G}}$ is zero over some atomic states. Likewise, if $p^*(v)$ is zero then $p^*(v) \log p_{\mathcal{G}}(v)/p_{\mathcal{H}}(v)$ is zero too. ■

3.7 Adding Arrows: an Example

The following example shows how the adding-arrows algorithm works.[44] Here we have four two-valued variables $V = \{A_1, A_2, A_3, A_4\}$ and we consider the

[44]This is an extension of an example in Chow and Liu (1968) from the spanning-tree case.

Table 3.2 *Probabilities of assignments*

$A_1 =$	$A_2 =$	$A_3 =$	$A_4 =$	Probability
0	0	0	0	0.100
0	0	0	1	0.100
0	0	1	0	0.050
0	0	1	1	0.050
0	1	0	0	0.000
0	1	0	1	0.000
0	1	1	0	0.100
0	1	1	1	0.050
1	0	0	0	0.050
1	0	0	1	0.100
1	0	1	0	0.000
1	0	1	1	0.000
1	1	0	0	0.050
1	1	0	1	0.050
1	1	1	0	0.150
1	1	1	1	0.150

Table 3.3 *Values for $\mathcal{G}_0$*

A_i	A_j	Par	$I(A_i, A_j \mid Par)$
A_1	A_2	$\emptyset$	0.079
A_1	A_3	$\emptyset$	0.00005
A_1	A_4	$\emptyset$	0.0051
A_2	A_3	$\emptyset$	0.189
A_2	A_4	$\emptyset$	0.0051
A_3	A_4	$\emptyset$	0.0051

subspace of nets whose graphs are directed-path singly connected and have no variables with more than two parents. The target distribution can be specified by Table 3.2.

We start off with a discrete graph $\mathcal{G}_0$. Then we work out the mutual information weights for each possible arrow that may be added to $\mathcal{G}_0$, as in Table 3.3.

Now $I(A_2, A_3)$ is highest so we spawn two graphs, $\mathcal{G}_{1a}$ with the arrow $A_2 \longrightarrow A_3$ and $\mathcal{G}_{1b}$ with the arrow $A_3 \longrightarrow A_2$. At the next stage for $\mathcal{G}_{1a}$ we must calculate mutual information values involving A_3, but conditional on A_2, $I(A_1, A_3|A_2)$ and $I(A_3, A_4|A_2)$, since A_3 is the parent of A_2. In Table 3.4 we have the values for $\mathcal{G}_{1a}$, and the values for $\mathcal{G}_{1b}$ are in Table 3.5.

Thus $I(A_1, A_2|A_3)$ has the greatest value at this stage. We can eliminate $\mathcal{G}_{1a}$ and add $A_1 \longrightarrow A_2$ to $\mathcal{G}_{1b}$ to obtain $\mathcal{G}_2$ as in Fig. 3.2.

We cannot next add another arrow into A_2 since that would yield three parents. Therefore we have Table 3.6 for $\mathcal{G}_2$.

Table 3.4 *Values for $\mathcal{G}_{1a}$*

A_i	A_j	Par	$I(A_i, A_j \mid Par)$
A_1	A_2	$\emptyset$	0.079
A_1	A_3	$\emptyset$	0.00005
A_1	A_3	A_2	0.0833
A_1	A_4	$\emptyset$	0.0051
A_2	A_4	$\emptyset$	0.0051
A_3	A_4	$\emptyset$	0.0051
A_3	A_4	A_2	0.0013

Table 3.5 *Values for $\mathcal{G}_{1b}$*

A_i	A_j	Par	$I(A_i, A_j \mid Par)$
A_1	A_2	$\emptyset$	0.079
A_1	A_2	A_3	0.1626
A_1	A_3	$\emptyset$	0.00005
A_1	A_4	$\emptyset$	0.0051
A_2	A_4	$\emptyset$	0.0051
A_2	A_4	A_3	0.0013
A_3	A_4	$\emptyset$	0.0754

There are three contenders for maximum weight: $I(A_1, A_4), I(A_2, A_4)$ and $I(A_3, A_4)$. Thus we can spawn five graphs $\mathcal{G}_{3a}, \ldots, \mathcal{G}_{3e}$ by adding respectively $A_1 \longrightarrow A_4, A_4 \longrightarrow A_1, A_2 \longrightarrow A_4, A_3 \longrightarrow A_4$, and $A_4 \longrightarrow A_3$ to $\mathcal{G}_2$. These are depicted in Figs 3.3–3.7.

Now no more arrows can be added to $\mathcal{G}_{3b}, \mathcal{G}_{3c}$, or $\mathcal{G}_{3e}$ without violating acyclicity, directed-path single-connectedness or the two-parent bound. The only possible additions are $A_3 \longrightarrow A_4$ to $\mathcal{G}_{3a}$ or $A_1 \longrightarrow A_4$ to $\mathcal{G}_{3d}$ with weights shown in Table 3.7 and Table 3.8, respectively. Each of these additions would result in the same graph, $\mathcal{G}_4$ as shown in Fig. 3.8.

All that remains is to determine the associated probability specifiers $\mathcal{S}_4$ from Table 3.2 (where a_i^1 represents assignment $A_i = 1$ and a_i^0 represents assignment $A_i = 0$):

$$p(a_1^1) = 0.55$$

$$p(a_3^1) = 0.55$$

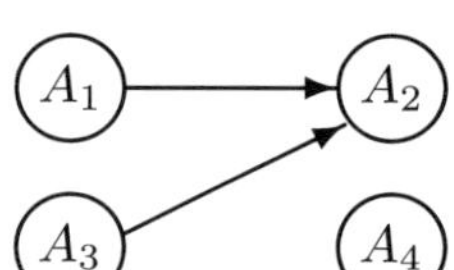

FIG. 3.2. $\mathcal{G}_2$.

Table 3.6 *Values for $\mathcal{G}_2$*

A_i	A_j	Par	$I(A_i, A_j \mid Par)$
A_1	A_3	$\emptyset$	0.00005
A_1	A_4	$\emptyset$	0.0051
A_2	A_4	$\emptyset$	0.0051
A_3	A_4	$\emptyset$	0.0051

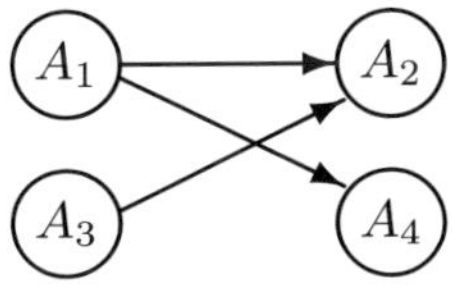

FIG. 3.3. $\mathcal{G}_{3a}$.

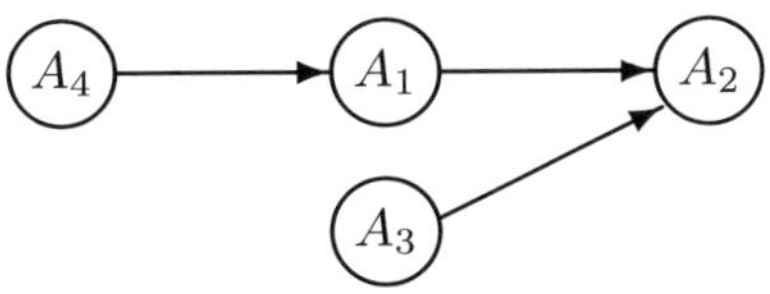

FIG. 3.4. $\mathcal{G}_{3b}$.

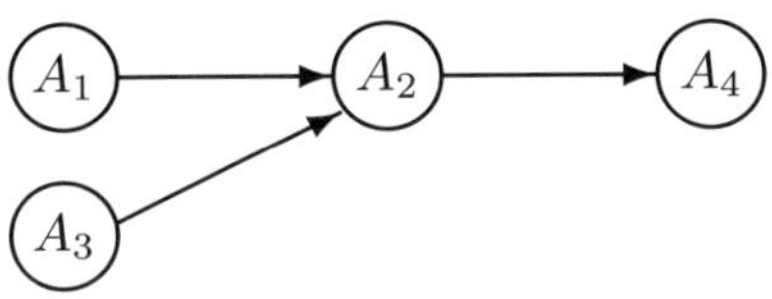

FIG. 3.5. $\mathcal{G}_{3c}$.

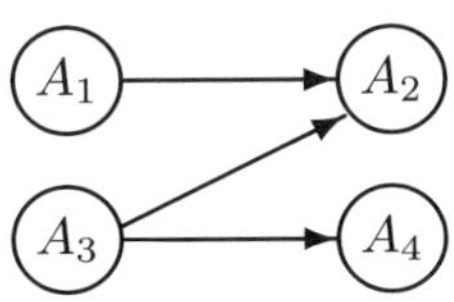

FIG. 3.6. $\mathcal{G}_{3d}$.

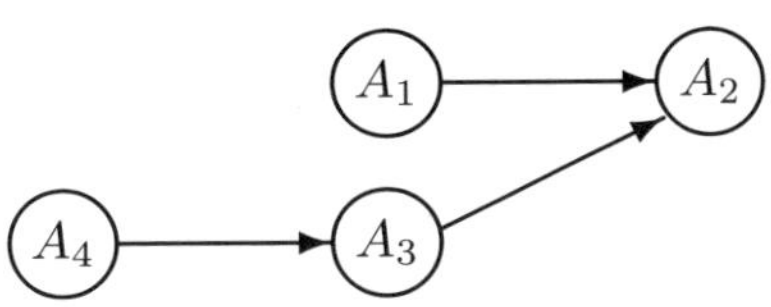

FIG. 3.7. $\mathcal{G}_{3e}$.

Table 3.7 *Values for $\mathcal{G}_{3b}$*

A_i	A_j	Par	$I(A_i, A_j \mid Par)$
A_4	A_3	A_1	0.00005

Table 3.8 *Values for $\mathcal{G}_{3d}$*

A_i	A_j	Par	$I(A_i, A_j \mid Par)$
A_4	A_1	A_3	0.00005

$$p(a_2^1|a_1^1a_3^1) = 1$$
$$p(a_2^1|a_1^1a_3^0) = 0.4$$
$$p(a_2^1|a_1^0a_3^1) = 0.6$$
$$p(a_2^1|a_1^0a_3^0) = 0$$
$$p(a_4^1|a_1^1a_3^1) = 0.5$$
$$p(a_4^1|a_1^1a_3^0) = 0.6$$
$$p(a_4^1|a_1^0a_3^1) = 0.4$$
$$p(a_4^1|a_1^0a_3^0) = 0.5.$$

Then we output the Bayesian net $(\mathcal{G}_4, \mathcal{S}_4)$ as our approximation to Table 3.2.

3.8 The Approximation Subspace

For the adding-arrows algorithm to work well, the approximation subspace $\mathbb{S}$ must satisfy certain regularity conditions:

- the discrete net $(\mathcal{D}, \mathcal{S}_\mathcal{D}) \in \mathbb{S}$,
- if $(\mathcal{G}, \mathcal{S}_\mathcal{G}) \in \mathbb{S}$ then $(\mathcal{H}, \mathcal{S}_\mathcal{H}) \in \mathbb{S}$ for each subgraph $\mathcal{H}$ of $\mathcal{G}$ on V (i.e. $\mathcal{H}$ has the same variables as $\mathcal{G}$ and no arrows that are not in $\mathcal{G}$).

The motivation behind these conditions is straightforward: for the adding-arrows algorithm to be able to output a net $(\mathcal{G}, \mathcal{S}_\mathcal{G})$ in $\mathbb{S}$, it must be able to consecutively add the arrows in $\mathcal{G}$ to the discrete net, all the while remaining in $\mathbb{S}$. Note that in the presence of the second condition, the first condition is equivalent to the condition that $\mathbb{S}$ be non-empty.

In order to examine the adding-arrows algorithm it helps to formulate a precise measure of the success of an approximation to a target network. By

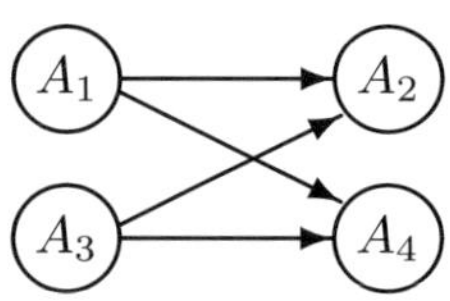

FIG. 3.8. $\mathcal{G}_4$.

Table 3.9 *Percentage successes of example graphs*

Graph	$\sum w_i$	σ
$\mathcal{G}_0$	0	0
$\mathcal{G}_{1a}$	.189	51.3
$\mathcal{G}_{1b}$	.189	51.3
$\mathcal{G}_2$	.3516	95.4
$\mathcal{G}_{3a}$	.3567	96.8
$\mathcal{G}_{3b}$	.3567	96.8
$\mathcal{G}_{3c}$	.3567	96.8
$\mathcal{G}_{3d}$	.3567	96.8
$\mathcal{G}_{3e}$	.3567	96.8
$\mathcal{G}_4$	.35675	96.8

Theorem 3.7 as arrows are added to the graph $\mathcal{G}$ in a Bayesian network its induced probability function p more closely approximates a target function p^* (as long as the corresponding specification $\mathcal{S}_\mathcal{G}$ is determined from p^*). Thus the worst approximation to p^* is afforded by the function q determined by the *discrete network* $(\mathcal{D}, \mathcal{S}_\mathcal{D})$, whose graph $\mathcal{D}$ contains all variables in V as nodes but no arrows, and whose specification $\mathcal{S}_\mathcal{D} = \{p(a_i) : a_i@A_i \subseteq V\}$. We can then measure the *percentage success* of an approximation network p by

$$\sigma = 100\left[\frac{d(p^*,q) - d(p^*,p)}{d(p^*,q)}\right].$$

By adding arrows one moves from the discrete network to the target network and the success of the approximation network is the percentage of the total distance that has been covered. From the proof of Theorem 3.6 we saw that

$$d(p^*,p) = -H(p^*) - \sum_{i=1}^{n} I(A_i, Par_i) + \sum_{i=1}^{n} H(p^*_{\lceil A_i}).$$

Hence

$$d(p^*,q) = -H(p^*) + \sum_{i=1}^{n} H(p^*_{\lceil A_i}),$$

and

$$\sigma = 100\left[\frac{\sum w_i}{d(p^*,q)}\right],$$

where $\sum w_i$ is the sum of the arrow weights of approximation network $(\mathcal{G}, \mathcal{S}_\mathcal{G})$. So once we calculate $d(p^*,q)$ it is rather easy to determine the percentage success of various approximation networks.

Consider the example of §3.7. Here $d(p^*,q) = 0.3687$ and the percentage successes are displayed in Table 3.9.

Figure 3.9 shows the percentage success of networks produced by the adding-arrows algorithm for a range of $n = |V|$ in various approximation subspaces.

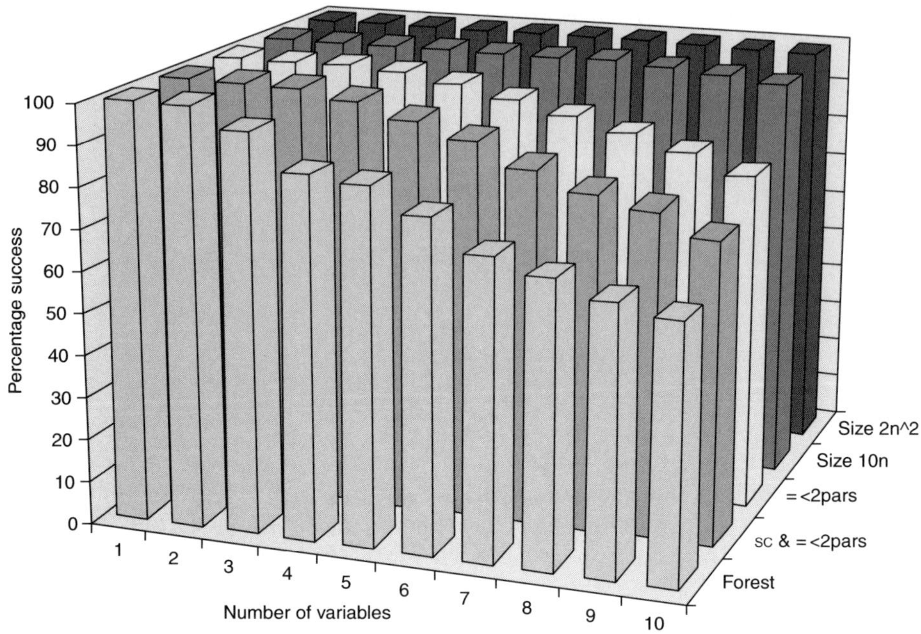

FIG. 3.9. Percentage success with various approximation subspaces.

First a target net $(\mathcal{G}^*, \mathcal{S}^*)$ was randomly generated as follows. A directed acyclic graph $\mathcal{G}^*$ is chosen at random: an ancestral order on the n binary variables is u-randomly picked;[45] then for each variable a u-random number of successors in the order are chosen to be its children, and then those children are picked from the successors at u-random. Thus the weight is on graphs of middling complexity, with very highly connected or disconnected graphs less likely.[46] The specifying probabilities in $\mathcal{S}^*$ were then generated at u-random from machine reals.

Next, approximation nets were generated by the adding-arrows method. The experiment was repeated so that the average success could be estimated. The front row shows the percentage success in the subspace of nets whose graphs are trees or forests.[47] Note that this subspace occupies a smaller proportion of the space of all nets as n increases (the subspace contains nets whose graphs

[45]The expression *u-random* is short for uniformly at random: i.e. each choice in a finite partition has the same probability of being chosen.

[46]Alternatively one can generate graphs as follows. For each pair of nodes decide whether they should be joined by an arrow at random—an arrow being as likely as none—and then if there is to be an arrow decide the direction at random—with one direction as likely as the other. Reject graphs that turn out not to be acyclic. Thus medium dense graphs are again most likely. It turns out that this procedure gives very similar resulting trends. Melancon *et al.* (2000) discuss the generation of random directed acyclic graphs. Ide and Cozman (2002) apply a similar method to the random generation of Bayesian nets.

[47]This is the space considered by Chow and Liu (1968).

have up to $n-1$ arrows whereas the whole space contains nets whose graphs have up to $n(n-1)/2$ arrows) and so nets within this subspace are likely to be worse approximations to a target function as n increases. In the second row the subspace contains nets with singly connected graphs where variables have no more than two parents. We can see that the approximations are on average significantly closer to the target distribution than the forest-based approximations. Further improvement is to be noted in the third row, where single-connectedness is dropped. Likewise for the fourth and the back row, where the subspaces contain nets of maximum size (i.e. number of specified probabilities bounded above by) $10n$ and $2n^2$ respectively. Thus Fig. 3.9 clearly indicates the ability of the adding-arrows algorithm to exploit larger approximation subspaces to yield better approximations.

While this experiment involved simulations with target functions selected at random, the same story can be told with more realistic targets if we consider target functions determined by databases of real observations, as follows.

In general a database of observations takes the form of a list of observed assignments $D = (u_1, \ldots, u_k)$, where each $u_i@U_i \subseteq V$. If $A_i \in V$ but $A_i \notin U_j$ for each $j = 1, \ldots, k$ (no observation is made of A_i) then A_i is called an *unobserved variable*. If each $U_i = V$—every observation observes every variable—then the database has no *missing values*. In such a case we can identify the probability function determined by the database with a frequency function (see §2.4): supposing the database to be the first k elements of an infinite collective of observations $\mathcal{V} = (v_1, v_2, v_3, \ldots)$ we can define

$$p^*(v) = \mathit{freq}_{\mathcal{V}}(v) = \lim_{n \longrightarrow \infty} \frac{|v|^n_{\mathcal{V}}}{n},$$

and estimate these values by $\mathit{freq}^k_{\mathcal{V}}(v)$, the frequency of v in the database, which we can also denote by $\mathit{freq}_D(v)$.

There are two complicating scenarios. First, if there are missing values or unobserved variables then the task of identifying $p^*(v)$ is more subtle: we need to identify a suitable probability function p^* that satisfies the constraints $p^*(u_i) \approx \mathit{freq}_D(u_i)$ for $i = 1, \ldots, k$. This problem is discussed in detail in Chapter 5 and for simplicity in this section we shall only consider databases with no missing values. Second, there may be *sampling bias*: frequencies determined by the database may differ systematically from the frequency distribution of the population from which the database is sampled, because of biases in the sampling mechanism. It may be that the target probability function is the population distribution rather than the sampled distribution, in which case one needs to know the bias in order to determine the target. For simplicity's sake we shall take the database distribution to be the target distribution here.

The adding-arrows algorithm was run on a range of databases with no missing values from the Machine Learning Repository,[48] and the final percentage

[48](Blake and Merz, 1998)

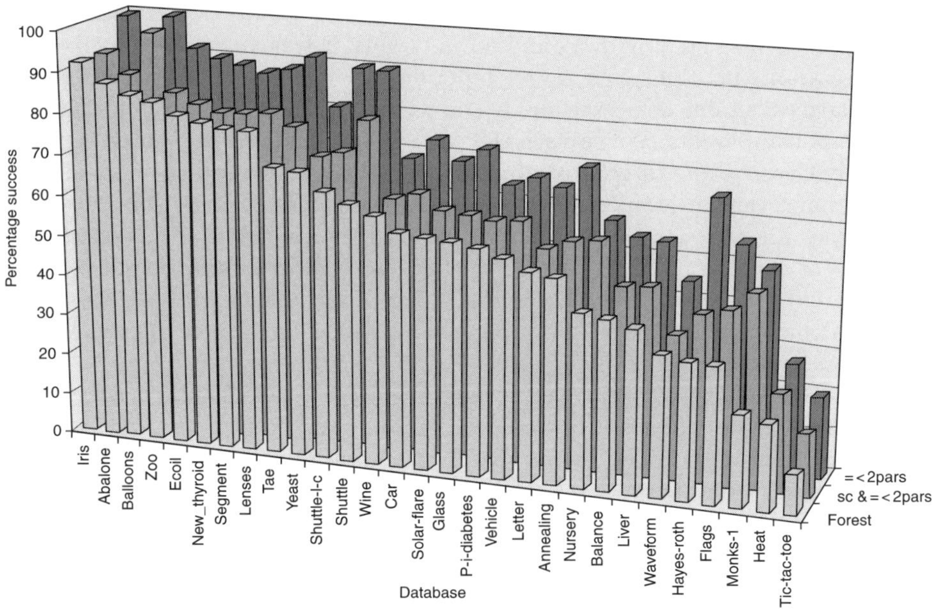

FIG. 3.10. Databases under structural constraints.

success was measured.[49] Fig. 3.10 shows the improvement that the relaxation of structural constraints makes on the approximation. On average the approximation networks that were both singly connected and limited to two parents per node were a further 5.4% towards the target distribution than the tree-shaped networks, while the approximation networks from the two-parent subspace were 14.7% closer on average. Thus varying the subspace affords significant increase in distribution fit on real data as well as simulated data. Note that this increase in fit does not require an excessive sacrifice in terms of complexity: the singly connected two-parent nets were on average less than 1% larger than the tree nets (the percentage is taken over the maximum size, ie. the size of a complete net), while the two-parent nets were on average less than 4% larger than the tree nets.[50]

Consider, e.g., the Pima Indians Diabetes database.[51] This database measures the occurrence of diabetes and several other relevant variables. There are nine

[49]Note that some databases involve continuous variables—these were discretised.

[50]Figure 3.10 involves only subspaces defined structurally because those defined in terms of size which were used in the simulations in Fig. 3.9 were not appropriate in this context. Many of the variables in the databases have more than two values. Consequently a size constraint of $10n$ or $2n^2$ can be very low for such a database—lower than the complexity of a tree for instance. Thus general size constraints should take into account the ranges of the variables, which makes them rather more complicated than in the binary case.

[51](Smith *et al.*, 1988)

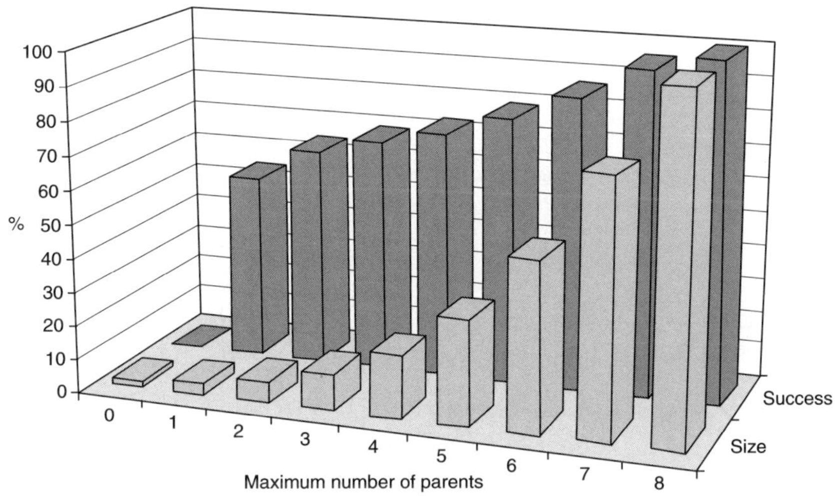

FIG. 3.11. Bounds on the number of parents.

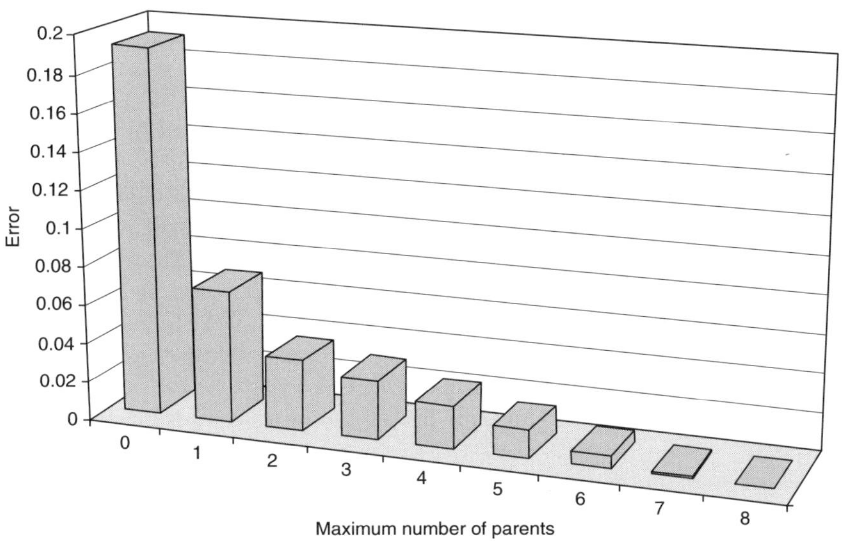

FIG. 3.12. Diagnostic error.

variables and those that have a continuous range of values can be discretised into two-valued variables. On such a domain a Bayesian net can have size at most 511, which is small enough for us to be able to generate complex networks for the purposes of comparison.

First we see that varying the approximation subspace allows one to vary the balance between closeness of approximation and size of approximating nets.

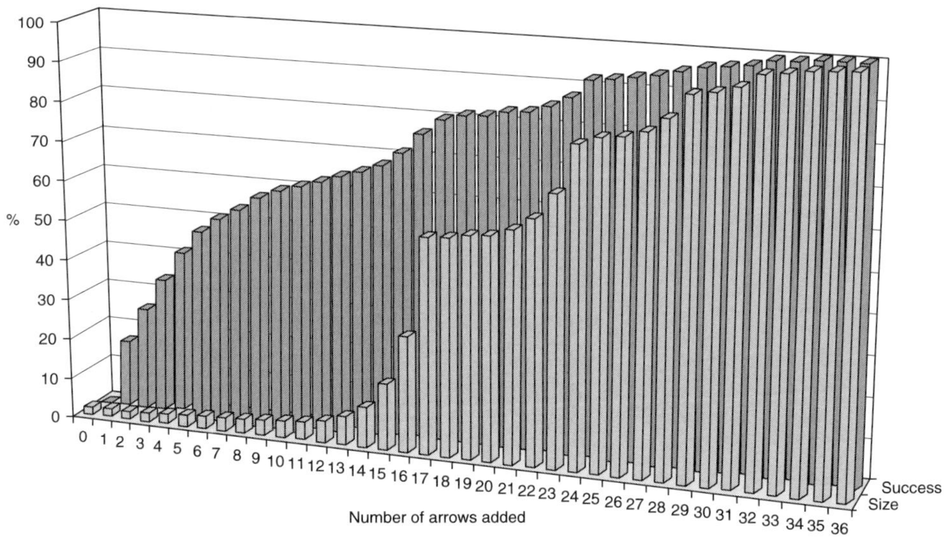

FIG. 3.13. Approximation subspace is the whole space of nets.

Consider the approximation subspaces $\mathbb{S}_k$ containing nets where no variable has more than k parents, for $k = 0, \ldots, 8$. Figure 3.11 displays percentage success of the nets produced by the adding-arrows algorithm, as well as their size as a percentage of the maximum size, 511. If the maximum number of parents k is relatively small then the approximation nets achieve a good degree of approximation for low size. Note too that if the network closely approximates the target distribution then diagnostic success is rendered more likely. That is, the diagnostic error $|p^*(a_i|u) - p(a_i|u)|$ is likely to be low. We can see this in the diabetes example by measuring the error for an assignment $a_i@A_i \in V$ and an assignment $u@U \subseteq V$ involving m other variables, repeating this for each i and m, and averaging. Figure 3.12 shows that the average diagnostic error decreases to zero as k increases, but also that the error is well below 0.05 even for a maximum of $k = 2$ parents.

We can also examine the adding-arrows strategy on an arrow-by-arrow basis. Figure 3.13 gives the percentage success and size as arrows are added to a discrete graph for $\mathbb{S} = \mathbb{B}$, the whole space of Bayesian nets. We see that success rises sharply, but that without any constraints, size also rises sharply before long. Figure 3.14 shows what happens with $\mathbb{S}_3$, a three-parent bound: we still get the sharp rise in success (although there is a limit to the final success) but the size is kept low. By way of comparison with Fig. 3.13, Fig. 3.15 shows what happens when arrows are added randomly (no weighting is used to select arrows) and $\mathbb{S} = \mathbb{B}$. We lose the sharp rise in success, and rise in size is also gentler. Clearly the use of the mutual information weight in Fig. 3.13 allows a quicker approximation to the target distribution.

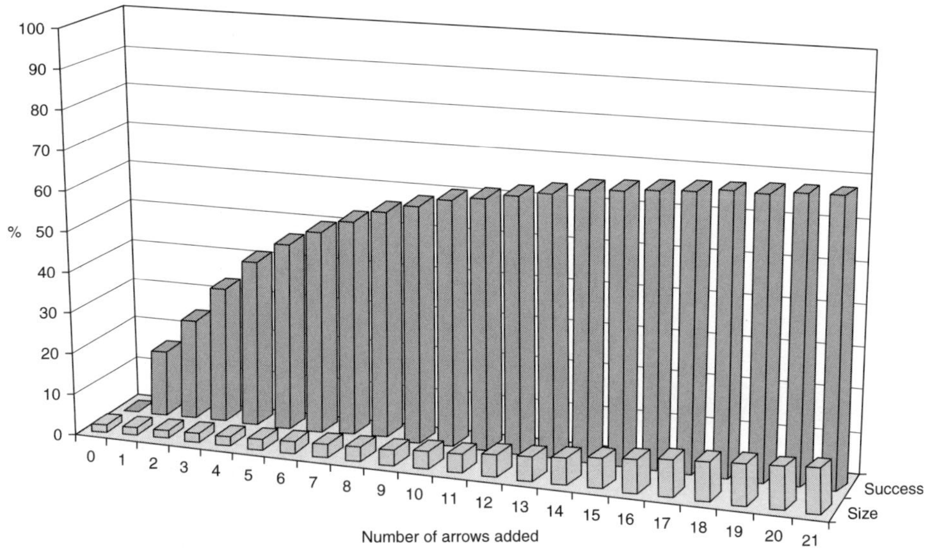

FIG. 3.14. Approximation subspace defined by a three-parent bound.

The last example was useful because there were few enough variables that we could generate networks of up to maximum complexity for the purposes of comparison. Now we shall apply the adding-arrows approach to a larger problem. 105 characteristics were obtained from pregnant women for research into the question of whether a mother's vegetarianism causes smaller babies—these variables sum up the state of the women's nutritional intake, health, and pregnancy.[52]

We can generate an approximation net over some or all of these variables in exactly the same way as before. Taking a subset of 23 variables, the maximum size of a net is about 19 million. In Fig. 3.16 we can see how increasing k again increases the distribution fit while controlling the size (size only rose to 0.06%). In Fig. 3.17 the approximation subspaces further require that the graph be singly connected. While this significantly reduces the amount of progress towards the target distribution, it ensures that probability values can be calculated in polynomial time and further reduces the size of the approximation network (size only rose to 0.01 percent). Thus we see again that computational and storage reductions can be traded for degree of approximation.

As to which approximation subspace is the most appropriate will depend on the application. While one would like to closely approximate a database distribution, one would not want to over-fit the distribution (i.e. fit the database distribution $freq_D$ rather than the target distribution $freq_{\mathcal{V}}$ which it approximates) and of course one may want to sacrifice some fit in order to lower the computational resources required by the approximation network. Unlike many

[52](Drake *et al.*, 1998)

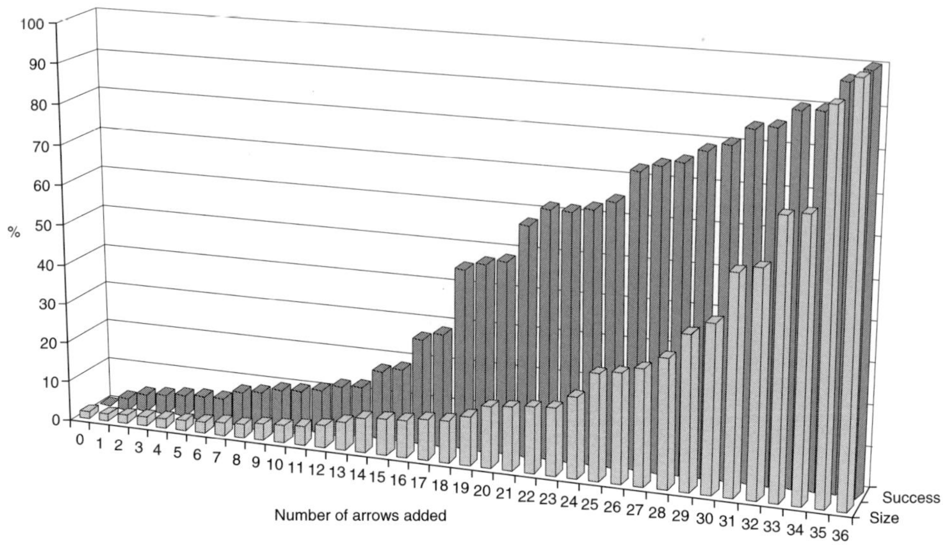

FIG. 3.15. Random arrows.

proposals for constructing Bayesian networks,[53] the mutual information weighting approach leaves the choice of approximation subspace open. This is a good thing: there is little point in prescribing one particular compromise between degree of approximation and computational complexity if different compromises suit different applications.

Note though that if necessary one can easily modify the adding-arrows algorithm to produce a technique for constructing a Bayesian net that does not require a choice of approximation subspace. The *balanced adding-arrows algorithm* works the same way as the standard adding-arrows algorithm except that each arrow $A \longrightarrow B$ is weighed by the conditional mutual information $I(A, B|Par_B)$ *divided by the increase in size that would arise if the arrow were added.* This balances degree of fit with increase in size, and, as Fig. 3.18 shows, achieves a good approximation for low size on the Pima Indians Diabetes database, at least until the last few arrows are added. One can then fix $\mathbb{S} = \mathbb{B}$ and halt the balanced adding-arrows algorithm when, say, size increases faster than success.[54]

3.9 Greed of Adding Arrows

The adding-arrows algorithm is a *greedy search*: instead of determining the weight of each network in subspace $\mathbb{S}$ of the space $\mathbb{B}$ of Bayesian nets and selecting those nets of maximum weight, the adding-arrows algorithm takes an incremental

[53](Neapolitan, 2003)

[54]The Minimum Description Length approach outlined in §8.6 is another variant of the mutual-information approach that does not leave choice of approximation subspace open.

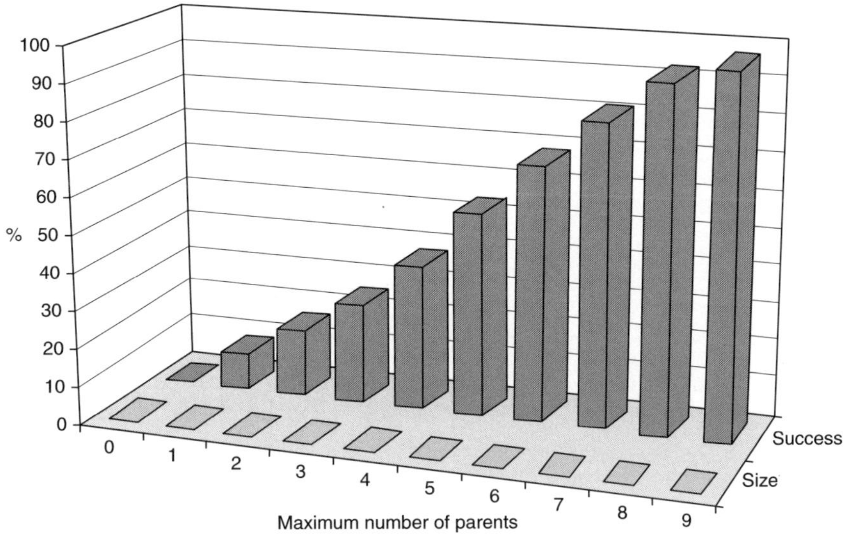

FIG. 3.16. Maximum number of parents k.

Table 3.10 *Specification* $\mathcal{S}^*$

$p(a^0) = 0.78164$	$p(a^1) = 0.21836$
$p(b^0) = 0.829402$	$p(b^1) = 0.170598$
$p(c^0\|a^0b^0) = 0.252754$	$p(c^1\|a^0b^0) = 0.747246$
$p(c^0\|a^0b^1) = 0.878842$	$p(c^1\|a^0b^1) = 0.121158$
$p(c^0\|a^1b^0) = 0.637654$	$p(c^1\|a^1b^0) = 0.362346$
$p(c^0\|a^1b^1) = 0.008118$	$p(c^1\|a^1b^1) = 0.991882$
$p(d^0\|a^0b^0) = 0.012421$	$p(d^1\|a^0b^0) = 0.987579$
$p(d^0\|a^0b^1) = 0.690939$	$p(d^1\|a^0b^1) = 0.309061$
$p(d^0\|a^1b^0) = 0.852748$	$p(d^1\|a^1b^0) = 0.147252$
$p(d^0\|a^1b^1) = 0.634175$	$p(d^1\|a^1b^1) = 0.365825$

approach, at each stage only searching the subspace of $\mathbb{S}$ consisting of nets whose graphs have one more arrow than current nets. This incremental approach is much faster than the former approach, but while the former will yield optimal nets, the adding-arrows method may not, as we see from the following example.

Example 3.8 Let $\mathbb{S}$ be the subspace of directed-path singly connected nets with no more than two parents and let target probability function p^* be defined by a Bayesian net with graph $\mathcal{G}^*$ as in Fig. 3.19 and probability tables as Table 3.10. Note that $(\mathcal{G}^*, \mathcal{S}^*) \in \mathbb{S}$. Now the adding-arrows algorithm may be applied as

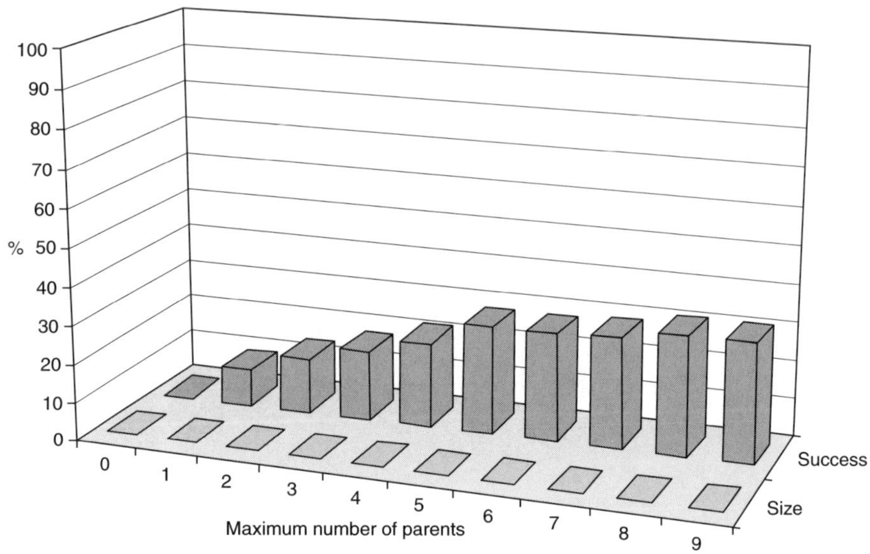

FIG. 3.17. Single-connectedness and k-parent bound.

follows—the relevant arrow weights are given in descending order in Table 3.11. First start with the discrete graph $\mathcal{G}_0$. Arrows between A and D have maximum weight, so construct graphs $\mathcal{G}_{1a}$ with arrow $A \longrightarrow D$ and $\mathcal{G}_{1b}$ with arrow $D \longrightarrow A$. At the next step the maximum weight arrow is $B \longrightarrow D$ added to $\mathcal{G}_{1a}$ to give $\mathcal{G}_2$ as in Fig. 3.20 ($\mathcal{G}_{1b}$ is eliminated). Finally $D \longrightarrow C$ has maximum weight at the next step (note that $C \longrightarrow D$ cannot be added to $\mathcal{G}_2$ without breaking the two-parent bound), yielding $\mathcal{G}_3$ as in Fig. 3.21 (any further arrows would break single-connectedness or acyclicity). By determining a probability specification $\mathcal{S}_3$ from p^* we can form a Bayesian net involving $\mathcal{G}_3$. Then the adding-arrows approach yields $(\mathcal{G}_3, \mathcal{S}_3) \in \mathbb{S}$ as an approximation to p^*. This approximation is reasonable—it scores 84% on our success measure (i.e. $(\mathcal{G}_3, \mathcal{S}_3)$ is 84% of the distance from the discrete net to the target $(\mathcal{G}^*, \mathcal{S}^*)$). However, it is not optimal: the target net itself is optimal, that is, $(\mathcal{G}^*, \mathcal{S}^*)$ is the best approximation in $\mathbb{S}$ to p^*.

Although there are cases in which the adding-arrows algorithm fails to find an optimal approximation, these cases appear to be surprisingly rare. One can perform experiments to ascertain their pervasiveness, and one finds that on average the measure of success is very close to 100%. The black bars in Fig. 3.22 show what happens when we generate n-variable nets $(\mathcal{G}^*, \mathcal{S}^*) \in \mathbb{S}$ at random and approximate them by the adding-arrows method. Here $\mathbb{S}$ contains directed-path singly connected nets with a bound of two parents maximum. There is not much to see: in each case the average success is greater than 99.7%. The black bars in Fig. 3.23 show the situation in which $\mathbb{S}$ contains nets with at most four

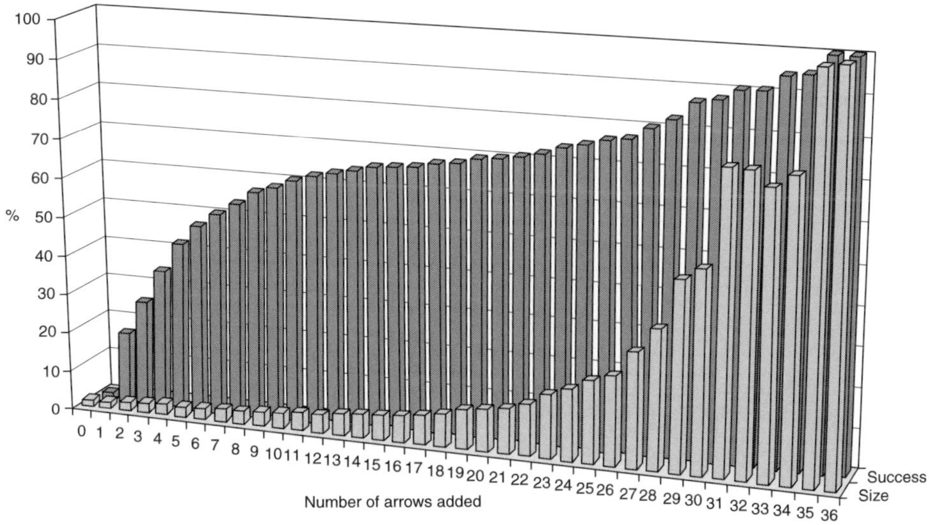

FIG. 3.18. Weighted by size.

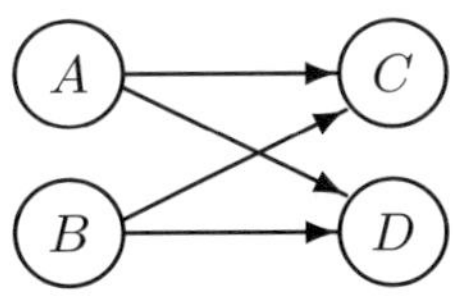

FIG. 3.19. Graph $\mathcal{G}^*$.

parents (there is no restriction to singly connected nets) and it tells a similar story: average success exceeding 98%.

We thus have an important justification for using the adding-arrows method: it yields good approximations *on average.*

Table 3.11 *Mutual information arrow weights*

$I(A,D) = 0.18758$
$I(B,D \mid A) = 0.177769$
$I(A,B \mid D) = 0.103899$
$I(B,D) = 0.0738702$
$I(C,D \mid A) = 0.0550221$
$I(C,D) = 0.0523379$
$I(B,C) = 0.036018$
$I(A,C \mid D) = 0.0128952$
$I(A,C) = 0.0102111$
$I(A,B) = 0$

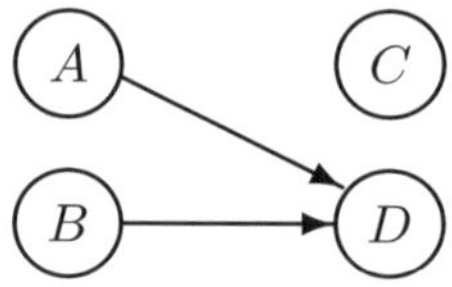

FIG. 3.20. Graph $\mathcal{G}_2$.

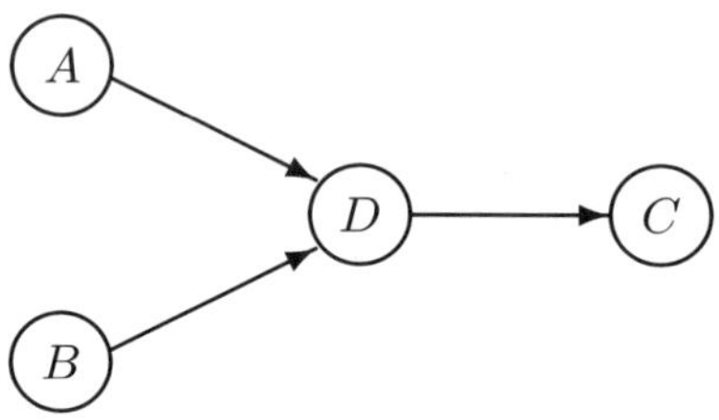

FIG. 3.21. Graph $\mathcal{G}_3$.

While the adding-arrows algorithm performs well at finding a close approximation to a target function, it performs less well at recovering a target network. The *recovery* problem is this: suppose the target probability function is represented by a net $(\mathcal{G}^*, \mathcal{S}^*)$ within the subspace $\mathbb{S}$; will the adding-arrows algorithm recover $(\mathcal{G}^*, \mathcal{S}^*)$ itself? i.e. will $(\mathcal{G}^*, \mathcal{S}^*)$ be among the nets output by the adding-arrows algorithm? Example 3.8 shows that the answer can be negative—there are cases in which the algorithm will fail to recover a target net. Moreover, if we perform simulations to find out how often a successful recovery occurs on average, we find that the algorithm can perform quite poorly. While the white bars

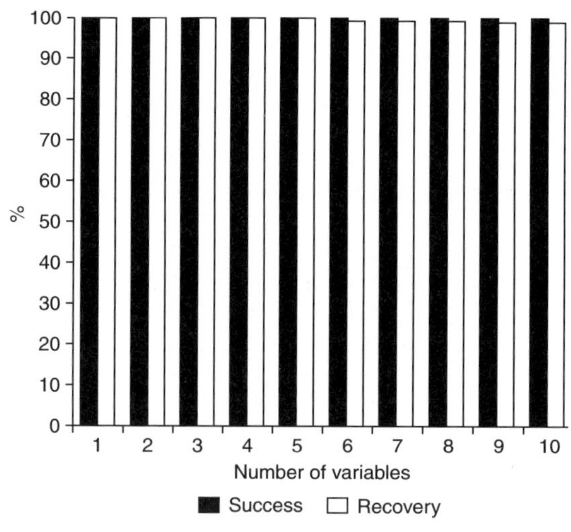

FIG. 3.22. Singly connected, two-parent bound.

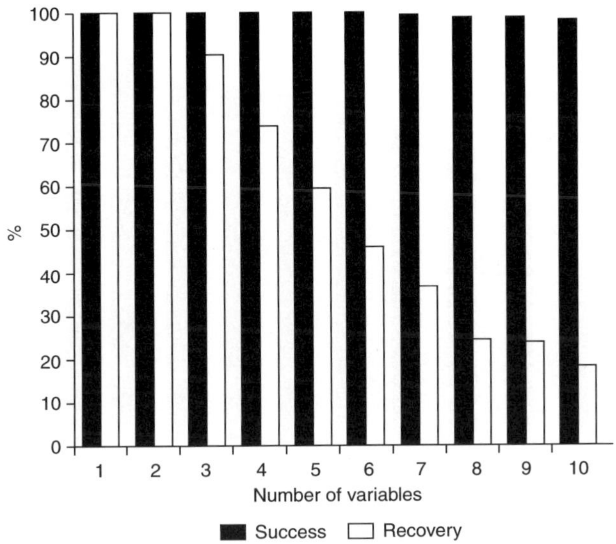

FIG. 3.23. Four parent bound.

in Fig. 3.22 show that the recovery rate can be high in some subspaces, the white bars in Fig. 3.23 show that in other subspaces the average recovery can decrease dramatically with the number of variables. However, in our context recovery is not as important a desideratum as accuracy of approximation. Indeed there are cases in which recovery fails because arrows in the target net are redundant; the algorithm then outputs nets of lower complexity; this is clearly preferable to outputting the target net itself.

Of course some applications may require a closer approximation or better recovery than the adding-arrows algorithm can yield. There are some simple changes one can make to the adding-arrows algorithm to increase its capability (at the expense of computational complexity of course). For example, one could search for more than one arrow to add at a time, choosing to add those arrows whose inclusion would increase network weight the most. Or one could reverse the direction of an arrow, or remove an arrow and add another arrow, according to prospective gains in network weight. All these approaches help to reduce the greed of the adding-arrows algorithm.

3.10 Complexity of Adding Arrows

The most direct way of finding a maximum weight net is to weigh each net in the approximation subspace $\mathbb{S}$ and select those with maximum weight. However, $\mathbb{S}$ can be very large and this method is not feasible in general.[55] One of the

[55]The number of directed acyclic graphs on n variables is asymptotically $n!2^N/M\rho^n$ where $N = n(n-1)/2$, $M \approx 0.574$ and $\rho \approx 1.488$; the number of directed acyclic graphs with k arrows

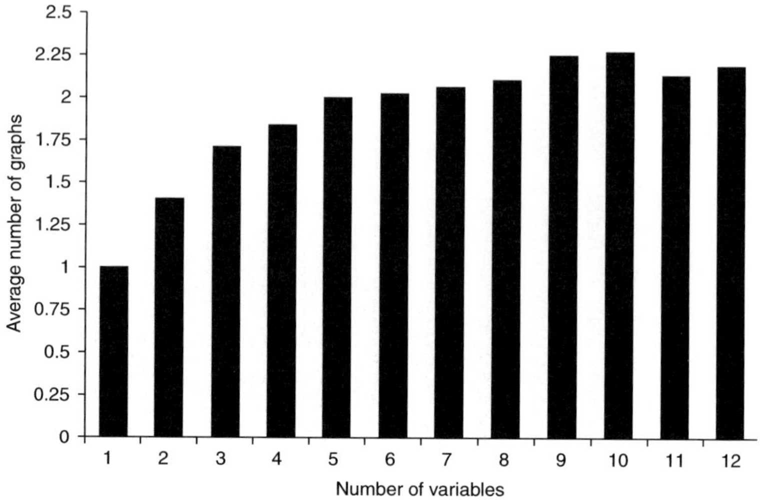

FIG. 3.24. Average number of graphs stored at steps of the adding-arrows algorithm, where the approximation subspace is the whole space of Bayesian nets.

motivations behind the adding-arrows approach is the need for a computationally tractable method. In this section, we will briefly investigate the tractability of adding arrows, sketching the main computational costs, and seeing how they vary with approximation subspace.

There are two considerations to take into account: the space complexity and the time complexity of the algorithm. Note that the approximation subspace $\mathbb{S}$ is chosen to be a space that contains nets of size within available bounds; hence the space complexity can be estimated by the number of nets in $\mathbb{S}$ that must be stored at each step of the algorithm. This number can in turn be estimated from simulations. When acyclicity is the only restriction on the proliferation of nets, i.e. when the approximation space is the whole space of Bayesian nets, $\mathbb{S} = \mathbb{B}$, Fig. 3.24 shows the average number of graphs that need to be stored at each step in this case. Although there is too little data to say for sure, it appears that the average number of graphs is bounded by a constant, 3. Fig. 3.25, dealing with the two-parent bound approximation subspace, shows the average number of graphs under consideration to increase linearly with n. (Introducing the two-parent bound increases complexity because it increases the likelihood of an arrow being added between variables with no parents—such arrows can go either way and their introduction leads to a doubling of the number of graphs.)

Next to time complexity. The main calculations are those of determining arrow weights, determining probability specifications, and checking to see whether a new net is in $\mathbb{S}$. We may suppose that the latter task can be performed quickly—

is of a similar order as long as k is not close to 0 or $n(n-1)/2$—see Bender *et al.* (1986).

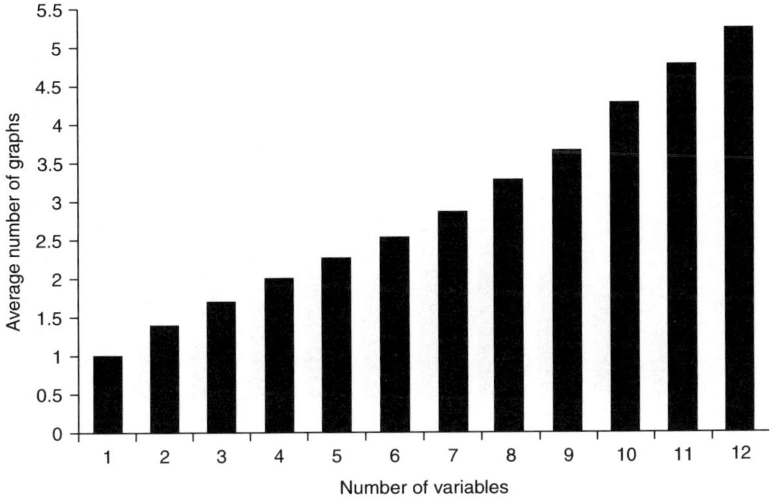

FIG. 3.25. Average number of graphs stored at steps of the adding-arrows algorithm, where the approximation subspace is the set of nets whose variables have no more than two parents.

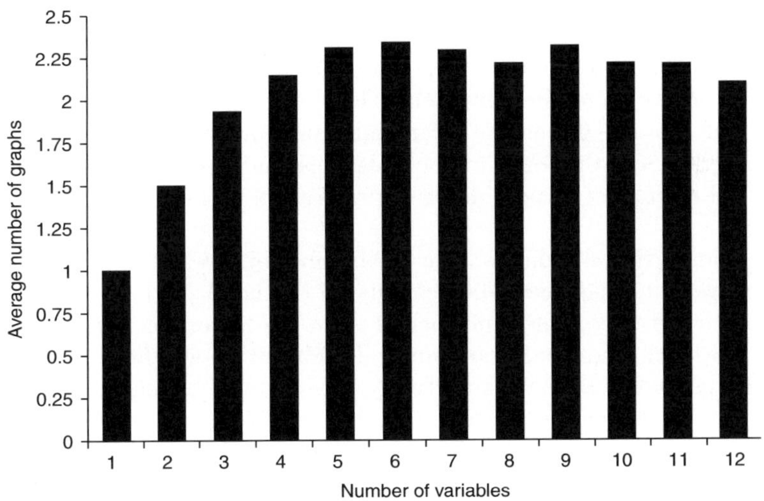

FIG. 3.26. Average number of nets output by the adding-arrows algorithm, where the approximation subspace is the whole space of Bayesian nets.

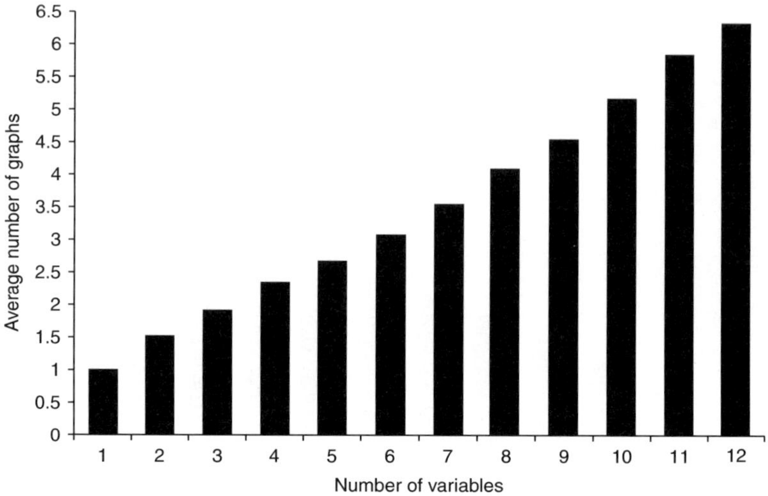

FIG. 3.27. Average number of nets output by the adding-arrows algorithm, where the approximation subspace is the set of nets whose variables have no more than two parents.

$\mathbb{S}$ can be chosen with this desideratum in mind. The length of time it takes to determine a probability specification will also depend on $\mathbb{S}$, and this may be borne in mind when choosing $\mathbb{S}$. Moreover if membership of $\mathbb{S}$ depends solely on the graph in a net, then no specifications need to be determined until output stage; Fig. 3.26 suggests that for $\mathbb{S} = \mathbb{B}$ the average number of specifications that need to be determined (i.e. the average number of nets output by the algorithm) is bounded above by a constant, while Fig. 3.27 indicates linear growth with a two-parent bound. Otherwise—if membership of $\mathbb{S}$ depends on specification as well as graph—the number of specifications that need to be determined will depend on the number of nets under consideration at each stage (Figs 3.24 and 3.25).

Time complexity also depends on the number of conditional mutual information arrow weights that need to be calculated by the algorithm. At the first step we start with the discrete net and each of the $n(n-1)$ possible arrows needs to be weighed. (Note that unconditional mutual information weight of arrow $A \longrightarrow B$ is the same as that of $B \longrightarrow A$ so actually only $n(n-1)/2$ weights need to be calculated.) At subsequent steps there may be several graphs under consideration. For such a graph, suppose arrow $A \longrightarrow B$ was most recently added: then other arrows into B whose addition would keep the net in $\mathbb{S}$ need to be re-weighed to take into account the new parent A. There are at most $n - 2$ such arrows. Letting s be the average number of nets under consideration at any step of the algorithm, we might then expect the total number of weights that need to be ascertained to be of the order $n^2 + kns$, where k is the total number of arrows

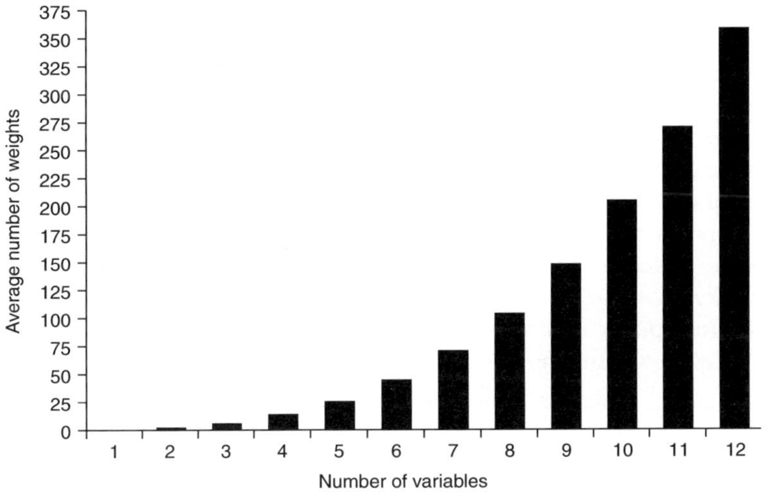

FIG. 3.28. Average number of weights calculated by the adding-arrows algorithm, where the approximation subspace is the whole space of Bayesian nets.

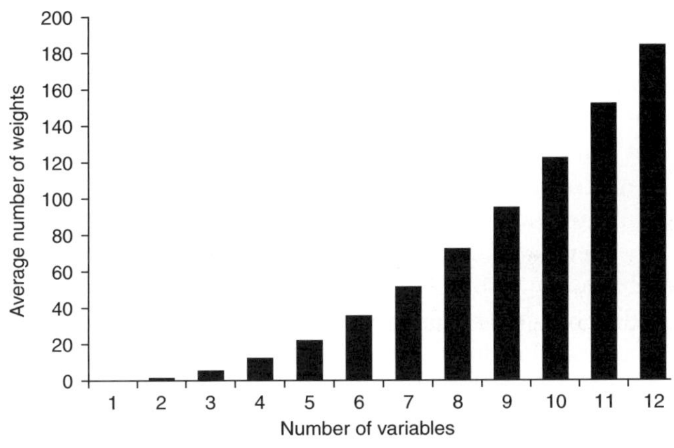

FIG. 3.29. Average number of weights calculated by the adding-arrows algorithm, where the approximation subspace is the set of nets whose variables have no more than two parents.

added. The first term n^2 comes from the initial arrows weighed and the second kns from the k subsequent steps for each graph (this second term is likely to be an overestimate since different graphs will frequently need to weigh the same arrow and each weight only needs to be calculated once.).

For the approximation space $\mathbb{S} = \mathbb{B}$ a complete net may be derived, $k \leq$

$n(n-1)/2$, but s appears to be bounded by a constant, so we would also expect the number of weights to increase with the cube of n. Fig. 3.28 is consistent with this assessment. For the approximation space of nets whose variables have no more than r parents, $k < nr$ increases linearly with n. Hence, for nets with a two-parent bound, where we have suggested that s increases linearly with n, we might expect the average number of calculated weights to increase roughly with the cube of n. Fig. 3.29 is consistent with this hypothesis—in fact here the increase appears to be somewhat slower.

Thus the space complexities and time complexities of the adding arrows algorithm vary to some extent with approximation subspace $\mathbb{S}$. In particular for the structural approximation subspaces under consideration here one would not expect the average number of weights that need to be found to grow more rapidly than n^3.

3.11 The Case for Adding Arrows

We have seen in this chapter how Bayesian nets can be used to represent probability functions. While inference in Bayesian nets is an important problem, perhaps the key problem is that of constructing a Bayesian net within a subspace of Bayesian nets that represents a good approximation to a target function. The optimal approximation is the net with maximum mutual information weight.

The adding-arrows algorithm is only one out of a plethora of proposals for constructing Bayesian nets, but it has several things going for it:

- It is conceptually very simple. The idea is simply that one can construct a Bayesian net approximation to a target function by repeatedly adding arrows with maximum mutual information weight (§3.6).
- There is a straightforward justification of this strategy: as long as the weight of a new arrow is positive (corresponding to probabilistic dependence), the new net formed will be closer to the target function than the old one (Theorem 3.7).
- The knowledge engineer has a parameter, namely the approximation subspace $\mathbb{S}$, that can be varied according to the computational resources available in a particular application (§3.8). Different contexts will demand different approximation subspaces, and the algorithm does not provide an ad hoc criterion for choosing $\mathbb{S}$.
- Although the algorithm is a greedy search, it achieves very close approximations of target functions (§3.9).
- The computational complexity of the algorithm is polynomial rather than exponential in n (§3.10).

4

CAUSAL NETS: FOUNDATIONAL PROBLEMS

Section 4.1 will present the strategy of using causal knowledge to construct a Bayesian network. The remainder of the chapter will highlight some of the chief difficulties with this strategy.

4.1 Causally Interpreted Bayesian Nets

There is another, simpler, suggestion for constructing a Bayesian net: just take the graph representing the causal relationships among the variables of interest. Thus to construct a Bayesian net on V, first construct a directed acyclic graph $\mathcal{C}$ by including an arrow from A to B if and only if A is a direct cause of B, and then determine the corresponding probability tables in $\mathcal{S}$ as usual. The graph in the Bayesian net $(\mathcal{C}, \mathcal{S})$ is given a causal interpretation and so the network is called a *causally interpreted Bayesian network*, or more simply a *causal net*. The notation $\mathcal{C}$ for the graph, instead of $\mathcal{G}$, signifies the presence of a causal interpretation.

The strategy of building a Bayesian net around a causal graph was originally put forward in the 1980s,[56] and has been widely applied in the construction of probabilistic expert systems. This type of procedure was used to construct an expert system for colonoscopy, for instance.[57] The aim was to produce a system for guiding an endoscope up a patient's colon, using a camera image to assist the guiding process. The colon centre is called the lumen (which we represent as variable L), showing up as a large dark region (LD) on the screen. It is important to avoid pockets in the colon wall called diverticula (D), which appear as small dark regions (SD). In order to distinguish the two types of region, the size (S) of the region was measured as were its mean light intensity M and its intensity variance V. Fig. 4.1 was taken as a depiction of the causal relationships among these variables, and a causal net was constructed by adding the appropriate probability tables. (Further variables were also taken into account so the causal net involving Fig. 4.1 was only actually a part of the final net.)

This way of constructing a Bayesian net requires prior knowledge of causal relationships and hinges on three key assumptions about the nature of causality. First, it is assumed that the concept of direct causality is a relation between variables. Second, that the causal graph on V will be acyclic. Third, that $(\mathcal{C}, \mathcal{S})$ will

[56](Pearl, 1988; Neapolitan, 1990)

[57](Sucar *et al.*, 1993; Sucar and Gillies, 1994; Kwoh and Gillies, 1996)

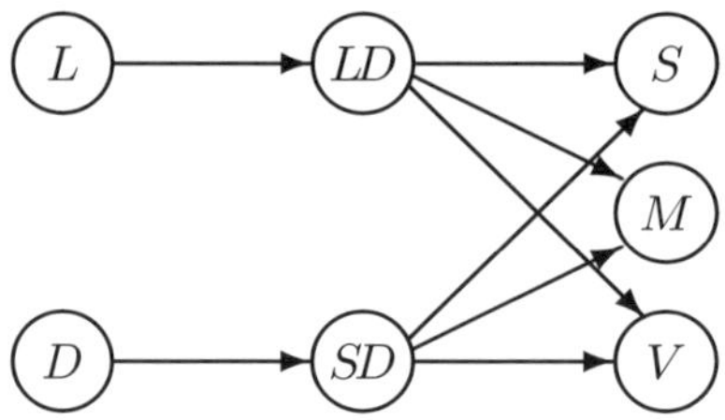

FIG. 4.1. Causal graph for part of a colonoscopy system.

be a Bayesian network, i.e. that the causal graph will satisfy the Markov Condition with respect to the probability function of interest. This latter assumption can be phrased as follows:

Causal Markov Condition Each variable is probabilistically independent of its non-effects, conditional on its direct causes.[58]

The first assumption, that direct causality relates variables, has certainly been disputed. Philosophers tend to take events as the relata of causality, although events themselves are understood in a number of ways. Other contenders for causal relata are properties, sentences, and propositions. It is also possible to think of causality not as relation at all but as a set of facts, say.[59] Although there are a variety of views on this issue, it seems a harmless idealisation to construe causality as a relation between variables—an event can be thought of as a single-case two-valued variable that takes one value if it occurs and takes the other value if it does not occur, a property can be thought of as a repeatable two-valued variable that takes one value when instantiated and the other when not instantiated, &c.—and such an idealisation rarely conflicts with causal intuitions. The assumption that causality is an acyclic relation is more contentious. Causal cycles are in fact widespread: poverty causes crime which causes further poverty; a weak immune system leads to disease which can further weaken the immune system; property price increases cause a rush to buy which in turn causes further price increases. However, it is possible to iron out these cycles by construing different instantiations of the causes and effects as different variables: if the first property price increase is a different variable to the second increase then there is chain of causal connections from one increase to the next, rather than a cycle between price increase and rush to buy. Thus causal cycles are a feature of repeatable variables rather than single-case variables. If such problems arise one can restrict attention to single-case variables.

[58]Here the non-effects and direct causes of a variable are those determined by the causal graph $\mathcal{C}$. Note in particular that the set of direct causes of a variable depends on the set of variables under consideration: if $V = \{A, B, C\}$ with causal graph $A \longrightarrow B \longrightarrow C$ then $A \longrightarrow C$ will be the causal graph induced on variable set $V' = \{A, C\}$; the two graphs disagree as to the direct cause of C though they agree as to causal relations on the variables they share.

[59]Mellor (1995) argues that causality is not a relation but a set of facts; Menzies (2003) takes issue with this position and maintains that causality is a relation.

The Causal Markov Condition is altogether more problematic. The most obvious issue is that its truth or falsity may depend on how one interprets probability and causality. We will discuss interpretations of causality in detail in Chapter 7 and Chapter 9, but for now we can assume that causality, like probability, can be construed as either a physical relation or a mental relation. Physical causality is a feature of the world inasmuch as causal relations exist as mind-independent entities, whereas with mental causality the relations are part of an agent's epistemic state. As with the interpretations of probability, neither concept precludes the viability of the other, and mental causal relations may just be an agent's imperfect knowledge of physical causal relations.

The question then is whether the Causal Markov Condition holds for different interpretations of causality and probability. In the next few sections I will argue that the condition does not hold for common interpretations. However in Chapter 6 we shall see that the Causal Markov Condition does hold under the objective Bayesian interpretation of probability (developed in Chapter 5) and a suitable interpretation of causality.

4.2 Physical Causality, Physical Probability

We shall first examine the Causal Markov Condition as interpreted as a claim about the relationship between physical causality and physical probability.[60] I will show here that this claim is highly problematic, rendering the physical interpretation an untenable foundation for causal nets.

The Causal Markov Condition is related to another condition known as the *Principle of the Common Cause*. This principle is a development of Mill's Fifth Canon of Inductive Reasoning which says, 'Whatever phenomenon varies in any manner whenever another phenomenon varies in some particular manner, is either a cause or an effect of that phenomenon, or is connected with it through some fact of causation.'[61] Hans Reichenbach formulated the principle in close to its current form.[62] The Principle of the Common Cause claims that if two variables are probabilistically dependent then one is the cause of the other or they are effects of common causes and those common causes *screen off* one variable from the other, i.e. render the two variables probabilistically independent. We shall write $A \longrightarrow B$ for 'A directly causes B' and $A \rightsquigarrow B$ for 'A causes B' (we have the recursive relationship $A \rightsquigarrow B$ if $A \longrightarrow B$ or $A \rightsquigarrow C \longrightarrow B$ for some C). Then

Principle of the Common Cause if $A \not\perp\!\!\!\perp B$ then $A \rightsquigarrow B$ or $B \rightsquigarrow A$ or there is a $U \subseteq V$ such that $C \in U$ implies $C \rightsquigarrow A$ and $C \rightsquigarrow B$, and $A \perp\!\!\!\perp B \mid U$.

[60]A Bayesian net is 'Bayesian' in the sense that it is updated using Bayesian conditionalisation—there is no requirement that the probabilities in its probability specification be given a Bayesian interpretation (see the note at the end of §2.7). Sucar *et al.* (1993) and Gillies (2002, 2003) explicitly argue for a physical interpretation of the probabilities in a Bayesian net. Neapolitan (1990, §2.5.2) argues that frequencies should be used where possible.

[61](Mill, 1843, p. 287)

[62](Reichenbach, 1956, §19, pp. 157–167)

Proposition 4.1 *The Causal Markov Condition implies the Principle of the Common Cause.*

Proof: Suppose the Causal Markov Condition holds, and that A and B are neither cause and effect nor effects of common causes. Then they are D-separated by $\emptyset$: if there are paths between them each path must contain a node whose arrows meet head to head. Thus $A \perp\!\!\!\perp B$.

Contrapositively, if $A \rightleftharpoons B$ then A and B are either cause and effect or effects of common causes U. In the latter case, these common causes D-separate A and B, and so $A \perp\!\!\!\perp B \mid U$. ■

The Principle of the Common Cause, having been around for longer than the Causal Markov Condition, has received more critical attention. The Principle of the Common Cause is normally construed as a link between physical causality and physical probability, and is championed as an important way in which causal relations can be inferred from observed probabilistic dependencies. However, a number of counterexamples to the Principle of the Common Cause have been put forward, as we shall see in the remainder of this section. By Proposition 4.1, these counterexamples are also counterexamples to the Causal Markov Condition. Hence if the counterexamples are cogent, they put paid to the Causal Markov Condition as physically interpreted.

The Principle of the Common Cause asserts that any probabilistic dependence must have a causal explanation. Thus any situation in which variables are probabilistically dependent, but in which this dependence is not accounted for by causal relationships among the variables, is a counterexample to the principle. In fact probabilistic dependencies arise not only via causal connections, but also accidentally or because the variables are related through meaning, through logical connections, through mathematical connections, because they are related by (non-causal) physical laws, or because they are constrained by local laws or boundary conditions. We shall deal with each of these counterexample scenarios in turn.

First, probabilistic dependencies can arise just by accident. Elliott Sober produced the following counterexample to the Principle of the Common Cause:

> Consider the fact that the sea level in Venice and the cost of bread in Britain have both been on the rise in the past two centuries. Both, let us suppose, have monotonically increased. Imagine that we put this data in the form of a chronological list; for each date, we list the Venetian sea level and the going price of British bread. Because both quantities have increased steadily in time, it is true that higher than average sea levels tend to be associated with higher than average bread prices. The two quantities are very strongly positively correlated.
>
> I take it that we do not feel driven to explain this correlation by postulating a common cause. Rather, we regard Venetian sea levels and British bread prices as both increasing for somewhat isolated endogenous reasons. Local conditions in Venice have increased the sea level and rather different local conditions in Britain have driven up the cost of bread. Here,

> postulating a common cause is simply not very plausible, given the rest of what we believe.[63]

Here Sober calls the existence of a common cause into question—there is a causal explanation of the correlation, but it is not an explanation involving common factors, so in a sense the correlation is accidental. Postulating a common cause conflicts with intuitions here: there just appears to be no common causal mechanism.[64]

Second, probabilistic dependencies can be explained by variables having related meaning. Consider the following two variables, 'Flu (F) taking possible assignments f^1 ('flu is present) and f^0 ('flu is absent), and orthomyxoviridae infection (O) taking assignments o^1 and o^0. Now 'flu is just a type—a subclassification—of orthomyxoviridae infection. Hence these variables are probabilistically dependent: $p(o^1|f^1) = 1 \neq p(o^1)$ (assuming that not everyone has an orthomyxoviridae infection). Neither variable can be said to be a cause of the other, since the variables do not even correspond to distinct events, and there is no causal mechanism linking the occurrence of one with the occurrence of the other. At a stretch one could say that the two variables have common causes, namely the causes, C say, of 'flu. But these common causes do not screen off the dependence: $p(o^1|c^1 f^1) = 1 \neq p(o^1|c^1)$ (assuming that the presence c^1 of causes of 'flu does not always lead to the presence of 'flu). Hence the Principle of the Common Cause fails.

One might argue that if two variables in a causal net have overlapping meaning, then there is some redundancy and one of them should be left out of the net. This is not a good suggestion for a number of reasons. One can lose valuable information from a Bayesian net by deleting a variable, since both the original variables may be important to the application of the network. Meaning overlap can vary—e.g. 'over six feet' and 'tall' differ in overlap according to whether these predicates are applied to people or buildings—and it may be useful to retain related variables. In some cases one may even want to include synonyms in a Bayesian net, e.g. in a network for natural language reasoning. Furthermore, removing a variable can invalidate the Causal Markov Condition if the removed variable is a common cause of other variables. Or one simply may not know that two variables have related meaning: Yersin's discovery that the black death coincides with *Pasteurella pestis* was a genuine example of scientific inference, not the sort of thing one can do at one's desk while building an expert system.

[63](Sober, 1988, p. 215)

[64]There have been several suggestions for salvaging the Principle of the Common Cause in the face of this counterexample. Sober has replied to some of these in Sober (2001). Yule (1926) studied similar correlations between time series and reached similar conclusions: 'Now it has been said that to interpret such correlations as implying causation is to ignore the common influence of a time-factor. ... I cannot regard time *per se* as a causal factor ... what one feels about such a correlation is, not that it must be interpreted in terms of some very indirect catena of causation, but that it has no meaning at all; that in non-technical terms it is simply a fluke' (pg. 4).

Probabilistic dependencies can also be explained by logical relations. For instance, logically equivalent sentences are necessarily perfectly correlated,[65] and if one sentence logically implies another, the probability of the latter must be greater than or equal to that of the former. Thus one should be wary of causal nets which involve logically complex variables. Suppose C causes complaints D, E, and F, and that we have three clinical tests, one of which can determine whether or not a patient has both D and E, another tells us whether or not the patient has one of E and F, and the third tells us whether the patient has C. Thus there is no direct way of determining $p(d|c), p(e|c)$, or $p(f|c)$ for assignments c, d, e, and f to C, D, E, and F respectively, but one can find $p(de|c)$ and $p(e \vee f|c)$.[66] One might then be tempted to incorporate $C \longrightarrow (DE), C \longrightarrow (E \vee F)$ in a causal graph, so that the probability specification of the corresponding causal net can be determined empirically. In such a situation, however, C will not screen node DE off from node $E \vee F$ and the Principle of the Common Cause, and thus Causal Markov Condition, fails.

This problem seriously affects situations where causal relata are genuinely logically complex, as happens with context-specific causality. A may cause B *only if* the patient has genetic characteristic C: if the patient has any other genetic characteristic then there is no possible causal mechanism from A to B. Then the conjunction AC is the cause of B, not A or C on their own. However, A may be able to cause D in everyone, so the causal graph would need to contain a node AC and a second node A. One would not expect these two nodes to be screened off by any common causes.[67]

Next we turn to mathematical relations as a probabilistic correlator. Consider the colonoscopy causal net described in §4.1. This causal net was constructed around the causal graph of Fig. 4.1, but then the Causal Markov Condition was tested and found to fail: the mean and variance variables were found to be probabilistically dependent when, according to the causal graph under the Causal Markov Condition, they should not have been. Neither variable causes the other, and the only plausible common causes failed to screen off the variables. Mean and variance are related mathematically, not causally: we have that $VarX = EX^2 - (EX)^2$, where $VarX$ is the variance of random variable X, and E signifies expectation so that EX is the mean of X. To take the simplest example, if X is a Bernoulli random variable and $EX = x$ then $VarX = x(1-x)$, making the mean and variance perfectly correlated. In the endoscopy case, the light intensity will have a more complicated distribution, but the mean value will still constrain the variance, counting for at least a part of the observed probabilistic dependence. The developers of the colonoscopy system tried to resolve this failure of the Causal Markov Condition. The first strategy was to remove

[65] At least according to standard notions of probability defined over logical sentences—see §11.9.

[66] Here $\vee$ is the symbol for *or*. $\neg, \wedge, \rightarrow, \leftrightarrow$ are symbols for *not*, *and*, *implies* and *if and only if* respectively. See §11.2.

[67] See §10.2 for an alternative way of representing context-specific causality.

one of the two dependent variables.[68] This marginally improved the performance when predicting the presence of the lumen, but the loss of information led to worse performance when predicting the presence of the diverticulum. The second strategy was to introduce an extra common cause in order to screen off the two variables.[69] While this move improved the success rate of the causal net, it raised fundamental problems. First it is not clear what the new node represents (it was just called a 'hidden node'), so a causal interpretation may no longer be appropriate for the graph. Second, the probabilities relating the new node to the other nodes had to be ascertained: this could only be done mathematically, by finding what the probabilities should be if the introduction of the new node allowed the unwanted correlation to be fully screened off, and could not be tested empirically or equated with any physical probability distribution. Therefore the Bayesian network lost both the physical causal and the physical probabilistic components of its interpretation. A physical interpretation of the causal net is just not feasible, given non-causal dependencies like this.

Moving through our list of non-causal inducers of probabilistic dependencies, we come to physical laws. Many physical-law counterexamples to the Principle of the Common Cause are analogous to the following one, expressed by Frank Arntzenius:[70]

> Suppose that a particle decays into 2 parts, that conservation of total momentum obtains, and that it is not determined by the prior state of the particle what the momentum of each part will be after the decay. By conservation, the momentum of one part will be determined by the momentum of the other part. By indeterminism, the prior state of the particle will not determine what the momenta of each part will be after the decay. Thus there is no prior screener off.

Suppose variables M_1 and M_2 are the momenta of the two parts. Since the momentum of one part determines that of the other part, $p(m_1|m_2) = 1 \neq p(m_1)$ for some $m_1@M_1, m_2@M_2$, and so $M_1 \rightleftharpoons M_2$. Neither momentum can be said to be a cause of the other (and because of the symmetry of the example, to insist otherwise would break the Bayesian net acyclicity requirement). If there is a common cause, then it is presumably the prior state S of the particle, but this common cause fails to screen off the momenta, for $p(m_1|m_2s) = 1 \neq p(m_1|s)$ by indeterminism. Hence the Principle of the Common Cause fails.[71]

Finally, the philosophical literature contains several examples of how local non-causal constraints and initial conditions can account for dependencies among

[68] (Sucar and Gillies, 1994)

[69] (Kwoh and Gillies, 1996)

[70] Arntzenius (1992, pp. 227–228), from van Fraassen (1980, p. 29).

[71] Such physical arguments against the Principle of the Common Cause are widespread. Butterfield (1992) looks at Bell's theorem and concludes (pg. 41) that, 'the violation of the Bell inequality teaches us a lesson, ... namely, some pairs of events are not screened off by their common past.' Arntzenius (1992) has other examples and also argues on a different front against the Principle of the Common Cause assuming determinism. See also Healey (1991) and Savitt (1996, pp. 357–360) for a survey.

causal variables. Nancy Cartwright, for instance, points out that

> independence is not always an appropriate assumption to make. ... A typical case occurs when a cause operates subject to constraint, so that its operation to produce one effect is not independent of its operation to produce another. For example, an individual has \$10 to spend on groceries, to be divided between meat and vegetables. The amount that he spends on meat may be a purely probabilistic consequence of his state on entering the supermarket; so too may be the amount spent on vegetables. But the two effects are not produced independently. The cause operates to produce an expenditure of n dollars on meat if and only if it operates to produce an expenditure of $10-n$ dollars on vegetables. Other constraints may impose different degrees of correlation.[72]

Wesley Salmon gives another counterexample to the screening condition.[73] Pool balls are set up such that the black is pocketed (B) if and only if the white is (W). A beginner is about to play who is just as likely as not to pot the black if she attempts the shot (S), and is very unlikely to pot the white otherwise. Thus if we let b, w, and s be assignments representing the occurrence of B, W, and S respectively, $p(b \leftrightarrow w) = 1$ and $p(b|s) = 1/2$, so $1/2 = p(w|s) \neq p(w|sb) = 1$ and the cause S does not screen off its effects B and W from each other. As Salmon says:

> It may be objected, of course, that we are not entitled to infer ... that there is no event prior to B which does the screening. In fact, there is such an event—namely, the compound event which consists of the state of motion of the cue-ball shortly after they collide. The need to resort to such artificial compound events does suggest a weakness in the theory, however, for the causal relations among S, B and W seem to embody the salient features of the situation. An adequate theory of probabilistic causality should, it seems to me, be able to handle the situation in terms of the relations among these events, without having to appeal to such *ad hoc* constructions.[74]

In response to the problem of non-causal constraints inducing probabilistic dependencies, one might admit defeat in domains such as quantum mechanics,[75] or troubleshooting pool players, but maintain that most applications of intelligent reasoning may be unaffected. But non-causal constraints occur just about anywhere, including central diagnosis problems, for example. When diagnosing circuit boards, one may be constrained by the fact that two components cannot fail simultaneously, for if one of them fails the circuit breaks and the other one cannot fail. Suppose there is a common cause C for the failures. Then C fails to screen failure F_1 off from failure F_2 for $p(f_2|cf_1) = 0 \neq p(f_2|c)$. In medicine the opposite is the case: failure of one component in the human body increases the chances of failure of another, as resources are already weakened. In both these

[72] (Cartwright, 1989, p. 113–114)

[73] (Salmon, 1980*b*, pp. 150–151; Salmon, 1984, pp. 168–169)

[74] (Salmon, 1980*b*, p. 151, my notation)

[75] As Spirtes *et al.* (1993, pp. 63–64) do.

cases the constraints are very general and not the sort of thing one would want to call causes.

4.3 Mental Causality, Physical Probability

We have seen that the Causal Markov Condition is implausible when both causality and probability are interpreted physically. In this section, we shall assess the condition under a mental interpretation of causality and a physical interpretation of probability.

There are various ways one can interpret causality mentally, but we can dismiss one possibility easily: the Causal Markov Condition does not stand a chance when causality is given a strictly subjective interpretation. Recall that strict subjectivism as an interpretation of probability holds that an agent's degrees of belief are rational if and only if they are probabilities—the agent is free to choose any probability function as her belief function. A strict subjectivist interpretation of causality can be thought of analogously: an agent is rational if her causal beliefs take the form of a directed acyclic graph and any directed acyclic graph will do. Now suppose probability is interpreted physically, and causality is strictly subjective. The Causal Markov Condition under this combination of interpretations says that each variable is probabilistically independent of its non-effects conditional on its direct causes, for whichever causal graph the agent adopts and for physical probability. Now given any variable $A \in V$ and sets of variables $U \subseteq T \subseteq V$ such that $A \notin T, U$, there is *some* directed acyclic graph in which U are deemed to be the direct causes of A and T its non-effects. The Causal Markov Condition then implies that $A \perp\!\!\!\perp T \mid U$, for physical probability. Since this holds for each choice of A, T, and U, it follows that all variables in V must be probabilistically independent! Clearly too strong an assumption.

A second mental interpretation of causality construes a causal graph $\mathcal{C}$ to be an agent's knowledge of physical causal relations. Of course in practice the agent's knowledge may well be incomplete or inaccurate, in which case $\mathcal{C}$ will not match the physical causal graph $\mathcal{C}^*$.

So how does the Causal Markov Condition fare under this second mental interpretation of causality? Not very well if the agent's causal knowledge can vary widely from the physical causal graph. Just as with strict subjectivist causality, if the agent is free to choose one of many causal graphs then the Causal Markov Condition will assert a great number of probabilistic independencies, few of which can be expected to hold. But what if the agent's causal graph is quite close to the physical picture? One line of reasoning goes something like this: if the Causal Markov Condition holds physically ($\mathcal{C}^*$ with respect to physical probability p^*), and the agent's causal graph $\mathcal{C}$ is similar to the physical causal graph $\mathcal{C}^*$, then the Causal Markov Condition will hold closely enough for practical purposes, in the sense that the probability function p determined by a Bayesian net $(\mathcal{C}, \mathcal{S}^*)$, where the specification $\mathcal{S}^*$ is induced by p^*, will be close enough to physical probability p^* to be put to practical use.

It is such a position that I want to argue against in this section. There are two flaws in the above reasoning. First, as we saw in §4.2, there is often reason to doubt the Causal Markov Condition holds of physical causality and physical probability. Second, even if the Causal Markov Condition were to hold of physical interpretations, small differences between the agent's causal graph and the physical causal graph can lead to significant differences in the probability functions determined by the corresponding causal nets. It is this second claim that I want to argue for here.

I shall argue as follows. Even if we make the assumption that the Causal Markov Condition holds of $\mathcal{C}^*$ with respect to p^*, we assume that the agent's specification $\mathcal{S}^*$ agrees with the corresponding physical probabilities p^*, and assume that her causal knowledge is correct ($\mathcal{C}$ is a subgraph of $\mathcal{C}^*$), then if, as one would expect, her causal knowledge is incomplete (a strict subgraph), p may not be close enough to p^* for practical purposes.

There are two basic types of incompleteness. The agent may well not know about all the variables ($\mathcal{C}$ has fewer nodes than $\mathcal{C}^*$) or even if she does, she may not know about all the causal relations between the variables ($\mathcal{C}$ has fewer arrows than $\mathcal{C}^*$).

To deal with the first case, suppose $\mathcal{C}$ is just $\mathcal{C}^*$ minus one variable A and the arrows connecting it to the rest of the graph. Even if $\mathcal{C}^*$ satisfies the Causal Markov Condition with respect to p^* then $\mathcal{C}$ can only be guaranteed (for all p^*) to satisfy the Causal Markov Condition if all the direct causes of A are direct causes of A's direct effects, each pair B, C of its direct effects have an arrow between them say from B to C, and the direct causes of each such B are direct causes of C.[76] Needless to say, such a state of affairs is rather unlikely and a failure of the Causal Markov Condition will have practical repercussions.

It is possible to run a simulation to indicate just how close the agent's function p will be to the physical function p^*, the results of which form Fig. 4.2. The left-hand bars show the performance of causal nets formed by removing a single node and its incident arrows from nets known to satisfy the Causal Markov Condition. For $n = 2, \ldots, 10$ causal nets $(\mathcal{C}^*, \mathcal{S}^*)$ on n two-valued variables were randomly generated, and for each net a random variable was removed to form the agent's net $(\mathcal{C}, \mathcal{S}^*)$, a random assignment of variables u was chosen and $p(a|u)$ calculated for each assignment $a@A$ where variable A does not occur in u. The new nets were deemed successful if their values for $p(a|u)$ differed from the values determined by the original nets by less than 0.05, that is, $|p(a|u) - p^*(a|u)| < 0.05$. For each n the percentage success was calculated over a number of trials[77] and each bar in the chart represents such a percentage. The right-hand bars represent the percentage success where half the nodes[78] and their incident arrows were removed.

[76] See Pearl *et al.* (1990, p. 82).

[77] At least 2000 trials for each n, and more in cases where convergence was slow.

[78] In fact the nearest integer less than or equal to half the nodes was chosen.

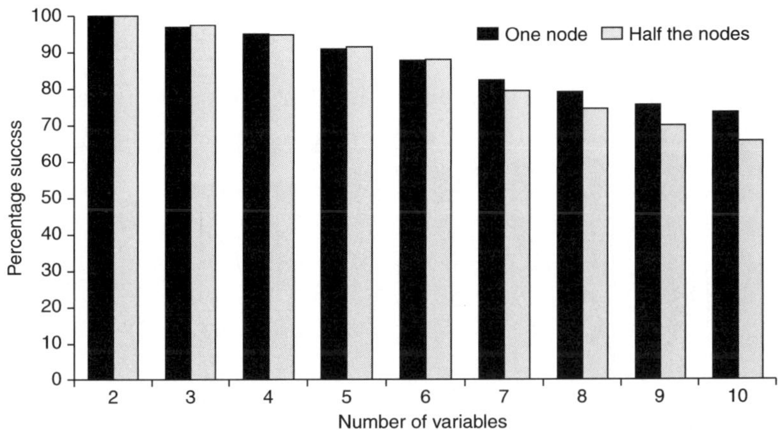

FIG. 4.2. Nodes removed.

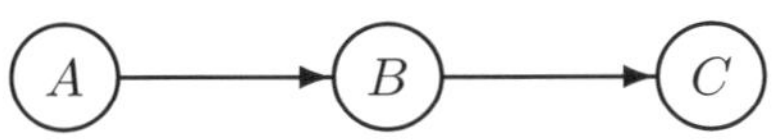

FIG. 4.3. Physical causal graph $\mathcal{G}^*$.

Such experiments are computationally time-consuming and only practical for small values of n. While one should be wary of reading too much into a small data set, the results do suggest a trend of decreasing success rate as the sizes of the networks increase. Thus it appears plausible that if one removes a node and its incident arrows from a large net that satisfies the Causal Markov Condition, then the resulting net will not be useful, in the sense that the probability values it determines will not be sufficiently close to physical probability. Moreover, removing more nodes from a causal net is likely to further reduce its probability of success, as the graph shows.

This trend may be surprising, in that if one removes a node from a large causal graph one is changing a smaller portion of it than if one removes a node from a small graph, so one might expect that removing a node changes the resulting probability function less as the original number of nodes n increases. But one must bear in mind that the Causal Markov Condition is non-local: removing a node can imply an independency between two nodes which are very far apart in the graph. Thus removing a node from a small graph is likely to change fewer implied independencies than removing a node from a large graph.

There are a couple of ways in which this simulation may be unrealistic, and it is worth exploring some variants to see whether they yield similar conclusions.

FIG. 4.4. B and its incident arrows removed.

FIG. 4.5. B removed but its incident arrows redirected.

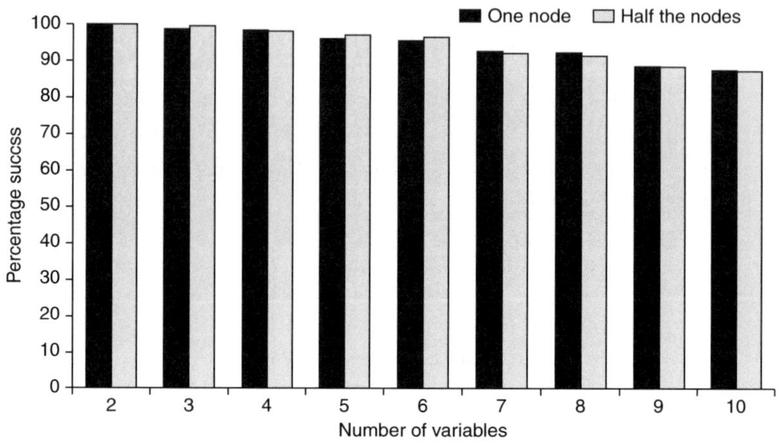

FIG. 4.6. Nodes removed—arrows re-routed.

For instance, if one does not know about some intermediary cause in a physical causal graph, one may yet know about the causal chain on which it exists. Thus if Fig. 4.3 represents the physical causal graph and one does not know about B, one may know that A causes C, as in Fig. 4.5 rather than Fig. 4.4. In this case removing B's incident arrows introduces an independency which is not implied by the original graph, whereas redirecting them does not. It can be seen from simulations that while redirecting rather than removing arrows improves success (see Fig. 4.6) the qualitative lesson remains: the general trend is still that success decreases as the number of nodes increases.

There is another way that the simulation may be unrealistic. Some types of cause may be more likely to be unknown than others, so perhaps one should not remove a node at random in the simulation. However, if we adjust for this factor we should not expect our conclusions to be undermined. To the extent that effects are more likely to be observable and causes to be unobservable, one will be more likely to know about nodes in the latter parts of causal chains than in the earlier parts. But while removing a leaf in a graph will not introduce any new independence constraints, removing common causes can do so. Thus if an agent is less likely to know about causes than effects, her causal knowledge $\mathcal{C}$ is even less likely to satisfy the Causal Markov Condition than a graph with nodes removed at random.

There may be other factors which render the simulation inappropriate, based on the way the networks are chosen at random. Here I made it as likely as not that two nodes have an arrow between them, and as likely as not that an arrow is in one direction as in another, while maintaining acyclicity. Thus the graphs are unlikely to be highly dense or highly sparse. I chose the specifying probabilities uniformly over machine reals in $[0, 1]$. Roughly half the nodes ($n/2$ nodes if n is even otherwise $(n-1)/2$ nodes) were chosen to occur in u and the nodes and their values were selected uniformly. In the face of a lack of knowledge about the large-scale structure of a physical causal graph I suggest these explications of 'at random' are appropriate. In any case, the trend indicated by the simulation does not seem to be sensitive to changes in the way a network is chosen at random.

In sum then, for a $\mathcal{C}^*$ large enough to be a physical causal graph the removal of an arbitrary node is likely to change the independencies implied by the graph, and to significantly change the resulting probability function determined by the causal net. This much is arguably true whether or not the physical situation $(\mathcal{C}^*, p^*)$ satisfies the Causal Markov Condition itself, for if the condition fails in the physical case, removing arbitrary nodes is hardly likely to make it hold.

Having looked at what happens when an agent is ignorant of causal variables, we shall now turn to the case where she is ignorant of causal relations.

Suppose then that $\mathcal{C}$ is formed from $\mathcal{C}^*$ by deleting an arrow, say from node A to node B. Then $\mathcal{C}$ cannot be guaranteed to satisfy the Causal Markov Condition with respect to p^*. For suppose $A, C_1, \ldots, C_k$ are the direct causes of B in $\mathcal{C}^*$. Then the Causal Markov Condition on $\mathcal{C}$ with respect to p^* requires that A be independent of B, conditional on $C_1, \ldots, C_k$, which is not implied by the Causal Markov Condition on $\mathcal{C}^*$ with respect to p^*.

The situation is worse if the following condition holds, which I shall call the *Causal Dependence* principle. This corresponds to the intuition that a cause will either increase the probability of a direct effect, or, if it is a preventative, make the effect less likely, as long as the effect's other direct causes are controlled for (i.e. held fixed). More precisely,

Causal Dependence $A \rightleftharpoons B \mid C_1, \ldots, C_k$ for direct causes $A, C_1, \ldots, C_k$ of B.

Now if $\mathcal{C}^*$ satisfies Causal Dependence with respect to p^* and the arrow between A and B is removed to give $\mathcal{C}$ as before then the Causal Markov Condition will *definitely fail* for $\mathcal{C}$ with respect to p^*. This is simply because the Causal Markov Condition on $\mathcal{C}$ with respect to p^* requires that A and B be independent conditional on $C_1, \ldots, C_k$ which contradicts the assumption that Causal Dependence holds for $\mathcal{C}^*$ with respect to p^*. Note that this conclusion only depends on the local situation involving A, B and the other direct causes $C_1, \ldots, C_k$ of B, so that further changes elsewhere in the graph cannot rectify the situation.[79] Note also that this result does *not* require that physical causality $\mathcal{C}^*$ satisfy the Causal Markov Condition with respect to physical probability p^*. Thus if the Causal Dependence principle holds of physical causality it is extremely unlikely that the Causal Markov Condition will hold of an agent's causal knowledge.

[79]If one or more of the other direct causes or their arrows to B are also absent in $\mathcal{C}$, then the Causal Markov Condition may be reinstated, although this would be a freak occurrence and the extra change may break a further independence relation elsewhere in the graph.

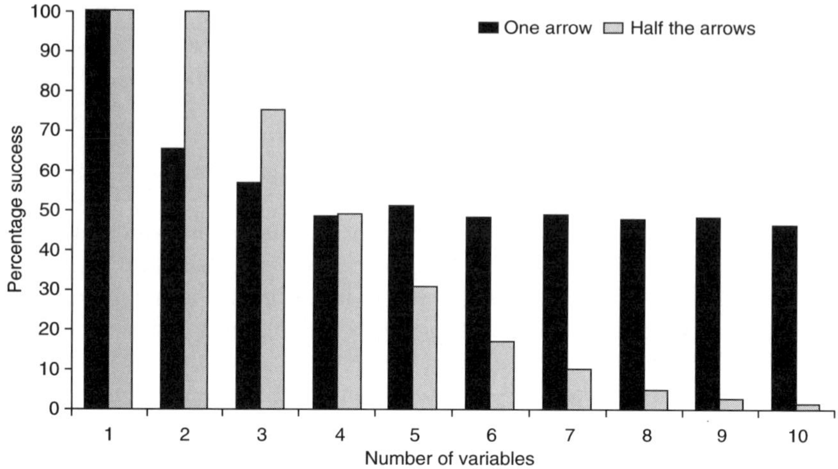

FIG. 4.7. Arrows removed.

Of course, we are arguing against the Causal Markov Condition by appealing to an alternative principle here and the sceptical reader may not be convinced by this tactic. Indeed we shall see in §7.3 that while Causal Dependence may normally hold, it does admit counterexamples. On the other hand, many proponents of the Causal Markov Condition also accept Causal Dependence, often in the guise of another principle called *faithfulness* (see §8.3 and subsequent sections). In any case, as before we can perform a simulation to indicate the general trends. The left-hand bars of Fig. 4.7 represent the results of the same simulation as before (Causal Dependence is not assumed to hold), except with a random arrow rather than a node removed. In this case there is no clear downward trend, but success rate is uniformly low. If more arrows are removed, then for all but small n the resulting network is less likely still to yield successful predictions, as the right-hand bars of Fig. 4.7 show, and again we see a downward trend as the number of nodes in $\mathcal{C}^*$ increases.

In sum, understanding causality in terms of the mental state of an agent—either strictly subjective causal beliefs or knowledge of physical causal relations—leads to serious doubts about the validity of the Causal Markov Condition and consequently the utility of causal nets.

4.4 Physical Causality, Mental Probability

Analogous problems occur when probability is given a mental interpretation.

If probability is given a strict subjectivist interpretation, then an agent is rational whatever her degrees of belief, as long as they satisfy the axioms of probability. In particular there is no requirement that the agent's degrees of belief yield any particular probabilistic independencies. Yet the Causal Markov Condition, where causality interpreted physically, implies that the agent's de-

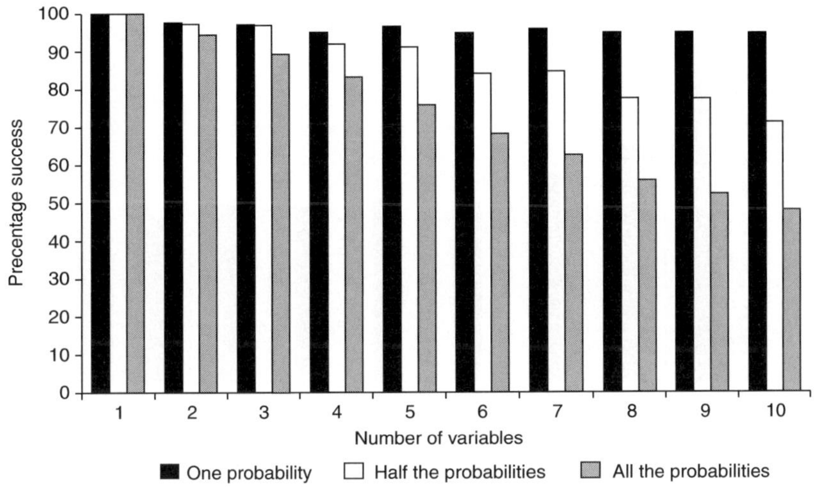

FIG. 4.8. Node probabilities perturbed.

grees of belief must satisfy certain independence relationships. Thus the Causal Markov Condition conflicts with a strict subjectivist notion of probability.

A second mental interpretation of probability interprets an agent's degrees of belief as estimates of physical probabilities. Thus the probabilities in the specification $\mathcal{S}$ of an agent's causal net are only approximations to the probabilities in $\mathcal{S}^*$, the specification that is induced by physical probability.

However, causal nets do not fare well under this interpretation either. The probability function p determined by the agent's causal net $(\mathcal{C}^*, \mathcal{S})$ need not be close to p^* determined by $(\mathcal{C}^*, \mathcal{S}^*)$, where $\mathcal{C}^*$ represents physical causal relations, $\mathcal{S}^*$ the corresponding physical probability specification and where the probabilities in $\mathcal{S}$ are approximations to those in $\mathcal{S}^*$. This can be shown from a simulation run along the same lines as those of §4.3. The left-hand bars of Fig. 4.8 show what happens if $\mathcal{S}$ is constructed by perturbing the physical probability specifiers (in $\mathcal{S}^*$) of one variable by 0.03. The middle bars show the percentage success if half the variables' probabilities are perturbed by 0.03, and the right-hand bars give the case where all variables have their probabilities perturbed. Thus small differences between an agent's degrees of belief that feature in probability tables in her causal net and the corresponding physical probabilities get amplified by the causal net and can lead to large differences between her probabilistic predictions and the physical probabilities that she is supposed to be estimating.

4.5 Mental Causality, Mental Probability

In practice the inadequacies of probabilistic and causal knowledge will occur together, making it even less likely that p is close enough to p^* for practical purposes. Again we can run a simulation, this time exhibiting the differences between knowledge and reality by modifying *both* components of a supposed

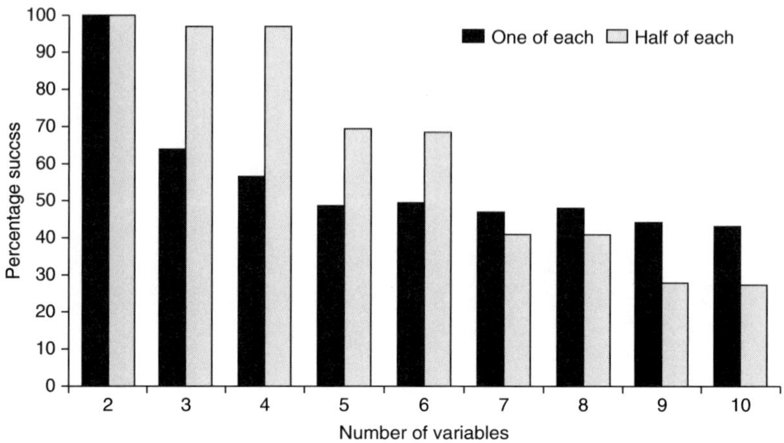

FIG. 4.9. Nodes and arrows removed, node probabilities perturbed.

physical causal net $(\mathcal{C}^*, \mathcal{S}^*)$ to construct an agent's causal net $(\mathcal{C}, \mathcal{S})$, and then as before measuring how well probabilities determined by the agent's net reflect those determined by the physical net. The left-hand bars of Fig. 4.9 show what happens if a node is removed (arrows re-routed), then an arrow is removed, and then one node's probabilities are perturbed by 0.03. The right-hand bars show what happens if half the nodes then half the remaining arrows are removed, then half the remaining nodes are perturbed.

Thus epistemic limitations can lead, significantly often, to practical problems: the probability function determined by an agent's causal net, representing the agent's knowledge of physical causal relations and her estimates of physical probabilities, may differ too much from the physical function to be of practical use.

A strict subjectivist interpretation of both causality and probability will also create problems for causal nets. On the one hand strict subjectivism says that the causal graph and probability specifiers are unrestricted, other than the graph being directed and acyclic and the specifiers being probabilities. On the other hand the Causal Markov Condition asserts that a number independence relationships must obtain. The tolerance of the interpretations clearly conflicts with the restrictions imposed by the Causal Markov Condition.

In sum, while the ability to build a Bayesian net around a causal graph would offer a neat solution to the Bayesian net construction problem, this approach relies on the validity of the Causal Markov Condition, which appears implausible under standard interpretations of probability and causality. In order to provide a justification of the Causal Markov Condition we shall need to invoke the objective Bayesian interpretation of probability, to which we turn now.

5

OBJECTIVE BAYESIANISM

In order to gain a deeper understanding of causal nets we will need to appeal to the objective Bayesian interpretation of probability. This chapter is devoted to a detailed development of this position. Later, in Chapter 6, we will see how objective Bayesianism leads to a coherent methodology for employing causal nets.

5.1 Objective versus Subjective

The Bayesian interpretation of probability is widely adopted for three key reasons. First it provides an interpretation of probability over single-case variables, and we tend to be interested in the probability of single cases: the probability that your car will break down in the next year, or the probability that you will live to 80, for instance. Second, it interprets a wide variety of probability statements which other interpretations cannot deal with: there is no obvious collective, or repeatable experiment, or chance fixer, that determines the probability that the continuum hypothesis is true,[80] yet many mathematicians can ascribe a degree of belief in this hypothesis. Third, it allows one to make decisions (e.g. using a probabilistic decision theory) even when there is little information concerning physical probabilities.

As discussed in §2.7, there are two types of Bayesian interpretation of probability. *Subjective Bayesianism* (also known as *strict subjectivism* or *strict personalism*) maintains that an agent's belief function is rational if and only if it is coherent (i.e. immune to a Dutch book), and in turn her belief function is coherent if and only if it is a probability function. Subjective Bayesianism is often viewed as objectionable because of its arbitrariness: two individuals with the same facts to hand can ascribe radically different probabilities to 'smoking causes cancer', for instance, and each individual is viewed as equally rational. The applications of probability, be they scientific, industrial, commercial, or political, tend to demand consensus of opinion rather than relativism. (Were probability more widely applied in the arts, subjective Bayesianism might be the interpretation of choice.)

Objective Bayesianism (or *epistemic probability*) on the other hand, maintains that rationality goes beyond coherence: further constraints need to be satisfied before an agent's degrees of belief can be deemed rational. The intention is to produce an interpretation of probability which captures the desirable features of

[80] This is the hypothesis that there is no cardinal number between the cardinality of the integers and that of the real numbers.

Bayesianism outlined above, while fixing the probability that an agent ought to ascribe to an assignment as a function of her factual knowledge.[81]

There are two types of further constraint that tend to be imposed on rational belief:

Empirical Information about the world ought to constrain degrees of belief. For example, knowing that a die rolls a six with frequency 1/3 ought to constrain your degree of belief in the next roll yielding a six to equal 1/3. The adoption of empirical constraints on their own leads to what is called *empirically based subjective probability*.[82]

Logical Lack of information about the world ought to constrain degrees of belief. For example, knowing only that an experiment I am about to perform has five outcomes should constrain your degree of belief in each outcome to 1/5. Adopting only logical constraints yields what might be called *logically based subjective probability*.[83]

Objective Bayesianism is the name given to a Bayesian interpretation of probability that appeals to both empirical and logical constraints.[84]

Before discussing the particular form such constraints might take, we shall take a look at their origins.

5.2 The Origins of Objective Bayesianism

Many of the ideas encapsulated in objective Bayesianism are attributable to Jakob Bernoulli. Bernoulli maintained that 'probability is a degree of certainty and differs from absolute certainty as a part differs from the whole,'[85] and he recognised both physical and mental probability (though he referred to them as 'objective' and 'subjective' respectively):

> The certainty of any event is observed either objectively and in itself, and it does not signify anything other than the very truth of the existence or the future existence of that event; or the certainty is observed subjectively and according to ourselves, and it lies in the measure of our knowledge about this truth of present or future existence.[86]

[81] I prefer the terminology 'epistemic probability' for this position because it emphasises the close link between knowledge and probability. However, the usual nomenclature is 'objective Bayesianism', and 'epistemic probability' has been used in the past to refer to subjective Bayesianism, so to avoid confusion I will stick with 'objective Bayesianism'.

[82] Proponents include Howson and Urbach (1989); Lewis (1980) and Neapolitan (1990, §2.4).

[83] This should be distinguished from the logical interpretation of probability, discussed in §11.10, which seeks to interpret probability primarily in terms of logical entailment relations rather than in terms of an agent's degree of belief. This distinction is often obscured because key proponents of the logical interpretation—e.g. Keynes (1921)—also accepted a link between probability and degree of belief.

[84] Warning: these distinctions are not widely adhered to in the literature: Franklin (2001), for example, conflates the logical interpretation of probability and objective Bayesianism.

[85] (Bernoulli, 1713, §IV.I)

[86] (Bernoulli, 1713, §IV.I)

Bernoulli was interested in the mental aspect—how we ought to make judgements of certainty. He provided an account where 'equally possible' cases receive equal probability. The probability of a proposition is then the proportion of such cases in which the proposition is true:

> it is clear that the power which any proof has depends upon a multitude of cases in which it can exist or not exist, in which it can indicate or not indicate the thing, or even in which it can indicate the opposite of the thing. And so, the degree of certainty or the probability which this proof generates can be computed from these cases by the method [as follows] ...
>
> ... we assume that b is the number of cases for which it can happen that some proof exists; that c is the number of cases for which it can happen that this proof does not exist; and that $a = b + c$. ... Moreover, I assume that all cases are equally possible, or that they all can happen with equal ease; for in other cases discretion must be applied, and any case which occurs rather readily must be counted as many times as it occurs more readily than others. For example, a case which occurs three times more readily than the other cases must be counted as three cases, each of which can occur with ease equal to that of any of the other cases.
>
> ... such a proof proves b/a of the thing or of the certainty of the thing.[87]

For Laplace cases are 'equally possible' if we are equally undecided about their occurrence:

> We know that of three or a greater number of events a single one of them ought to occur; but nothing induces us to believe that one of them will occur rather than the others. In this state of indecision it is impossible for us to announce their occurrence with certainty. It is, however, probable that one of these events, chosen at will, will not occur because we see several cases equally possible which exclude its occurrence, while only a single one favours it.
>
> The theory of chance consists in reducing all the events of the same kind to a certain number of cases equally possible, that is to say, to such as we may be equally undecided about in regard to their existence, and in determining the number of cases favourable to the event whose probability is sought. The ratio of this number to that of all the cases possible is the measure of this probability, which is thus simply a fraction whose numerator is the number of favourable cases and whose denominator is the number of all cases possible.[88]

Laplace's rule may be formulated thus: if we are indifferent as to which of a number of possible outcomes will occur, we should ascribe each outcome equal probability. The application of this constraint on degree of certainty requires knowledge of which outcomes are *possible* and on a *lack* of information pertaining to the individual outcomes themselves; consequently the rule can be thought of

[87](Bernoulli, 1713, §IV.III)

[88](Laplace, 1814, pp. 6–7)

as a logical (rather than empirical) constraint.

Laplace's rule is called the Principle of Indifference by John Maynard Keynes, who argued in favour of its qualified application. Keynes' goal was to produce an objective interpretation of probability:

> in the sense important to logic, probability is not subjective. It is not, that is to say, subject to human caprice. A proposition is not provable because we think it so. When once the facts are given which determine our knowledge, what is probable or improbable in these circumstances has been fixed objectively, and is independent of our opinion.[89]

But the Principle of Indifference was Keynes' only tool for determining probabilities—his interpretation appealed only to this logical constraint, disregarding empirical constraints.

Bernoulli was aware of the limitations of basing probability on purely logical constraints. He argued that empirical knowledge is also required to constrain probability:

> It has been shown in the preceding chapter—from the numbers of cases in which proofs of any given thing can exist or not exist, can indicate or not indicate or even indicate the opposite—how the strengths of these proofs and the probabilities proportional to them can be calculated and estimated. And there we concluded that for correctly forming conjectures about anything at all, nothing is required other than that the number of these cases be accurately determined and that it be found out how much more easily some cases can happen than others. But here, finally, we seem to have met our problem, since this may be done only in a very few cases and almost nowhere other than in games of chance the inventors of which, in order to provide equal chances for the players, took pains to set up so that the numbers of cases would be known and fixed for which gain or loss must follow, and so that all these cases could happen with equal ease. For in several other occurrences which depend upon either the work of nature or the judgement of men, this by no means is the situation. And so, for example, the numbers of cases in dice are known: for in each die there are clearly as many cases as there are sides, and they are all equally likely. Because of the similarity of the sides and the balanced weight of the die, there is no reason why one of the sides should be more prone to fall than another, as there would be reason if the sides were of different shapes or if the die was made of a material heavier on one side than on another. And so likewise, the numbers of chances for drawing forth a white or black pebble from an urn are known, and it is known that all chances are equally likely: for the numbers of pebbles of each kind are known and determinate, and there is no reason why this pebble or that pebble should come forth rather than any other one.
>
> But what mortal will ever determine, for example, the number of diseases—i.e., the number of cases—which are able to seize upon the uncountable parts of the human body at any age and which can inflict death upon us? And what mortal will ever determine how much more

[89](Keynes, 1921, p. 4)

> likely this disease than that disease, pestilence than dropsy, dropsy than fever will destroy a man so that then a conjecture can be formed about the relationship between life and death in future generations? Who likewise will reckon up the innumerable cases of mutations to which the air is daily exposed, so that he can then guess after any given month, not to mention after any given year, what the constitution of the air will be? Again, who has well enough examined the nature of the human mind or the amazing structure of our body so that in games which depend wholly or in part on the acumen of the former or the agility of the latter, he could dare to determine the cases in which this player or that can win or lose? For these and other such things depend upon causes completely hidden from us, and since moreover these things will forever deceive our effort because of the innumerable variety of their combinations, it would clearly be unwise to wish to learn anything in this way.
>
> But indeed, another way is open to us here by which we may obtain what is sought; and what you cannot deduce a priori, you can at least deduce a posteriori—i.e., you will be able to make a deduction from many observed outcomes of similar events. For it must be presumed that every single thing is able to happen and not to happen in as many cases as it was previously observed to have happened and not to have happened in like circumstances. For if, for example, an experiment was once conducted on 300 men of the age and constitution of which Titius is now, and you observed that 200 of them had died before passing the next ten years and that the others had further prolonged their lives, you could safely enough conclude that the number of cases in which Titius must pay his debt to nature within the next ten years is twice the number of cases in which he can pay his debt after ten years. And so, if anyone has observed the weather for the past several years and has noted how many times it was calm or rainy; or if anyone has judiciously watched two players and has seen how many times this one or that one has emerged victorious: in this way he has detected what the ratio probably is between the number of cases in which the same events, with similar circumstances prevailing, are able to happen and not to happen later on.[90]

Thus any Principle of Indifference may be over-ridden by empirical knowledge. Bernoulli again:

> For example: three ships set sail from port; after some time it is announced that one of them suffered shipwreck; which one is guessed to be the one that was destroyed? If I considered merely the number of ships, I would conclude that the misfortune could have happened to each of them with equal chance; but because I remember that one of them had been eaten away by rot and old age more than the others, had been badly equipped with masts and sails, and had been commanded by a new and inexperienced captain, I consider that this ship, more probably than the others, was the one to perish.[91]

[90] (Bernoulli, 1713, §IV.IV)

[91] (Bernoulli, 1713, §IV.II)

Laplace also emphasised the dependence of probability on both knowledge and lack of knowledge:

> The curve described by a simple molecule of air or vapour is regulated in a manner just as certain as the planetary orbits; the only difference between them is that which come from our ignorance.
>
> Probability is relative, in part to this ignorance, in part to our knowledge.[92]

In sum then, we can see in the writings of Bernoulli, Laplace, and Keynes the main ideas behind objective Bayesianism. Bernoulli and Laplace were concerned with ascertaining probabilities interpreted as mental degrees of certainty. Bernoulli highlighted equipossibility as a route to measuring probabilities, which Laplace explicated in terms of indifference. Keynes put forward the idea that such a notion of probability might be objective rather than subjective. Bernoulli emphasised the importance of experience as well as indifference in determining probabilities.

We are left with two chief problems:

- How exactly does empirical information constrain degrees of belief? Is there an empirical rule analogous to the logical Principle of Indifference? This question will be addressed in §5.3.
- How exactly does indifference constrain degrees of belief in the presence of empirical information? The Principle of Indifference requires a total absence of empirical information, but in most situations we will have a mixture of information and indifference. We will look at this problem in §5.4.

5.3 Empirical Constraints: The Calibration Principle

There is one empirical constraint on rational belief that is relatively uncontroversial:

Truth Principle If an agent knows u to be true then she should have maximum degree of belief in u, $p(u) = 1$.

The standard argument behind the Bayesian approach, the Dutch Book argument, at most requires that an agent give probability one to *logical* truths,[93] not to truths empirically observed. Thus the truth principle introduces new content to Bayesianism and requires justification. However, most Bayesians admit the truth principle through the back door, by insisting that all probabilities be implicitly conditional on an agent's background information b, in which case if u is in b then $p(u) = p(u|b) = 1$.

In fact one can justify the truth principle using a modification of the Dutch Book argument. If an agent sets betting quotient $p(u) < 1$ and the stake-chooser is privy to the same information as she is, then choosing a negative stake will

[92](Laplace, 1814, p. 6)

[93]One can argue that even this constraint needs to be relaxed—see §11.9.

force the agent to lose money whatever happens. Here the background information circumscribes 'whatever happens' to eventualities consistent with the information, rather than all logically possible eventualities.

One purported objection to the truth principle is based on the observation that much of what we think we know to be true is defeasible—background information is not incontrovertible. However, some claim, if we give probability 1 to such information we can never reduce our degree of belief in it to below 1. This claim is made on the supposition that an agent updates her degrees of belief via Bayesian conditionalisation: (if an agent learns w between times t and $t+1$ then her new belief function should be her old belief function conditional on w, $p_{t+1}(v) = p_t(v|w)$ for each $v@V$). Now, the argument goes, if u is known at t and $p_t(u) = 1$ then $p_{t+1}(u) = p_t(u|w) = 1 - p_t(\neg u|w) = 1 - p_t(w|\neg u)p_t(\neg u)/p_t(w) = 1$ too because $p(\neg u) = 0$. So u can never become less certain, even if w contradicts u. But this argument is flawed in two respects. First it is fallacious: if w contradicts u and $p_t(u) = 1$ then $p_t(w) = 0$ and so $p_t(u|w)$ is unconstrained. Thus Bayesian conditionalisation does not prevent certainties from becoming less certain—it leaves this question open. Second, Bayesian conditionalisation is not the only way of updating degrees of belief. If the agent adopts *cross entropy updating* instead (see §§5.7 and 12.11) then it is easy to lower the probability of u as and when it is retracted from the agent's stock of knowledge.

The truth principle can be viewed as a special case of the following constraint:

Mental–Physical Calibration Principle If an agent knows the chance $p^*(u)$ of u then she should set her degree of belief in u to that probability, $p(u) = p^*(u)$.

Note that chance and not frequency or propensity is employed here because u, as the object of a degree of belief, is an assignment to a single-case variable not a repeatable variable. On any account of chance, if (single-case) u is known to be true then the chance of u is 1 (and known to be so) in which case $p(u) = 1$ too. Thus the truth principle follows.

Notice that the Calibration Principle tells an agent what to do only in very precise circumstances: when she knows a chance. In practice the principle will have to be augmented to be more widely applicable. For instance, an agent will rarely know exact values of chances—more often she will know approximate values.[94] In this case the Calibration Principle should presumably be extended to insist that she set her degree of belief in u to her best estimate of the chance, if she has one. As noted above, an agent's background knowledge is defeasible; consequently as estimates of chances improve her knowledge will be replaced rather than augmented and her degrees of belief will change accordingly.

Similarly, suppose the agent knows that $p^*(u)$ is r or s, where these are real numbers between 0 and 1. How should this knowledge constrain her degree of belief $p(u)$ in u? Certainly $p(u)$ is not constrained to be r or s. For example, if u is

[94]Note that scientific theories may posit exact values for chances, e.g., a particle may have spin up with the same probability as spin down, i.e. probability 1/2.

determined (a statement about the past, for instance) then its chance is arguably 0 or 1. If the agent knows this, but does not know whether or not u is actually true, then she is hardly compelled to believe u either fully or not at all. Indeed, these values seem the least rational to ascribe to u, given the lack of knowledge. A better value would be $p(u) = 1/2$, or at least some other non-extreme value. The Calibration Principle leaves this question open, as it stands, and should be extended to deal with such cases. One could argue that disjunctive knowledge of chances is not knowledge at all and should be ignored when setting degrees of belief. Then the agent would be free to give past u whatever degree of belief she likes. However, this move does not seem appropriate if r and s are very close, say 0.99 and 1. Then the disjunctive knowledge conveys a lot of information about u. A better strategy would be to restrict $p(u)$ to the interval $[r, s]$, aware as usual of the defeasible character of such a constraint. More generally, if n possible values are given for $p^*(u)$ then one can restrict $p(u)$ to lie in their convex hull, i.e. the closed interval between the value nearest 0 and the value nearest 1. Arguably this strategy is also best to deal with conjunctive knowledge of chances. If the agent has information that $p^*(u) = 0.8$ *and* has information that $p^*(u) = 1$ and neither piece of information defeats the other (perhaps they are the testimonies of equally reliable witnesses) then rather than disregard these conflicting statements, it seems better to treat them disjunctively as defining an interval $[0.8, 1]$ of rational degrees of belief.

We also have to tread carefully when presented with a piece of knowledge like $p^*(u) \neq 1/2$ (Laplace's example is of a biased coin where the direction of the bias is unknown.) It does not seem right that this should constrain degree of belief directly: there is no indication as to whether $p^*(u) > 1/2$ or $p^*(u) < 1/2$ and so, in the face of indifference $p(u) = 1/2$ might be quite rational.[95] (Likewise, knowing that u and w are probabilistically dependent with respect to p^* offers no constraint in the absence of knowing the direction of dependence.) On the other hand, suppose an agent knows just that $p^*(u) > 1/2$. Should she then restrict her degree of belief to $p(u) > 1/2$? It does not seem clear that the chance information precludes $p(v) = 1/2$, which seems a rational assignment of degree of belief given that $p^*(v)$ might be practically indistinguishable from 1/2. In this case, then, taking the closure of the interval $(1/2, 1]$ seems natural when forming a constraint on degree of belief. Thus we see again that the knowledge that $p^*(u) \in X \subseteq [0, 1]$ constrains $p(u)$ to lie in the smallest closed convex set Y containing X.

Note that if the agent's knowledge consists of a set of linear constraints $\sum_{i=1}^{k} a_i p^*(u_i) \geq b_i$ then p^* must lie in a closed convex subset of the set $\mathbb{P}$ of all

[95] Laplace (1814, p. 56): 'But if there exist in the coin an inequality which causes one of the faces to appear rather than the other without knowing which side is favored by this inequality, the probability of throwing heads at the first throw will always be $\frac{1}{2}$; because of our ignorance of which face is favored by the inequality the probability of the simple event is increased if this inequality is favorable to it, just so much as it is diminished if the inequality is contrary to it.'

probability functions,[96] in which case this constraint can carry over directly to p. Perhaps the most natural example of a non-linear constraint is an independence constraint. Suppose $V = \{A, B\}$ where both A and B are two-valued with values a^1, a^0 and b^1, b^0 respectively. Suppose the agent knows that $A \perp\!\!\!\perp_{p^*} B$ (i.e. $p^*(ab) = p^*(a)p^*(b)$ for all $a@A$ and $b@B$) and that A and B are mutually exclusive, i.e. a^1 occurs if and only if b^0 occurs. Should her degrees of belief satisfy the same independence relationship? Only two probability functions satisfy these constraints, defined by $x = (p(a^1b^1), p(a^1b^0), p(a^0b^1), p(a^0b^0)) = (0, 1, 0, 0)$ and $x' = (0, 0, 1, 0)$ respectively. It does not seem plausible that an agent should be forced to commit herself to one of these extreme functions as her belief function, and thus one can can argue that knowledge of physical probabilistic independencies should not constrain degrees of belief to satisfy corresponding mental probabilistic independencies. Thus p may lie in the smallest closed convex set of probability functions encompassing x and x', which is the set of probability functions induced by the exclusivity constraint on its own.

Other extensions of the Calibration Principle are relatively straightforward. The knowledge that $p^*(u) \in [r, s]$ can directly constrain $p(u)$ to lie in this interval. (This type of information rarely crops up in practice without having some distinguished point in the interval as a best candidate for $p^*(u)$—statistics may tell us that $p^*(u)$ is likely to lie in an interval around r, in which case r itself is a straightforward best estimate of $p^*(u)$.)

So we see that there are a number of ways in which the Calibration Principle can be fleshed out in order to make it more widely applicable. We end up with something like the following:

Mental–Physical Calibration Principle If an agent knows that $f(p^*_{\downharpoonright U}) \in X$ for $U \subseteq V$ then her belief function p should satisfy the constraint $p_{\downharpoonright U} \in Y$ where Y is the smallest closed convex set of probability functions on U that contains $f^{-1}X$.

In the rest of this section we shall take a look at the rationale behind the Calibration Principle.

The principle has three main points in its favour. First, it is intuitively plausible. As David Lewis pointed out, if you know a coin is fair (i.e. has a chance of 0.5 of tossing heads) then your degree of belief in a heads will be 0.5.[97] That we often use chances to inform our degrees of belief is beyond question.

Second, if one adopts a physical notion of chance one can argue that success in the physical world requires latching on to its chances. Just as the Dutch book argument shows that betting quotients must be probabilities to avoid loss whatever happens, so similar arguments show that betting quotients should reflect physical chances to avoid loss in the actual course of events: if an agent knows $p^*(u)$ yet sets $p(u) \neq p^*(u)$ then any stake-chooser party to the same information can select stakes that force her to lose money in the long run. Note that u is

[96] (Paris, 1994, Proposition 6.1)

[97] (Lewis, 1980, p. 84)

single-case so strictly speaking there is no long run when betting on u. To get the argument to work the agent must make a large number of bets on outcomes like u that have the same chance. Alternatively one can argue that if the agent repeatably ignores chances when determining her degrees of belief then in the long run she can be forced to lose money, even if there is only a single bet for each chance she ignores.[98]

Third, if one adopts an ultimate belief notion of chance then the Calibration Principle is practically tautologous. According to the ultimate belief notion of chance (§2.8) chances are just what our degrees of belief ought to be if we had all possible information about the world up to the time at which the chance is determined. In which case it is unavoidable that degrees of belief ought to be set to chances as they are known. Note that circularity becomes a concern if one adopts the ultimate belief notion of chance—degrees of belief are reckoned using chances via the Calibration Principle yet chances themselves are defined in terms of degrees of belief. The circularity is not vicious though. The Calibration Principle is not a definition of rational degree of belief, it is an epistemological mechanism by which one may calculate rational degrees of belief. On the other hand the ultimate belief notion of chance is not an epistemological tool, but an ontological definition or analysis of chance. Obviously one cannot find out the chance of u by learning everything about the world at a particular time and then working out one's rational degree of belief in u—one finds out about chances via frequencies or propensities as in the case of physical chance (although as we shall see shortly it is by no means obvious as to exactly how the link between chance and frequency might explicated).

While the Calibration Principle seems natural and plausible, there are a number of potential difficulties that need to be addressed.

First of all, one can object that the Calibration Principle seems *too strong* a constraint on rational belief. The Calibration Principle aims to ensure that degrees of belief are measured according to the same scale as chances (an agent is *perfectly calibrated* if $p(u) = p^*(u)$ for each u). But is calibration an important goal? What is important, one can claim, is predictive accuracy rather than calibration. An agent's *prediction* for set U of variables is deemed to be the assignment u to U that the agent awards maximum degree of belief. Then her *predictive accuracy* is the proportion of her predictions that are correct. Predictive accuracy is used widely in machine learning and data mining as a test for success for a system's classification accuracy. While one can argue that calibration will yield predictive accuracy, calibration is clearly not *required* for predictive accuracy. Korb, Hope and Hughes, however, make the following compelling case for calibration over predictive accuracy.

> Predictive accuracy entirely disregards the confidence of the prediction. In binomial classification, for example, a prediction of a mushroom's ed-

[98]One might even argue that in a single case an agent's expected loss will be positive if she fails to bet according to a known chance, by using the chance to determine the mathematical expectation of her loss. However, this assumes another kind of Calibration Principle: that the agent's expected loss is determined by the mathematical expectation.

> ibility with a probability of 0.51 counts exactly the same as a prediction of edibility with a probability of 1.0. Now, if *we* were confronted with the first prediction, we might rationally hesitate to consume such a mushroom. The predictive accuracy measurement does not hesitate. According to standard evaluation practice in machine learning and data mining every prediction is as good as every other. Any business, or animal, which behaved this way would have a very short life span.[99]

Thus predicting u does not necessarily mean accepting u for practical purposes: the belief of 0.51 that the mushroom is edible may lead to a prediction of its edibility but does not warrant a practical acceptance of its edibility. Decision making depends on more than prediction, and it is here that calibration becomes important.

On the other hand, one can accept that calibration is an important desideratum and claim that the Calibration Principle is *too weak*. The reason being, while the Calibration Principle tells us how to calibrate degrees of belief with known chances, it does not tell us that we ought to obtain any chances in the first place. An agent with her head in the sand who makes no empirical observations will satisfy the Calibration Principle although she may be very poorly calibrated. Thus if calibration is a goal, something stronger is required. I sympathise with this line of argument, but I would maintain that the role of objective Bayesianism is to elucidate the relationship between background knowledge and rational degree of belief. While knowledge-gathering is an important task, it is a different task. An agent ought to gather knowledge properly, set her degrees of belief appropriately, make good decisions based on those degrees of belief, behave ethically, and so on—Bayesianism only deals with the second of these tasks.

Subjective Bayesians often put forward the following sort of objection to a Calibration Principle. One can accept the virtues of calibration but argue that degrees of belief tend naturally to the corresponding chances through repeated Bayesian conditionalisation as new empirical observations are made. Thus any further calibration via the Calibration Principle is unnecessary. As mentioned in §2.8 de Finetti, a strict subjectivist, showed how degrees of belief converge to frequencies under the assumption that prior degrees of belief are exchangeable, i.e. invariant under permutations in the ordering of outcomes (thus one's degree of belief in a coin tossing heads, tails, tails is that same as it tossing tails, tails, heads).[100] While exchangeable degrees of belief are appropriate in some situations—notably when the outcomes under consideration are probabilistically independent—they are inappropriate when confronted with processes that are known to have temporal dependence.[101] Certainly, there are no circumstances under which a strict subjectivist could argue that an agent's degrees of belief *ought* to be exchangeable, because strict subjectivists hold that to be rational it is sufficient that the agent's degrees of belief are probabilities—no

[99] (Korb *et al.*, 2001, p. 277)

[100] (de Finetti, 1937)

[101] See Gillies (2000, pp. 75–77) for discussion of this point.

further constraints are warranted. Thus de Finetti's argument only goes through if exchangeability just happens to be satisfied. Moreover, convergence arguments only deal with calibration in the long run, i.e. after a great many observations have been made. But unless the Calibration Principle is adopted, agents open themselves up to avoidable poor calibration in the short term. For example, suppose an agent learns that $p^*(u) = r$. If a truth principle is adopted then the agent is committed to forming new degree of belief $p_{t+1}(p^*(u) = r) = 1$, and by Bayesian conditionalisation $p_{t+1}(u) = p_t(u|p^*(u) = r)$. But without a Calibration Principle this can be any value at all, and certainly need not be r. Presumably if calibration is important then an agent should calibrate at the earliest opportunity, and this is only possible with a Calibration Principle.[102]

Another important objection stems from interpretational problems. Bayesianism is normally conceived as ascribing probabilities to single cases, not to repeatably instantiatable variables. Thus chance is used in Calibration Principle, not frequency or propensity. But, the objection goes, chance is an overly metaphysical theory: while it is clear as to how probabilities are to be measured under the frequency and propensity theories, it is not so easy to ascertain chances. The standard suggestion is this: a chance $p^*(u)$ is measured by determining the features of the world that determine $p^*(u)$ (the *chance fixers*), using these to produce a list of repeatable conditions (which define a reference class of outcomes), generating a collective from these repeatable conditions, and then measuring the frequency in this collective. The first step is the stumbling block: if I want to measure the chance of my car breaking down in the next year, there are bound to be a large number of chance fixers—to do with the car itself, driving conditions, amount of usage, and so on—and I would find it very hard to list them all correctly. If only a subset of chance fixers are identified, or there are mistakes in the list of identified chance fixers then there is no guarantee that the associated frequency will resemble the chance to be measured. Thus while the chance interpretation may provide a metaphysics of single-case probability, it poses a serious epistemological difficulty, namely determining a suitable reference class from the single case in question (this is the reference class problem of §2.5). And of course if we cannot measure chances then we can not apply the Calibration Principle.

Can we use frequencies or propensities in the Calibration Principle instead of chances? Yes, talk of chances can be eliminated, but again we have a reference class problem: if the mental probability of a single-case variable is to be set to the physical probability of a repeatably instantiatable variable then we need to determine a suitable reference class from the single case. If I want to set my degree of belief in my car breaking down in the next year, should I look at the propensity of cars of the same make breaking down, or cars of the same age, or

[102]Note that Dawid (1982) shows that if an agent's degrees of belief are coherent then she should believe she is perfectly calibrated to degree 1. However, this leaves open the question of whether she actually is well calibrated, so cannot be used to argue for the redundancy of a Calibration Principle.

cars of the same specification, or vehicles that I have owned? A good suggestion is: take the narrowest reference class for which you have frequency data. So if I know cars of the same make break down with propensity 0.1 but cars of the same make and age break down with propensity 0.2, I should set my belief to the latter figure. This 'principle of the narrowest reference class' fails though if data is available for more than one narrowest reference class. If I also know that cars of the same age and specification as mine break down with propensity 0.3, then should I set my degree of belief to 0.2 or 0.3?

I think the best way to deal with the reference class problem is to treat each narrowest reference class propensity as an estimate of the chance we are interested in. Thus I have two conflicting reports of the chance of my car breaking down in the next year, 0.2 and 0.3. I suggested earlier that when faced with multiple estimates of a chance, the best we can do is constrain degree of belief to lie in the convex hull determined by the estimates, i.e. the smallest closed interval containing the estimates, $[0.2, 0.3]$ in this case. If we do that, then the Calibration Principle avoids reference class problems and becomes more readily applicable.

We see then that the Calibration Principle—suitably extended to deal with disjunctive information and so on—forms a defensible empirical constraint on rational belief. Application of the principle depends on the totality of information available: one should apply the principle to the *best* estimate of the chance to hand (e.g. the *narrowest* reference class) and its application differs if there are multiple best estimates. In fact Bernoulli himself argued that probability judgements should be based on all available evidence:

> It is not enough to weigh one or another proof, but everything must be sought out which can come within our realm of knowledge and which appears to have any connection at all with proving the thing.[103]

Many objections to versions of the Calibration Principle are misguided because they have ignored some relevant background knowledge. One objection proceeds as follows:[104] suppose we have observed only sixes in a finite number of throws of a die; then the Calibration Principle leads us to assign probability 1 to a six at the next toss; but this would be far too bold, especially if the number of observed throws is small. Such an objection reveals a flawed application of the Calibration Principle rather than a flaw in the Calibration Principle itself. Here we do not only have an observed frequency of sixes, but we also know that the outcomes were generated by a die, that dice are roughly symmetrical and that fully symmetrical dice yield a six in about a sixth of throws, in the long run. Clearly, this extra knowledge should lead us to be more cautious, especially if the number of observed throws is small and thus the observed frequency is only a weak approximation of the limiting frequency. (If we were merely told that an experiment has six possible outcomes and that only outcome 6 had occurred in the past, then we would be more justified in applying the Calibration Principle

[103](Bernoulli, 1713, §IV.II)

[104](Uffink, 1996, §2)

using just the frequency information, giving probability 1 to outcome 6 on the next trial.)

Keynes emphasised that we need to take qualitative as well as quantitative information into account.

> Bernoulli's second axiom, that in reckoning a probability we must take everything into account, is easily forgotten in these cases of statistical probabilities. The statistical result is so attractive in its definiteness that it leads us to forget the more vague though more important considerations which may be, in a given particular case, within our knowledge. To a stranger the probability that I shall send a letter to the post unstamped may be derived from the statistics of the Post Office; for me those figures would have but the slightest bearing on the question.[105]

This is perhaps the key challenge for proponents of empirical constraints: how can one sharpen qualitative information into quantitative constraints on rational degrees belief? (Of course every scientist faces the challenge of sharpening phenomenal information into the language of her science, and it should be no surprise that knowledge engineers are in the same boat.) Now by adopting an interval-based approach to empirical constraints I think that the sharpening challenge can by and large be met. Consider Keynes' Post Office example: I know that I am scattier than the average member of the populace, but I do not know quantitatively how much scattier, so this knowledge only constrains my degree of belief that I have posted a letter unstamped to lie between the Post Office average and 1. On the other hand, I have found that in the past my letters have reliably found their recipients on almost all occasions: on more than 90% of occasions, I am sure. Taking this knowledge into account, my degree of belief would lie between the Post Office average and 0.1.

To what extent are these bounds objective? Would not a more wary agent give a lower bound of 80% stamped postings? I am assuming here that a bound marks the boundary between knowledge and conjecture: I know (defeasibly!) that my postings are 90% reliable, but I am not sure about greater reliability. Indeed, a more wary agent may have stronger demands on knowledge and on the same experience only give 80% as the boundary between knowledge and conjecture. Standards for knowledge may well be subjective (though there is much agreement), in which case the bounds are subjective too. On the other hand, there might be a rational standard of knowledge that one ought to adopt and which varies only according to context—perhaps moderately wary in day-to-day life and sceptical when faced with philosophical argument—if so, one may be able to make a case for objective bounds. The important thing to note is that subjective standards for knowledge do not put paid to objective Bayesianism, which demands only that degrees of belief be determined objectively from *given* background knowledge. If the standards for knowledge differ, so will the knowledge and so will the rational degrees of belief.

[105](Keynes, 1921, p. 322)

In sum it seems plausible that qualitative information can be sharpened into quantitative bounds on degree of belief, if not point-valued degrees of belief. To lend this claim further credibility, we will see in §5.8 that qualitative causal information can be translated into quantitative constraints. In the mean time we shall suppose that the sharpening challenge can be met and that empirical knowledge imposes, via the Calibration Principle, a set of quantitative constraints on an agent's degrees of belief.

5.4 Logical Constraints: The Maximum Entropy Principle

We came across one logical constraint in §5.2: the Principle of Indifference advocates equal probability to each of a number of basic outcomes, if an agent is indifferent as to which will occur. This can be formulated in our framework as follows:

Principle of Indifference If nothing in an agent's knowledge favours one assignment to V over another, then $p(v) = 1/||V||$ for each $v@V$.

There are are broadly speaking three problems with the Principle of Indifference. The first does not affect us here: the principle leads to paradoxes on infinite domains.[106] Keynes himself acknowledged this problem but argued that the principle is perfectly applicable on finite domains, where the alternatives are 'basic', that is, not subdivisible into further alternatives. Here V is finite and the assignments to V are the most specific descriptions of states of affairs, and hence basic. Arguably the role of the infinite is to help us reason about the large but finite universe we occupy; that a principle cannot be easily extended from finite domains to infinite domains can only lead us to conclude that the infinite will not be of much help, and we will have to stick with reasoning directly about the finite.

The second problem is how we understand indifference. If the agent knows nothing at all then trivially her knowledge does not favour one assignment over another. In that case the Principle of Indifference is readily applicable. But an agent will rarely know nothing at all. If the arguments of §5.3 are accepted, her knowledge will take the form of a set of constraints on her degrees of belief, and it may be hard to tell whether these constraints favour any one assignment over the others. Thus the Principle of Indifference needs to be rendered more precise so that one can tell exactly when it is applicable.

The third problem is that very often an agent's knowledge *will* favour one assignment over another. The Principle of Indifference does not tell her how to set her degrees of belief in that situation. Thus the principle is incomplete; if an agent's background knowledge is to fix her degrees of belief then more needs to be said.

Edwin Jaynes put the case thus:

> The problem of specification of probabilities in cases where little or no information is available, is as old as the theory of probability. Laplace's

[106] See Keynes (1921) for a catalogue of the paradoxes.

> "Principle of Insufficient Reason" was an attempt to supply a criterion of choice, in which one said that two events are to be assigned equal probabilities if there is no reason to think otherwise. However, except in cases where there is an element of symmetry that clearly renders the events "equally possible," this assumption may appear just as arbitrary as any other that might be made. Furthermore, it has been very fertile in generating paradoxes in the case of continuously variable random quantities, since intuitive notions of "equally possible" are altered by a change of variables. Since the time of Laplace, this way of formulating problems has been largely abandoned, owing to the lack of any constructive principle which would give us a reason for preferring one probability distribution over another in cases where both agree equally well with the available information.[107]

Jaynes put forward the *Maximum Entropy Principle*, which generalises the Principle of Indifference:

> The principle of maximum entropy may be regarded as an extension of the principle of insufficient reason (to which it reduces in case no information is given except enumeration of the possibilities x_i), with the following essential difference. The maximum entropy distribution may be asserted for the positive reason that it is uniquely determined as the one which is maximally noncommital with regard to missing information, instead of the negative one that there was no reason to think otherwise. Thus the concept of entropy supplies the missing criterion of choice which Laplace needed to remove the apparent arbitrariness of the principle of insufficient reason, and in addition it shows precisely how this principle is to be modified in case there are reasons for "thinking otherwise".[108]

Jaynes' principle is this:

Maximum Entropy Principle An agent ought to adopt, out of all the probability functions that satisfy the constraints imposed by her background knowledge, a function p that maximises entropy,

$$H = -\sum_{v@V} p(v) \log p(v).$$

Note that by continuity, $0 \log 0 = 0$. The Maximum Entropy Principle is also known simply as *maxent*.

Suppose background knowledge imposes a set π of quantitative constraints on an agent's belief function p, via the Calibration Principle. This narrows down the set of rational probability functions to a set $\mathbb{P}_\pi = \{x \in \mathbb{P} : x \text{ satisfies } \pi\}$, where $\mathbb{P}$ is the set of all probability functions and x is the vector of parameters $x^v = p(v)$ (see §2.2). The Maximum Entropy Principle further narrows down the set of probability functions considered rational to $\mathbb{H}_\pi = \{x \in \mathbb{P}_\pi : x \text{ maximises } H(x)\}$ where $H(x) = -\sum_{v@V} x^v \log x^v$. Let $\mathbb{O}$ signify the set of probability

[107] (Jaynes, 1957, p. 622)

[108] (Jaynes, 1957, p. 623)

functions considered optimal: an agent ought to adopt a probability function from $\mathbb{O}$. Subjective Bayesians argue that $\mathbb{O} = \mathbb{P}$; empirically based subjectivist Bayesians claim $\mathbb{O} = \mathbb{P}_\pi$; objective Bayesians maintain that $\mathbb{O} = \mathbb{H}_\pi$. Note that if $\mathbb{P}_\pi$ is convex then there will be at most one function in $\mathbb{H}_\pi$, while if $\mathbb{P}_\pi$ is closed then there will be at least one function in $\mathbb{H}_\pi$. In §5.3 I advocated a convex hull approach where constraints restrict degrees of belief to closed convex sets. In this case $\mathbb{P}_\pi$ will be closed and convex and $\mathbb{H}_\pi$ will consist of a single probability function. Thus π determines a unique optimal belief function, and rational belief is objective in that it only depends on background knowledge.[109]

In §5.5 we shall look at how the x-parameters x^v for $x \in \mathbb{H}_\pi$ can be determined. For the remainder of this section we shall evaluate the rationale behind the Maximum Entropy Principle.

The most common justification for the Maximum Entropy Principle is that articulated by Jaynes above. It seems clear that if a belief function is to represent background knowledge then it should express the background knowledge and only the background knowledge, i.e. it should satisfy the constraints imposed by background knowledge but be maximally non-committal (or uncertain) in other respects. Now entropy is the standard measure of the amount of uncertainty of a probability function, and hence a belief function should be one from all those that satisfy the constraints imposed by background knowledge which maximises entropy. The argument that entropy best measures uncertainty proceeds by observing that up to multiplicative constant, entropy is the only function $H(x)$ which satisfies the following desiderata:[110]

- H should be continuous in x.
- 'With equally likely events there is more choice, or uncertainty, when there are more possible events.'[111] If the x^v are all equal (i.e. $x^v = 1/||V||$), then H should be a monotonic increasing function of $||V||$.
- 'If a choice be broken down into two successive choices, the original H should be the weighted sum of the original values of H.'[112] For example, $H(1/2, 1/3, 1/6) = H(1/2, 1/2) + 1/2H(2/3, 1/3)$; choosing one of three alternatives with probabilities $1/2, 1/3, 1/6$ can be thought of as first choosing one of two alternatives each of probability $1/2$ and then with probability $1/2$ (i.e. if the second alternative is chosen) choosing two more alternatives of probability $2/3, 1/3$.

[109] Note that this objectivity does not extend to countably infinite domains of variables—see Williamson (1999).

[110] See Shannon (1948, §6); Shannon and Weaver (1949); Paris (1994, pp. 77–78) and Jaynes (2003, chapter 11).

[111] (Shannon, 1948, §6)

[112] (Shannon, 1948, §6)

While some variants of the entropy measure of uncertainty have been thought to go against intuition,[113] entropy itself remains the most widely adopted explication of uncertainty of a probability function. No doubt this is partly due to the fact that the entropy measure of uncertainty has led to very fruitful implications in communication and information theory: as Shannon remarked, the above justification 'is given to lend a certain plausibility to some of our later definitions. The real justification of these definitions, however, will reside in their implications'.[114]

Paris and Vencovská give an alternative justification of the Maximum Entropy Principle. They cite a number of intuitively plausible conditions that any principle for determining a probability function from background knowledge ought to satisfy, and go on to show that the Maximum Entropy Principle is the only principle which satisfies these conditions. The conditions are:[115]

Irrelevant Information p should be invariant to irrelevant information being added to π, i.e. $C \cap C' = \emptyset$ implies $\mathbb{O}_{\pi \restriction C} = \mathbb{O}_{\pi,\pi' \restriction C}$, where π, π' are constraints on $C, C' \subseteq V$ respectively, and $\mathbb{O}_{\restriction C}$ is the set of optimal probability functions restricted to C.

Equivalence p should be invariant to reformulation of π, i.e. $\mathbb{P}_\pi = \mathbb{P}_{\pi'}$ implies $\mathbb{O}_\pi = \mathbb{O}_{\pi'}$.

Renaming p should be invariant under renaming of assignments to V. Suppose $V = \{A_1, \ldots, A_n\}, V' = \{A'_1, \ldots, A'_n\}$ and that $||A_i|| = ||A'_i||$ for $i = 1, \ldots, n$; let $J = ||V||$ and σ be the bijection from assignments $\{v_1, \ldots, v_J\}$ to V to assignments $\{v'_1, \ldots, v'_J\}$ to V' given by $\sigma(v_i) = v'_i$; let π' be formed from π by applying this bijection; then $p' \in \mathbb{O}_{\pi'}$ if and only if $p'\sigma \in \mathbb{O}_\pi$.

Relativisation if π and π' agree on constraints involving assignments consistent with u then $\mathbb{O}_\pi$ and $\mathbb{O}_{\pi'}$ agree on assignments consistent with u.

Obstinacy p should be invariant under learning new information consistent with p. $\mathbb{O}_\pi \cap \mathbb{P}_{\pi'} \neq \emptyset$ implies $\mathbb{O}_{\pi,\pi'} = \mathbb{O}_\pi \cap \mathbb{P}_{\pi'}$.

Independence If π contains no information about the relationship between B and C other than their probabilities conditional on A, then p should render B and C independent conditional on A, i.e. $\pi = \{p(b|a) = r_1, p(c|a) = r_2, p(a) = r_3\}$ implies $B \perp\!\!\!\perp_p C \mid A$ for $p \in \mathbb{O}_\pi$.

Continuity The property of being a rational probability function should not die in the limit. If $\mathbb{P}_{\pi_i} \longrightarrow \mathbb{P}_\pi$ (with respect to Blaschke distance) and $p_i \in \mathbb{O}_{\pi_i}$ then $\lim_{i \longrightarrow \infty} p_i \in \mathbb{O}_\pi$.

[113]Notably conditional entropy was originally misinterpreted by Shannon, and this led to criticism in Uffink (1995, §4) and Seidenfeld (1979).

[114](Shannon, 1948, p. 393)

[115]See §3 of Paris and Vencovská (2001) for precise formulations.

Then Paris and Vencovská show that the optimal probability functions are those obtained by the Maximum Entropy Principle, $\mathbb{O}_\pi = \mathbb{H}_\pi$.[116]

Some have objected to the Maximum Entropy Principle, claiming that it inherits problems that beset the Principle of Indifference, in particular, representation dependence. Suppose, e.g., that $V = \{C\}$ where C takes values *true* or *false* depending on whether or not a particular object is colourful, and let $V' = \{R, B, G\}$, two-valued variables true or false according to whether the particular object is red, blue, or green respectively. If there are no constraints then maxent on V will yield a function p_V for which $p_V(c) = 1/2$ for $c@C$, but maxent on V' will yield $p_{V'}(rbg) = 1/8$ for $r@R, b@B, g@G$. Now $C = \mathit{false}$ corresponds to $R = \mathit{false} \cdot B = \mathit{false} \cdot G = \mathit{false}$ yet $p_V(C = \mathit{false}) = 1/2 \neq 1/8 = p_{V'}(R = \mathit{false} \cdot B = \mathit{false} \cdot G = \mathit{false})$. Thus the probability given by maxent to the colourfulness of the object depends on how the domain of variables is represented. Clearly the problem with this objection is that we know of a correspondence between 'not colourful' and 'not red, blue, or green' but the agent does not: if we were to formulate the problem from the perspective we enjoy, then we should consider $V'' = \{C, R, B, G\}$ and the constraint $C = \mathit{false} \leftrightarrow R = \mathit{false} \cdot B = \mathit{false} \cdot G = \mathit{false}$ in which case no inconsistency will arise. Changes in representation often contain implicit changes in knowledge (see Chapter 12 for further discussion of this point) and this implicit knowledge must be made explicit if the Maximum Entropy Principle is to be applied effectively.[117]

Two other objections to the Maximum Entropy Principle are altogether more serious and need to be addressed in some detail. These two objections were articulated by Judea Pearl in his pioneering book on Bayesian nets:

> computational techniques for finding a maximum-entropy [ME] distribution (Cheeseman, 1983) are usually intractable, and the resulting distribution is often at odds with our perception of causation.[118]

Indeed, the problem of computing the parameters $x \in \mathbb{H}_\pi$ that maximise entropy has often been considered too difficult to perform in practice and we shall look at this problem in some detail in the next few sections; the problem of how causal knowledge impinges on the entropy maximisation process has also been little understood and we shall address this question in §5.8.

In sum, objective Bayesianism is two faceted: empirical knowledge constrains rational degree of belief through the Calibration Principle; lack of further knowledge constrains rational degree of belief through the Maximum Entropy Principle. In the remainder of this chapter we shall look at the relationships between

[116] (Paris and Vencovská, 2001). Note that there are other axiomatic derivations of the Maximum Entropy Principle—see e.g. Shore and Johnson (1980), Tikochinsky *et al.* (1984), Uffink (1995) for a criticism, and Csiszár (1991).

[117] Halpern and Koller (1995) argue that no reasonable way of setting probabilities is independent of representation. Paris and Vencovská (1997) defend the Maximum Entropy Principle from the charge of representation dependence.

[118] (Pearl, 1988, p. 463)

objective Bayesianism, Bayesian nets, and causality. In the next chapter we shall see how objective Bayesianism can offer us a way round the difficulties that plague the causal interpretation of Bayesian nets (discussed in Chapter 4).

5.5 Maximising Entropy Efficiently

The chief difficulty when applying the Maximum Entropy Principle is that the number of x-parameters x^v in the entropy expression $H(x)$ is exponential in the size of the domain V—therefore when the domain size is large it can be impractical to determine the values of the parameters that maximise entropy. The object of the following sections is to put forward a principled and practical way of reducing the number of parameters required in the entropy maximisation process.

The key idea is this. By analysing the structure of the constraints imposed by background knowledge, it is possible to determine a host of conditional probabilistic independencies that the maximum entropy probability function p will satisfy. In §5.6 we shall see that the independence structure of p is most naturally represented by a Markov network. By transforming this Markov network into a Bayesian network (§5.7), we can exploit these independencies to reparameterise the entropy expression, thereby reducing the computational complexity of the maximisation task.

Apart from simplifying the entropy maximisation problem, this reparameterisation strategy yields the following advantages. First, we are left with a Bayesian network representation of an agent's belief function: this is desirable in that it may allow efficient storage and updating of the belief function (§§5.7, 12.11). Second, the approach allows further computational savings when the background knowledge includes knowledge of causal relationships (§5.8).

We shall suppose that an agent's background knowledge imposes a number of constraints $\pi = \{\pi_1, \ldots, \pi_m\}$ on the set of probability functions that she may adopt. Associated with each constraint π_i is the set $C_i \subseteq V = \{A_1, \ldots, A_n\}$ of variables involved in the constraint: e.g. if π_i is the constraint that the mean of variable A_1 is $1/3$ then the associated constraint set is $C_i = \{A_1\}$. Let $z_i^{c_i} =_{df} p(c_i)$ where $c_i @ C_i$, and let z_i be the vector of these parameters. Each constraint π_i on C_i will be assumed to be an equality constraint of the form $f_i(z_i) = 0$ or an inequality constraint of the form $f_i(z_i) \geq 0$ (a constraint which restricts probabilities to a closed interval can be thought of as two inequality constraints). Note that z_i is determined by x through the relationship $z_i^{c_i} = \sum_{v @ V, v \sim c_i} x^v$. As usual we denote the set of constrained probability functions by $\mathbb{P}_\pi$, so

$$\mathbb{P}_\pi = \{x \in \mathbb{P} : f_1(z_1) \geqq 0, \ldots, f_m(z_m) \geqq 0\},$$

where $\geqq$ is either $\geq$ or $=$ according to the constraint. We shall assume throughout that the constraints $\pi_1, \ldots, \pi_m$ are consistent in the sense that $\mathbb{P}_\pi \neq \emptyset$, since maximising entropy subject to inconsistent constraints is a trivial task.[119]

[119]However, finding out whether π is inconsistent may not be easy.

Under the standard x-parameterisation, the entropy equation is

$$H(x) = -\sum_{v@V} x^v \log x^v. \tag{5.1}$$

The Maximum Entropy Principle requires that a parameter vector $x \in \mathbb{P}_\pi$ is found that maximises $H(x)$. If, as we have argued, $\mathbb{P}_\pi$ is closed and convex, then there will be a unique such x, and typically one might use numerical optimisation techniques or Lagrange multiplier methods to find it. But, as mentioned in §3.3, there are $\prod_{i=1}^n ||A_i||$ x-parameters. One of the x-parameters is determined by additivity from the others, and so there are $(\prod_{i=1}^n ||A_i||) - 1$ free x-parameters, a number exponential in n. This is a problem for numerical optimisation methods because as n becomes large there will quickly become too many parameters to be stored and adjusted, and there may even be too many terms in eqn 5.1 to be summed in available time. Lagrange multiplier methods suffer analogously: a system of equations (consisting of the m constraint equations and $\prod_{i=1}^n ||A_i||$ partial derivatives of the Lagrange equation with respect to the x-parameters) must be solved for x, and this system of equations will quickly become unhandleable as n increases.

Unfortunately there appears to be no fully general solution to the complexity problem: the task of finding an approximation to the maximum entropy function is NP-complete[120] and the task of finding a likely approximation is RP-complete,[121] and so if NP $\neq$P $\neq$ RP then there is no polynomial time algorithm for performing these tasks and any algorithm will be intractable in the worst case as n increases. The best we can hope for is an algorithm which performs well on the type of problem that occurs in practice and badly only rarely. This at least would be an improvement on naive numerical and Lagrange multiplier approaches which perform uniformly badly.

The approach outlined in the following sections is based on the premise that in practice the sizes of the constraint sets C_i are usually small in comparison with n, as n becomes large. Constraints often consist of observed means of single variables, marginals of small sets of variables, hypothesised deterministic connections among small sets of variables, causal connections among pairs of variables, independence relationships among small sets of variables, and so on. The point is that there is a limit to the amount we normally observe and to the connections among variables posited by background knowledge, in that while there may be many observations and many connections, each observation and connection will relate only few variables. The number of possible observations pertinent to a joint distribution over V increases exponentially with n, but, I suggest, our ability to observe increases sub-exponentially.

If such an assumption is correct, then as n grows there are many conditional independencies that the entropy-maximising probability function p will satisfy.

[120](Paris, 1994, Theorem 10.6)

[121](Paris, 1994, Theorem 10.7)

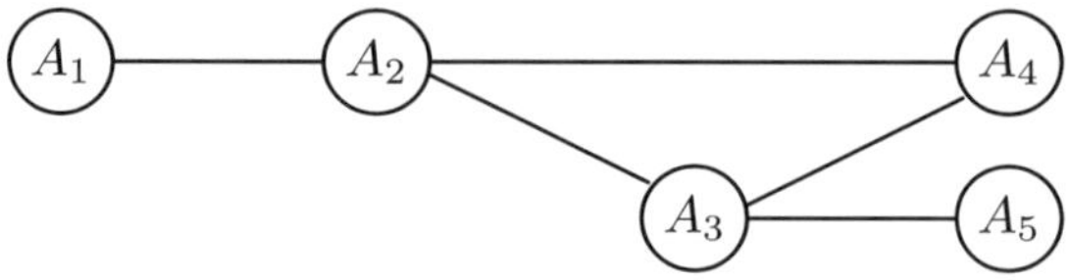

FIG. 5.1. Example constraint graph.

We can identify these independencies just from the constraint sets C_i, and exploit them to simplify the task of determining p, as we shall now see.

5.6 From Constraints to Markov Network

Define an undirected *constraint graph* $\mathcal{G}$ as follows. Take as vertices the variables in V. Include an edge between two variables $A_i, A_j \in V$ if and only if A_i and A_j occur in the same constraint set C_k.

Suppose, e.g., that $V = \{A_1, \ldots, A_5\}$ and that there are four constraints $\pi_1, \ldots, \pi_4$ constraining $C_1 = \{A_1, A_2\}, C_2 = \{A_2, A_3, A_4\}, C_3 = \{A_3, A_5\}$, $C_4 = \{A_4\}$ respectively. Then the constraint graph $\mathcal{G}$ is depicted in Fig. 5.1.

The constraint graph is useful because it represents conditional independencies that a maximum entropy function p satisfies. For $X, Y, Z \subseteq V$, Z *separates* X from Y in undirected graph $\mathcal{G}$ if every path from a vertex in X to a vertex in Y goes through some vertex in Z. Then:

Theorem 5.1 *If Z separates X from Y in the constraint graph $\mathcal{G}$ then $X \perp\!\!\!\perp_p Y \mid Z$ for any p satisfying the constraints which maximises entropy.*

Proof: The first step is to use standard Lagrange multiplier optimisation. By theorems of Lagrange and Runge-Kutta,[122] if $x \in \mathbb{P}_\pi$ is a local maximum of H then there are constants $\mu, \lambda_1, \ldots, \lambda_m \in \mathbb{R}$, called *multipliers*, such that

$$\frac{\partial H}{\partial x^v} + \mu + \sum_{i=1}^{m} \lambda_i \frac{\partial f_i}{\partial x^v} = 0 \tag{5.2}$$

for each assignment $v@V$, where μ is the multiplier corresponding to the additivity constraint $\sum_{v@V} x^v = 1$, and where $\lambda_i = 0$ for each inequality constraint which is not effective at x (i.e. for each inequality constraint π_i such that $f_i(x) > 0$).

Now the argument of f_i is the vector z_i of probabilities of assignments to C_i. Moreover, $z_i^{c_i} = \sum_{v@V, v\sim c_i} x^v$, so

$$\frac{\partial f_i}{\partial x^v} = \frac{\partial f_i}{\partial z_i^{c_i}} \frac{\partial z_i^{c_i}}{\partial x^v} = \frac{\partial f_i}{\partial z_i^{c_i}} .1$$

where c_i is the assignment to C_i that is consistent with v. Furthermore,

[122] See, e.g., Sundaram (1996, Theorems 5.1 and 6.1).

$$\frac{\partial H}{\partial x^v} = -1 - \log x^v,$$

so eqn 5.2 can be written

$$\log x^v = -1 + \mu + \sum_{i=1}^{m} \lambda_i \frac{\partial f_i}{\partial z_i^{c_i}},$$

where each $c_i \sim v$. Thus,

$$x^v = e^{\mu - 1} \prod_{i=1}^{m} e^{\lambda_i (\partial f_i / \partial z_i^{c_i})}. \tag{5.3}$$

Hence the local maximum x is representable as a product of functions, each of which depends only on variables in a single constraint set C_i (the leading term is a constant). The probability function p corresponding to x is said to *factorise* according to the constraint sets $C_1, \dots C_m$, and since these sets are complete subsets of $\mathcal{G}$, p is said to *factorise* according to $\mathcal{G}$.[123] The *Global Markov Condition* says that if Z separates X from Y in $\mathcal{G}$ then $X \perp\!\!\!\perp_p Y \mid Z$, and this condition is a straightforward consequence of factorisation according to $\mathcal{G}$.[124] Thus the theorem follows for local maxima p, and in particular for global maxima p. ∎

The converse does not hold in general. For example, a constraint π_1 that asserts the independence of A_1 and A_2 must of course be satisfied by the maximum entropy function p, but would not correspond to any separation in the constraint graph $\mathcal{G}$. However, there is a partial converse to Theorem 5.1: separation in $\mathcal{G}$ captures all the conditional independencies of p that are due to structure of the constraint sets and not the constraints themselves. More precisely, suppose that as before we are given disjoint $X, Y, Z \subseteq V$ and constraint sets $C_1, \dots, C_m$ and we construct the corresponding constraint graph $\mathcal{G}$; then

Theorem 5.2 *If, for all $\pi_1, \dots, \pi_m$ constraining variables in $C_1, \dots, C_m$ respectively, $X \perp\!\!\!\perp_p Y \mid Z$ where p is a function satisfying $\pi_1, \dots, \pi_m$ that maximises entropy, then Z separates X from Y in $\mathcal{G}$.*

Proof: We shall show the contrapositive, namely that if Z does not separate X from Y in $\mathcal{G}$ then there is some $\pi = \{\pi_1, \dots, \pi_m\}$ constraining $C_1, \dots, C_m$ such that, for $p \in \mathbb{H}_\pi$, $X \rightleftharpoons_p Y \mid Z$.

So suppose $A_{i_1}, \dots, A_{i_k}$ is a shortest path from some $A_{i_1} \in X$ to some $A_{i_k} \in Y$ avoiding vertices in Z. The task is then to find some $\pi_1, \dots, \pi_m$ that render A_{i_1} and A_{i_k} probabilistically dependent conditional on Z for the maximum entropy p.

[123] (Lauritzen, 1996, pp. 34–35)

[124] (Lauritzen, 1996, Proposition 3.8)

For $j = 1, \ldots, k-1$, A_{i_j} and $A_{i_{j+1}}$ are connected by an edge in $\mathcal{G}$, so they are in the same constraint set, which we can call C_j without loss of generality. Moreover no three vertices on the path are in the same constraint set, for we could otherwise construct a shorter path from A_{i_1} to A_{i_k} avoiding Z. Thus $C_1, \ldots, C_{k-1}$ are distinct. For each such constraint set C_j let π_j consist of the constraint $p(a^*_{i_j}|a^*_{i_{j+1}}) = 1$ for some distinguished assignments $a^*_{i_j}, a^*_{i_{j+1}}$ to $A_{i_j}, A_{i_{j+1}}$ respectively; moreover add the constraint $p(a^*_{i_1}) = 1/2$ to π_1. (It is straightforward to see that each π_j can be written in the form $f_j(z_j) = 0$.) Let all other constraints $(\pi_k, \ldots, \pi_m)$ be vacuous. The constraints $\pi_1, \ldots, \pi_m$ thus defined are clearly consistent, and constrain $C_1, \cdots, C_m$ respectively.

Note that by rewriting the constraints $\pi_1, \ldots, \pi_{k-1}$ and discarding the vacuous constraints $\pi_k, \ldots, \pi_m$, one can repose the optimisation problem as one involving constraint sets $C'_1, \ldots, C'_{k-1}$, where $C'_j = \{A_{i_j}, A_{i_{j+1}}\}$ for $j = 1, \ldots, k-1$. These constraint sets lead to a constraint graph $\mathcal{G}'$ in which the only edges are those between A_{i_j} and $A_{i_{j+1}}$ for $j = 1, \ldots, k-1$. By applying Theorem 5.1 to $\mathcal{G}'$, we see that $A_{i_j} \perp\!\!\!\perp_p \{A_{i_{j+2}}, \ldots, A_{i_k}\} \mid A_{i_{j+1}}$ for $j = 1, \ldots, k-2$, and (since none of $A_{i_1}, \ldots, A_{i_k}$ are in Z) $A_{i_1} \perp\!\!\!\perp_p Z \mid A_{i_k}$ and $A_{i_1} \perp\!\!\!\perp_p Z$. So for any $z@Z$,

$$
\begin{aligned}
p(a^*_{i_1}|a^*_{i_k} z) &= p(a^*_{i_1}|a^*_{i_k}) \\
&= \sum_{a_{i_2}, \ldots, a_{i_{k-1}}} p(a^*_{i_1}|a_{i_2} \cdots a_{i_{k-1}} a^*_{i_k}) p(a_{i_2}|a_{i_3} \cdots a_{i_{k-1}} a^*_{i_k}) \cdots \\
&\quad \cdots p(a_{i_{k-2}}|a_{i_{k-1}} a^*_{i_k}) p(a_{i_{k-1}}|a^*_{i_k}) \\
&= \sum_{a_{i_2}, \ldots, a_{i_{k-1}}} p(a^*_{i_1}|a_{i_2}) p(a_{i_2}|a_{i_3}) \cdots \\
&\quad \cdots p(a_{i_{k-2}}|a_{i_{k-1}}) p(a_{i_{k-1}}|a^*_{i_k}) \\
&= 1
\end{aligned}
$$

(the last step follows since $p(a_{i_j}|a^*_{i_{j+1}}) = 0$ if $a_{i_j} \neq a^*_{i_j}$). On the other hand, $p(a^*_{i_1}|z) = p(a^*_{i_1}) = 1/2 \neq 1 = p(a^*_{i_1}|a^*_{i_k} z)$, so $A_{i_1} \rightleftharpoons A_{i_k} \mid Z$, as required. ■

This allows us to adopt the following terminology. Suppose p is a function satisfying $\pi_1, \ldots, \pi_m$ that maximises entropy. We shall say that an independence $X \perp\!\!\!\perp_p Y \mid Z$ is an *constraint-set independence* if Z separates X from Y in the constraint graph $\mathcal{G}$—the independence is attributable to the structure of the constraint sets, in the sense that any set of constraints on the same constraint sets would induce the independence. Otherwise the independence is a *constraint independence*—the independence is forced by the particular constraints themselves and some other set of constraints on the same constraint sets would yield a dependence $X \rightleftharpoons_p Y \mid Z$.

In sum, the constraint graph $\mathcal{G}$ offers a practical representation of the constraint-set independencies—the independencies satisfied by the maximum entropy function on account of the structure of the constraint sets.

Let z denote the parameter matrix with rows z_i, for $i = 1, \ldots, m$. Then $(\mathcal{G}, z)$ is called a *Markov network* with respect to the factorisation of eqn 5.3. Having worked out the values of the constant multipliers $\mu, \lambda_1, \ldots, \lambda_m$ in eqn 5.3 one can recast the entropy maximisation problem as follows. Given z, one can determine x from the factorisation, and hence the task of finding the x-parameters of the maximum entropy function can be reduced to that of finding the z-parameters of the maximum entropy function. While there were $(\prod_{i=1}^{n} ||A_i||) - 1$ free x-parameters, these are now determined by $\sum_{i=1}^{m}(\prod_{A_j \in C_i} ||A_j||) - 1$ free z-parameters. Note that one would expect the number of values $||A_j||$ that variable A_j can take to be independent of the number of variables n and subject to practical limits. Suppose then that some constant K provides an upper bound for the $||A_j||$. At the end of §5.5 I suggested that the sizes $|C_i|$ of the constraint sets would also be subject to practical limits: suppose that the $|C_i|$ are bounded above by a constant L. Then there are at most $m(K^L - 1)$ free z-parameters. Thus if the number of constraints m increases linearly with n then so does the number of required z-parameters—a dramatic reduction from the number of x-parameters (bounded above by $K^n - 1$) required under the original formulation of the problem.[125]

While the Markov network formulation offers the possibility of a reduction in the complexity of entropy maximisation, it leaves us with two tasks: (i) to find the values of the multipliers in the factorisation, and (ii) to find the values of the z-parameters which yield maximum entropy. Neither of these tasks are straightforward in general: (i) the multipliers must be determined from a system of $(\prod_{i=1}^{n} ||A_i||)$ equations (one factorisation for each $v@V$), and (ii) the z-parameters must be determined either from the same large system of equations or numerically from an analogue of the large summation expression for entropy, eqn 5.1.

It is somewhat easier, in fact, to move to a second reparameterisation. Having reduced the complexity of the problem by exploiting independencies, we shall move from a Markov network parameterisation to a Bayesian network parameterisation. This will allow some simplification of the above two tasks and will leave us with a practical representation of the agent's belief function to which standard algorithms for inference and updating can more easily be applied.

5.7 From Markov to Bayesian Network

An undirected graph is *triangulated* if for every cycle involving four or more vertices there is an edge in the graph between two vertices that are non-adjacent in the cycle. The first step towards a Bayesian network representation of the maximum entropy probability function is to construct a triangulated graph $\mathcal{G}^T$ from the constraint graph $\mathcal{G}$. Of course this move is trivial when, as is often the case, the constraint graph $\mathcal{G}$ is already triangulated. For example Fig. 5.1

[125]In fact, the x-parameters are determined by their marginals on the cliques (maximal complete subgraphs) of $\mathcal{G}$ (see Lauritzen, 1996, p. 40). There are at most n cliques, so if clique-size and the K_j are bounded above, then the x-parameters are determined by a number of parameters that is *at worst* linear in n.

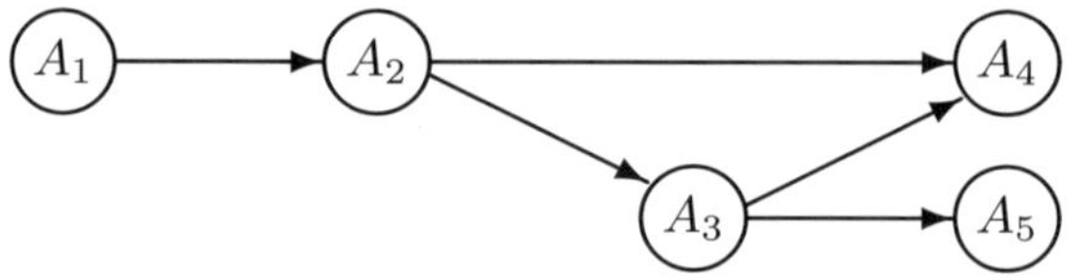

FIG. 5.2. Example directed constraint graph.

is already triangulated. If $\mathcal{G}$ is not already triangulated, one of a number of standard triangulation algorithms can be applied to construct $\mathcal{G}^T$.[126]

Next, re-order the variables in V according to *maximum cardinality search* with respect to $\mathcal{G}^T$: choose an arbitrary vertex as A_1; at each step select the vertex which is adjacent to the largest number of previously numbered vertices, breaking ties arbitrarily. Let $D_1, \ldots, D_l$ be the cliques of $\mathcal{G}^T$, ordered according to highest labelled vertex. Let $E_j = D_j \cap (\bigcup_{i=1}^{j-1} D_i)$ and $F_j = D_j \backslash E_j$, for $j = 1, \ldots, l$.

In our example involving Fig. 5.1, $A_1, \ldots, A_5$ are already ordered according to a maximum cardinality search,

$$D_1 = \{A_1, A_2\}, \quad D_2 = \{A_2, A_3, A_4\}, \quad D_3 = \{A_3, A_5\},$$

$$E_1 = \emptyset, \quad E_2 = \{A_2\}, \quad E_3 = \{A_3\},$$

$$F_1 = \{A_1, A_2\}, \quad F_2 = \{A_3, A_4\}, \quad F_3 = \{A_5\}.$$

Finally, construct an acyclic *directed constraint graph* $\mathcal{H}$ as follows. Take variables in V as vertices. Step 1: add an arrow from each vertex in E_j to each vertex in F_j, for $j = 1, \ldots, l$. Step 2: add further arrows to ensure that there is an arrow between each pair of vertices in $D_j, j = 1, \ldots, l$, taking care that no cycles are introduced (there is always some orientation of an added arrow which will not yield a cycle). In our example, an induced directed constraint graph $\mathcal{H}$ is depicted in Fig. 5.2.

D-separation (defined in §3.2) plays the role in the directed constraint graph that separation played in the undirected constraint graph and yields a directed version of Theorem 5.1:

Theorem 5.3 *If Z D-separates X from Y in the directed constraint graph $\mathcal{H}$ then $X \perp\!\!\!\perp_p Y \mid Z$ for any p satisfying the constraints which maximises entropy.*

Proof: Since $\mathcal{G}^T$ is triangulated, the ordering yielded by maximum cardinality search is a *perfect* ordering (for each vertex, the set of its adjacent predecessors is complete in the graph).[127] Because the cliques are ordered according to highest labelled vertex where the vertices have a perfect ordering, the clique order has the *running intersection property* (for each clique, its intersection with the union of its predecessors is contained in one of its predecessors).[128] Now p factorises

[126]See e.g. Neapolitan (1990, §3.2.3) and Cowell *et al.* (1999, §4.4.1).

[127](Neapolitan, 1990, Theorem 3.2)

[128](Neapolitan, 1990, Theorem 3.1)

according to the cliques of $\mathcal{G}^T$, since it factorises according to $C_1, \ldots, C_m$ and these sets are complete in $\mathcal{G}^T$ and so are subsets of its cliques. These three facts imply that $p(v) = \prod_{i=1}^{l} p(f_i|e_i)$ for each $v@V$, where f_i, e_i are the assignments to F_i, E_i respectively which are consistent with v.[129]

Take an arbitrary component $p(f_i|e_i)$ of this factorisation. Each member of E_i is a parent (in $\mathcal{H}$) of each member of F_i and the members of F_i form a complete subgraph of $\mathcal{H}$ so we can write $F_i = \{A_{i_1}, \ldots, A_{i_k}\}$ where the parents of A_{i_j} are $Par_{i_j} =_{df} E_i \cup \{A_{i_1}, \ldots, A_{i_{j-1}}\}$. Hence,

$$\begin{aligned} p(f_i|e_i) &= p(a_{i_1} \cdots a_{i_k}|e_i) \\ &= \prod_{j=1}^{k} p(a_{i_j}|e_i a_{i_1} \cdots a_{i_{j-1}}) \\ &= \prod_{j=1}^{k} p(a_{i_j}|par_{i_j}), \end{aligned}$$

where a_{i_j} and par_{i_j} are the assignments to A_{i_j}, Par_{i_j} respectively that are consistent with v. Furthermore, each variable A_i occurs in precisely one F_j, so

$$p(v) = \prod_{i=1}^{n} p(a_i|par_i) \tag{5.4}$$

for each $v \in V$. When eqn 5.4 holds, p is said to *factorise* with respect to $\mathcal{H}$, and $\mathcal{H}$ together with the specified values of $p(a_i|par_i)$ form a Bayesian net. It follows by Proposition 3.2 that if Z D-separates X from Y in $\mathcal{H}$ then $X \perp\!\!\!\perp_p Y \mid Z$.[130] ■

In general the directed constraint graph $\mathcal{H}$ is not as comprehensive a representation of independencies as the undirected constraint graph $\mathcal{G}$. If $\mathcal{G}$ is not already triangulated then some constraint-set independencies will not be implied by the directed constraint graph $\mathcal{H}$. To see this note that if $\mathcal{G} \neq \mathcal{G}^T$ then there must be two variables A_i and A_j which are not directly connected in $\mathcal{G}$, and so which are separated by some (possibly empty) Z in $\mathcal{G}$, but which are directly connected in $\mathcal{G}^T$ and thus in $\mathcal{H}$, and which are therefore not D-separated by Z in $\mathcal{H}$. On the other hand if $\mathcal{G} = \mathcal{G}^T$ then we do have an analogue of Theorem 5.2:

Theorem 5.4 *Suppose $\mathcal{G}$ is triangulated. If, for all $\pi_1, \ldots, \pi_m$ constraining variables in $C_1, \ldots, C_m$ respectively, $X \perp\!\!\!\perp_p Y \mid Z$ where p is a function satisfying $\pi_1, \ldots, \pi_m$ that maximises entropy, then Z D-separates X from Y in $\mathcal{H}$.*

Proof: To check whether Z D-separates X from Y in $\mathcal{H}$ it suffices to check whether Z separates X from Y in the undirected *moral graph* formed by restricting $\mathcal{H}$ to X, Y, Z and their ancestors, adding an edge between any two parents

[129] (Neapolitan, 1990, Theorem 7.4)

[130] (See Neapolitan, 1990, Theorem 6.2)

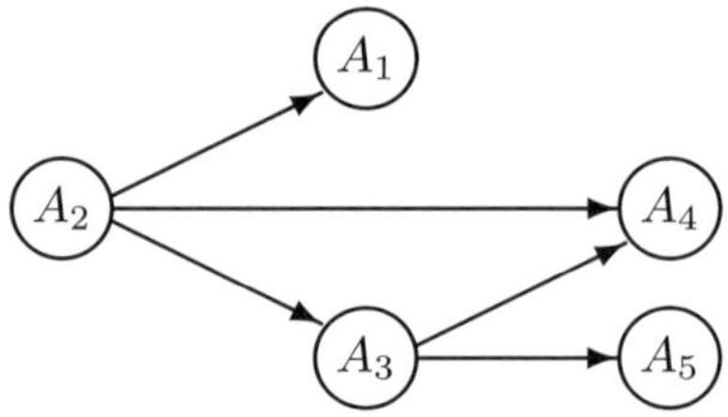

FIG. 5.3. Alternative directed constraint graph.

in this graph that are not already directly connected, and replacing all arrows by undirected edges.[131] But all parents of vertices in $\mathcal{H}$ are directly connected, so the moral graph is a subgraph of $\mathcal{G}^T = \mathcal{G}$. By Theorem 5.2 if $X \perp\!\!\!\perp_p Y \mid Z$ for all such p then Z separates X from Y in $\mathcal{G}$. Hence Z separates X from Y in any subgraph of $\mathcal{G}$ that contains X, Y, and Z, and in particular in the moral graph, as required. ■

Thus if $\mathcal{G}$ is triangulated then $\mathcal{H}$ represents each constraint-set independence of p.

As in §3.1, given some set $U \subseteq V$ containing A_i and its parents according to $\mathcal{H}$, and $u@U$, define parameter $y_i^u = p(a_i|par_i)$, where a_i, par_i are the assignments to A_i, Par_i respectively that are consistent with u. Let y_i be the vector of parameters y_i^u as u varies on A_i and its parents, and let y be the matrix with the y_i as rows, $i = 1, \ldots, n$. In this notation eqn 5.4 corresponds to

$$x^v = \prod_{i=1}^{n} y_i^v \tag{5.5}$$

for each $v@V$, and $(\mathcal{H}, y)$ is thus a Bayesian net.

Thanks to the factorisation of eqn 5.5, the task of finding the x-parameters that maximise entropy can be reduced to that of finding the corresponding y-parameters. The number of free y-parameters required is determined by the cliques $D_1, \ldots, D_l$ in $\mathcal{H}$: there are $\sum_{i=1}^{l}(\prod_{A_j \in D_i} ||A_j||) - 1$. Thus if clique-size $|D_i|$ is bounded above by constant R and the number of values $||A_j||$ bounded above by K, there are at most $n(K^R - 1)$ free y-parameters. If $\mathcal{G} \neq \mathcal{G}^T$ then the Bayesian network representation of p will require more parameters than the Markov network representation of §5.6. However, the Bayesian net representation is more convenient for the following reasons.

First, there are no unknown multipliers in eqn 5.5. In contrast, in order to reconstruct the maximum entropy function from its Markov network representation via eqn 5.3, the values of constants $\mu, \lambda_1, \ldots, \lambda_m$ must be determined.

Second, the entropy equation can be reformulated in terms of the y-parameters as follows:

[131] (Cowell *et al.*, 1999, Corollary 5.11)

$$
\begin{aligned}
H &= -\sum_{v@V} x^v \log x^v \\
&= -\sum_{v@V} \left(\prod_{j=1}^{n} y_j^v\right) \log \prod_{i=1}^{n} y_i^v \\
&= -\sum_{v@V} \left(\prod_{j=1}^{n} y_j^v\right) \sum_{i=1}^{n} \log y_i^v \\
&= -\sum_{i=1}^{n} \sum_{v@V} \left(\prod_{j=1}^{n} y_j^v\right) \log y_i^v \\
&= -\sum_{i=1}^{n} \sum_{v@Anc_i'} \left(\prod_{A_j \in Anc_i'} y_j^v\right) \log y_i^v,
\end{aligned}
$$

where $Anc_i' = \{A_i\} \cup Anc_i$ consists of A_i and its ancestors in $\mathcal{H}$ (other terms cancel in the last step by additivity). In our example, Fig. 5.2 induces an entropy equation of the form

$$
\begin{aligned}
H = &- \sum_{v@A_1} y_1^v \log y_1^v - \sum_{v@\{A_1,A_2\}} y_1^v y_2^v \log y_2^v - \sum_{v@\{A_1,A_2,A_3\}} y_1^v y_2^v y_3^v \log y_3^v \\
&- \sum_{v@\{A_1,A_2,A_3,A_4\}} y_1^v y_2^v y_3^v y_4^v \log y_4^v - \sum_{v@\{A_1,A_2,A_3,A_5\}} y_1^v y_2^v y_3^v y_5^v \log y_5^v.
\end{aligned}
$$

Note that roughly speaking there are fewest components in the sum of the entropy equation when the sets of ancestors Anc_i' are smallest, and that when constructing $\mathcal{H}$, judicious use of maximum cardinality search and orientation of arrows can lead to a directed constraint graph with minimal ancestor sets. In our example, Fig. 5.3 (where the vertices are labelled according to the original ordering, not that given by maximum cardinality search) is an alternative directed constraint graph, which leads to the following entropy equation:

$$
\begin{aligned}
H = &- \sum_{v@A_2} y_2^v \log y_2^v - \sum_{v@\{A_1,A_2\}} y_1^v y_2^v \log y_1^v - \sum_{v@\{A_2,A_3\}} y_2^v y_3^v \log y_3^v \\
&- \sum_{v@\{A_2,A_3,A_4\}} y_2^v y_3^v y_4^v \log y_4^v - \sum_{v@\{A_2,A_3,A_5\}} y_2^v y_3^v y_5^v \log y_5^v.
\end{aligned}
$$

This version of the entropy equation is more economical in the sense that the largest ancestor sets are smaller than those induced by Fig. 5.2.

Having rewritten the entropy equation in terms of a y-parameterisation one can then use numerical techniques or Lagrange multiplier methods to find the values of the y-parameters that maximise H. If using the latter approach, note that there is an additivity constraint for each $i = 1, \ldots, n$ and each $u@Par_i$, of the form

$$\sum_{a_i @ A_i} y_i^{a_i u} = 1,$$

and each such constraint will require its own multiplier μ_i^u. Thus for assignment a_i to A_i and u to its parents, the partial derivative of the Lagrange equation takes the form

$$\frac{\partial H}{\partial y_i^{a_i u}} + \mu_i^u + \sum_{i=1}^{m} \lambda_i \frac{\partial f_i}{\partial y_i^{a_i u}} = 0$$

for

$$\frac{\partial H}{\partial y_i^{a_i u}} = - \sum_{A_k : A_i \in Anc'_k} \; \sum_{w @ Anc'_k, w \sim a_i u} \left(\prod_{A_j \in Anc'_k, j \neq i} y_j^w \right) [\log y_k^w + I_{k=i}]$$

where $I_{k=i} = 1$ if $k = i$ and 0 otherwise, and where as before $\lambda_i = 0$ for each inequality constraint π_i which is not effective at $y_i^{a_i u}$.

The third advantage of the Bayesian net parameterisation is this: the reparameterisation converts the general entropy maximisation problem into the special case problem of determining the parameters of a Bayesian net that maximise entropy; therefore we can apply existing techniques that have been developed for the special case to solve the general problem. Garside, Holmes, Markham, and Rhodes have developed a number of efficient algorithms which determine the parameters of a Bayesian net that maximise entropy. Their approach uses Lagrange multiplier methods on the original version of the entropy equation (eqn 5.1), subject to the restriction that the constraints must be linear. They have also developed specialised algorithms that deal with the cases in which the directed graph in the Bayesian net is a tree or inverted tree.[132] Schramm and Fronhöfer have investigated an alternative solution to the same problem, using an efficient system for maximising entropy that works by minimising cross entropy iteratively.[133]

Fourth, a Bayesian net is a good representation of an agent's belief function, given the uses such a function is normally put to, because Bayesian nets can be amenable to efficient calculations and updating. As discussed in §3.4, there is now a large literature and set of computational tools for calculating marginal probabilities from a Bayesian net, and in particular conditional probabilities of the form $p(a_i|u)$, where $a_i@A_i$ and $u@U \subseteq (V\backslash\{A_i\})$.[134] Many such algorithms also implement Bayesian conditionalisation to update p on evidence u. Bayesian conditionalisation may be generalised to *minimum cross entropy updating*, which has

[132](Rhodes and Garside, 1995; Garside and Rhodes, 1996; Garside *et al.*, 1998; Holmes and Rhodes, 1998; Rhodes and Garside, 1998; Holmes, 1999; Holmes *et al.*, 1999; Markham and Rhodes, 1999; Garside *et al.*, 2000)

[133](Schramm and Fronhöfer, 2002)

[134]See, e.g., Jordan (1998, part 1) and Cowell *et al.* (1999, chapter 6).

similar justifications to those of the Maximum Entropy Principle.[135] A minimum cross entropy update x_{t+1} of x_t is a parameter vector satisfying new constraints which minimises cross entropy distance to the old function x_t,

$$d(x_{t+1}, x_t) = \sum_{v@V} x_{t+1}^v \log \frac{x_{t+1}^v}{x_t^v}.$$

By converting this to our y-parameterisation, it is not hard to see that the Bayesian network representation of p_{t+1} will be the same as the Bayesian network representation of p_t on all variables except those in the new constraint sets and their predecessors under an ancestral ordering. Numerical methods or Lagrange multiplier methods can then be used with respect to the y-parameter formulation, in order to identify the new Bayesian network representation. This strategy is explained in more detail in §12.11.

5.8 Causal Constraints

We saw in §5.4 that Pearl highlighted two problems with entropy maximisation: the computational problem and the problem that 'the resulting distribution is often at odds with our perception of causation'.[136] Having addressed the first problem we shall now turn to the relationship between maximum entropy and causality.

Pearl argued that it is counterintuitive that adding an effect variable can lead to a change in the marginal distribution over the original variables:

> For example, if we first find an ME [i.e. maxent] distribution for a set of n variables $X_1, \ldots, X_n$ and then add one of their consequences, Y, we find that the ME distribution $P(x_1, \ldots, x_n, y)$ constrained by the conditional probability $P(y|x_1, \cdots, x_n)$ changes the marginal distribution of the X variables ... and introduces new dependencies among them. This is at variance with the common conception of causation, whereby hypothesizing the existence of unobserved future events is presumed to leave unaltered our beliefs about past and present events. This phenomenon was communicated to me by Norm Dalkey and is discussed in Hunter (1989).[137]

This problem is exemplified in 'Pearl's puzzle', which Daniel Hunter describes as follows.

> The puzzle is this: Suppose that you are told that three individuals, Albert, Bill and Clyde, have been invited to a party. You know nothing about the propensity of any of these individuals to go to the party nor about any possible correlations among their actions. Using the obvious abbreviations, consider the eight-point space consisting of the events $ABC, AB\bar{C}, A\bar{B}C$, etc. (conjunction of events is indicated by concatenation). With no constraints whatsoever on this space, MAXENT yields

[135] (Williams, 1980)

[136] (Pearl, 1988, p. 463)

[137] (Pearl, 1988, pp. 463–464)

> equal probabilities for the elements of this space. Thus $Prob(A) = Prob(B) = 0.5$ and $Prob(AB) = 0.25$, so A and B are independent. It is reasonable that A and B turn out to be independent, since there is no information that would cause one to revise one's probability for A upon learning what B does. However, suppose that the following information is presented: Clyde will call the host before the party to find out whether Al or Bill or both have accepted the invitation, and his decision to go to the party will be based on what he learns. Al and Bill, however, will have no information about whether or not Clyde will go to the party. Suppose, further, that we are told the probability that Clyde will go conditional on each combination of Al and Bill's going or not going. ...
>
> When MAXENT is given these constraints ... A and B are no longer independent! But this seems wrong: the information about Clyde should not make A's and B's actions dependent.[138]

To start with, when there are no constraints, the undirected constraint graph on A, B, C has no edges so by Theorem 5.1 the maximum entropy function yields all variables probabilistically independent. However, when the probability distribution of C conditional on A and B is added as a constraint, the undirected constraint graph on A, B, C has an edge between each pair of variables. Thus by Theorem 5.2 there is some conditional probability distribution which renders A and B probabilistically dependent for the maximum entropy function. This dependence does indeed seem counterintuitive here.

The difficulty is that while we have taken into account the probability distribution of C conditional on A and B as a constraint on maximising entropy, we have ignored the further fact that A and B are causes of C. The key question is: how does causal information constrain the entropy maximisation process?

Hunter's answer to this conundrum is that causal statements are counterfactual conditionals and that the constraint in this example should be thought of as a set of probabilities of counterfactual conditionals rather than as a conditional probability distribution. Under Hunter's analysis of counterfactuals and probabilities of counterfactuals, a reconstruction of the above example retains the probabilistic independence of A and B when the constraint is added.

Hunter's response is in my opinion unconvincing, for two reasons. First, the counterfactual conception of causal relations adopted by Hunter is problematic. As Hunter himself acknowledges, his possible-worlds account of counterfactuals is rather simplistic.[139] More importantly though, the connection between causal relations and counterfactuals that Hunter adopts is implausible. Hunter says,

> the suggestion is that the relations between Al's and Bill's actions on the one hand and Clyde's on the other are expressible as counterfactual conditionals, that there is a certain probability that if Al and Bill *were* to go to the party, then Clyde *would not* go, and so on. The information to MAXENT should be probabilities of counterfactuals rather than

[138](Hunter, 1989, p. 91)

[139](Hunter, 1989, p. 95)

conditional probabilities.[140]

This type of information is written in Hunter's notation using statements of the form $Prob(AB \Box\!\!\rightarrow C) = 0.1$. But such a statement expresses uncertainty about a counterfactual connection: the probability that were Al and Bill to go then Clyde would go is 0.1. It does not express what we require, namely certain knowledge about a chancy causal connection, which would be better represented by $AB \Box\!\!\rightarrow (Prob(C) = 0.1)$: if Al and Bill were to go then Clyde would go with probability 0.1. In Pearl's puzzle we are told the exact causal relationships between A, B, and C, and Hunter misrepresents these as uncertain relationships. Moreover, correcting Hunter's representation of the causal connections seems unlikely to resolve Pearl's puzzle. In fact depending on how probability is interpreted one can even argue that $AB \Box\!\!\rightarrow (Prob(C) = 0.1)$ if and only if $Prob(C|AB) = 0.1$. For instance, under the Bayesian interpretation of probability $Prob(C|AB) = 0.1$ can be taken to mean that the agent in question would award betting quotient 0.1 to C were AB to occur; under the propensity interpretation it can be taken to mean that AB events have a (counterfactual) propensity to produce C events with probability 0.1. If this equivalence holds then Pearl's puzzle must still obtain, despite the counterfactual analysis.[141]

The second difficulty with Hunter's analysis is that while it resolves Pearl's puzzle, it fails to resolve a minor modification of Pearl's puzzle. In the original puzzle we are provided with the probability distribution of C conditional on A and B. Suppose instead we are provided with the distribution of C conditional on A, and the distribution of C conditional on B. In this case, the undirected constraint graph contains an edge between A and C and an edge between B and C; thus while $A \perp\!\!\!\perp_p B \mid C$ for maximum entropy p, there must be constraints with respect to which p will render A and B unconditionally dependent; this yields a puzzle analogous to that of the original problem. However, Hunter's counterfactual reconstruction fails to eliminate the dependence of A and B in this modified puzzle.[142] In defence, Hunter argues that his counterfactual analysis warrants the counterintuitive conclusion in the case of the modified puzzle, because according to his analysis situations in which A and B are positively correlated are more probable than situations in which A and B are negatively correlated. However, in the light of the above doubts about Hunter's analysis I suggest that intuition should prevail and that this new puzzle needs resolving.

In fact, I think that Pearl's puzzle and its modification can be resolved without having to appeal to a counterfactual analysis, any formulation of which is likely to be contentious. The resolution that I propose depends on making explicit the way in which qualitative causal relationships constrain entropy maximisa-

[140](Hunter, 1989, p. 95)

[141]The relationship between causality and counterfactuals is in fact much more subtle than indicated here—see Lewis (1973)—and many believe that there is no close relationship on account of these difficulties—see Sosa and Tooley (1993, chapters 12–14).

[142](Hunter, 1989, pp. 101–104)

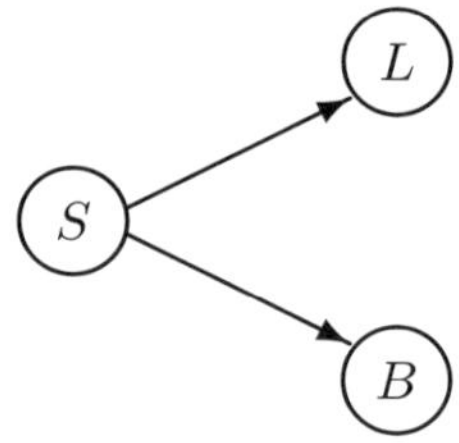

FIG. 5.4. Smoking, lung cancer and bronchitis.

tion. Having made this constraint explicit, we shall see that it leads to a general framework for maximising entropy subject to causal knowledge. Finally, at the end of this section we shall see that the framework can be applied to resolve both Pearl's puzzle and its modification.

Causality satisfies a fundamental asymmetry, which can be elucidated with the help of the following example.[143] Suppose an agent is concerned with two variables L and B signifying lung cancer and bronchitis respectively. Initially she knows of no causal relationships between these variables, but she may have other background knowledge which leads her to adopt probability function p_1 as her belief function. We shall suppose that L and B are independent or not strongly dependent according to p_1. Then the agent learns that smoking S causes each of lung cancer and bronchitis, which can be represented by a directed graph, Fig. 5.4. The agent may also learn probabilistic information relating to the strength of the causal relationships and their direction (the agent may learn that that smoking positively causes rather than prevents lung cancer and bronchitis). One can argue that this new knowledge should impact on the agent's degrees of belief concerning L and B, making them more dependent. The reasoning is as follows: if an individual has bronchitis, then this may be because he is a smoker, and smoking may also have caused lung cancer, so the agent should believe the individual has lung cancer given bronchitis to a greater extent than before—the two variables become dependent (or more dependent if dependent already). Thus p_2, the new probability function determined with respect to her current knowledge (which includes the causal knowledge) might be expected to differ from p_1 over the original domain $\{L, B\}$.

Next the agent learns that both lung cancer and bronchitis cause chest pains C, giving the causal graph of Fig. 5.5, and perhaps also learns about the strength and direction of the causal relationships. But in this case one can *not* argue that L and B should be rendered more dependent. If an individual has bronchitis then he may well have chest pains, but this does not render lung cancer any more probable because there is already a perfectly good explanation for any chest pains. One cannot reason via a common effect in the same way that one can via a common cause, since learning of the existence of a common effect

[143](Williamson, 2001*b*)

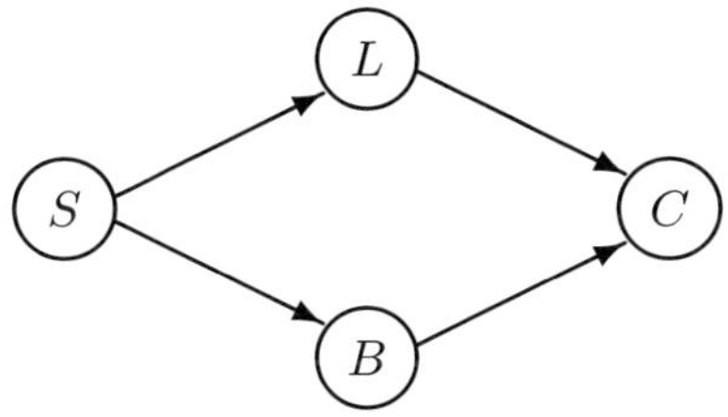

FIG. 5.5. Smoking, lung cancer, bronchitis, and chest pains.

is irrelevant to an agent's current degrees of belief. Thus the new probability function p_3 ought to agree with p_2 on the domain of p_2, $\{S, L, B\}$.

This central asymmetry of causality can be explicated by what I call the *Causal Irrelevance* principle. This says roughly that if an agent has initial belief function p_U on domain U and then learns of the existence of new variables which are not causes of any of the variables in U, then the restriction to U of her new belief function p^V on $V \supseteq U$ should agree with p^U on U, written $p^V_{\restriction U} = p^U$. This condition can be rendered precise as follows.

Suppose that entropy is to be maximised subject to causal constraints κ, detailing all known causal connections and absences of causal connections between variables, as well as the probabilistic constraints $\pi = \{\pi_1, \ldots, \pi_m\}$ that we have considered in previous sections. In the case where κ is *complete* knowledge of causal relations, κ can be represented by a directed acyclic causal graph $\mathcal{C}$ on V: all and only the causal relation in $\mathcal{C}$ hold among variables in V. Let $p_{\kappa,\pi}$ denote the probability function (on domain V) that an agent ought to adopt given her knowledge, κ and π. Given $U \subseteq V$ let κ_U be knowledge on U induced by κ (the constraints in κ that involve only variables in U). Define π_U to be the subset of those constraints in π which only involve variables in U, $\pi_U = \{\pi_i : C_i \subseteq U, 1 \le i \le m\}$. We shall denote the probability function *defined on domain* U that an agent ought to adopt given knowledge κ_U, π_U by $p^U_{\kappa_U,\pi_U}$. We shall say that $V\backslash U$ is *irrelevant* to U if $p_{\kappa,\pi\restriction U} = p^U_{\kappa_U,\pi_U}$, i.e. if the knowledge that involves variables not in U has no bearing on rational belief over U.

A set of variables $U \subseteq V$ is *ancestral* with respect to κ, or *κ-ancestral*, if it is non-empty and closed under possible causes as determined by κ: if variable $A_i \in U$ then any variable that might be a cause of A_i (i.e. is not ruled out as a cause of A_i by κ) is in U. Note that if U_1 and U_2 are κ-ancestral then so are $U_1 \cap U_2$ and $U_1 \cup U_2$. π is *compatible* with probability function p^U defined on domain U if there is a probability function defined on domain V which extends p^U and satisfies π. π is *compatible* on U if it is compatible with every probability function p^U defined on U that satisfies κ_U and π_U. Then:

Causal Irrelevance If U is κ-ancestral and π is compatible on U then $V\backslash U$ is irrelevant to U, i.e. $p_{\kappa,\pi\restriction U} = p^U_{\kappa_U,\pi_U}$.

The requirement that U be ancestral with respect to κ is just the requirement that $V\backslash U$ must not contain any causes of variables in U. In the trivial case in which U is a singleton, κ_U contains no causal information and we set $p_{\kappa_U,\pi\downharpoonright U} = p^U_{\pi_U}$, which may be found by maximising entropy subject to π_U. We shall call U a *relevance set* if it is κ-ancestral and π is compatible on U. It need not be the case that the intersection and union of relevance sets are themselves relevance sets, but we do have the following property:

Proposition 5.5 *If U is a relevance set with respect to V, κ, π and W is a relevance set with respect to U, κ_U, π_U then W is a relevance set with respect to V, κ, π.*

Recall our example. Here $V = \{S, L, B, C\}$. Causal knowledge κ is represented by Fig. 5.5 and the κ-ancestral sets are $\{S\}, \{S, L\}, \{S, B\}, \{S, L, B\}, \{S, L, B, C\}$. Suppose the agent has the following probabilistic knowledge concerning the strength and direction of causal connections: $\pi = \{p(l^1|s^1) = 0.2, p(l^1|s^0) = 0.01, p(b^1|s^1) = 0.3, p(b^1|s^0) = 0.05, p(c^1|l^1b^1) = 0.99, p(c^1|l^1b^0) = 0.95, p(c^1|l^0b^1) = 0.8, p(c^1|l^0b^0) = 0.1\}$. Consider first the set $U = \{S, L, B\}$. Now any probability function on U that satisfies $\pi_U = \{p(l^1|s^1) = 0.2, p(l^1|s^0) = 0.01, p(b^1|s^1) = 0.3, p(b^1|s^0) = 0.05\}$ can be extended to one satisfying π (take a Bayesian net representing the original function and add arrows from L and B to C and the probability specifiers $p(c^1|l^1b^1) = 0.99, p(c^1|l^1b^0) = 0.95, p(c^1|l^0b^1) = 0.8, p(c^1|l^0b^0) = 0.1$). U is also κ-ancestral so Causal Irrelevance applies: $p_{\kappa,\pi\downharpoonright U} = p^U_{\kappa_U,\pi_U}$, C is irrelevant to U and the degrees of belief the agent should adopt over U are the same as those that she ought to adopt under causal knowledge κ_U of Fig. 5.4 and probabilistic knowledge π_U.

Now consider $U' = \{L, B\}$. Although π_U is compatible on U', U' is not κ-ancestral. Thus Causal Irrelevance does not apply, S is not irrelevant to U', and $p_{\kappa_U,\pi_U\downharpoonright U'}$ need not equal $p^{U'}_{\kappa_{U'},\pi_{U'}}$. Here the condition that U be κ-ancestral plays and important role: U' contains information which bears on degrees of belief over U, since it says that L and B are both dependent on common cause S which would admit the inference that L and B are themselves dependent; moreover, varying the dependency between say L and S would incline one to vary the dependency between L and B.

Compatibility also plays a crucial role in the Causal Irrelevance principle. If π were to include knowledge that an individual in question actually has chest pains $p(c^1) = 1$, then arguably the agent's degree of belief that the individual has lung cancer ought to be raised, and so too her degree of belief that he has bronchitis and her degree of belief that he is a smoker. Thus learning of probabilistic information that is not compatible *can* provide evidence to change current beliefs. Even if U is ancestral $V \backslash U$ becomes relevant to U if π contains information information that is incompatible on U.

The claim is that Causal Irrelevance captures a key way in which causal knowledge constrains rational belief. Thus it is not enough to maximise entropy subject to quantitative constraints π: one ought to take qualitative causal knowledge κ into account too, and this qualitative knowledge can be sharpened into quantitative constraints on degree of belief by the Causal Irrelevance principle.

To be explicit:

Causal to Probabilistic Transfer Let $U_1, \ldots, U_k$ be all the relevance sets in V. Then $p_{\kappa,\pi} = p_{\pi',\pi}$, the probability function p satisfying constraints in π' and π which maximises entropy, where $\pi' = \{p_{\lfloor U_i} = p^{U_i}_{\kappa_{U_i},\pi_{U_i}} : i = 1, \ldots, k\}$.

Note that V itself is trivially always a relevance set, with corresponding constraint $p_{\lfloor V} = p^{V}_{\kappa_V,\pi_V} = p_{\kappa,\pi}$, which is vacuous. We may therefore ignore V when applying the Transfer principle. By Proposition 5.5, for each relevance set U the set $\mathbb{P}_{\kappa,\pi}$ of probability functions on V satisfying constraints imposed by κ and π is a subset of the set $\mathbb{P}^{V}_{\kappa_U,\pi_U}$ of probability functions on V satisfying constraints imposed by κ_U and π_U.

A word on consistency. Since π is compatible on all the relevance sets U_i, π is consistent with each individual new constraint $p_{\lfloor U_i} = p^{U_i}_{\kappa_{U_i},\pi_{U_i}}$. However, this is no guarantee that the whole set of constraints $\pi \cup \pi'$ will be consistent—there may be no probability function that satisfies $\pi \cup \pi'$. As an example take two-valued variables $V = \{A, B\}$, κ-ancestral sets $U_1 = \{A\}, U_2 = \{B\}, U_3 = V$, and $\pi = \{p(a^1) = p(b^1), p(a^1) = 3/4\}$. Now $p^{U_1}_{\kappa_{U_1},\pi_{U_1}}(a^1) = 3/4$ but $p^{U_2}_{\kappa_{U_2},\pi_{U_2}}(b^1) = 1/2$ so while π is consistent with transferred constraints $p_{\lfloor U_1} = p^{U_1}_{\kappa_{U_1},\pi_{U_1}}$ and $p_{\lfloor U_2} = p^{U_2}_{\kappa_{U_2},\pi_{U_2}}$ individually, it is not consistent with them when taken together. We shall of course be interested just in the case where $\pi \cup \pi'$ is consistent.

The Transfer principle allows us to directly transfer causal constraints represented by κ into probabilistic constraints π'.[144] Observing that the constraint set for constraint $p_{\lfloor U_i} = p^{U_i}_{\kappa_{U_i},\pi_{U_i}}$ is just U_i, we can apply the techniques of §§5.6 and 5.7 to find a Bayesian net that represents the entropy maximiser $p_{\kappa,\pi}$. However, this method for constructing a Bayesian net will not lead to an efficient representation of $p_{\kappa,\pi}$ as it stands. This is because the constraint sets U_i generated by π' are often large subsets of V. Indeed V itself occurs as a constraint set (albeit a trivial one since the corresponding constraint can be eliminated without altering the results). This creates a problem for the techniques of §5.6, which depend on small constraint sets for viability. But a bit of further analysis shows that one can eradicate this extra complexity. Surprisingly, one can in fact ignore causal constraints when constructing a constraint graph, just taking $\mathcal{G}_\pi$, the constraint graph for π, as a representation of probabilistic independencies satisfied by $p_{\kappa,\pi}$:

Theorem 5.6 *If Z separates X from Y in the constraint graph $\mathcal{G}_\pi$ of π then $X \perp\!\!\!\perp_{p_{\kappa,\pi}} Y \mid Z$.*

[144]Note that the transfer principle implicitly assumes that Causal Irrelevance is the *only* way that causal knowledge impinges on degree of belief: where there are no relevance sets we proceed by maximising entropy as normal. This is only intended as a first, rather general, approximation: in certain specific contexts there may be other ways in which causal knowledge constrains degree of belief—clearly the Transfer principle would need to be augmented in such cases.

Proof: We prove the following hypothesis by induction on k: for any V, κ, π with k non-trivial relevance sets $U_1, \ldots, U_k \neq V$, $p_{\kappa,\pi}$ factorises with respect to $\mathcal{G}_\pi$. Then the Global Markov Condition follows as in the proof of Theorem 5.1.

If $k = 0$ there are no non-trivial causal constraints to be transferred into probabilistic constraints and $p_{\kappa,\pi} = p_\pi$ factorises with respect to $\mathcal{G}_\pi$ by Theorem 5.1.

Now take arbitrary k. By the proof of Theorem 5.1 $p =_{df} p_{\kappa,\pi}$ factorises according to the constraint sets of κ, π, i.e. the constraint sets $C_1, \ldots, C_m$ of π and the relevance sets $U_1, \ldots, U_k$ which are the constraint sets of transferred causal constraints π'. Graphically, p factorises with respect to the union $\mathcal{G}_\pi \cup \mathcal{K}^{U_1} \cup \cdots \cup \mathcal{K}^{U_k}$, where $\mathcal{K}^{U_i}$ is the complete graph on U_i.

Writing κ_i and π_i for κ_{U_i} and π_{U_i} respectively, consider U_i, κ_i, π_i for arbitrary $i, 1 \leq i \leq k$. On this domain there must be fewer than k non-trivial relevance sets, for otherwise by Proposition 5.5 these relevance sets are relevance sets with respect to V, κ, π, and together with U_i itself number more than k, contradicting our assumption of k non-trivial relevance sets. Therefore by the induction hypothesis, $p^{U_i}_{\kappa_i,\pi_i}$ factorises with respect to $\mathcal{G}^{U_i}_{\pi_i}$ and hence with respect to $\mathcal{G}_\pi$.

Take U_1 and let $T = V \backslash U_1$. Now $p(v) = p(t|u_1)p(u_1)$ and we can write $p = p_{\downharpoonright T|U_1} p_{\downharpoonright U_1}$ where $p_{\downharpoonright T|U_1}$ (the probability function on T conditional on U_1 induced by p) factorises with respect to $\mathcal{G}_\pi \cup \mathcal{K}^{U_2} \cup \cdots \cup \mathcal{K}^{U_k}$.[145] Since $p_{\downharpoonright U_1} = p^{U_1}_{\kappa_1,\pi_1}$ factorises with respect to $\mathcal{G}_\pi$, p itself then factorises with respect to $\mathcal{G}_\pi \cup \mathcal{K}^{U_2} \cup \cdots \cup \mathcal{K}^{U_k}$. Repeating this reduction for $U_2, \ldots, U_k$ we see that p factorises with respect to $\mathcal{G}_\pi$. ■

Theorem 5.6 leads to a modification of our recipe for constructing a Bayesian net representation of the entropy maximising probability function when we have causal as well as probabilistic constraints:

- take the constraint graph $\mathcal{G}_\pi$ for constraints in π as a representation of independencies pf $p_{\kappa,\pi}$ (*not* the constraint graph $\mathcal{G}_{\kappa,\pi}$ for constraints in κ, π);
- construct a directed constraint graph $\mathcal{H}_\pi$ from $\mathcal{G}_\pi$ as in §5.7, and adopt this as the graph in the Bayesian net representation of $p_{\kappa,\pi}$;
- determine corresponding probability tables as in §5.7, remembering to take causal constraints κ into account by transferring them into probabilistic constraints π'.

In certain circumstances one can exploit the structure of the causal constraints to further simplify the entropy maximisation process. Suppose that κ determines a causal ordering (a total ancestral order: each $\{A_1, \ldots, A_i\}$ is κ-ancestral); then the Bayesian network representation of $p_{\kappa,\pi}$ is particularly neat when π is compatible on each $U_i = \{A_1, \ldots, A_i\}$, for $i = 1, \ldots, n$, as we see from the following results.

[145] See e.g. Cowell *et al.* (1999, Proposition 5.7 and its proof).

Theorem 5.7 *Suppose that the relevance sets include $U_i = \{A_1, \ldots, A_i\}$, for $i = 1, \ldots, n$. Construct directed acyclic graph $\mathcal{H}$ on V by including an arrow to a variable A_i from each predecessor A_j that occurs in some constraint set containing A_i but none of its successors: $A_j \longrightarrow A_i$ iff $j < i$ and $A_i, A_j \in C_k \subseteq U_i$ for some $k, 1 \leq k \leq m$. Then Z D-separates X from Y in $\mathcal{H}$ implies $X \perp\!\!\!\perp_{p_{\kappa,\pi}} Y|Z$.*

Proof: By Corollary 3.5 it is enough to show that $A_i \perp\!\!\!\perp_{p_{\kappa,\pi}} U_{i-1} \mid Par_i^{\mathcal{H}}$ for each $i = 1, \ldots, n$. Clearly $A_i \perp\!\!\!\perp_{p_{\kappa,\pi}} U_{i-1} \mid Par_i^{\mathcal{H}}$ if and only if $A_i \perp\!\!\!\perp_{p_{\kappa,\pi \downharpoonright U_i}} U_{i-1} \mid Par_i^{\mathcal{H}}$. Since U_i is a relevance set, $p_{\kappa,\pi \downharpoonright U_i} = p^{U_i}_{\kappa_{U_i},\pi_{U_i}}$ so we need to show that $A_i \perp\!\!\!\perp_{p^{U_i}_{\kappa_{U_i},\pi_{U_i}}} U_{i-1} \mid Par_i^{\mathcal{H}}$. But $Par_i^{\mathcal{H}}$ is the set of variables in U_i that occur with A_i in constraints of π_{U_i}, so $Par_i^{\mathcal{H}}$ separates A_i from $U_{i-1} \backslash Par_i^{\mathcal{H}}$ in the constraint graph $\mathcal{G}_{\pi_{U_i}}$. Applying Theorem 5.6, $A_i \perp\!\!\!\perp_{p^{U_i}_{\kappa_{U_i},\pi_{U_i}}} U_{i-1} \mid Par_i^{\mathcal{H}}$. ■

Note in particular that this graph $\mathcal{H}$ corresponding to independencies of $p_{\kappa,\pi}$ is no larger (in the sense that it has no more arrows) than the directed constraint graph $\mathcal{H}_\pi$ that would be determined from the constraint graph $\mathcal{G}_\pi$ using the techniques of §5.7.

Thus under the conditions of Theorem 5.7 $(\mathcal{H}, y)$ forms a Bayesian network representation of $p_{\kappa,\pi}$, where the y parameters are defined by $y_i^u = p(a_i|par_i)$ as in §5.7. We saw in §5.7 that in the absence of causal knowledge the y parameters are the parameters that maximise $H = \sum_{i=1}^n H_i$ where

$$H_i = -\sum_{v @ Anc'_i} \left(\prod_{A_j \in Anc'_i} y_j^v \right) \log y_i^v.$$

However when we have a causal ordering the situation is simpler yet: we can determine the y_1 parameters by maximising H_1, then the y_2 parameters by maximising H_2 subject to the y_1 parameters having been fixed in the previous step, and so on:

Theorem 5.8 *Suppose as in Theorem 5.7 that the $U_i = \{A_1, \ldots, A_i\}$ are relevance sets for $i = 1, \ldots, n$ and $\mathcal{H}$ contains just arrows to A_i from predecessors that occur in the same constraint set in π_{U_i}. Then $p_{\kappa,\pi}$ is represented by the Bayesian network $(\mathcal{H}, y)$ where for $i = 1, \ldots, n$ the y_i maximise H_i subject to the constraints in κ_{U_i}, π_{U_i}.*

Proof: We shall use induction on i. For the base case $i = 1$, we have that $y_i^u = p_{\kappa,\pi}(a_1) = p^{U_1}_{\kappa_{U_1},\pi_{U_1}}(a_1) = p_{\pi_{U_1}}(a_1)$ for $a_1 \sim u$ since the causal knowledge is trivial in this case. This is found by maximising entropy H on domain U_1 subject only to π_{U_1}, which is just maximising H_1 subject to π_{U_1}. Assume the inductive hypothesis for case $i-1$ and consider case i. Here we have that $y_i^u = p_{\kappa,\pi}(a_i|par_i) = p^{U_i}_{\kappa_{U_i},\pi_{U_i}}(a_i|par_i)$. We find the y_i^u by maximising H on domain U_i, i.e. $\sum_{j=1}^i H_j$, subject to κ_{U_i}, π_{U_i}. Now the $y_j^u, j = 1, \ldots, i-1$, are fixed by the inductive hypothesis, and hence so are the $H_j, j = 1, \ldots, i-1$. This it suffices to maximise H_i with respect to parameters y_i and subject to κ_{U_i}, π_{U_i}. ■

Thus when the $U_i = \{A_1, \ldots, A_i\}$ are relevance sets the general entropy maximisation task, which requires simultaneously finding the y parameters that maximise H, reduces to the simpler task of sequentially finding the y_i parameters that maximise H_i, as i runs through $1, \ldots, n$. Clearly this can offer enormous efficiency savings, both for numerical optimisation techniques and Lagrange multiplier methods. In the Lagrange multiplier case partial derivatives are simpler and each partial derivative involves only one free parameter.

In particular, if the $U_i = \{A_1, \ldots, A_i\}$ are the *only* relevance sets then all the transferred causal constraints $p_{\downharpoonright U_i} = p^{U_i}_{\kappa_{U_i}, \pi_{U_i}}$ are adhered to by the sequential maximisation procedure and can consequently be ignored when determining the parameters. Thus it suffices to sequentially maximise H_i with respect to parameters y_i subject only to π_{U_i}. When using Lagrange multiplier methods one can then derive an analogue of eqn 5.3:

$$y_i^u = e^{(\mu_i^u/\pi)-1} \prod_{C_k \subseteq U_i} e^{(\lambda_k/\pi)(\partial f_k/\partial y_k^u)},$$

where the constant $\pi = \sum_{w@Anc_i, w\sim u} \prod_{A_j \in Anc_i} y_j^w$ is fixed by having determined y_j^u for $j < i$ earlier in the sequential maximisation.

There is a second, more important special case. Suppose that the causal knowledge κ is complete, determining a causal graph $\mathcal{C}$ on V, and that each variable A_i occurs only with its direct causes $Par_i^{\mathcal{C}}$ in the constraint sets of π. If all κ-ancestral sets are relevance sets then the independence graph $\mathcal{H}$ is just $\mathcal{C}$, the causal graph, and $(\mathcal{C}, y)$ offers a Bayesian network representation of $p_{\kappa,\pi}$.

For example suppose that each probabilistic constraint takes the form of the probability of an assignment to a variable conditional on an assignment to its parents. Then compatibility of these constraints on the U_i is guaranteed. If *each* probability of the form $y_i^u = p(a_i|par_i)$ is given as a constraint then the probability function $p_{\kappa,\pi}$, represented as above by the Bayesian net $(\mathcal{C}, y)$, is fully determined by the causal graph and the probabilistic constraints and no work is required to maximise entropy.[146] If some of these parameters are given then sequential maximisation can be used to determine the others.[147]

We have another example of this special case when background knowledge takes the form of a *structural equation model*.[148] Such a model can be thought of as a causal graph $\kappa = \mathcal{C}$ together with, for each variable A_i, an equation $A_i = f_i(Par_i, E_i)$ determining the value of each effect A_i as a function of the values of its direct causes Par_i and an error variable E_i that is not itself a variable in V.

[146] This situation is dealt with in detail in Williamson (2001*b*).

[147] This is essentially the context in which Lukasiewicz (2000) advocated sequential entropy maximisation. The framework here clearly provides a justification for that type of approach.

[148] (Pearl, 2000, §1.4.1)

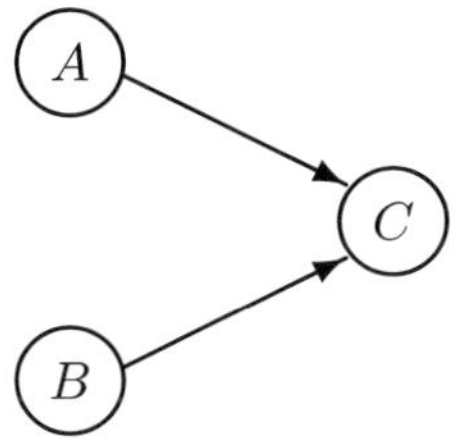

FIG. 5.6. Causal graph of Pearl's puzzle.

(The error variables are normally assumed to be probabilistically independent, but we need not assume this here.) Moreover, these equations are interpreted causally: A_i is fixed by its direct causes; effects do not determine their causes. Now for each equation the constraint set consists of A_i and its direct causes. Under this interpretation constraint equations are compatible on κ-ancestral sets of variables, since each equation provides information about the effect variable and not its direct causes. Hence the directed constraint graph $\mathcal{H}$, determined via Theorem 5.7, is just the causal graph $\mathcal{C}$ and by determining y-parameters via Theorem 5.8 we generate a Bayesian net $(\mathcal{C}, y)$ representation of $p_{\kappa,\pi}$, where $\pi = \{a_i = f_i(par_i, e_i) : a_i@A_i, par_i@Par_i, e_i@E_i, i = 1, \ldots, n\}$.[149] The y-parameters may be found as follows. Form an extended domain V' which includes the error variables. Then maximise entropy subject to deterministic constraints π among the variables in V'. The Bayesian net representation is trivial to determine: in the directed constraint graph $\mathcal{H}'$, the parents of A_i include the error variable E_i as well as the direct causes of A_i in $\mathcal{C}$, and each parameter $p(a_i|par_i e_i)$ is 1 or 0 according to whether $f_i(par_i, e_i)$ is a_i or not. Then the y-parameters of the original network V can be determined from this extended network over V' via the identity $p(a_i|par_i) = \sum_{e_i} p(a_i|par_i e_i)p(e_i|par_i) = \sum_{e_i} p(a_i|par_i e_i)p(e_i)$ [since $e_i \perp\!\!\!\perp Par_i$ in the extended network] $= \sum_{e_i} I_{f_i(par_i,e_i)=a_i} p(e_i)$ [where the indicator $I_{f_i(par_i,e_i)=a_i}$ is 1 or 0 according to whether $f_i(par_i, e_i) = a_i$ or not] $= \sum_{e_i} I_{f_i(par_i,e_i)=a_i} 1/||E_i||$ [maximising entropy gives $p(e_i) = 1/||E_i||$ since no constraints convey any information about E_i], and this is just the proportion of assignments e_i to E_i for which $f_i(par_i, e_i) = a_i$.

The situation in Pearl's puzzle resembles the former example. In Pearl's puzzle the causal information κ takes the form of causal graph Fig. 5.6, and the conditional probability distribution of C conditional on A and B. This conditional probability distribution is compatible on $\{A, B\}$. By Causal Irrelevance C is irrelevant to $\{A, B\}$. Our analysis now tells us that the agent's probability function over $\{A, B, C\}$ is represented by a Bayesian network $(\mathcal{C}, y)$, where $\mathcal{C}$ is the graph capturing the causal information and the y-parameters consist of the given conditional distribution together with $p(a^1) = 1/2$ and $p(b^1) = 1/2$

[149] This provides a justification of the Causal Markov Condition for structural equation models. The standard justification in this context appeals to a further assumption that error terms are independent—see Pearl (2000, Theorem 1.4.1).

found by sequential entropy maximisation. In particular this probability function agrees with that formed on domain $\{A, B\}$ under no constraints. Thus we do not have any puzzling counterintuitive change in degrees of belief.

Moreover, the same reasoning goes through in the modification of Pearl's puzzle. Here we are given the same causal knowledge but the distribution of C conditional on A and that of C conditional on B, not that of C conditional on A and B. We now have to use sequential maximisation to provide the distribution of C conditional on A and B as parameters for a Bayesian network representation, but (as long as the conditional distributions are compatible on $\{A, B\}$) Causal Irrelevance still rids us of any counterintuitive dependency between A and B. Note that compatibility depends in this example on the constraints themselves: if $\pi = \{p(c^1|a^1) = 1, p(c^1|a^0) = 0, p(c^1|b^1) = 0, p(c^b|b^0) = 1\}$ then π is not compatible on $\{A, B\}$ since it is not compatible with $p(a^1) = p(b^1) = 1$, for example.

In this chapter, we have seen that objective Bayesianism interprets probability mentally, as rational degree of belief, dependent on the background knowledge of an agent. Empirical information imposes constraints on degree of belief via the Calibration Principle and lack of information constrains degree of belief via the Maximum Entropy Principle. Objective Bayesianism is objective to the extent that these principles narrow down degree of belief: it is plausible, I have argued, that they narrow it down to a single probability function, in which case objective Bayesianism is fully objective, but even if they allow some latitude for choice of belief function, the position is near the opposite end of the objectivity scale from de Finetti's strict subjectivism.

The typical sticking points for objective Bayesianism are its computational complexity and its handling of qualitative causal information, but I hope to have shown that these hurdles can be overcome, the former by appealing to a Bayesian net reparameterisation of the entropy maximisation problem and the latter by using the Causal Irrelevance principle to sharpen causal constraints.

6

TWO-STAGE BAYESIAN NETS

In this chapter, we shall see how objective Bayesianism as developed in Chapter 5 can be invoked to save the causal interpretation of Bayesian networks from the objections posed in Chapter 4.

6.1 Causal Nets Maximise Entropy

We have seen some of the problems that face a causal interpretation of Bayesian nets in Chapter 4. If both causality and probability are interpreted physically then the Causal Markov Condition can fail because probabilistic dependencies may be accidental or have non-causal explanations (§4.2). Moreover, standard mental interpretations face their own problems (§§4.3–4.5). The Causal Markov Condition can hardly be expected to hold if one (or both) of the interpretations is strictly subjective, because the condition operates as a strong constraint while strict-subjectivism posits freedom from restrictions. If one (or both) of causality and probability is interpreted as an agent's knowledge of the corresponding physical quantity then even if the physical situation satisfies the Causal Markov Condition, any gap between knowledge and reality can lead to poor performance of the agent's causal net.

So can causal nets be justified, or should they be abandoned?

In fact they can be justified: there is a clear objective Bayesian justification of causal nets that appeals to the techniques of Chapter 5. Suppose that an agent has the components of a causal net as her background knowledge: the causal relations embodied in the causal graph $\mathcal{C}$ and the probability tables of the specification $\mathcal{S}$. (The independencies encapsulated in the Causal Markov Condition are not assumed to be part of the agent's background knowledge—it is the Causal Markov Condition that is in question here.) This background knowledge can be translated into precise quantitative constraints on the agent's degrees of belief. The causal graph constrains the agent's belief function p via Causal Irrelevance, and p must yield the probabilities in the probability specification as marginals. This situation corresponds to one of the special cases mentioned at the end of §5.8, and there we saw that the agent's belief function p, which is determined from the quantitative constraints by maximising entropy, can be represented by a Bayesian net, namely the Bayesian net $(\mathcal{C}, \mathcal{S})$ itself. So, given knowledge described by the constraints in a causal net, one ought to adopt as one's belief function the function induced by the causal net itself. This justifies the use of causal nets: a causal net $(\mathcal{C}, \mathcal{S})$ is an optimal probability model given the information $\mathcal{C}$, $\mathcal{S}$. It also justifies the Causal Markov Condition, which must hold when probability is interpreted as the belief function an agent should adopt on the basis of background knowledge $\mathcal{C}, \mathcal{S}$.

6.2 Refining Bayesian Nets

Now even though the probability function determined by the causal net may be most rational from an objective Bayesian point of view, the simulation of §4.3 showed that it may not be close enough to physical probability for practical purposes. As Jaynes pointed out (Jaynes considers robot agents):

> Quite generally, as the robot's state of knowledge ... changes, probabilities [determined by it] may change from independent to dependent or *vice versa*; yet the real properties of the events remain the same. Then one who attributed the property of dependence or independence to the events would be, in effect, claiming for the robot the power of psychokinesis. We must be vigilant against this confusion between reality and a state of knowledge about reality, which we have called the 'mind projection fallacy'.[150]

What can be done when the agent's belief function does not mirror a target probability function?

Perhaps the best strategy here is to modify the causal net in order that it may better represent the target. In §3.5 we saw that by adding arrows to a Bayesian net according to a conditional mutual information arrow weighting, one can decrease the cross entropy distance between the probability function determined by the Bayesian net and a target probability function, all the while remaining within a subspace of the space Bayesian nets whose members allow computationally tractable inference. Thus one can gather new probabilistic information which can be used to calculate arrow weightings and thereby restructure the network.

Likewise, new causal information can also motivate restructuring the net. Suppose one learns of a new direct causal relationship. Arguably, by the Causal Dependence principle introduced in §4.3, any such relation implies the probabilistic dependence of cause and effect, conditional on the effect's other direct causes. But then by adding an arrow corresponding to the causal relation (and the associated probability specifiers) one can produce a modified net that will better approximate target probability, as demonstrated by Theorem 3.7.

Note that while adding arrows corresponding to new causal relations leaves the causal interpretation of the Bayesian net intact, adding arrows according to mutual information need not: the new arrows need not correspond to direct causal relationships. Thus while the original net is a causal net, a causal interpretation of the modified net may be untenable.

6.3 A Two-Stage Methodology

This leads to a two-stage methodology for employing Bayesian nets. When background knowledge takes the form of the components of a causal net,

[150](Jaynes, 2003, p. 92)

Stage One adopt the probability function determined by the causal net as a rational belief function (this, according to the objective Bayesian interpretation of probability, is the best probability function one can adopt given such knowledge),

Stage Two refine this Bayesian net to better correspond to a target probability function (the justification of this stage is down to the motivation behind the calibration principle of §5.3).

Or more generally whatever the form an agent's background knowledge actually takes, first construct a Bayesian net that best represents that knowledge using the methods of §§5.6–5.8, and second collect new information and refine the net using the techniques of §3.5.

7

CAUSALITY

The task of the next three chapters is to discuss the nature of causality and investigate the possibility of discovering causal structure via the automated learning of Bayesian networks. This chapter will introduce theories of causality.

7.1 Metaphysics of Causality

While the mathematical theory of probability is well-developed and its axioms and main definitions have remained stable for a number of years,[151] there is no consensus regarding the mathematisation of causality.[152] Neither is there much agreement as to what causality is. In this chapter, we shall explore some of the array of opinions on the nature of causality. In the next chapter, we shall consider how one can learn causal relationships.

There are three varieties of position on causality. One can argue that the concept of causality is of heuristic use only and should be eliminated from scientific discourse: this was the tack pursued by Bertrand Russell, who maintained that science appeals to functional relationships rather than causal laws.[153] Alternatively one can argue that causality is a fundamental feature of the world and should be treated as a scientific primitive—this claim is usually the result of disillusionment with purported philosophical analyses, several of which appeal to the asymmetry of time in order to explain the asymmetry of causation, a strategy that is unattractive to those who want to analyse time in terms of causality. Or one can maintain that causal relations can be reduced to other concepts not involving causal notions. This latter position is dominant in the philosophical literature, and there are four main approaches which can be described roughly as follows. The mechanistic theory, discussed in §7.2, reduces causal relations to physical processes. The probabilistic account (§7.3) reduces causal relations to physical probabilistic relations. The counterfactual account (§7.4) reduces causal relations to counterfactual laws. The agent-oriented account (§7.5) reduces causal relations to the ability of agents to achieve goals by manipulating their causes.[154]

[151]See Billingsley (1979) for an overview of the mathematical theory of probability. Its axioms were put forward in Kolmogorov (1933).

[152]Pearl (2000) has developed a mathematical theory of causality, but this formalisation has yet to enjoy support as widespread as the support for the mathematical theory of probability.

[153](Russell, 1913). Russell later modified his views on causality, becoming more tolerant of the notion.

[154]See the introduction to Sosa and Tooley (1993) for more discussion on the variety of interpretations of causality.

In §2.3 we saw that three distinctions can be used to classify interpretations of probability—these can also be applied to interpretations of causality. An interpretation of causality can deal with either single-case or repeatable causes and effects. We will suppose here that causality is a relation between variables (as mentioned in §4.1 this claim has been disputed, but even if strictly false is a harmless idealisation) and that these variables are single-case or repeatable according to the interpretation of causality in question. An interpretation of causality is mental if it views causality as a feature of an agent's epistemic state and physical if a feature of the world external to an agent. An interpretation is subjective if two agents with the same background knowledge can disagree as to causal relationships yet both be correct, and objective if causal relationships are not a matter of arbitrary choice. In Chapter 9, I shall argue in favour of an interpretation of causality analogous to the objective Bayesian interpretation of probability; this interpretation does not correspond to any of the dominant views of causality, which we shall now explore.

7.2 Mechanisms

The mechanistic account of causality aims to understand the physical processes that link cause and effect, interpreting causal statements as saying something about such processes. Wesley Salmon[155] and Phil Dowe[156] are two influential proponents of this type of position. They argue that a causal process is one that transmits[157] or possesses[158] a conserved physical quantity, such as energy-mass, linear momentum or charge, from start (cause) to finish (effect).

The mechanistic account is clearly a physical interpretation of causality, since it identifies causal relationships with physical processes. Such a notion of cause relates single cases, since only they are linked by physical processes, although causal regularities or laws may be induced from single-case causal connections. Causal mechanisms are understood objectively: if two agents disagree as to causal connections then at least one is wrong.

The main limitation of this approach is its rather narrow applicability: most of our causal assertions are apparently unrelated to the physics of conserved quantities. While it may be possible that physical processes such as those along which quantities are conserved could suggest causal links to physicists, such processes are altogether too low-level to suggest causal relationships in economics, for instance. One could maintain that the economists' concept of causality is the same as that of physics and is reducible to physical processes but one would be forced to accept that the epistemology of such a concept is totally unrelated to its metaphysics. This is undesirable: if the grounds for knowledge of a causal connection have little to do with the nature of the causal connection as it is

[155](Salmon, 1980*a*, 1984, 1997, 1998)

[156](Dowe, 1993, 1996, 1999, 2000*a*,*b*)

[157](Salmon, 1997, §2)

[158](Dowe, 2000*b*, §V.1)

analysed then one can argue that it cannot be the causal connection that we have knowledge of, but something else.[159] On the other hand one could keep the physical account and accept that the economists' causality differs from the physicists' causality. But this position faces the further questions of what economists' causality is, and why we think that cause is a single concept when in fact it is not. These problems clearly motivate a more unified account of causality.

7.3 Probabilistic Causality

Probabilistic causality has a wider scope than the mechanistic approach: here the idea is to understand causal connections in terms of probabilistic relationships between variables, be they variables in physics, economics, or wherever. There is no firm consensus among proponents of probabilistic causality as to what probabilistic relationships among variables constitute causal relationships, but typically they appeal to the intuitions behind the Principle of the Common Cause introduced in §4.2: if two variables are probabilistically dependent then one causes the other or they are effects of common causes which screen off the dependence. Indeed, Hans Reichenbach applied the Principle of the Common Cause to an analysis of causality, as a step on the way to a probabilistic analysis of the direction of time.[160] Similarly Patrick Suppes argued that causal relations induce probabilistic dependencies and that screening off can be used to differentiate between variables that are common effects and variables that are cause and effect.[161] However, both these analyses fell foul of a number of criticisms,[162] and more recent probabilistic approaches adopt Causal Dependence (see §4.3) and the Causal Markov Condition (see §4.1) as necessary conditions for causality, together with other less central conditions which are sketched in Chapter 8.[163] Sometimes Causal Dependence is only implicitly adopted: the causal relation may be defined as the smallest relation that (i.e. the causal graph $\mathcal{C}^*$ is the graph with the smallest number of arrows that) satisfies the Causal Markov Condition, in which case Causal Dependence must hold (if there is an arrow from C to E in $\mathcal{C}^*$ then $C \rightleftharpoons E \mid D$, where D is the set of E's other direct causes, since otherwise that arrow would be redundant in $\mathcal{C}^*$.)

Probabilistic causality is normally applied to repeatable rather than single-case variables—in principle either is possible, as long as the chosen interpretation of probability handles the same kind of variables. Invariably causality is interpreted as a physical, mind-independent concept (this will be challenged in Chapter 9) and thus objective.

The chief problem that besets probabilistic causality is the dubious status of the probabilistic conditions to which the account appeals. We saw in §4.2 that the

159 See Benacerraf (1973) for a parallel argument in mathematics.

160 (Reichenbach, 1956)

161 (Suppes, 1970)

162 (See Salmon, 1980*b*, §§2–3)

163 See Pearl (1988, 2000); Spirtes *et al.* (1993); McKim and Turner (1997); Korb (1999).

Principle of the Common Cause and the Causal Markov Condition as predicated of a physical notion of cause and probability face serious objections. While these conditions may hold in many situations, the counterexamples we encountered clearly show that they do not hold invariably; yet a probabilistic analysis of cause requires them to hold invariably. The Causal Dependence condition faces its own barrage of counterexamples, and we shall explore one type of counterexample in the remainder of this section.[164]

First note that the Causal Dependence condition is often augmented with claims about the direction of causation. The condition itself says that if C is a direct cause of E then $C \rightleftharpoons E \mid D$, where D is the set of E's other direct causes. The augmented condition distinguishes directions of causation thus:

- if assignment c to C is a direct *positive cause* of assignment e to E then $p(e|cd) \geq p(e|c'd)$ for all $d@D$ and $c'@C$ with strict inequality in at least one case;
- if $c@C$ is a direct *preventative* or *negative cause* of $e@E$ then $p(e|cd) \leq p(e|c'd)$ for all $d@D$ and $c'@C$ with strict inequality in at least one case;
- if $c@C$ is a direct *mixed cause* of $e@E$ then $p(e|cd) > p(e|c'd)$ for some $c'@c$ and $d@D$ and $p(e|cd) < p(e|c'd)$ for some other $c'@c, d@D$.

If C and E take two assignments c^1, c^0 and e^1, e^0, and if c^1, e^1 indicate presence, occurrence or truth of C and E respectively while c^0, e^0 stand for their absence, failure to occur or falsity, then one can adopt the following terminology:

- C is a positive cause of E means c^1 is a positive cause of e^1, and
- C is a preventative of E means c^1 is a preventative of e^1.

Many of the counterexamples to Causal Dependence in the philosophical literature are directed at this augmented version—however, they can often be adapted to refute the original version as well.

Consider Rosen's golf ball example.[165] Here a golfer takes a shot (s) but the golf ball bounces off a tree (t) into the hole for a birdie (b). Thus bouncing the ball off the tree positively causes the ball to enter the hole. The problem here is that while the golfer may anyway be unlikely to get a birdie, he will be even less likely to get one by bouncing the ball off a tree. Thus positive causation can be accompanied by a decrease in probability, $p(b|ts) < p(b|t's)$, where t' signifies no bounce off the tree.

Salmon gave three possible responses to the golf ball example.[166] One can argue that the descriptions of the causal relata are not specific enough: as one specifies more background conditions relevant to the bounce off the tree, the probability of a birdie will increase. Alternatively one might say that the causal

[164] For discussion of other counterexamples see e.g. Salmon (1971, p. 64); Hesslow (1976); Skyrms (1980, p. 108); Cartwright (1983, pp. 23–25); Tooley (1987, pp. 234–235); Mellor (1988); Humphreys (1989, pp. 41–42); Eells (1991); Hitchcock (1993); Papineau (1994, pp. 339–440); Mellor (1995); Menzies (1996) and Noordhof (1998, §2).

[165] (Suppes, 1970, p. 41)

[166] (Salmon, 1980*b*)

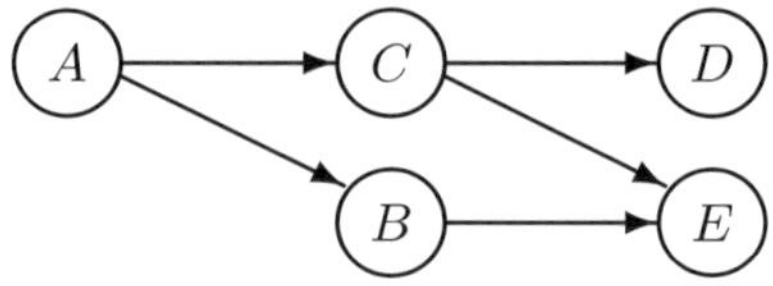

FIG. 7.1. Dowe's decay example.

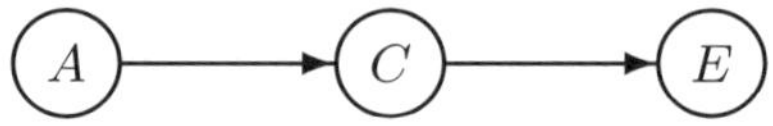

FIG. 7.2. Modified decay example.

chains are underspecified: if we take causes local enough to their effects, each link in the causal chain will correspond to probability-raising and will be deemed an instance of positive causality. A third option is to relativise to causal process: 'Once the player has swung on the approach shot, and the ball is travelling toward the tree and not toward the hole, the probability of the ball's going into the hole if it strikes the limb is greater—given the general direction it is going—than if it does not make contact with the tree at all.'[167] Salmon was sceptical though as to whether any of these strategies will be effective in all problematic situations, and gave an atomic energy-level example as an instance of their failure. Dowe presented the following variant of Salmon's problematic case and argued cogently that it defeats all of Salmon's strategies.[168] An unstable atom can decay via the pathways shown in Fig. 7.1. Each variable takes two possible values, e.g. c^1 if the atom decays to particle C and c^0 if it does not become C. We are also told that $p(c^1) = 1/4$ and $p(e^1|c^1) = 3/4$, and that in fact a particular atom actually decayed via $A \longrightarrow C \longrightarrow E$. Thus C actually positively caused E, although c^1 lowers the probability of e^1: $p(e^1|c^1) = 3/4 < 15/16 = p(e^1)$.

Note though that although positive causation is accompanied in Dowe's example by probability lowering, this is not as it stands a counterexample to the augmented dependence principle, which requires us to consider probabilities conditional on E's other causes, in this case B. The question thus is whether $p(e^1|c^1b^1) \geq p(e^1|c^0b^1)$ and $p(e^1|c^1b^0) \geq p(e^1|c^0b^0)$ and there is a strict inequality in at least one of these cases. Now c^1 and b^1 are mutually exclusive, thus $p(c^1b^1) = p(c^0b^0) = 0$ and $p(e^1|c^1b^1)$ and $p(e^1|c^0b^0)$ are unconstrained—we do not have enough information to decide whether the probabilistic condition holds.

However, we can reformulate Dowe's example as follows. Dowe's case is equivalent to Fig. 7.2 where c^0 corresponds to a decay via the B pathway (i.e. b^1) in Dowe's example, and e^0 corresponds to d^1. As before we have $p(e^1|c^1) < p(e^1)$, but now this does count against the augmented dependence principle: C is a positive cause of E (C did actually positively cause E) but C lowers the probability of E conditional on E's other direct causes (of which there are now none).

[167](Salmon, 1980*b*, p. 227)

[168](Dowe, 2000*b*, §II.6)

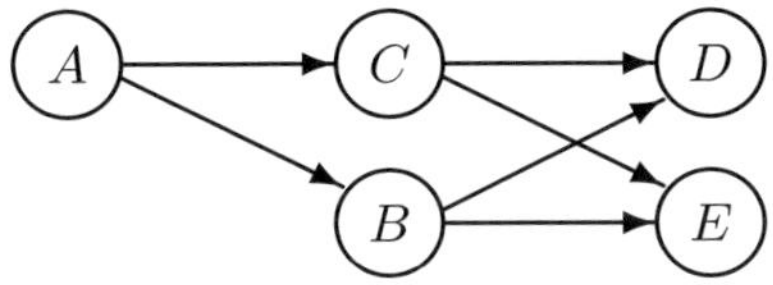

FIG. 7.3. Modified decay example.

As originally formulated, Causal Dependence only requires that cause and direct effect be dependent conditional on the effect's other direct causes (not that positive causation be accompanied by raising of conditional probability) and we have dependence in this example, so the original formulation survives. But we can further modify the example: if $p(c^1) = 1$ then $p(e^1|c^1) = p(e^1)$, $C \perp\!\!\!\perp E$, yet C causes E so Causal Dependence as originally formulated fails.

The lesson that is normally drawn from this type of objection is that the Causal Dependence condition is implausible when the variables under consideration are single-case. The fact is that hitting the tree positively caused the birdie in the particular case under consideration, and the decay via C positively caused the decay via E in the single case, even though the corresponding probabilities both decreased. However, when considering *repeatable* variables in these examples the situation changes. Intuitively hitting the tree in general *prevents* a birdie which is just what the augmented Causal Dependence principle associates with probability decrease.

However the decay example proves fatal even when variables are repeatably instantiatable. Suppose as before that B and C atoms can decay to E atoms, but that they can also both decay to D atoms too, as in Fig. 7.3. b^1 and c^1 are mutually exclusive, as are d^1 and e^1, so Fig. 7.2 remains an equivalent causal picture. Now if B and C atoms have an equal propensity to produce E atoms, $p(e^1|c^1) = p(e^1|c^0)$, then $E \perp\!\!\!\perp C$ even though C is the direct cause of E. This directly contradicts Causal Dependence. (The augmented version is thereby also untenable: C is a positive cause of E but in no case does c^1 raise the probability of e^1.) Thus although Causal Dependence may often hold, it does not hold invariably.

In sum then, probabilistic causality appeals to the Principle of the Common Cause, the Causal Markov Condition or Causal Dependence, but these conditions simply do not hold in a number of cases.

7.4 Counterfactuals

The counterfactual account, developed in detail by David Lewis,[169] reduces causal relations to subjunctive conditionals: E *depends causally* on C if and only if (i) if C were to occur then E would occur (or its chance of occurring would be significantly raised) and (ii) if C were not to occur then E would not occur (or its chance of occurring would be significantly lowered). The causal relation

[169](Lewis, 1973)

is then taken to be the transitive closure of Causal Dependence: C causes E if E depends causally on C or if E depends causally on some D and C causes D. The subjunctive conditionals (called *counterfactual* conditionals if the antecedent is false) are in turn given a semantics in terms of possible worlds: 'if C were to occur then E would occur' is true if and only if (i) there are no possible worlds in which C is true or (ii) E holds at all the possible worlds in which C holds that our closest to our own world. So causal claims are claims about what goes on in possible worlds that are close to our own.[170]

Lewis's counterfactual theory was developed to account for causal relationships between single-case events (which can be thought of as single-case variables which take the values 'occurs' or 'does not occur'), and the causal relation is intended to be mind-independent and objective.

Many of the difficulties with this view stem from Lewis' reliance on possible worlds. Possible worlds are not just a dispensable façon de parler for Lewis, they are assumed to exist in just the way our world exists. But we have no physical contact with these other worlds, which makes it hard to see how their goings-on can be the object of our causal claims and hard to see how we discover causal relationships. Moreover it is doubtful whether there is an objective way to determine which worlds are closest to our own if we follow Lewis' suggestion of measuring closeness by similarity—two worlds are similar in some respects and different in others and choice or weighting of these respects is a subjective matter. Causal relations, on the other hand, do not seem to be subjective. Instead of analysing causal relations, of which we have at least an intuitive grasp, in terms of subjunctive conditionals and ultimately possible worlds, which many find mysterious, it would be more natural to proceed in the opposite direction. Thus we might be better-off appealing to causality to decide whether E would (be more likely to) occur were C to occur,[171] and depending on the answer we could then say whether a world in which C and E occurs is closer to our own than one in which C occurs but E does not.

7.5 Agency

The agency account, whose chief proponents are perhaps Huw Price and Peter Menzies,[172] analyses causal relations in terms of the ability of agents to achieve goals by manipulating their causes. According to this account, C causes E if and only if bringing about C would be an effective way for an agent to bring about E. Here the strategy of bringing about C is deemed effective if a rational decision theory would prescribe it as a way of bringing about E. Menzies and

[170]Lewis modified his account in Lewis (2000), but the changes made have little bearing on our discussion. See Lewis (1986) for Lewis' account of causal explanation.

[171]See Pearl (2000, chapter 7), for an analysis of counterfactuals in terms of causal relations. Dawid (2001) argues that counterfactuals are irrelevant and misleading for an analysis of causality.

[172](Price, 1991, 1992*a*,*b*; Menzies and Price, 1993)

Price argue that the strategy would be prescribed if and only if it raises the 'agent probability' of the occurrence of E.[173]

Menzies and Price do not agree as to the interpretation of these probabilities: Menzies maintains that they are chances, while Price seems to have a Bayesian conception.[174] Consequently it is not entirely clear whether they view causality as a physical or mental notion. On the one hand, they claim that there would be causal relations without agents,[175] while on the other they say, 'we would argue that when an agent can bring about one event as a means to bringing about another, this is true in virtue of certain basic intrinsic features of the situation involved, these features being essentially non-causal though not necessarily physical in character',[176] and maintain that the concept of cause is a 'secondary quality', relative to human responses or capacities.[177] From this relativity one might expect cause to be subjective, but they say that causation is significantly more objective than other secondary quantities like colour or taste.[178] The events they consider are single-case.[179]

The chief problems that beset the agency approach are inherited from those faced by the probabilistic and counterfactual approaches. First, the agency approach assumes a version of Causal Dependence for agent probabilities—we saw in §7.3 that this condition does not always hold.[180] Of course, where a causal connection is not accompanied by probabilistic dependence, such as in the atomic decay example of §7.3, bringing about a cause is not a good strategy for bringing about its effects. Second, the agency account appeals to subjunctive conditionals[181] (C causes E if and only if, *were* an agent to bring about C, that *would* be a good strategy for bringing about E) and so qualms about the utility of a counterfactual account can equally be applied to the agency approach.

[173](Menzies and Price, 1993)

[174](Menzies and Price, 1993, p. 190)

[175](Menzies and Price, 1993, §6)

[176](Menzies and Price, 1993, p. 197)

[177](Menzies and Price, 1993, pp. 188, 199)

[178](Menzies and Price, 1993, p. 200)

[179]Price's views are discussed in more detail in Williamson (2004*a*).

[180]In fact the version assumed by the agency approach does not restrict attention to direct causes and does not demand that dependence be conditional on the effect's other causes. This type of dependence condition is rarely advocated since it faces a wider range of counterexamples than Causal Dependence in the form used here—see the references given in §7.3.

[181](Menzies and Price, 1993, §5)

8

DISCOVERING CAUSAL RELATIONSHIPS

8.1 Epistemology of Causality

Different views on the nature of causality lead to different suggestions for discovering causal relationships. The mechanistic view of causality, for instance, leads naturally to a quest for physical processes, while proponents of probabilistic causality prescribe searching for probabilistic dependencies and independencies.

However, there are two very general strategies for causal discovery which cut across the metaphysical positions. Whatever view one holds on the nature of causality, one can advocate either *hypothetico-deductive* or *inductive* discovery of causal relationships. Under a hypothetico-deductive account (§8.2) one hypothesises causal relationships, deduces predictions from the hypothesis, and then tests the hypothesis by seeing how well the predictions accord with what actually happens. Under an inductive account (§8.3), one makes a large number of observations and induces causal relationships directly from this mass of data. We shall discuss each of these approaches in turn in this chapter, and give an overview of some recent proposals for discovering causal relationships.

8.2 Hypothetico-Deductive Discovery

According to the hypothetico-deductive account, a scientist first hypothesises causal relationships and then tests this hypothesis by seeing whether predictions drawn from it are borne out. The testing phase may be influenced by views on the nature of causality: a causal hypothesis can be supported or refuted according to whether physical processes are found that underlie the hypothesised causal relationships, whether probabilistic consequences of the hypothesis are verified, and whether experiments show that by manipulating the hypothesised causes one can achieve their effects.

Karl Popper was an exponent of the hypothetico-deductive approach. For Popper a causal explanation of an event consists of natural laws (which are universal statements) together with initial conditions (which are single-case statements) from which one can predict by deduction the event to be explained. The initial conditions are called the 'cause' of the event to be explained, which is in turn called the 'effect'.[182] Causal laws, then, are just universal laws, and are to be discovered via Popper's general scheme for scientific discovery: (i) hypothesise the laws; (ii) deduce their consequences, rejecting the laws and returning to step (i) if these consequences are falsified by evidence. Popper thus combines what

[182](Popper, 1934, §12)

is known as the *covering-law* account of causal explanation with a hypothetico-deductive account of learning causal relationships.

The covering-law model of explanation was developed by Hempel and Oppenheim[183] and also Railton,[184] and criticised by Lewis.[185] While such a model fits well with Popper's general account of scientific discovery, neither the details nor the viability of the covering-law model are relevant to the issue at stake: a Popperian hypothetico-deductive account of causal discovery can be combined with practically any account of causality and causal explanation.[186] Neither does one have to be a strict falsificationist to adopt a hypothetico-deductive account. Popper argued that the testing of a law only proceeds by falsification: a law should be rejected if contradicted by observed evidence (i.e. if falsified), but should never be accepted or regarded as confirmed in the absence of a falsification. This second claim of Popper's has often been disputed, and many argue that a hypothesis is confirmed by evidence in proportion to the probability of the hypothesis conditional on the evidence.[187] Given this probabilistic measure of confirmation—or indeed any other measure—one can accept the hypothesised causal relationships according to the extent to which evidence confirms the hypothesis. Thus the hypothetico-deductive strategy for learning causal relationships is very general: it does not require any particular metaphysics of causality, nor a covering-law model of causal explanation, nor a strict falsificationist account of testing.

Besides providing some criterion for accepting or rejecting hypothesised causal relationships, the proponent of a hypothetico-deductive account must do two things: (i) say how causal relationships are to be hypothesised; (ii) say how predictions are to be deduced from the causal relationships.

Popper fulfilled the latter task straightforwardly: effects are predicted as logical consequences of laws given causes (initial conditions). The viability of this response hinges very closely on Popper's account of causal explanation, and the response is ultimately inadequate for the simple reason that no one accepts the covering-law model as Popper formulated it: more recent covering-law models are significantly more complex, coping with chance explanations.[188]

Popper's response to the former task was equally straightforward, but perhaps even less satisfying:

> my view of the matter, for what it is worth, is that there is no such thing as a logical method of having new ideas, or a logical reconstruction of this process. My view may be expressed by saying that every discovery

[183](Hempel and Oppenheim, 1948)

[184](Railton, 1978)

[185](Lewis, 1986, §VII)

[186]Even the eliminativist position of Russell (1913), in which he argued that talk of causal laws should be eradicated in favour of talk of functional relationships, ties in well with Popper's logic of scientific discovery. Both Popper and Russell, after all, drew no sharp distinction between causal laws and the other universal laws that feature in science.

[187]See Howson and Urbach (1989); Earman (1992).

[188]E.g. Railton (1978).

> contains 'an irrational element', or 'a creative intuition'[189]

Popper accordingly placed the question of discovery firmly in the hands of psychologists, and concentrated solely on the question of the justification of a hypothesis.

The difficulty here is that while hypothesising may contain an irrational element, Popper has failed to shed any light on the rational element which must surely play a significant role in discovery. Popper's scepticism about the existence of a logic need not have precluded him from discussing the act of hypothesis from a normative point of view: both Popper in science and Pólya in mathematics remained pessimistic about the existence of a precise logic for hypothesising, yet Pólya managed to identify several imprecise but important heuristics.[190] One particular problem is this: a theory may be refuted by one experiment but perform well in many others; in such a case it may need only some local revision, to deal with the domain of application on which it is refuted, rather than wholesale rehypothesising. Popper's account says nothing of this, giving the impression that with each refutation one must return to a blank sheet and hypothesise afresh. The hypothetico-deductive method as stated neither gives an account of the progress of scientific theories in general, nor of causal theories in particular.

Any hypothetico-deductive account of causal discovery which fails to probe either the hypothetico or the deductive aspects of the process is clearly lacking. These are, in my view, the key shortcomings of Popper's position. I shall try to shed some light on these aspects when I present a new type of hypothetico-deductive account in §9.9. For now, we shall turn to a competing account of causal discovery, inductivism.

8.3 Inductive Learning

Francis Bacon developed a rather different account of scientific learning. First one makes a large amount of careful observations of the phenomenon to be explained, by performing experiments if need be. One compiles a table of positive instances (cases in which the phenomenon occurs),[191] a table of negative instances (cases in which the phenomenon does not occur),[192] and a table of partial instances (cases in which the phenomenon occurs to a certain degree).[193]

> We have chosen to call the task and function of these three tables the *Presentation of instances to the intellect.* After the *presentation* has been made, *induction* itself has to be put to work. For in addition to the *presentation* of each and every instance, we have to discover which nature appears constantly with a given nature or not, which grows with it or decreases with it; and which is a limitation (as we said above) of a more general nature. If the mind attempts to do this affirmatively from the

[189] (Popper, 1934, p. 32)
[190] (Pólya, 1945, 1954*a*,*b*)
[191] (Bacon, 1620, §II.XI)
[192] (Bacon, 1620, §II.XII)
[193] (Bacon, 1620, §II.XIII)

> beginning (as it always does if left to itself), fancies will arise and conjectures and poorly defined notions and axioms needing daily correction, unless one chooses (in the manner of the Schoolmen) to defend the indefensible.[194]

Thus Bacon's method consists of presentation followed by induction of a theory from the observations. It is to be preferred over a hypothetico-deductive approach because it avoids the construction of poor hypotheses in the absence of observations, and it avoids the tendency to defend the indefensible:

> Once a man's understanding has settled on something (either because it is an accepted belief or because it pleases him), it draws everything else also to support and agree with it. And if it encounters a larger number of more powerful countervailing examples, it either fails to notice them, or disregards them, or makes fine distinctions to dismiss and reject them, and all this with much dangerous prejudice, to preserve the authority of its first conceptions.[195]

Note that while Bacon's position is antithetical to Popper's hypothetico-deductive approach, it is compatible with Popper's falsificationism—indeed Bacon claims that 'every *contradictory instance* destroys a conjecture'.[196] The first step of the inductive process, *exclusion*, involves ruling out a selection of simple and often rather vaguely formulated conjectures by means of providing contradictory instances.[197] The next step is a *first harvest*, which is a preliminary interpretation of the phenomenon of interest.[198] Bacon then produces a seven-stage process of elucidating, refining, and testing this interpretation—only the first stage of which was worked out in any detail.[199]

Present-day inductivists claim that causal relationships can be hypothesised algorithmically from experimental and observational data, and that suitable data would yield the correct causal relationships. Usually, but not necessarily, the data takes the form of a database of past cases: a set V of repeatably instantiatable variables are measured, each entry of the database $D = (u_1, \ldots, u_k)$ consists of an observed assignment of values to some subset U_i of V. Such an account of learning is occasionally alluded to in connection with probabilistic analyses of causality and has been systematically investigated by researchers in the field of artificial intelligence, including groups in Pittsburgh,[200] Los Angeles,[201] and Monash,[202] proponents of a Bayesian learning approach,[203] and computationally-

[194] (Bacon, 1620, §II.XV)
[195] (Bacon, 1620, §I.XLVI)
[196] (Bacon, 1620, §II.XVIII)
[197] (Bacon, 1620, §§II.XVIII-XIX)
[198] (Bacon, 1620, §II.XX)
[199] (Bacon, 1620, §§II.XXI-LII)
[200] (Spirtes *et al.*, 1993; Glymour, 1997; Scheines, 1997; Mani and Cooper, 1999, 2000, 2001)
[201] (Pearl, 1999, 2000)
[202] (Dai *et al.*, 1997; Wallace and Korb, 1999; Korb and Nicholson, 2003)
[203] (Cooper, 1999, 2000; Heckerman *et al.*, 1999; Tong and Koller, 2001; Yoo *et al.*, 2002)

minded psychologists.[204] Several of these approaches are sketched in the ensuing sections.

These approaches seek to learn various types of causal model. The simplest type of causal model is just a *causal graph* which shows only qualitative causal relationships. A *causal net* is slightly more complex, containing the quantitative information $p(a_i|par_i)$ in addition to a causal graph. A *structural equation model* is a third type of causal model—this can be thought of as a causal graph together with an equation for each variable in terms of its direct cause variables, $A_i = f_i(Par_i, E_i)$, where f_i is some function and E_i is an error variable, where all error variables are assumed to be probabilistically independent.

The mainstream of these inductivist AI approaches have the following feature in common. In order that causal relationships can be gleaned from statistical relationships, the approaches assume the Causal Markov Condition holds of physical causality and physical probability.[205] Of course a causal net contains the Causal Markov Condition as an inbuilt assumption. In the case of structural equation models the Causal Markov Condition is a consequence of the representation of each variable as a function just of its direct causes and an error variable, given the further assumption that all error variables are probabilistically independent.

The inductive procedure then consists in finding the class of causal models—or under some approaches a single 'best' causal model—whose probabilistic independencies implied via the Causal Markov Condition are consistent with independencies inferred from the data. Other assumptions are often also made, such as minimality (no submodel of the causal model also satisfies the Causal Markov Condition), faithfulness (all independencies in the data are implied via the Causal Markov Condition), linearity (all variables are linear functions of their direct causes and uncorrelated error variables), causal sufficiency (all common causes of measured variables are measured), context generality (every individual possesses the causal relations of the population), no side effects (one can intervene to fix the value of a variable without changing the value of any non-effects of the variable), and determinism. However, these extra assumptions are less central than the Causal Markov Condition: approaches differ as to which of these extra assumptions they adopt and the assumptions tend to be used just to facilitate the inductive procedure based on the Causal Markov Condition, either by helping to provide some justification of the inductive procedure or by increasing the purported efficiency or efficacy of algorithms for causal induction.

The brunt of criticism of the inductive approach tends to focus on the Causal Markov Condition and the ancillary assumptions outlined above. We have already discussed at length the difficulties that beset the Causal Markov Condition (see §4.2 and subsequent sections); in cases where this condition fails the induc-

[204](Waldmann and Martignon, 1998; Glymour, 2001; Tenenbaum and Griffiths, 2001; Waldmann, 2001; Hagmayer and Waldmann, 2002)

[205]There are inductive AI methods that take a totally different approach to causal learning, such as that in Karimi and Hamilton (2000, 2001), and Wendelken and Shastri (2000). However, non-Causal-Markov approaches are well in the minority.

tive approach will simply posit the wrong causal relationships. It is plain to see that the ancillary conditions are also very strong and these face numerous counterexamples themselves. The proof, inductivists claim, will be in the pudding. However, the reported successes of inductive methods have been questioned,[206] and these criticisms lend further doubt to the inductive approach as a whole and the Causal Markov Condition in particular as its central assumption.[207]

In the next chapter, we shall see that the inductive and hypothetico-deductive approaches can be reconciled by using the inductive methods as a way of hypothesising a causal model, then deducing its consequences and restructuring the model if these are not borne out (perhaps because of failure of the Causal Markov Condition).

For the rest of this chapter we shall take a tour of some recent proposals for inducing causal relationships.

8.4 Constraint-Based Induction

Peter Spirtes, Clark Glymour, and Richard Scheines developed an account of causal discovery in the last decade of the twentieth century.[208] Their approach was to induce a partially directed causal graph from independence constraints embodied in a database of past case data. Undirected edges in this graph indicate causal relations of unknown direction. They developed the *PC algorithm* (apparently named after its authors, Peter and Clark)[209] to construct the graph:[210]

- Start off with a complete undirected graph on V;
- for $n = 0, 1, 2, \ldots$ remove any edges $A - B$ if $A \perp\!\!\!\perp B \mid X$ for some set X of n neighbours of A;
- for each structure $A - B - C$ in the graph with A and C not adjacent, substitute $A \longrightarrow B \longleftarrow C$ if B was not found to screen off A and C in the previous step;
- repeatedly substitute
  (i) $A \longrightarrow B \longrightarrow C$ for $A \longrightarrow B - C$ with A and C non-adjacent;
  (ii) $A \longrightarrow B$ for $A - B$ if there is a chain of arrows from A to B.

In order to argue for the correctness of this algorithm, Spirtes, Glymour and Scheines make the following fundamental assumptions about the relationship between causality and probability (understood to be the frequency distribution determined by the database):

[206](Humphreys and Freedman, 1996; Humphreys, 1997; Freedman and Humphreys, 1999; Woodward, 1997)

[207]See Dash and Druzdzel (1999); Hausman (1999); Hausman and Woodward (1999); Glymour and Cooper (1999, part 3); Lemmer (1996); Lad (1999); Cartwright (1997, 1999, 2001) for further discussion of the inductive approach.

[208](Spirtes *et al.*, 1993)

[209](Pearl, 2000, p. 50)

[210](Spirtes *et al.*, 1993, §5.4.2)

Causal Markov Condition Each variable in V is probabilistically independent of its non-effects conditional on its direct causes;

Minimality No proper subgraph on V of the causal graph on V satisfies the Causal Markov Condition;

Faithfulness The only probabilistic independencies among V are those derivable from the causal graph via the Causal Markov Condition;

Causal Sufficiency all common causes of variables in V are themselves in V.

Note that Faithfulness implies Minimality in the presence of the Causal Markov Condition. Faithfulness is a very strong assumption: there may be no graph which captures all and only the independencies satisfied by the database distribution, and if there is, there is rarely any guarantee that it will coincide with the causal graph. The PC algorithm has been modified to deal with situations in which Causal Sufficiency fails, but this modification does not always work.[211] In such cases the PC algorithm has been superseded by the *FCI algorithm* (where FCI stands for Fast Causal Inference), which is at least asymptotically correct—assuming of course the Causal Markov Condition and Faithfulness.[212]

Judea Pearl advocates a constraint-based approach very similar to that of Spirtes, Glymour and Scheines.[213] Pearl takes causal models to be structural equation models, thereby assuming the Causal Markov Condition.[214] By invoking Occam's razor, Pearl argues that when inducing causal models from data one ought to infer only minimal models—so Minimality is also assumed—in which case one can infer that A causes B if and only if A causes B in every minimal causal graph that implies (via the the Causal Markov Condition) the independencies in the data.[215] Finally Faithfulness and Causal Sufficiency must also be satisfied to guarantee that induced causal models latch on to genuine causal relationships. Verma and Pearl put forward the *IC algorithm* (IC standing for Inductive Causation) to perform the induction,[216]although Pearl subsequently advocated use of the PC algorithm with two extra substitutions appended to the final step:[217]

- repeatedly substitute:
  ...
  (iii) $A \longrightarrow B$ for $A - B$ if there are two chains $A - C \longrightarrow B$ and $A - D \longrightarrow B$ with C and D not adjacent;
  (iv) $A \longrightarrow B$ for $A - B$ if there is a chain $A - C \longrightarrow D \longrightarrow B$ with C and B not adjacent.

[211](Spirtes *et al.*, 1993, §§6.2, 6.3)
[212](Spirtes *et al.*, 1993, §6.7)
[213](Pearl, 2000, chapter 2)
[214](Pearl, 2000, §2.2)
[215](Pearl, 2000, §2.3)
[216](Verma and Pearl, 1990)
[217](Pearl, 2000, §2.5)

Then the modified PC algorithm will find all the arrows that correspond to inferable causal relations. If Causal Sufficiency fails, the IC algorithm can be further modified to identify possible unmeasured (or 'latent') variables, but guarantees of correctness are weaker than before.[218]

8.5 Bayesian Induction

The Bayesian approach to inducing causal relationships was developed by Cooper, Heckerman, Herskovitz, and Meek.[219] The basic idea here is to induce the causal graph $\mathcal{C}$ that maximises the posterior probability

$$p(\mathcal{C}|D) = \frac{p(\mathcal{C})p(D|\mathcal{C})}{\sum_{\mathcal{C}'} p(\mathcal{C}')p(D|\mathcal{C}')},$$

where D is a database of observed past case data. Now

$$p(D|\mathcal{C}) = \int p(D|\mathcal{C}, \mathcal{S}_{\mathcal{C}})p(\mathcal{S}_{\mathcal{C}})d\mathcal{S}_{\mathcal{C}}$$

with the integral over probability specifications $\mathcal{S}_{\mathcal{C}}$ that would accompany $\mathcal{C}$ in a Bayesian net. (Note that this approach requires that p be defined not only over variables in V, but over causal graphs, probability specifications and databases too.) Assuming the Causal Markov Condition, $\mathcal{C}$ and $\mathcal{S}_{\mathcal{C}}$ form a Bayesian net from which one can calculate $p(D|\mathcal{C}, \mathcal{S}_{\mathcal{C}})$. To further aid calculation, it is assumed that probability specifiers are themselves probabilistically independent and that their prior distribution takes the form of a Dirichlet distribution.[220]

Despite the adoption of these simplifying assumptions, the Bayesian approach can be computationally intractable,[221] and the constraint-based methods of §8.4, the information-theoretic methods of §8.6 or greedy approaches similar to the adding-arrows method of §3.5 tend to be preferred in practice.

8.6 Information-Theoretic Induction

One strategy for inducing causal relations from data involves first defining a *scoring function* that attaches a score to each causal model given the data, and then searching for the causal model with the highest score (or lowest score, depending on whether the scoring function gives higher or lower scores to better models). The posterior probability $p(\mathcal{C}|D)$ can be thought of as a Bayesian scoring function, for instance.

Often a scoring function will favour models that fit the data best and which are simplest, maintaining some kind of balance between these two desiderata. Under the information-theoretic approach, the simplicity of a hypothesis is measured in terms of its optimal description length while its fit with data is measured

[218] (Pearl, 2000, §2.6)

[219] (Cooper and Herskovits, 1992; Heckerman *et al.*, 1999)

[220] See Heckerman *et al.* (1999) for the details.

[221] See Chickering (1996) and Heckerman *et al.* (1999, §3).

in terms of the length of a description of the data using the hypothesis (a hypothesis that fits the data well can be exploited to provide a short description of the data).

The *Minimum Description Length* (MDL) approach takes causal models to be causal nets (and thus takes the Causal Markov Condition for granted) and aims to find the causal net that minimises sum of the length of a description of the net and the length of a description of the data.[222] The description length of the net is measured by:

$$DL(\mathcal{C}, \mathcal{S}) = \sum_{i=1}^{n} [|Par_i| \log_2 n + d(||A_i|| - 1)||Par_i||] ,$$

where d is the number of bits required to describe a numerical value (one must specify each of the $|Par_i|$ parents of each variable A_i, taking $\log_2 n$ bits, and then each of its $(||A_i||-1)||Par_i||$ probability specifiers,[223] taking d bits). Information theory tells us that to optimally encode the database we need to construct the code using the probability distribution p^* of the data.[224] The best estimate of this distribution is the distribution p determined by the induced causal model. If we use this induced distribution then the description length of an encoding of the database is approximately

$$\begin{aligned} DL(D, \mathcal{C}, \mathcal{S}) &= -k \sum_{v} p^*(v) \log_2 p(v) \\ &= k\,[H(p^*) + d(p^*, p)] , \end{aligned}$$

where as usual H is entropy and d is cross-entropy distance. The aim is then to find the causal net that minimises the total description length $DL(\mathcal{C}, \mathcal{S}) + DL(D, \mathcal{C}, \mathcal{S})$. One can adapt the adding-arrows technique for minimising cross entropy (§3.5) to provide a greedy search for the MDL causal net, as follows.[225] For each number $j = 0, \ldots, n(n-1)/2$ of arrows that a causal graph on V may contain, use the methods of §3.5 to search for a Bayesian net with exactly j arrows whose induced probability function p is closest to the target function p^* (in terms of cross entropy distance). Then for each of these $n(n-1)/2+1$ nets determine the total description length, selecting the net which minimises this value.

The *Minimum Message Length* (MML) approach is very similar to MDL.[226] The aim is still to find the causal model that minimises the description of the model and the data. But under the MML approach a causal model is construed as

[222] (Rissanen, 1978; Lam and Bacchus, 1994*a*)

[223] There are $||A_i||||Par_i||$ specifiers $p(a_i|par_i)$ in the probability table of variable A_i, but these are determined by additivity from the values of $(||A_i|| - 1)||Par_i||$ specifiers.

[224] (Cover and Thomas, 1991, §5; Lam and Bacchus, 1994*a*, §3.2)

[225] (Lam and Bacchus, 1994*a*, §4)

[226] (Wallace and Boulton, 1968; Wallace and Korb, 1999; Korb and Nicholson, 2003, §8.5)

a structural equation model whose error terms have a Gaussian distribution and whose variables are totally ordered by temporal priority.[227] Thus the MML approach also takes the Causal Markov Condition for granted. The MML approach takes the message length of a hypothesis H to be

$$ML(H) = -\log p(H)$$

and the message length of the data given a hypothesis to be

$$ML(D, H) = -\log p(D|H)$$

and the aim is to minimise total message length

$$ML(H) + ML(D, H) = -\log p(D|H)p(H) = -\log p(DH),$$

which is equivalent to the Bayesian approach of maximising $p(H|D)$ in the case in which all databases have the same prior probability $p(D)$.[228] A hypothesis H is a group of causal models that differ in only minor ways: two models are part of the same hypothesis if they differ only with respect to the inclusion of small effects, with respect to the total order of the variables, or if they are equivalent with respect to implied independencies.[229] A hypothesis is induced using a *Markov Chain Monte Carlo* algorithm—the algorithm moves from one hypothesis to another randomly in such a way that each hypothesis is visited with frequency $p(DH)$, and it outputs the hypothesis which receives most visits after a fixed number of steps.[230]

8.7 Shafer's Causal Conjecturing

Glenn Shafer developed an account of causal inference as a part of his programme to provide a new framework for probability theory: the framework of probability trees, defined over Moivrean events (which are subsets of a sample space), Humean events (which are instantaneous events) and corresponding variables.[231] Many of the principal ideas can be imported into our framework as follows.

One can construct a tree of possible values of a sequence of repeatable variables: a dummy root node branches to the possible values of the first variable, each of whose values branch to the possible values of the second variable, and so on. For example, consider the sequence of variables (B, T) where B concerns John's betting behaviour and takes assignments b and b' signifying 'bets on heads' and 'refuses to bet' respectively, and T concerns a coin toss and takes assignments h for 'heads occurs' and t for 'tails occurs' respectively; the corresponding

[227](Wallace and Korb, 1999, §7.3). The MML approach has also been applied to causal models construed as causal nets whose variables are totally ordered—Korb and Nicholson (2003, §8.6.5).

[228](Wallace and Korb, 1999, §7.2)

[229](Wallace and Korb, 1999, §7.5)

[230](Wallace and Korb, 1999, §§7.6–7.7; Korb and Nicholson, 2003, §8.6)

[231](Shafer, 1996, 1999)

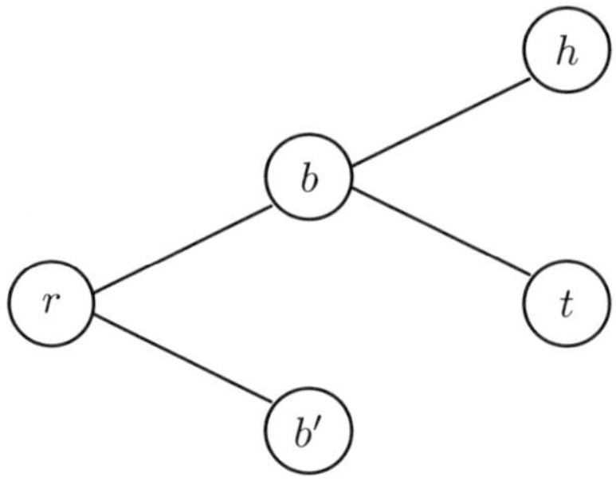

FIG. 8.1. A tree constructed from a sequence of variables.

tree is depicted in Fig. 8.1 (the root node is called r). A *probability tree* is then constructed by labelling each edge with the probability of the assignment that the edge leads to, conditional on the assignments between it and the root. Thus the edge between b and h in Fig. 8.1 is labelled by $p(h|b)$.

A node in a probability tree is called a *situation*. A situation can be identified with the pathway that leads up to it, represented by the assignment of values along that pathway. Thus the node at the top right of Fig. 8.1 can be represented by the assignment bh.[232]

Shafer accepts a version of the Principle of the Common Cause.[233] He argues that the causal independence of two variables implies that they are probabilistically independent, conditional on each situation;[234] conversely, probabilistic dependence implies causal dependence. Shafer distinguishes three kinds of causal connection, 'linear sign', 'scored sign', and 'tracking', the first two being useful in the context of using regression to predict the expected value of a variable and the latter applied to the more general problem of determining the probability of a variable.[235] In the case of tracking, the direct causes of a variable screen it off from its situation: this is just the Causal Markov Condition in the probability tree framework.[236] While Shafer's framework is rather radical, the techniques he proposes for inferring causal relationships are more traditional: causal relations are discovered by performing randomised experiments and using linear regression techniques.[237]

[232]Note that Shafer also identifies a situation with the set of pathways in the tree going through that node—see Shafer (1996, §2.1).

[233](Shafer, 1996, §5.3)

[234](Shafer, 1996, §5.1; Shafer, 1999, §2.3)

[235](Shafer, 1999, §2.4)

[236]The relationship between the Causal Markov Condition and the probability tree framework is further discussed in Shafer (1996, Proposition 15.3 and §15.5).

[237](Shafer, 1996, §§14.5–14.6)

8.8 The Devil and the Deep Blue Sea

Unfortunately neither Popper's hypothetico-deductive approach nor the recent inductivist proposals from AI offer a viable account of the discovery of causal relationships. Popper's hypothetico-deductive approach suffers from underspecification: the hypothesis of causal relationships remains a mystery and Popper's proposals for deducing predictions from hypotheses were woefully simplistic. On the other hand, the key shortcoming of the inductive approach is this: given the counterexamples to the Causal Markov Condition of Chapter 4 the inductive approach cannot guarantee that the induced causal model or class of causal models will tally with causality as we understand it—the causal models that result from the inductive approach will satisfy the Causal Markov Condition, but the true causal picture may not. While this objection may put paid to the dream of using Causal Markov formalisms for learning causal relationships via a purely inductive method, neither the formalisms nor the inductive method should be abandoned because, as we shall see in §9.6, Causal Markov methods are a special case of a new framework for inducing a causal model from data. In §9.9 we shall see that this inductive framework features as the first step in a modified hypothetico-deductive account of causal discovery.

9

EPISTEMIC CAUSALITY

In this chapter, I shall present an account of causality which coheres well with the objective Bayesian interpretation of probability adopted in Chapter 5, and which motivates a new approach to the problem of discovering causal relationships.

9.1 Mental yet Objective

Epistemic causality embodies the following position. The causal relation is mental rather than physical: a causal structure is part of an agent's representation of the world, just as a belief function is, and causal claims do not directly supervene on mind-independent features of the world.[238] But causality is objective rather than subjective: some causal structures are more warranted than others on the basis of the agent's background knowledge, so if two people disagree about what causes what, one may be right and the other wrong. Thus epistemic causality sits between a wholly subjective mental account and a physical account of causality, just as objective Bayesianism sits between strict subjectivism and physical probability.

Consider by way of example a topological graph such as the London tube map. The nodes signify tube stations and the arcs refer to collections of train lines between those stations. Thus the interpretation of the graph consists of physical mind-independent things. On the other hand an association graph, in which the nodes signify words and two nodes are linked if an agent associates those words with each other, is a subjective entity since two agents are likely to construct quite different association graphs yet neither be wrong in any sense. A causal graph, according to the epistemic theory, occupies an intermediate position. The nodes refer to physical events (or whatever the relata of causality are) and an arrow signifies that one node is a direct cause of another. These arrows have no physical interpretation—instead a causal graph embodies an agent's way of representing these events. Yet this graph is not arbitrary: there is a sense in which causal claims are correct or incorrect.

While epistemic causality and objective Bayesianism both occupy the middle ground between physical and subjective positions, there is an important difference between the two views which concerns attitudes to physical interpretations. It is relatively uncontroversial that there is a viable physical notion of probability (although the viability of a physical concept of chance has been questioned, it is straightforward to show that various versions of the frequency theory satisfy the

[238] Of course this is not to say that the mental cannot be reduced to, or does not itself supervene on, the physical.

axioms of probability). In contrast it is by no means clear that there is a viable physical notion of causality. Thus there are two routes open to the proponent of epistemic causality. One can adopt an epistemic interpretation of cause but keep an open mind about the viability of a physical interpretation. On the other hand one might argue that there is no need for a physical notion of cause given an epistemic interpretation, and that failure of attempts to produce such a notion show that there simply is none—I shall call this the *anti-physical* position.

The origins of epistemic causality can be attributed to Immanuel Kant and Frank Ramsey, who were both anti-physicalists. It will be instructive to examine their views to see their reasons for their positions.

9.2 Kant

To understand Kant's position we must first turn to David Hume, who argued that causal connection is not a feature of the external world:

> It appears that, in single instances of the operation of bodies, we never can, by our utmost scrutiny, discover any thing but one event following another; without being able to comprehend any force or power by which the cause operates, or any connexion between it and its supposed effect. ... One event follows another; but we never can observe any tie between them. They seem *conjoined*, but never *connected*.[239]

Causal connection is instead a mental phenomenon:

> But when one particular species of event has always, in all instances, been conjoined with another, we make no longer any scruple of foretelling one upon the appearance of the other, and of employing that reasoning, which can alone assure us of any matter of fact or existence. We then call the one object, *Cause*; the other, *Effect*. We suppose that there is some connexion between them; some power in the one, by which it infallibly produces the other, and operates with the greatest certainty and strongest necessity. It appears, then, that this idea of a necessary connexion among events arises from a number of similar instances which occur of the constant conjunction of these events; nor can that idea ever be suggested by any one of these instances, surveyed in all possible lights and positions. But there is nothing in a number of instances, different from every single instance, which is supposed to be exactly similar; except only, that after a repetition of similar instances, the mind is carried by habit, upon the appearance of one event, to expect its usual attendant, and to believe that it will exist. This connexion, therefore, which we *feel* in the mind, this customary transition of the imagination from one object to its usual attendant, is the sentiment or impression from which we form the idea of power or necessary connexion. Nothing farther is in the case. Contemplate the subject on all sides; you will never find any other origin of that idea.[240]

[239] (Hume, 1748, paragraph 58)
[240] (Hume, 1748, paragraph 59)

However, Hume did not analyse cause in terms of this mental connection, believing that the notion was not well-enough understood. Instead he offered a reduction of cause to physical facts:

> Yet so imperfect are the ideas which we form concerning it, that it is impossible to give any just definition of cause, except what is drawn from something extraneous and foreign to it. Similar objects are always conjoined with similar.[241]

Kant was quick to pick up on the shortcomings of this reduction:

> Now it is easy to show that there actually are in human knowledge judgements which are necessary and in the strictest sense universal, and which are therefore pure *a priori* judgements. If an example from the sciences be desired, we have only to look to any of the propositions of mathematics; if we seek an example from the understanding in its quite ordinary employment, the proposition, 'every alteration must have a cause', will serve our purpose. In the latter case, indeed, the very concept of cause so manifestly contains the concept of a necessity of connection with an effect and of the strict universality of the rule, that the concept would be altogether lost if we attempted to derive it, as Hume has done, from a repeated association of that which happens with that which precedes, and from a custom of connecting representations, a custom originating in this repeated association, and constituting therefore a merely subjective necessity.[242]

For Kant, cause is not a physical concept:

> To the synthesis of cause and effect there belongs a dignity which cannot be empirically expressed, namely, that the effect not only succeeds upon the cause, but that it is posited *through* it and arises *out of* it.[243]

But Kant also steers away from a subjective conception of cause, in as much as he recognises that causal information is not arbitrary:

> The concept of cause, for instance, which expresses the necessity of an event under a presupposed condition, would be false if it rested only on an arbitrary subjective necessity, implanted in us, of connecting certain empirical representations according to the rule of causal relation. I would not then be able to say that the effect is connected with the cause in the object, that is to say necessarily, but only that I am so constituted that I cannot think this representation otherwise than as thus connected. This is exactly what the sceptic most desires. For if this be the situation, all our insight, resting on the supposed objective validity of our judgements, is nothing but sheer illusion; nor would there be wanting people who would refuse to admit this subjective necessity, a necessity which can only be felt. Certainly a man cannot dispute with anyone regarding that which depends merely on the mode in which he is himself organised.[244]

[241](Hume, 1748, paragraph 60)

[242](Kant, 1781, B4–5)

[243](Kant, 1781, B124)

[244](Kant, 1781, B168)

One task for any epistemic account of causality is to explain why causality is not an arbitrary notion. Kant does this by appealing to his theory of a priori intuitions: space, time, and the law of causality are representations, lenses that we look through to systematise the world,

> We can extract clear concepts of them from experience, only because we have put them into experience, and because experience is thus itself brought about only by their means.[245]

9.3 Ramsey

In another era, Bertrand Russell's position resembled that of Hume. Russell argued that causal connection is not a physical notion: 'the reason why physics has ceased to look for causes is that, in fact, there are no such things.'[246] Like Hume, Russell believed that the concept of causality hinges on the notion of necessity and the production of an effect by a cause, and that these ideas are so unintelligible that the only option is to eliminate causality in favour of dealing with functional equations.[247]

Frank Ramsey was not satisfied and adopted an epistemic approach, as Kant had before him. He argued that while it is tempting to reduce cause to constant conjunction, a causal law is not simply a conjunction:

> when we regard it as a proposition capable of the two cases of truth and falsity, we are forced to make it a conjunction, and to have a theory of conjunctions which we cannot express for lack of symbolic power.
>
> [But what we can't say we can't say, and we can't whistle it either.]
>
> If then it is not a conjunction, it is not a proposition at all; and then the question arises in what way it can be right or wrong.[248]

Ramsey came up with two concepts of causality in order to answer this question. His original idea was that causal laws are 'consequences of those propositions which we should take as axioms if we knew everything and organised it as simply as possible in a deductive system.'[249] However, he later dropped that theory in favour of the view that 'a causal generalisation is not, as I then thought, one which is simple, but one we trust ... we may trust it because it is simple, but that is another matter.'[250] A causal law is more than a constant conjunction since 'we trust it to guide us in a new instance'.[251]

Ramsey provides a kind of counterfactual account of causality. But not the usual type of counterfactual account which implies that were the cause C to occur then the effect E would occur. Indeed as Ramsey noted it is easy to doubt

[245] See Kant (1781, B241).
[246] (Russell, 1913, p. 1)
[247] (Russell, 1913)
[248] (Ramsey, 1929, p. 146)
[249] (Ramsey, 1929, p. 150)
[250] (Ramsey, 1929, p. 150)
[251] (Ramsey, 1929, p. 151)

whether such a statement has any empirical content.[252] Instead, Ramsey presents an epistemic counterfactual account according to which a causal law is a human disposition: if C causes E is part of an agent's knowledge and the agent were to learn C then she would be disposed to believe E. Thus the agent's degree of belief in E conditional on C is high.[253]

Ramsey's view is that causal laws cannot be eliminated as Hume and Russell suggest, because they are useful in their capacity as dispositions: (note that in Ramsey's theory causal laws are one type of 'variable hypothetical')

> We can begin by asking whether these variable hypotheticals play an essential part in our thought; we might, for instance, think that they could simply be eliminated and replaced by the primary propositions which serve as evidence for them. ... But this would, I think, be wrong; apart from their value in simplifying our thought, they form an essential part of our mind. That we think explicitly in general terms is at the root of all praise and blame and much discussion. We cannot blame a man except by considering what would have happened if he had acted otherwise, and this kind of unfulfilled conditional cannot be interpreted as a material implication, but depends essentially on variable hypotheticals.[254]

Ramsey argued that these causal dispositions are mental rather than physical:

> The world, or rather that part of it with which we are acquainted, exhibits as we must all agree a good deal of regularity of succession. I contend that over and above that it exhibits no feature called causal necessity, but that we make sentences called causal laws from which (i.e. having made which) we proceed to actions and propositions connected with them in a certain way, and say that a fact asserted in a proposition which is an instance of causal law is a case of causal necessity. This is a regular feature of our conduct, a part of the general regularity of things; as always there is nothing in this beyond the regularity to be called causality, but we can again make a variable hypothetical about this conduct of ours and speak of it as an instance of causality.[255]

Ramsey, like Kant, wants to eliminate any arbitrariness, but he proffers a different account:

> if two systems both fit the facts, is not the choice capricious? We do, however, believe that the system is uniquely determined and that long enough investigation will lead us all to it. This is Peirce's notion of truth as what everyone will believe in the end; it does not apply to the truthful statement of matters of fact, but to the 'true scientific system'.[256]

[252] (Ramsey, 1929, p. 161)
[253] (Ramsey, 1929, p. 154)
[254] (Ramsey, 1929, pp. 153–154)
[255] (Ramsey, 1929, p. 160)
[256] (Ramsey, 1929, p. 161)

9.4 The Convenience of Causality

The following doctrines provide perhaps the most natural motivation for epistemic causality:

Convenience It is convenient to represent the world in terms of cause and effect.

Explanation Humans think in terms of cause and effect because of this convenience, not because there is something physical corresponding to cause which humans experience.

An anti-physical position, moreover, would make the further claim that there is no physical causal relation: by the explanation doctrine, a physical interpretation of causality is superfluous and unwarranted.

That causality is convenient explains why it is not arbitrary: roughly speaking if two agents have differing causal pictures then the superior convenience of one would explain its correctness. Hence the proponent of this type of epistemic causality is like the instrumentalist philosopher of science who argues that science offers an empirically fruitful systematisation and counts as knowledge even though some of its terms may not refer.

In this section, I will try to shed some light on the convenience of causality, but I will also have a few words to say on the explanation doctrine. Section 9.5 and subsequent sections will address a more formal characterisation of epistemic causality.

The thought that we have a notion of cause because it yields a convenient representation of knowledge can be found in the writings of Judea Pearl:[257]

> Human beings exhibit an almost obsessive urge to mold empirical phenomena conceptually into cause-effect relationships. The tendency is, in fact, so strong that it sometimes comes at the expense of precision and often requires the invention of hypothetical, unobservable entities (such as the ego, elementary particles, and supreme beings) to make theories fit the mold of causal schemata. When we try to explain the actions of another person, for example, we invariably invoke abstract notions of mental states, social attitudes, beliefs, goals, plans, and intentions. Medical knowledge, likewise, is organized into causal hierarchies of invading organisms, physical disorders, complications, syndromes, clinical states, and only finally, the visible symptoms.What are the merits of these fictitious variables called *causes* that make them worthy of such relentless human pursuit, and what makes causal explanations so pleasing and comforting once they are found? We take the position that human obsession with causation, like many other psychological compulsions, is computationally motivated. Causal models are attractive mainly because they provide effective data structures for representing empirical knowledge—

[257]This is Pearl's position as of 1988. He later changed his mind and adopted a physical concept of cause by reducing causal structure to systems of functional equations (Pearl, 2000). Pearl's latter position is compared with epistemic causality in Williamson (2004*a*).

> they can be queried and updated at high speed with minimal external supervision.[258]

Pearl makes two claims: that causes and effects themselves are often fictitious, and that humans represent the world causally because such a representation is computationally convenient. It is the latter idea that I wish to pursue here.

Pearl argues that causal models are convenient because they convey important information about relevance and irrelevance. Furthermore,

> In probability theory, the notion of informal relevance is given quantitative underpinning through the device of *conditional independence*, which successfully captures our intuition about how dependencies should change in response to new facts.[259]

By assuming the Causal Markov Condition Pearl shows that a causal graph conveys information about conditional independencies, and that by augmenting a causal graph with probabilities to form a Bayesian net, it offers a powerful mechanism for making predictions, diagnoses, and strategic decisions.

However, there are two significant problems with Pearl's explication of the convenience of causality.

The first difficulty is that Pearl's causal calculus seems too complicated to account for the utility of causality. Pearl develops a formalism, or computational model, not an informal account of human reasoning. Further work needs to be done before the explanation doctrine is justified: one must argue that the convenience of the formalism explains why informal human causal reasoning is effective, and is effective enough to account for us having a notion of cause. Pearl was optimistic that the formalism would provide a model of how humans actually reason, that the brain somehow incorporates Bayesian networks.[260] However, there is little evidence to lend substance to this hope.[261] A better strategy might be just to argue that informal causal reasoning often approximates formal causal reasoning, and the validity of the latter explains the effectiveness of the former. One can make an analogy here with the justification of informal deductive reasoning: it was not until formal systems of logic and their properties had been extensively studied that a convincing explanation for the effectiveness (and limitations) of informal deductive reasoning could be offered. For example one can argue that informal deductive reasoning is effective because it loosely approximates natural deduction in the first order predicate calculus which is sound and complete. Likewise one can argue that informal causal reasoning is effective because it loosely approximates reasoning via causal graphs and Bayesian nets, inference in which is sound and complete with respect to implied independencies and probability judgements respectively. The difficulty with this type of explanation is that it is hard to characterise informal reasoning. One problem is that

[258] (Pearl, 1988, p. 383)

[259] (Pearl, 1988, p. 80)

[260] (Pearl, 1988, §5.1)

[261] Research by Tversky and Kahneman (1977) may even be construed as evidence against this claim.

different people reason rather differently, and another is that reasoning changes with the years: for instance probabilistic judgements play a far greater role in informal causal inference these days than they did say in the nineteenth century. While careful empirical studies might provide scope for pursuing this line of argument, there is nothing like a compelling case at present.[262]

The second problem with Pearl's account of convenience is his reliance on the Causal Markov Condition. We saw in Chapters 4 and 6 that the Causal Markov Condition admits counterexamples and is only really plausible under an objective Bayesian account of probability where background knowledge takes a suitable form. This does not seem to be what Pearl has in mind: he argues in favour of the Causal Markov Condition as a generally valid condition holding with respect to physical probability, not as merely a default condition holding of rational belief.

So while Pearl was right to stress the convenience of causality, his account of this convenience is at best incomplete, at worst implausible.

I suggest instead that the convenience of causality can be accounted for by some rather weak principles. While we saw in §7.3 that the Causal Dependence condition of §4.3 does not always hold, the counterexamples were rather contrived and the condition does appear to hold much of the time. Hence,

Qualified Causal Dependence Normally causal relations are accompanied by probabilistic dependencies.

Strategy Normally, instigating causes is a good way to achieve their effects. On the other hand instigating effects is not normally a good way to bring about their causes.

This latter condition is the motivation behind the agency account of causality (§7.5), and provides an account of the asymmetry of causality.

While these principles are on their own too weak and imprecise to constitute a probabilistic or agency analysis of causality, they are strong enough to provide a foundation for epistemic causality, since they are strong enough to render the concept of cause useful. The concept of cause is useful because a causal connection is (i) a reliable (though not fully reliable) indicator of a probabilistic dependence, and thus allows us to make predictions and diagnoses, and (ii) helpful for making strategic decisions.

These two conditions are simple enough to explain why we think in terms of cause and effect—we do not have to posit a human faculty for reasoning with D-separation and Bayesian nets, just a human faculty for associating dependencies and strategies with causal relations. Yet they are powerful enough to yield a formal calculus, as we shall now see.

[262] Glymour (2001) sketches some directions that this type of research programme might take. See also Glymour (2003). Gopnik *et al.* (2004) claim that 'Children's causal learning and inference may involve computations similar to those for learning causal Bayes nets and for predicting with them' (p. 3), but others have argued that humans have a limited capacity for inferring causal relationships from observed probabilistic independencies and that temporal and agency considerations play a more prominent role—see e.g. Lagnado and Sloman (2004).

9.5 Causal Beliefs

Objective Bayesianism maintains that an agent's rational degrees of belief are determined by her background knowledge. In §5.8 we considered background knowledge that takes the form of causal constraints κ and probabilistic constraints π. We saw that the degrees of belief that the agent ought to adopt, represented by probability function $p_{\kappa,\pi}$, are determined by first by transferring causal constraints κ into new probabilistic constraints π' and then finding the most non-committal probability function that satisfies π' and π by maximising entropy.

Epistemic causality can make an analogous move: the causal beliefs that an agent ought to adopt are determined by her background knowledge. Given background knowledge consisting of a set κ of causal constraints and a set π of probabilistic constraints, an agent ought to adopt a causal graph $\mathcal{C}_{\kappa,\pi}$, determined from κ and π, as a representation of her causal beliefs. The agent's epistemic state thus contains her background knowledge κ, π, her degrees of belief $p_{\kappa,\pi}$ and her causal beliefs $\mathcal{C}_{\kappa,\pi}$.[263]

How then is $\mathcal{C}_{\kappa,\pi}$ to be determined from κ and π? The situation is again analogous to that of objective Bayesianism, which advocates choosing the most non-committal (i.e. the maximum entropy) probability function $p_{\kappa,\pi}$ that satisfies the constraints imposed by background knowledge κ, π. Here we need to choose the most non-committal causal graph $\mathcal{C}_{\kappa,\pi}$ that satisfies κ, π. This leaves two questions: How can a causal graph be non-committal? How does background knowledge constrain the choice of causal graph?

The first question can be given a straightforward answer. Each arrow in a causal graph asserts something about probabilistic dependencies (via the Qualified Causal Dependence principle) and about strategies (via the Strategy principle). A graph commits itself inasmuch as it makes such claims. So the most non-committal causal graph satisfying the constraints imposed by background knowledge is that with fewest arrows.

Next to the second question—how does background knowledge constrain the choice of causal graph? Clearly $\mathcal{C}_{\kappa,\pi}$ should satisfy all constraints in κ. But how does π bear on choice of $\mathcal{C}_{\kappa,\pi}$?

According to the Qualified Causal Dependence and Strategy principles, probabilistic knowledge π bears on causality to the extent that it contains information about dependencies and strategies. Now while causal relations are normally accompanied by probabilistic dependencies, that does not mean that probabilistic dependencies are normally accompanied by causal relations. Indeed in §4.2 we saw that while probabilistic dependencies can often be attributed to causal connections, they may also be attributed to other connections, such as connections through meaning, logical, mathematical or physical relations or boundary conditions, or they may be attributed not to connections at all but to isolated

[263] Note that while π might be derived from knowledge of physical probabilities via the calibration principle (§5.3), we do not assume there is such a thing as physical causality so we need to provide a rather different account as to the origins of causal constraints κ—see §9.8.

constraints, such as variation within time series in the example of British bread prices and Venetian sea levels. Nevertheless in many applications the following default rule may be appropriate: if background knowledge induces a probabilistic dependence, and the agent knows of no non-causal factors that explain the dependence, then she should attribute the dependence (or that much of the dependence that is unaccounted for) to causal relationships. It must be emphasised that this default rule is only plausible in applications where causal relations dominate. In mathematical applications, for instance, a dependency would by default indicate a non-causal relation (a logical, mathematical, or semantic relation), rather than a causal relation. Supposing though that this default rule is appropriate, what form of dependence is induced by a causal relation?

Qualified Causal Dependence asserts that Causal Dependence normally holds: normally a cause changes the probability of a direct effect when controlling for (i.e. conditional on) the direct effect's other causes. Such a dependency may be symmetric, however, since A may be dependent on B controlling for B's other causes and B may be dependent on A controlling for A's other causes. Yet causality is not symmetric and the Strategy principle picks up this asymmetry: if A causes B then intervening to change the value of A can change the value of B but intervening to change the value of B cannot change the value of A. An *intervention* (sometimes called a *divine intervention*) on A is a change in the value of A that is brought about without changing the values of any of A's direct causes in V.[264] Thus an intervention changes A via a causal pathway that is not captured by the modelling context V. For example, if $V = \{A, B\}$ and the only causal belief the agent has is $A \longrightarrow B$, then an intervention on A can be brought about using any causal mechanism (since there are no causes of A in V) but an intervention on B must be brought about without changing A. An intervention on A, then, involves holding fixed A's direct causes in V (or indeed some set of A's non-effects in V that includes A's direct causes in V).

We shall say then that there is a *strategic dependence* from A to B (or that B is *strategically dependent* on A), written $A \Rrightarrow B$, if A and B are probabilistically dependent when intervening on A and controlling for B's other causes, i.e. if $A \rightleftharpoons B \mid D_B \backslash A, C_A$ for some $D_A \subseteq C_A \subseteq NE_A$ (where D_B is the set of direct causes of B so $D_B \backslash A$ is the set of B's other causes, and NE_A is the set of A's non-effects, so C_A is a set of A's non-effects that includes its direct causes). Note that strategic dependencies do reflect the asymmetry of causality: it is not possible that A can be direct cause of B if B is a direct cause of A; similarly it is not possible that B can be strategically dependent on A if B is a direct cause of A, for otherwise $A \rightleftharpoons B | D_B \backslash A, C_A$ for some C_A containing B, which is trivially false.

Combining Strategy with Qualified Causal Dependence we get:

Strategic Causal Dependence Normally, if $A \longrightarrow B$ then $A \Rrightarrow B$.

[264]We make no assumption here that a divine intervention on A is always possible to carry out: clearly this is not the case if all ways of changing A are already included in V.

Moreover, it is only *direct* causal relations that explain strategic dependencies. Suppose A only indirectly causes B—then one would not expect $A \rightleftharpoons B \mid D_B \backslash A, C_A$ because now $D_B \backslash A = D_B$, i.e. all of B's direct causes are being controlled for, in particular, causes on all chains from A to B. Thus an indirect causal relation from A to B does not explain any strategic dependence $A \Rrightarrow B$. Similarly, if B is not an effect of A then one would not expect intervening on A to change B and any strategic dependence from A to B remains to be explained. Hence if a strategic dependence $A \Rrightarrow B$ is to be explained by a causal relation at all, it can only be $A \longrightarrow B$.

We now have a basis for a default rule: if background knowledge induces a strategic dependence from A to B, and the agent does not know of any non-causal inducer of this dependence, and a causal relation $A \longrightarrow B$ is compatible with causal knowledge, then she should attribute the dependence to a causal relation $A \longrightarrow B$. Note, however, that we are assuming that κ and π exhaust the agent's background knowledge, in which case the agent knows of no non-causal dependency-inducing relations at all. (One can relax this assumption by explicitly modelling any knowledge ν of non-causal dependency-inducing relations, in which case the following principle only applies for each strategic dependence not implied by ν—see §11.8.) Thus we get:

Probabilistic to Causal Transfer $\mathcal{C}$ satisfies κ and π if and only if $\mathcal{C}$ satisfies κ and κ' where probabilistic constraints π are transferred to causal constraints $\kappa' = \{A \longrightarrow B : A \Rrightarrow B$ for $p_{\kappa,\pi}$, and $A \longrightarrow B$ is consistent with $\kappa\}$.

Note that in order to determine whether $A \Rrightarrow B$, the set D_B of B's direct causes, the set D_A of A's direct causes and the set NE_A of A's non-effects must be determined from the constrained causal graph: $\mathcal{C}$ is defined in terms of $\mathcal{C}$ itself. Hence this Transfer principle is best viewed as a constraint on $\mathcal{C}$ as a whole rather than as an incremental way of adding arrows to produce $\mathcal{C}$. (The production of $\mathcal{C}$ will be discussed in §§9.6 and 9.9.)

In sum, then, given constraints κ, π, an agent should adopt, as a representation of her causal beliefs, a causal graph $\mathcal{C}_{\kappa,\pi}$ found by selecting, from all those directed acyclic graphs that satisfy the constraints (via the Probabilistic to Causal Transfer principle), a graph with fewest arrows.

9.6 Special Cases

In this section, we shall examine a couple of special cases of the formalism presented above.

κ is *strategically consistent* with π if κ does not block the transfer of strategic dependencies to arrows in the Probabilistic to Causal Transfer principle, i.e., if for each $\mathcal{C}$ satisfying κ and π, $A \Rrightarrow B$ implies $A \longrightarrow B$ in $\mathcal{C}$.

Theorem 9.1 *κ is strategically consistent with π if and only if, for each $\mathcal{C}$ satisfying κ and π the Causal Markov Condition holds (with respect to $p_{\kappa,\pi}$).*

Proof: Suppose $\mathcal{C}$ satisfies κ and π. First we show that if $A \Rightarrow B$ implies $A \longrightarrow B$, then the Causal Markov Condition holds. By Corollary 3.5, to prove the Causal Markov Condition it suffices to show that, assuming $V = \{A_1, \ldots, A_n\}$ is ordered ancestrally with respect to $\mathcal{C}$, $A_k \perp\!\!\!\perp A_1, \ldots, A_{k-1} \mid D_k$ for $k = 1, \ldots, n$ (writing D_i for D_{A_i}). We shall show by induction on $i = 1, \ldots, k-1$ that $A_k \perp\!\!\!\perp A_1, \ldots, A_i \mid D_k$.

First the base case $i = 1$. If $k = 1$ or $A_1 \in D_k$ then there is nothing to do. Otherwise $A_1 \not\longrightarrow A_k$ and so by assumption (i.e. $A \Rightarrow B$ implies $A \longrightarrow B$), $A_k \perp\!\!\!\perp A_1 \mid D_k \backslash A_1, C_1$ for each $D_1 \subseteq C_1 \subseteq NE_1$ (writing NE_i for NE_{A_i}). Now $D_k \backslash A_1 = D_k$ and $D_1 = \emptyset$ so in particular $A_k \perp\!\!\!\perp A_1 \mid D_k$.

Next the inductive step. It suffices to show that $A_k \perp\!\!\!\perp A_{i+1} \mid D_k, A_1, \ldots, A_i$ since by the inductive hypothesis $A_k \perp\!\!\!\perp A_1, \ldots, A_i \mid D_k$ and Contraction (§3.2) it then follows that $A_k \perp\!\!\!\perp A_1, \ldots, A_{i+1} \mid D_k$. If $A_{i+1} \in D_k$ there is nothing to do, otherwise $A_{i+1} \not\longrightarrow A_k$ and by assumption, $A_k \perp\!\!\!\perp A_{i+1} \mid D_k \backslash A_{i+1}, C_{i+1}$ for each $D_{i+1} \subseteq C_{i+1} \subseteq NE_{i+1}$. Now $D_k \backslash A_{i+1} = D_k$ and taking $C_{i+1} = \{A_1, \ldots, A_i\}$ we have that $A_k \perp\!\!\!\perp A_{i+1} \mid D_k, A_1, \ldots, A_i$ as required.

Conversely, we must show that if the Causal Markov Condition holds then $A \Rightarrow B$ implies $A \longrightarrow B$. To see this suppose $A \not\longrightarrow B$ in $\mathcal{C}$ but that $A \rightleftharpoons B | D_B \backslash A, C_A$ for some $D_A \subseteq C_A \subseteq NE_A$. Now if $B \not\leadsto A$ (B is not a cause of A), then by the contrapositive of Weak Union (§3.2) $A, C_A \rightleftharpoons B | D_B$ which contradicts the Causal Markov Condition since $\{A\} \cup C_A \subseteq NE_B$. On the other hand, if $B \leadsto A$ then by Weak Union $A \rightleftharpoons B, D_B, C_A \backslash D_A \mid D_A$ which contradicts the Causal Markov Condition since $\{B\} \cup D_B \cup C_A \backslash D_A \subseteq NE_A$. ■

Now to a second special case. κ is *strategically compatible* with π if any causal graph that satisfies π on its own (i.e. that satisfies π together with an empty set of causal constraints) also satisfies κ. Strategic compatibility implies strategic consistency.

Let $\mathbb{C}_{\kappa,\pi}$ be the set of minimal graphs satisfying κ, π, i.e., the set of rational causal graphs $\mathcal{C}_{\kappa,\pi}$. By Theorem 9.1,

Corollary 9.2 *If κ is strategically compatible with π then $\mathbb{C}_{\kappa,\pi}$ is the set of minimal graphs satisfying the Causal Markov Condition (with respect to $p_{\kappa,\pi}$).*

(Note that strategic consistency is not enough for Corollary 9.2: strategically consistent κ may posit causal relationships which do not appear in a minimal graph satisfying the Causal Markov Condition.)

As we saw in Chapter 8, many proposals for discovering causal relationships suggest constructing the minimal Bayesian net that best fits data. Corollary 9.2 provides a qualified justification of these proposals: *if* one adopts an epistemic view of causality and an objective Bayesian interpretation of probability, and *if* causal knowledge is strategically compatible with probabilistic knowledge, then the rational causal belief graphs are graphs in minimal Bayesian nets, and standard techniques for constructing minimal Bayesian nets can be applied to learning causal relations.

Since the Causal Markov Condition may hold with respect to the agent's causal belief graph and her degrees of belief, and since, as we saw in §§5.7 and 5.8, the Causal Markov Condition may hold with respect to the directed constraint graph and her degrees of belief, the question naturally arises as to the relationship between the agent's causal belief graph and the directed constraint graph.

Theorem 9.3 *Suppose that the undirected constraint graph is triangulated, that there are no constraint independencies and that κ is strategically compatible with π. Then the agent's causal belief graph $\mathcal{C}_{\kappa,\pi}$ can be set to the directed constraint graph $\mathcal{H}_\pi$.*

Proof: The directed constraint graph $\mathcal{H}_\pi$ satisfies the Causal Markov Condition with respect to $p_{\kappa,\pi}$ (Theorem 5.6, Theorem 5.3), and since there are no constraint independencies, no smaller graph has this property (Theorem 5.4). Hence by Corollary 9.2 $\mathcal{H}_\pi$ is a candidate for $\mathcal{C}_{\kappa,\pi}$. ■

This leads to a strategy for constructing the causal belief graph $\mathcal{C}_{\kappa,\pi}$ in the case where κ is strategically compatible with π: first construct the directed constraint graph $\mathcal{H}_\pi$, and then remove arrows from this graph to represent any constraint independencies until no more can be removed. (Conversely in cases where it is easy to determine $\mathcal{C}_{\kappa,\pi}$, this graph can be used instead of the directed constraint graph in a Bayesian net representation of $p_{\kappa,\pi}$—this will result in a more efficient representation if there are constraint independencies.)

Strategic compatibility has further consequences:

Theorem 9.4 *If κ is strategically compatible with π then for the agent's belief state $\mathcal{C}_{\kappa,\pi}, p_{\kappa,\pi}$, the following conditions hold:*
(i) $A \longrightarrow B$ if and only if $A \rightrightarrows B$,
(ii) Causal Dependence.

Proof: (i) $A \longrightarrow B$ implies $A \rightrightarrows B$ since by strategic compatibility and minimality the only arrows in $\mathcal{C}$ are those introduced by Probabilistic to Causal Transfer, and each of these corresponds to a strategic dependence. Conversely, by strategic compatibility and Probabilistic to Causal Transfer there is an arrow for each strategic dependence.[265]

(ii) Causal Dependence holds as follows. If $A \longrightarrow B$ then by part (i), $A \rightleftharpoons B \mid D_B\backslash A, C_A$ for some $D_A \subseteq C_A \subseteq NE_A$. By the contrapositive of Weak Union (§3.2), $A, C_A \rightleftharpoons B \mid D_B\backslash A$. Then by the contrapositive of Contraction, either $A \rightleftharpoons B \mid D_B\backslash A$ or $C_A \rightleftharpoons B \mid D_B\backslash A, A$. But the latter contradicts the Causal Markov Condition (which holds since by part (i) strategic compatibility implies strategic consistency), so $A \rightleftharpoons B \mid D_B\backslash A$, as required. ■

Notice that the Causal Markov Condition and Causal Dependence are posited of the agent's causal and probabilistic beliefs $\mathcal{C}_{\kappa,\pi}$ and $p_{\kappa,\pi}$, and are only default conditions inasmuch as they depend on κ being strategically consistent

[265]Hence Strategic Causal Dependence holds without exception.

and strategically compatible respectively with π. In particular, the conditions clearly cannot hold if the agent's causal and probabilistic background knowledge contains information contradicting them.

9.7 Uniqueness and Objectivity

The agent's causal beliefs $\mathcal{C}_{\kappa,\pi}$ are only objective inasmuch as they are uniquely determined by background knowledge κ, π. In the case of objective Bayesianism we saw that the belief function p is uniquely determined: the Calibration Principle constrains degrees of belief to lie within a closed convex set; in a closed convex set of probability functions there is a unique entropy maximiser. There is no such guarantee in the case of epistemic causality. For instance, if κ is strategically consistent with π and π implies that there are no probabilistic independencies among V then any complete directed acyclic graph on V will be a candidate for $\mathcal{C}_{\kappa,\pi}$, and there are $n!$ of these (where as usual $n = |V|$).

Objectivity, though, is a matter of degree. If $\mathcal{C}$ is uniquely determined by κ and π (the set $\mathbb{C}_{\kappa,\pi}$ of minimal graphs satisfying κ, π is a singleton) then we have full objectivity. At the other end of the spectrum if $\mathcal{C}$ can be any directed acyclic graph then we have no objectivity—the determination of $\mathcal{C}$ is fully subjective. In our framework we never have full subjectivity since by minimality if two graphs are in $\mathbb{C}_{\kappa,\pi}$ then they must have the same number of arrows. In this section we shall examine the extent to which the determination of $\mathcal{C}$ is objective, focussing on the case in which κ is strategically compatible with π.

There are results which suggest situations in which $\mathcal{C}_{\kappa,\pi}$ will be uniquely determined:

Theorem 9.5 *If κ provides a causal ordering of the variables and is strategically compatible with π then the following are equivalent:*
(i) $\mathcal{C}_{\kappa,\pi}$ is uniquely determined;
(ii) $p_{\kappa,\pi}$ satisfies the Intersection property of §3.2;
(iii) no two variables that depend on a third variable in V are equivalent, i.e., if $A \rightleftharpoons B, C$ then there is no bijection g such that $C = g(B)$ almost everywhere.[266]

Proof: (i) $\Leftrightarrow$ (ii). Assuming a fixed causal ordering of the variables, there is a unique minimal directed acyclic graph satisfying the Causal Markov Condition if and only if Intersection holds: this is shown in §5 of Armstrong and Korb (2003).

(ii) $\Leftrightarrow$ (iii). This shown in §6 of Armstrong and Korb (2003). ■

For example, the Intersection property is satisfied if $p_{\kappa,\pi}$ is strictly positive;[267] in that case under the assumptions of Theorem 9.5 on κ, $\mathcal{C}_{\kappa,\pi}$ is uniquely determined.

In general though, as pointed out above, $\mathbb{C}_{\kappa,\pi}$ will not be a singleton; we can analyse its composition using the following concepts.

[266] Some terminology: $C = g(B)$ *almost everywhere* if $C = g(B)$ for all values of B except perhaps those which have probability 0.

[267] (Pearl, 1988, §3.1.2)

Two directed acyclic graphs are *Markov equivalent* if they imply the same probabilistic dependencies via the Causal Markov Condition (see §3.2). Write $\mathcal{C} \sim \mathcal{C}'$ if $\mathcal{C}$ and $\mathcal{C}'$ are Markov equivalent and $[\mathcal{C}]$ for the Markov equivalence class $\{\mathcal{C}' : \mathcal{C}' \sim \mathcal{C}\}$ of $\mathcal{C}$.

The *skeleton* of a directed acyclic graph is the undirected graph formed by replacing arrows by undirected edges. A *v-structure* in a directed acyclic graph is a structure of the form $A \longrightarrow B \longleftarrow C$.

Theorem 9.6. (Verma and Pearl, 1990) *Directed acyclic graphs are Markov equivalent if and only if they have the same skeleton and the same v-structures.*

Thus a Markov equivalence class may be represented by an *essential graph*, a partially directed acyclic graph which contains an arrow from A to B iff every graph in the class contains that arrow and an (undirected) edge between A and B iff every graph in the class contains an arrow between A and B but graphs in the class differ as to the direction of the arrow.[268]

Proposition 9.7 *Suppose κ is strategically compatible with π. Then $\mathcal{C} \in \mathbb{C}_{\kappa,\pi}$ implies $[\mathcal{C}] \subseteq \mathbb{C}_{\kappa,\pi}$.*

Proof: Suppose $\mathcal{C} \in \mathbb{C}_{\kappa,\pi}$ and $\mathcal{C}' \sim \mathcal{C}$. By Markov equivalence, $\mathcal{C}'$ satisfies the Causal Markov Condition with respect to $p_{\kappa,\pi}$. By Theorem 9.6, all members of a Markov equivalence class have the same number of arrows, so $\mathcal{C}'$ is also minimal. Hence by Corollary 9.2, $\mathcal{C}' \in \mathbb{C}_{\kappa,\pi}$. ■

Hence (under the assumption of strategic compatibility) $\mathbb{C}_{\kappa,\pi}$ is a union of Markov equivalence classes, $\mathbb{C}_{\kappa,\pi} = [\mathcal{C}_1] \cup \cdots \cup [\mathcal{C}_M]$. The number of rational causal graphs $|\mathbb{C}_{\kappa,\pi}| = \sum_{i=1}^{M} |[\mathcal{C}_i]|$, so to get an idea of this number we need an idea of the number M of equivalence classes and the size of each equivalence class.

A directed acyclic graph $\mathcal{G}$ on V is *faithful* or *stable* with respect to a probability function p on V iff each independency of p is captured by $\mathcal{G}$ under the Markov Condition. If both the Markov Condition and Faithfulness hold then $\mathcal{G}$ represents all and only the independencies of p. p is *faithful* or *stable* if there is some directed acyclic graph $\mathcal{G}$ which is faithful with respect to p. Clearly,

Proposition 9.8 *If $p_{\kappa,\pi}$ is faithful then $M = 1$, i.e. $\mathbb{C}_{\kappa,\pi} = [\mathcal{C}]$ for some directed acyclic graph $\mathcal{C}$.*

In general though there is no guarantee that faithfulness will hold:

Example 9.9 (Pearl, 2000, §2.4). Suppose A, B, C can take values 0 or 1 and C takes value 1 if and only if A and B take the same value. Then each pair of variables is unconditionally independent but dependent conditional on the third variable. The three graphs of Figs 9.1–9.3 all satisfy the Causal Markov Condition here, but none are faithful: for instance Fig. 9.1 does not capture the unconditional independence between A and C.

[268] See Andersson *et al.* (1997).

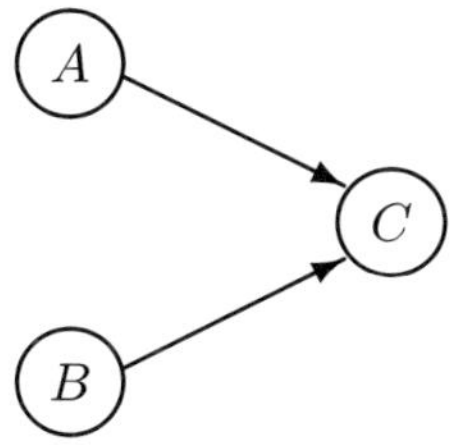

FIG. 9.1. Failure of faithfulness.

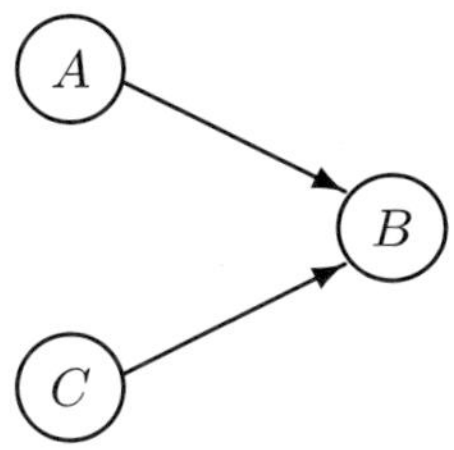

FIG. 9.2. Failure of faithfulness.

However, we can predict something about the faithfulness of $p_{\mathcal{K},\pi}$ on the basis of the techniques of §§5.6–5.8. There we saw that one can construct Markov and Bayesian net representations of $p_{\mathcal{K},\pi}$, that in the Markov net representation (an undirected analogue of) faithfulness will hold unless there are constraint independencies (i.e. constraints themselves force independencies),[269] and that in the Bayesian net representation faithfulness holds if it does in the Markov net and the Markov net is triangulated. Hence $M = 1$ unless there are constraint independencies or the undirected constraint graph is not triangulated.

Having discussed the number M of Markov equivalence classes in $\mathbb{C}_{\mathcal{K},\pi}$ we now turn to the sizes of these classes.

Gillispie and Perlman (2002) have a number of relevant numerical results in this respect. Given a domain of size n, the average number of elements of a Markov equivalence class, i.e. the number of directed acyclic graphs divided by the number of classes, tends to about 3.75 as n increases. About 27.4% of

[269]In fact $p_{\mathcal{K},\pi}$ may be faithful if constraints force independencies but the constraint graph itself will not be faithful to $p_{\mathcal{K},\pi}$.

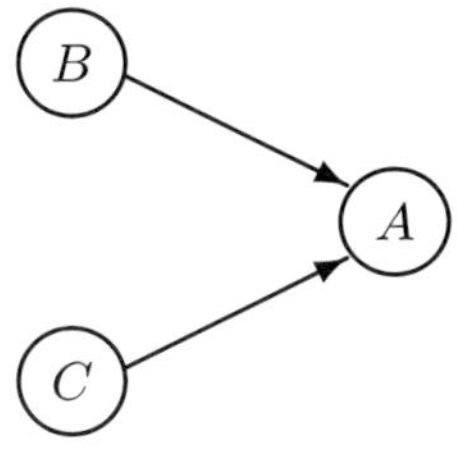

FIG. 9.3. Failure of faithfulness.

equivalence classes have only a single member. Now the space of directed acyclic graphs may not be representative of the space of causal graphs: causal graphs may normally be sparser than the average directed acyclic graph. However, the above figures appear to be fairly stable even if we bound the maximum number of parents a variable may have. Unless $k = 0$ or $k = 1$, the number of directed acyclic graphs whose variables have no more than k parents divided by the total number of directed acyclic graphs still appears to tend to about 4, (though there is too little numerical data to be very confident about this conclusion).

To sum up, investigations in this area—though admittedly very sketchy—suggest that epistemic causality is close to fully objective. There are a variety of natural situations in which $\mathcal{C}_{\kappa,\pi}$ will be uniquely determined from κ, π (Theorem 9.5). Failing that, in cases where faithfulness holds we should expect about four members of $\mathbb{C}_{\kappa,\pi}$: on average all but two of the arrows in $\mathcal{C}_{\kappa,\pi}$ will have their directions fully determined.

9.8 Causal Knowledge

An agent's degrees of belief $p_{\kappa,\pi}$ and causal beliefs $\mathcal{C}_{\kappa,\pi}$ are determined by her causal constraints κ and probabilistic constraints π imposed by background knowledge. As discussed in §5.3, the probabilistic constraints are imposed via the calibration principle. What constitutes causal knowledge and where do the constraints κ come from?

Of course we are not assuming that κ contains knowledge of physical causal relations, since we do not assume that there are such things as physical causal relations. But this is not to say that physical considerations play no part in κ: physical relationships may *constrain* causal relationships without *constituting* them.

Mechanisms, laws, and temporal considerations may impose constraints on causal relations, for example. Typically in science when one variable can induce a change in another we expect there to be some kind of mechanism linking the two quantities. (Here a mechanism is loosely interpreted as some sort of physical connection between two quantities, not in the precise sense of the transmission of conserved quantities discussed in §7.2.) Conversely, lack of any mechanism between two variables renders any causal connection between the two implausible. For example, before the germ theory of disease there was no known mechanism linking cadaverous matter and disease, and consequently there was widespread dismissal of Semmelweis' claim that the use of disinfectant after autopsy prevents death from puerperal fever in childbirth.[270] Thus the knowledge that there is no mechanism linking A and B may lead to the constraint that A and B are not causally connected, $A \not\rightsquigarrow B$ and $B \not\rightsquigarrow A$, in κ. Physical laws can have a bearing on causality too: if according to physical laws two entities are symmetric, then neither is the cause of the other, for causal relations are asymmetric and would serve to break the symmetry. Consider the particle example of §4.2: a particle

[270](Gillies, 2004)

decays into two parts, and the momentum M_1 of one determines the momentum M_2 of the other; if M_1 causes M_2 then by the symmetry of the problem M_2 causes M_1, which is not possible if causality is asymmetric. Thus symmetry of A and B can lead to a causal constraint of the form $A \not\rightsquigarrow B$ and $B \not\rightsquigarrow A$ in κ. If causality can only occur forwards in time then temporal knowledge will impose causal constraints: if B only occurs after A then $B \not\rightsquigarrow A$. For instance, if potting the ball occurs after it is struck, then the potting is not a cause of the striking.

While physical considerations tend to impose negative constraints, κ may also contain positive knowledge of causal relations: those of the agent's causal beliefs that are well tested and well entrenched in the agent's epistemic state. Obviously causal knowledge in this sense cannot figure in κ until the agent has some tried and tested causal beliefs; it cannot play a part in the formation of an initial causal belief graph.

To understand positive knowledge of causal relations we need a notion of causal relation that is not relativised to background knowledge. After Ramsey, we might understand such relations to be rational causal beliefs that are determined in the long run. (Just as objective probabilities are for de Finetti those degrees of belief determined in the long run after repeated conditionalisation—§2.8.) This idea of rational belief in the long run of course assumes that different agents will converge to the same beliefs in the long run—in the case of degrees of belief, de Finetti showed that this convergence occurs if agents' prior degrees of belief are exchangeable, and an analogous argument is needed in the case of epistemic causality. In the absence of such an argument the following option is more attractive.

In §2.8 we saw that Lewis provided a knowledge-independent objective single-case notion of probability by defining it to be those degrees of belief an agent ought to adopt were she to have all the relevant information in her background knowledge (apart from the probabilities themselves, of course). We can give a similar account of knowledge-independent objective causality by interpreting it as those causal beliefs that an agent ought to adopt were she to have all the relevant information as her background knowledge. Thus let κ^* include all physical constraints on causal relations (such as mechanistic, law-induced and temporal constraints) and π^* include all knowledge of chances (so that $p_{\kappa,\pi}$ is the chance function p^*), and suppose the agent also has full knowledge of non-causal dependency inducers (so that the only arrows added to the agent's causal belief graph via the Probabilistic to Causal Transfer principle correspond to strategic dependencies that are induced by causal relations). Then we can define the knowledge-independent *ultimate causal relations* on V to be the agent's causal belief graph $\mathcal{C}^* = \mathcal{C}_{\kappa^*,\pi^*}$. (If the domain V is taken to include all relevant variables, $V = V^*$, then we can also avoid relativising causal relations to domain.) Thus positive causal knowledge in an agent's causal background knowledge κ

can be interpreted as her knowledge of ultimate causal relations in $\mathcal{C}^*$.[271]

9.9 Discovering Causal Relationships: A Synthesis

In Chapter 8, we saw that Popper's account of causal discovery was hypothetico-deductive while most recent proposals are inductive. The epistemic view of causality developed in this chapter leads naturally to a hybrid of the hypothetico-deductive and inductive approaches, based on the following scheme:

Hypothesise A causal belief graph $\mathcal{C}_{\kappa,\pi}$ is induced from constraints κ and π;
Predict predictions are deduced from the hypothesised graph;
Test evidence is obtained to confirm or disconfirm the hypothesis;
Update the causal graph is updated in the light of the new evidence;

and the process continues by returning to the Predict phase.

This approach combines aspects of both the hypothetico-deductive and the inductive methods. The inductive method is incorporated in the first stage of the causal discovery process, Hypothesise. Here a causal graph is induced directly from background knowledge κ and π. However, one cannot be sure that the induced graph will represent the ultimate causal relations among the variables of interest, since background knowledge is only partial and may be imperfect. Hence the induced causal graph should be viewed as a tentative hypothesis, in need of evaluation, as occurs in the hypothetico-deductive method. Evaluation takes place in the Predict and Test stages. If the hypothesis is disconfirmed, rather than returning to the Hypothesise stage, changes are made to the causal graph in the Update stage, leading to the hypothesis of a new causal graph.

The Hypothesise stage requires a procedure for obtaining a causal graph from data. By Corollary 9.2 one can often utilise standard AI techniques, outlined in Chapter 8, for inducing a minimal causal graph that satisfies the Causal Markov Condition. It is worth pointing out that the first step of the inductive procedure, namely the choice of variables that are relevant to the question at stake, is often neglected in such accounts. A good strategy here seems to be simply to observe values of as many variables in the domain of interest as possible and rule out as irrelevant those that are uncorrelated with the key variables. For example in a study to determine whether a mother's vegetarianism causes smaller babies, 105 variables related to the women's nutritional intake, health, and pregnancy were measured and then the small subset of variables relevant to the key variables (vegetarianism and baby size) were determined statistically.[272]

The Predict step involves drawing predictions from an induced causal graph. Here Strategic Causal Dependence can be invoked—a direct causal relation will normally be accompanied by a strategic dependence. These predictions may not be invariable consequences of causal claims (otherwise the inductive method, and

[271] See Williamson (2004*a*) for further discussion of this ultimate belief interpretation of causal relations.

[272] (Drake *et al.*, 1998)

indeed a probabilistic analysis of causality, would be unproblematic) but might be expected to hold in most cases. From a Bayesian perspective the confirmation one should give to causal hypothesis $\mathcal{C}$ given an observed failure, f say, of the strategic dependence predictions from $\mathcal{C}$, is proportional to $p(f|\mathcal{C})$, the degree to which one expects the strategic dependence predictions to fail assuming $\mathcal{C}$ is correct, since Bayes' theorem gives $p(\mathcal{C}|f) = p(f|\mathcal{C})p(\mathcal{C})/p(f)$. Causal claims can be used to make other plausible (but not inevitable) predictions, by means of the physical indicators of causality mentioned in §9.8: causal relations are normally accompanied by mechanisms, cause and effect are not normally symmetric, and cause is normally temporally prior to effect.

The Test stage follows. The idea is first to collect more data—either by renewed observation or by performing experiments—in order to verify predictions made at the last stage, and second to use the new evidence and the predictions to evaluate the causal model. The hypothesised causal graph will dictate which variables must be controlled for when performing experiments. If some precise degree of confirmation is required, then, as indicated above, Bayesianism can provide this.

Finally the Update stage. It is not generally the degree of confirmation of the model as a whole which will decide how the causal model is to be restructured, but the results of individual tests of causal links. If, for instance, the hypothesised model predicts that C causes E, and an experiment is performed which shows that intervening to change the value of C does not change the distribution of E, controlling for E's other direct causes, then this evidence alone may be enough to warrant removing the arrow from C to E in the causal model. Finding out that the dependence between C and E is explained by a non-causal (e.g. logical) relationship between the variables might also lead to the retraction of the arrow from C to E. As degrees of belief calibrate better with chances, new strategic dependencies may become apparent; others may vanish; interventions which were hitherto impractical may be performed; if all direct causes of a variable are known an intervention becomes impossible. Improved knowledge of mechanisms may suggest removing arrows, while temporal considerations may warrant changing directions of arrows. The point is that the same procedures that were used to draw predictions from a causal model may be used to suggest alterations if the predictions are not borne out.

It is not hard to see how this approach might overcome the key shortcomings of the inductive and hypothetico-deductive methods. The key difficulty facing Causal Markov inductive methods is the possibility of failure of the Causal Markov Condition. But these methods have been replaced by the new inductive approach of §9.5, which figures in the Hypothesise stage, and which, as we saw in §9.6, generalises the Causal Markov methods, enabling causal relationships to be found even in cases where the Causal Markov Condition fails. The Hypothesise and Update stages give an account of the ways in which causal theories can be hypothesised, while the Predict and Test stages give a coherent story as to how causal theories should be evaluated, overcoming the problem of underspecification of the hypothetico-deductive method discussed in §8.2.

9.10 The Analogy with Objective Bayesianism

We have seen how epistemic causality and objective Bayesianism can be given a unified treatment. An agent's epistemic state contains degrees of belief together with causal beliefs. We idealise and represent these by a probability function and a directed acyclic graph respectively. Prior beliefs are those that satisfy background knowledge but are otherwise maximally non-committal. In the objective Bayesian case probabilistic background knowledge constrains degree of belief directly via the calibration principle, causal background knowledge constrains degree of belief indirectly via the Causal Irrelevance principle and Causal to Probabilistic Transfer, and the Maximum Entropy Principle is used to select the maximally non-committal probability function. In the case of epistemic causality, causal background knowledge constrains causal beliefs directly, probabilistic background knowledge constrains causal beliefs via Strategic Causal Dependence and Probabilistic to Causal Transfer, and minimality is used to select the maximally non-committal causal graph.

These prior beliefs are just beliefs—depending on the extent and reliability of initial data they may not correspond at all closely with chance and ultimate causal relations, in which case a process of calibration will need to take place if the beliefs are to be useful to the agent in her dealings with the world. As the agent obtains new data, mechanisms must be invoked to update prior beliefs into posterior beliefs. When objective Bayesian degrees of belief are represented using a Bayesian net, this leads to a two-stage methodology for using the Bayesian net. In the case of epistemic causality, this leads to a synthesis between the hypothetico-deductive and inductive accounts of discovering causal relationships.

This conception of belief formation and change is useful because it allows us to break a deadlock. On the one hand proponents of Causal Markov learning techniques cling to a purely inductive method despite the refutation of the Causal Markov Condition by counterexamples, even to the point of placing the condition beyond reproach.[273] On the other hand critics of the inductive method reject Causal Markov learning approaches outright on the basis of the Causal Markov counterexamples. The deadlock is broken by separating the Causal Markov learning techniques from the inductive method. The Causal Markov counterexamples provide reason to reject the inductive method, but learning techniques that rely on the Causal Markov Condition remain a valuable way of forming causal beliefs. When Causal Markov methods are applicable they form but the first, fallible step on the path to knowledge.

The objective Bayesian analogy also suggests a way to avoid inscrutable metaphysical questions about the nature of causality. Bayesianism has provided a purely epistemological framework in which to discuss the central issues surrounding probabilistic reasoning. By providing a degree-of-belief interpretation of

[273]Pearl (2000, p. 44): 'this Markov assumption is more a convention than an assumption'.

probability it has been able to avoid awkward concerns about the nature of mind-independent, single-case physical probabilities and in particular how we find out about them: the epistemology of an epistemic concept of probability is not so mysterious. Likewise by providing a causal-belief interpretation of causality we do not face questions about how causal relationships exist as mind-independent entities, and how we can come to know about such entities. By putting the epistemology first we can deal with causality as an epistemic, mental notion. We do not have to project our interpretation of nature onto nature itself, instead we can concentrate, as the prototypical inductivist Francis Bacon did, on methodology,

> our way and method (as we have often said clearly, and are happy to say again) is not to draw results from results or experiments from experiments (as the empirics do), but (as true Interpreters of Nature) from both results and experiments to draw causes and axioms, and from causes and axioms in turn to draw new results and experiments.[274]

And as with objective Bayesian probability, the epistemic view of causality does not render the concept subjective in the sense of being arbitrary or detached from worldly results:

> Human knowledge and human power come to the same thing, because ignorance of cause frustrates effect. For Nature is conquered only by obedience; and that which in thought is a cause, is like a rule in practice.[275]

Note though that the Bayesian analogy does not provide the whole story. One limitation of Bayesianism is its portrayal of the agent as a vessel receiving data, ignoring the fact that information is not just given to an agent, it must be gathered by the agent. Bayesianism tells an agent how she should update her degrees of belief on receipt of new evidence, but not what evidence to gather. But as Popper noted, it is not enough to say to an agent 'observe' and let her get on with it—the agent must use her beliefs to narrow her search for new evidence. Similarly a picture of causal belief change must shed some light on the gathering process; it should indicate which information to look for next. Thus the Predict and Test stages of §9.9, which do not appear in the standard Bayesian-style conception of belief change, are of vital importance.

The relationship between Bayesian nets and causality is more subtle than it might at first sight seem. The Causal Markov counterexamples show that causal relationships need not satisfy the Causal Markov Condition with respect to physical probability. On the other hand, we saw that there are circumstances in which degrees of belief satisfy the Causal Markov Condition with respect to causal background knowledge (§5.8) and causal beliefs (§9.6). This qualified justification of the Causal Markov Condition has methodological repercussions: a two-stage methodology for constructing Bayesian nets, and the qualified use of techniques for learning minimal Bayesian nets to learn causal relations.

[274](Bacon, 1620, §I.CXVII)
[275](Bacon, 1620, §I.III)

10

RECURSIVE CAUSALITY

In the final chapters of the book we turn to extensions and applications of the framework developed thus far. In this chapter, we extend Bayesian nets to cope with recursive causality. In Chapter 11, we see how Bayesian nets can be used to reason about logical relations, and finally in Chapter 12, we discuss how the framework might deal with changes in the domain V.

10.1 Overview

Causal relations can themselves take part in causal relations. The fact that smoking causes cancer (SC), for instance, causes government to restrict tobacco advertising (A), which helps prevent smoking (S), which in turn helps prevent cancer (C). This causal chain is depicted in Fig. 10.1, and further examples will be given in §10.2.

So causal models need to be able to treat causal relationships as causes and effects. This observation motivates an extension of the Bayesian net causal calculus to allow nodes that themselves take Bayesian nets as values. This type of net will be called a *recursive Bayesian net* (§10.3).

Because a recursive Bayesian net makes causal and probabilistic claims at different levels of its recursive structure, there is a danger that the net might contradict itself. Hence, we need to ensure that the net is consistent, as explained in §10.4. In §10.5 we see that under a new Markov condition a recursive Bayesian net determines a joint probability distribution over its domain.

Section 10.6 contains a comparison of this approach with other generalisations of Bayesian nets, and in §10.7 we see by analogy with recursive Bayesian nets how recursive causality can be modelled in structural equation models. A similar analogy motivates the application of recursive Bayesian nets to a non-causal domain, namely the modelling of arguments (§10.8).

10.2 Causal Relations as Causes

It is almost universally accepted that causality is an asymmetric binary relation, but the question of what the causal relation relates is much more controversial: as mentioned in §4.1 the relata of causality have variously taken to be single-case

FIG. 10.1. SC: smoking causes cancer; A: tobacco advertising; S: smoking; C: cancer.

FIG. 10.2. R: interest rate reduction; B: borrowing; I: investment; E: economic boost.

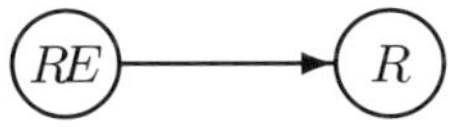

FIG. 10.3. RE: interest rate reduction causing economic boost; R: interest rate reduction.

events, properties, propositions, facts, sentences, and more. In this chapter we shall only add to the controversy, by dealing with cases in which causal relations themselves are included as relata of causality. The aim here is to shed light more on the processes of causal reasoning, especially formalisations of causal reasoning, than on the metaphysics of causality.

More generally we shall consider sets of causal relations, represented by causal graphs such as that of Fig. 10.1, as relata of causality. (A single causal relationship is then represented by a causal graph consisting of two nodes referring to the relata and an arrow from cause to effect.) If, as in Fig. 10.1, a causal graph $\mathcal{G}$ contains a causal relation or causal graph as a value of a node, we shall call $\mathcal{G}$ a *recursive causal graph* and say that it represents *recursive causality*.

Perhaps the best way to get a feel for the importance and pervasiveness of recursive causality is through a series of examples.

Policy decisions are often influenced by causal relations. As we have already seen, smoking causing cancer itself causes restrictions on advertising. Similarly, monetary policy makers reduce interest rates (R) because interest rate reductions boost the economy (E) by causing borrowing increases (B) which in turn allow investment (I). Here we have a causal chain as in Fig. 10.2 as a value of node RE in Fig. 10.3.

Policy need not be made for us: we often decide how we behave on the basis of perceived causal relationships. It is plausible that drinking red wine causes an increase in anti-oxidants which in turn reduces cholesterol deposits, and this apparent causal relationship causes some people to increase their red wine consumption. This example highlights two important points. First, it is a belief in the causal relationship which directly causes the policy change, not the causal relationship itself. The belief in the causal relationship may itself be caused by the relationship, but it may not be—it may be a false belief or it may be true by accident. Likewise, if a causal relationship exists but no one believes that it exists, there will be no policy change. Second, the policy decision need not be rational on the basis of the actual causal relationship that causes the decision: drinking red wine may do more harm than good.

A contract can be thought of as a causal relationship, and the existence of a contract can be an important factor in making a decision. A contract in which

FIG. 10.4. C: cocoa production; P: purchase.

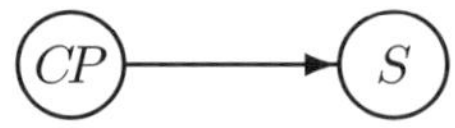

FIG. 10.5. CP: cocoa production causing payment; S school investment.

production of commodity C is purchased at price P may be thought of as a causal relationship $C \longrightarrow P$, and the existence of this causal relationship can in turn cause the producer to invest in further means of production, or even other commodities. For example, a Fair Trade chocolate company has a long-term contract with a cooperative of Ghanaian cocoa producers to purchase (P) cocoa (C) at a price advantageous to the producer as in Fig. 10.4. The existence of this contract (CP) allows the cooperative to invest in community projects such as schools (S), as in Fig. 10.5.

An insurance contract is an important instance of this example of recursive causality. Insuring a building against fire may be thought of as a causal relationship of the form 'insurance contract causes [fire F causes remuneration R]' or $[C \longrightarrow P] \longrightarrow [F \longrightarrow R]$ for short, where as before C is the commodity (i.e. the policy document) and P is payment of the premium. The existence of such an insurance policy can cause the policy holder to commit arson (A) and set fire to her building and thereby get remunerated: $[[C \longrightarrow P] \longrightarrow [F \longrightarrow R]] \longrightarrow A \longrightarrow F \longrightarrow R$. Causality in this relationship is nested at three levels. Insurance companies will clearly want to limit the probability of remuneration given that arson has occurred.

Thus we see that recursive causality is particularly pervasive in decision-making scenarios. However, recursive causality may occur in other situations too—situations in which it is the causal relationship itself, rather than someone's belief in the relationship, that does the causing. Pre-emption is an important case of recursive causality, where the pre-empting causal relationship prevents the pre-empted relationship: [poisoning causing death] prevents [heart failure causing death].[276] Context-specific causality may also be thought of recursively: a causal relationship that only occurs in a particular context (such as susceptibility to disease among immune-deficient people) can often be thought of in terms of the context causing the causal relationship.

Arguably prevention is sometimes best interpreted in terms of recursive causality: when taking mineral supplements prevents goitre, what is really happening is that taking mineral supplements prevents [poor diet causing goitre]—this is because there are other causes of goitre such as various defects of the thyroid gland, taking mineral supplements does not inhibit these causal chains and thus

[276]This seems to be a simpler and more natural way of representing pre-emption than the proposal of §§10.1.3, 10.3.3, 10.3.5 of Pearl (2000).

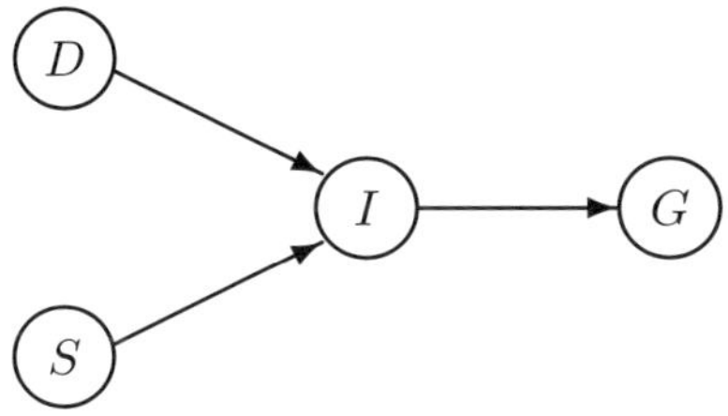

FIG. 10.6. D: poor diet; S: mineral supplements; I: iodine deficiency; G: goitre.

does not prevent goitre simpliciter. (In many such cases, however, the recursive nature can be eliminated by identifying a particular component of the causal chain which is prevented. Poor diet (D) causes goitre (G) via iodine deficiency (I), and mineral supplements (S) prevent iodine deficiency and so this example might be adequately represented by Fig. 10.6, which is not recursive. Of course the recursive aspect cannot be eliminated if no suitable intermediate variable I is known to the modeller.)

Recursive causality is clearly a widespread phenomenon. The question now arises as to how recursive causality can be treated more formally. In §10.3 causal nets are extended to cope with recursive causality and then in §§10.4 and 10.5 we shall examine two key characteristics of these extended causal models, their consistency and their ability to represent probability functions.

10.3 Extension to Recursive Causality

As noted in §10.2, causal relationships often act as causes or effects themselves. In a causal net, however, the nodes tend to be thought of as simple variables, not complex causal relationships. Thus we need to generalise the concept of causal net so that nodes in its causal graph $\mathcal{G}$ can signify complex causal relationships. On the other hand, we would like to retain the essential features of ordinary Bayesian nets, namely the ability to represent joint distributions efficiently, and the ability to perform probabilistic inference efficiently.

The essential step is this: we shall allow variables to take Bayesian nets as values. If a variable takes Bayesian nets as values we will call it a *network variable* to distinguish it from a *simple variable* whose values do not contain such structure. Thus S, which signifies 'payment of subsidy to farmer' and takes value *true* or *false* is a simple variable. (We shall write s^1 for the assignment $S = true$ and s^0 for $S = false$.) An example of a network variable is A, which stands for 'agricultural policy' and which has assignment a^1 to a value which is the Bayesian net containing the graph of Fig. 10.7 and the probability specification $\{p_{a^1}(f^1) = 0.1, p_{a^1}(s^1|f^1) = 0.9, p_{a^1}(s^1|f^0) = 0.2\}$, where F is a simple variable signifying 'farming', or assignment a^0 to Bayesian net with graph of Fig. 10.8 and specification $\{p_{a^0}(f^1) = 0.1, p_{a^0}(s^1) = 0.2\}$. Interpreting these nets causally, a^1 implies that A is a policy in which farming causes subsidy and a^0 implies that A is a policy in which there is no such causal relationship. For simplicity,

FIG. 10.7. Graph of a^1: farming causes subsidy.

FIG. 10.8. Graph of a^0: no causal relationship between farming and subsidy.

we shall consider network variables with at most two values, but the theory that follows applies to network variables which take any finite number of values.

A *recursive Bayesian net* is then a Bayesian net containing at least one network variable. A *recursive causal net* is a recursive Bayesian net with a causal interpretation: the graph in the net and the graphs in the values of the network variables are all interpreted as depicting causal relationships. For example the network with graph Fig. 10.9 and specification $\{p(l^1) = 0.7, p(a^1|l^1) = 0.95, p(a^1|l^0) = 0.4\}$, representing the causal relationship between lobbying and agricultural policy, is a recursive causal net, where the simple variable L stands for 'lobbying' and takes value *true* or *false*, and A is the network variable signifying 'agricultural policy' discussed above.

We shall allow network variables to take recursive Bayesian nets (as well as the standard Bayesian nets of §3.1) as values. In this way a recursive Bayesian net represents a hierarchical structure.

If a variable C is a network variable then each variable that occurs as a node in a Bayesian net that is a value of C is called a *direct inferior* of C, and each such variable has C as a *direct superior*. *Inferior* and *superior* are the transitive closures of these relations: thus E is inferior to C if and only if it is directly inferior to C or directly inferior to a variable D that is inferior to C. The variables that occur in the same local network as C are called its *peers*.

A recursive Bayesian net $(\mathcal{G}, \mathcal{S})$ conveys information on a number of levels. The variables that are nodes in $\mathcal{G}$ are *level 1*; any variables directly inferior to level 1 variables are *level 2*, and so on. The network $(\mathcal{G}, \mathcal{S})$ itself can be thought of as a value of a network variable B, and we can speak of B as the *level 0 variable*. (We have not specified the other possible values of B: for concreteness we can suppose that B is a single-valued network with b^0 the only possible assignment $B = (\mathcal{G}, \mathcal{S})$.) The *depth* of the network is the maximum level attained by a variable. A Bayesian net is *non-recursive* if its depth is 1; it is *well-founded* if its depth is finite. We shall restrict our discussion to *finite* nets: well-founded nets whose levels are each of finite size.

For $i \geq 0$ let V_i be the set of level i variables, and let $\mathcal{G}_i$ and $\mathcal{S}_i$ be the set of

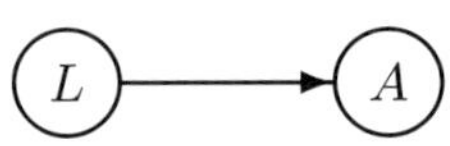

FIG. 10.9. Lobbying causes agricultural policy.

graphs and specifications respectively that occur in nets that are values of level i variables. Thus $V_0 = \{B\}, \mathcal{G}_0 = \{\mathcal{G}\}$, and $\mathcal{S}_0 = \{\mathcal{S}\}$. The domain of the recursive net is the set $V = \bigcup_i V_i$ of variables at all levels.

Note that V contains the level 0 variable B itself and thus contains all the structure of the recursive net. In our example, $V = \{B, L, A, F, S\}$ where the level 0 network variable B takes value whose graph is Fig. 10.9 and whose probability specification is $\{p(l^1) = 0.7, p(a^1|l^1) = 0.95, p(a^1|l^0) = 0.4\}$ and the only other network variable is A with assignment a^1 to a value that has graph of Fig. 10.7 and specification $\{p_{a^1}(f^1) = 0.1, p_{a^1}(s^1|f^1) = 0.9, p_{a^1}(s^1|f^0) = 0.2\}$ and assignment a^0 to a value that has graph of Fig. 10.8 and specification $\{p_{a^0}(f^1) = 0.1, p_{a^0}(s^1) = 0.2\}$; then V itself determines all the structure of the recursive Bayesian net in question. Consequently we can talk of 'recursive Bayesian net $(\mathcal{G}, \mathcal{S})$ on domain V' and 'recursive Bayesian net of V' interchangeably.

A network variable A_i can be thought of as a simple variable A'_i if one drops the Bayesian net interpretation of each of its values: A'_i is the *simplification* of A_i. A recursive net $(\mathcal{G}, \mathcal{S})$ can then be interpreted as a non-recursive net $(\mathcal{G}, \mathcal{S})'$ on domain $V'_1 = \{A'_i : A_i \in V_1\}$: then $(\mathcal{G}, \mathcal{S})'$ is called the *simplification* of $(\mathcal{G}, \mathcal{S})$.

A variable may well occur more than once in a recursive Bayesian net, in which case it might have more than one level.[277] Note that in a well-founded network no variable can be its own superior or inferior. A recursive causal net makes causal and probabilistic claims at all its various levels, and if variables occur more than once in the network, these claims might contradict each other. We shall examine this possibility now.

10.4 Consistency

A recursive causal net $(\mathcal{G}, \mathcal{S})$ can be interpreted as making causal and probabilistic claims about the world. At level 1 it asserts the causal relations in $\mathcal{G}$, the probabilistic independence relationships one can derive from $\mathcal{G}$ via the Causal Markov Condition, and the probabilistic claims made by the probability specification $\mathcal{S}$. But it makes claims at other levels too: for each network variable A_i in its domain, precisely one of its possible values (with its causal relationships, probabilistic independencies and probabilities) must be the case. A recursive causal net is consistent if these claims do not contradict each other.

In order to give a more precise formulation of the consistency requirement we need first to define consistency of non-recursive causal nets. There are three desiderata: consistency with respect to causal claims (*causal consistency*), consistency with respect to implied probabilistic independencies (*Markov consis-*

[277]While one might think that there will be no repetition of variables if all variables correspond to single-case events, this is not so. Single-case A causing single-case B causes an agent to change her belief about the relationship between A and B, this belief being represented by network variable C with B causing A in one value with A causing B in another value. Here A and B occur more than once in the net but are not repeatably instantiatable variables—they are single-case.

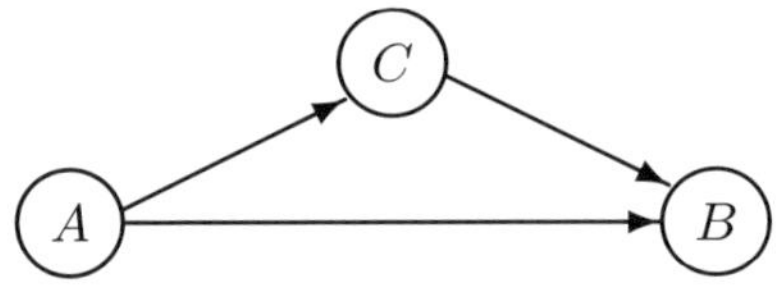

FIG. 10.10. Consistency example.

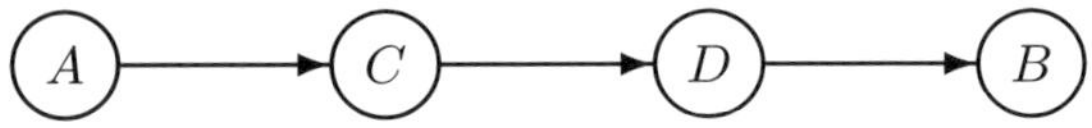

FIG. 10.11. Consistency example.

tency), and consistency with respect to probabilistic specifiers (*probabilistic consistency*).

First causal consistency. Recall from §3.2 that a chain $A \rightsquigarrow B$ from node A to node B is a graph on sequence of nodes beginning with A and ending with B such that there is an arrow from each node to its successor and no other arrows (the chain is *in* $\mathcal{G}$ if it is a subgraph of $\mathcal{G}$). A *subchain* of a chain c from A to B is a chain from A to B involving nodes in c in the same order, though not necessarily all the nodes in c. Thus Fig. 10.10 contains both the chain $A \longrightarrow C \longrightarrow B$ and its subchain $A \longrightarrow B$. The *interior* of a chain $A \rightsquigarrow B$ is defined as the subchain involving all nodes between A and B in the chain, not including A and B themselves.

The restriction $\mathcal{G}_{\downharpoonright W}$ of causal graph $\mathcal{G}$ defined on variables V to the set of variables $W \subseteq V$ is defined as follows: for variables $A, B \in W$, there is an arrow $A \longrightarrow B$ in $\mathcal{G}_{\downharpoonright W}$ if and only if $A \longrightarrow B$ is in $\mathcal{G}$ or, $A \rightsquigarrow B$ is in $\mathcal{G}$ and the variables in the interior of this chain are in $V \backslash W$. Thus $\mathcal{G}$ and $\mathcal{G}_{\downharpoonright W}$ agree as to the causal relationships among variables in W. It is not hard to see that for $X \subseteq W \subseteq V, \mathcal{G}_{\downharpoonright W \downharpoonright X} = \mathcal{G}_{\downharpoonright X}$.

Two causal graphs $\mathcal{G}$ on V and $\mathcal{H}$ on W are *causally consistent* if there is a third (directed and acyclic) causal graph $\mathcal{F}$ on $U = V \cup W$ such that $\mathcal{F}_{\downharpoonright V} = \mathcal{G}$ and $\mathcal{F}_{\downharpoonright W} = \mathcal{H}$. Thus $\mathcal{G}$ and $\mathcal{H}$ are causally consistent if there is a model $\mathcal{F}$ of the causal relationships in both $\mathcal{G}$ and $\mathcal{H}$. Such an $\mathcal{F}$ is called a *causal supergraph* of $\mathcal{G}$ and $\mathcal{H}$.

Figures 10.11 and 10.12 are causally consistent for instance, because the latter graph is the restriction of the former to $\{A, B, C\}$. However, Fig. 10.10 is not causally consistent with Fig. 10.11: they do not agree as to the causal chains between A, B, and C. Similarly Figs 10.10 and 10.12 are causally inconsistent.

Note that if $\mathcal{G}$ and $\mathcal{H}$ are causally consistent and nodes A and B occur in both $\mathcal{G}$ and $\mathcal{H}$ then there is a chain $A \rightsquigarrow B$ in $\mathcal{G}$ if and only if there is a chain $A \rightsquigarrow B$

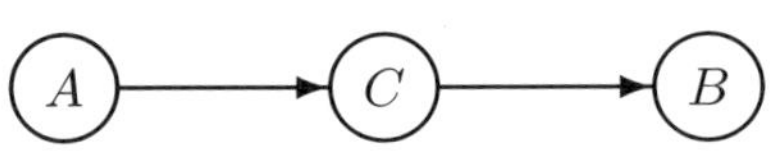

FIG. 10.12. Consistency example.

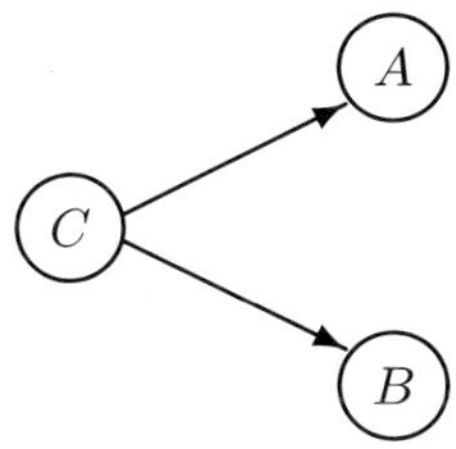

FIG. 10.13. Consistency example.

FIG. 10.14. Consistency example.

in $\mathcal{H}$. We will define two non-recursive causal nets to be *causally consistent* if their causal graphs are causally consistent.

The second important consistency requirement is Markov consistency. Two causal graphs $\mathcal{G}$ and $\mathcal{H}$ are *Markov consistent* if they posit (via the Causal Markov Condition) the same set of conditional independence relationships on the nodes they share. Figures 10.11 and 10.12 are Markov consistent because on their shared nodes A, C, B they each imply just that A and B are probabilistically independent conditional on C. Fig. 10.10 is not Markov consistent with either of these graphs because it does not imply this independency. Two non-recursive causal nets are *Markov consistent* if their causal graphs are Markov consistent.

Note that Markov consistency does not imply causal consistency: for instance two different complete graphs on the same set of nodes (graphs, such as Fig. 10.10, in which each pair of nodes is connected by some arrow) are Markov consistent, since neither graph implies any independence relationships, but causally inconsistent because where they differ, they differ as to the causal claims they make. Neither does causal consistency of a pair of causal graphs imply Markov consistency: Figs 10.13 and 10.14 are causally consistent but Fig. 10.14 implies that A and B are probabilistically independent, while Fig. 10.13 does not. In fact we have the following. Let $Com_{\mathcal{G}}(X)$ be the set of closest common causes of $X \subseteq V$ according to $\mathcal{G}$, that is, the set of causes C of X that are causes of at least two nodes A and B in X for which some pair of chains from C to A and C to B only have node C in common. Then,

Theorem 10.1 *Suppose $\mathcal{G}$ and $\mathcal{H}$ are causal graphs on V and W respectively. $\mathcal{G}$ and $\mathcal{H}$ are Markov consistent if they are causally consistent and their shared nodes are closed under closest common causes ('cccc' for short), $Com_{\mathcal{G}}(V \cap W) \cup$*

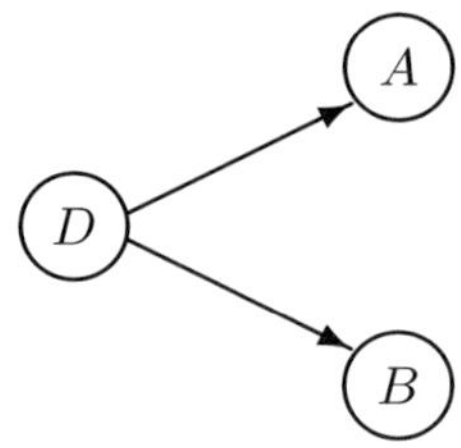

FIG. 10.15. Consistency example.

$Com_{\mathcal{H}}(V \cap W) \subseteq V \cap W$.

Proof: Suppose $X \perp\!\!\!\perp_{\mathcal{G}} Y \mid Z$ for some $X, Y, Z \subseteq V \cap W$. Then for each $A \in X$ and $B \in Y$, Z D-separates A from B in $\mathcal{G}$. $\mathcal{G}$ and $\mathcal{H}$ are causally consistent so there is a causal supergraph $\mathcal{F}$ on $V \cup W$ ($\mathcal{G} = \mathcal{F}_{\downharpoonright V}$ and $\mathcal{H} = \mathcal{F}_{\downharpoonright W}$). Now consider a path between A and B in $\mathcal{F}$. Such a path either (a) is a chain ($A \rightsquigarrow B$ or $B \rightsquigarrow A$), (b) contains some C where $C \rightsquigarrow A$ and $C \rightsquigarrow B$, or (c) contains a $\longrightarrow C \longleftarrow$ structure. In case (a) there must be in $\mathcal{G}$ a subchain of this chain which is blocked by Z so the original chain in $\mathcal{F}$ must also be blocked by Z. Similarly in case (b), since $\mathcal{G}$ and $\mathcal{H}$ are cccc there must be a blocked subpath in $\mathcal{G}$ which has $C \rightsquigarrow A$ and $C \rightsquigarrow B$. In case (c), either there is a corresponding subpath in $\mathcal{G}$ which is blocked, or C and its descendants are not in Z so the path in $\mathcal{F}$ is blocked in any case. Thus $X \perp\!\!\!\perp_{\mathcal{F}} Y \mid Z$. Next take the restriction $\mathcal{F}_{\downharpoonright W} = \mathcal{H}$. Paths between A and B in $\mathcal{H}$ must be blocked by Z since they are subpaths of paths in $\mathcal{F}$ that are blocked by Z and all variables in Z occur in $\mathcal{H}$. Thus $X \perp\!\!\!\perp_{\mathcal{H}} Y \mid Z$, as required. ∎

While (under the assumption of causal consistency) closure under closest common causes is a sufficient condition for Markov consistency, it is not a necessary condition: Figs 10.13 and 10.15 are Markov consistent because neither imply any independencies just among their shared nodes A and B, but the set of shared nodes is not cccc.

Markov consistency is quite a strong condition. It is not sufficient merely to require that the pair of causal graphs imply sets of conditional independence relations that are consistent with each other—in fact any two graphs satisfy this property. The motivation behind Markov consistency is based on Causal Dependence: a cause and its direct effect are usually probabilistically dependent conditional on the effect's other direct causes so probabilistic independencies that are not implied by the Causal Markov Condition are unlikely. For example, while the fact that C causes A and B (Fig. 10.13) is consistent with A and B being unconditionally independent (Fig. 10.14), it makes their independence unlikely: if A and B have a common cause then the occurrence of assignment a of A may be attributable to the common cause which then renders b more likely (less likely, if the common cause is a preventative), in which case A and B are unconditionally dependent. Thus Figs 10.13 and 10.14 are not compatible, and

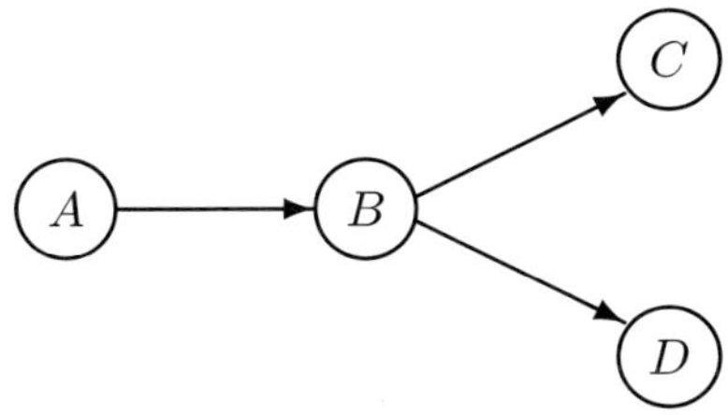

FIG. 10.16. B is the closest common cause of C and D.

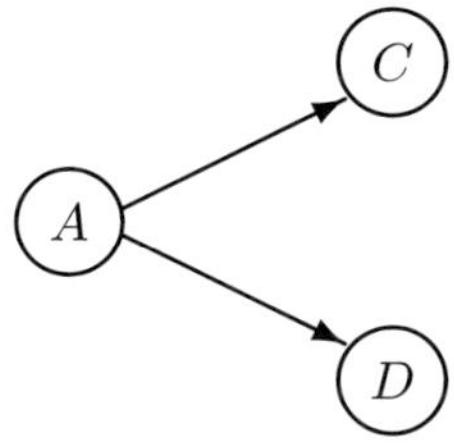

FIG. 10.17. A is the closest common cause of C and D.

we need the stronger condition that independence constraints implied by each graph should agree on the set of nodes that occur in both graphs.

Finally we turn to probabilistic consistency. Two causally consistent non-recursive Bayesian nets $(\mathcal{G}, \mathcal{S})$ and $(\mathcal{H}, \mathcal{T})$, defined over V and W respectively, are *probabilistically consistent* if there is some non-recursive Bayesian net $(\mathcal{F}, \mathcal{R})$, defined over $V \cup W$ and where $\mathcal{F}$ is a causal supergraph of $\mathcal{G}$ and $\mathcal{H}$, whose induced probability function satisfies all the equalities in $\mathcal{S} \cup \mathcal{T}$. Such a network is called a *causal supernet* of $(\mathcal{G}, \mathcal{S})$ and $(\mathcal{H}, \mathcal{T})$.

Lemma 10.2 *Suppose two non-recursive Bayesian nets $(\mathcal{G}, \mathcal{S})$ and $(\mathcal{H}, \mathcal{T})$ are causally consistent, probabilistically consistent and cccc. Then there is a causal supernet $(\mathcal{F}, \mathcal{R})$ of $(\mathcal{G}, \mathcal{S})$ and $(\mathcal{H}, \mathcal{T})$ that is cccc with $(\mathcal{G}, \mathcal{S})$ and $(\mathcal{H}, \mathcal{T})$.*

Proof: Because $(\mathcal{G}, \mathcal{S})$ and $(\mathcal{H}, \mathcal{T})$ are causally and probabilistically consistent, there is a supernet $(\mathcal{E}, \mathcal{Q})$, of $(\mathcal{G}, \mathcal{S})$ and $(\mathcal{H}, \mathcal{T})$. If $\mathcal{E}$ is cccc with $\mathcal{G}$ and $\mathcal{H}$ then we set $(\mathcal{F}, \mathcal{R}) = (\mathcal{E}, \mathcal{Q})$ and we are done. Otherwise, if $\mathcal{E}$ is not cccc with $\mathcal{G}$ say, then there is some Y-structure of the form of Fig. 10.16 in $\mathcal{E}$, where Fig. 10.17 is

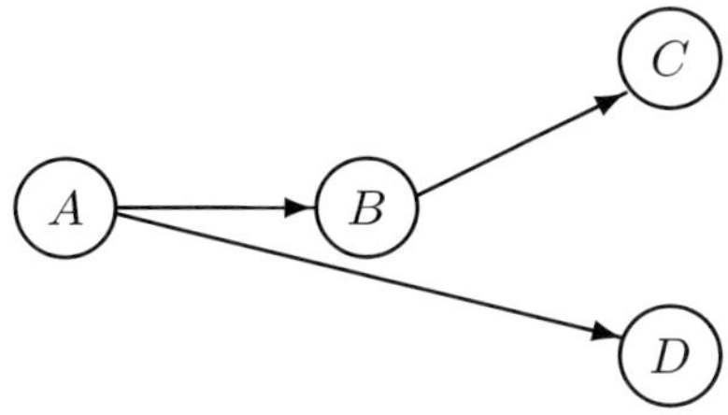

FIG. 10.18. A is the closest common cause of C and D.

the corresponding structure in $\mathcal{G}$. (In these diagrams take the arrows to signify the existence of causal chains rather than direct causal relations.) Note that B must be in $\mathcal{G}$ or $\mathcal{H}$, since the domain of a causal supergraph of $\mathcal{G}$ and $\mathcal{H}$ is the union of the domains of $\mathcal{G}$ and $\mathcal{H}$; B cannot be in $\mathcal{G}$ since otherwise by causal consistency the chain from A to C in $\mathcal{G}$ would go via B; hence B is in $\mathcal{H}$. Note also that not both of C and D can be in $\mathcal{H}$, for otherwise $\mathcal{G}$ and $\mathcal{H}$ are not cccc. Suppose then that D is not in $\mathcal{H}$. Then the chain from B to D is not in $\mathcal{G}$ or $\mathcal{H}$. Construct $\mathcal{F}$ by taking $\mathcal{E}$, removing the chain from B to D and including a chain from A to D, as in Fig. 10.18. (Do this for all such Y-structures not replicated in $\mathcal{G}$.) $\mathcal{F}$ remains a causal supergraph of $\mathcal{G}$ and $\mathcal{H}$, since the chain from B to $\mathcal{H}$ was redundant. Moreover $\mathcal{F}$ is now cccc with $\mathcal{G}$. Next construct the associated probability specification $\mathcal{R}$ by determining specifiers from $(\mathcal{E}, \mathcal{Q})$. Thus if the causal chain from A to D is direct we can set $p(d|a) = \sum_b p_{(\mathcal{E},\mathcal{Q})}(d|b)p_{(\mathcal{E},\mathcal{Q})}(b|a)$ in $\mathcal{R}$. It is not hard to see that $p_{(\mathcal{F},\mathcal{R})}$ agrees with $p_{(\mathcal{E},\mathcal{Q})}$ on the specifiers in $\mathcal{S}$ and $\mathcal{T}$ so the new net is also a causal supernet of $(\mathcal{G}, \mathcal{S})$ and $(\mathcal{H}, \mathcal{T})$. If $\mathcal{E}$ is not cccc with $\mathcal{H}$ then repeat this algorithm to yield a causal supernet of $(\mathcal{G}, \mathcal{S})$ and $(\mathcal{H}, \mathcal{T})$ that is cccc with $(\mathcal{G}, \mathcal{S})$ and $(\mathcal{H}, \mathcal{T})$. ■

Note that the requirement that $\mathcal{G}$ and $\mathcal{H}$ are cccc in the above result is essential. If $\mathcal{G}$ is Fig. 10.16 and $\mathcal{H}$ is Fig. 10.17 then there is no causal supergraph of $\mathcal{G}$ and $\mathcal{H}$ that is cccc with $\mathcal{G}$ and $\mathcal{H}$.

Theorem 10.3 *Suppose two non-recursive Bayesian nets are causally consistent, probabilistically consistent and cccc. Then they determine the same probability function over the variables they share.*

Proof: Suppose $(\mathcal{G}, \mathcal{S})$ and $(\mathcal{H}, \mathcal{T})$ are causally and probabilistically consistent and cccc. Then by Lemma 10.2 there is a causal supernet $(\mathcal{F}, \mathcal{R})$ that is cccc with both nets. By Theorem 10.1 $\mathcal{F}$ is Markov consistent with $\mathcal{G}$ and $\mathcal{H}$.

Next note that $(\mathcal{G}, \mathcal{S})$ and $(\mathcal{F}, \mathcal{R})$ determine the same probability function over variables $V = \{A_1, \ldots, A_n\}$ of $(\mathcal{G}, \mathcal{S})$:

$$p_{(\mathcal{G},\mathcal{S})}(v) = \prod_{i=1}^{n} p_{(\mathcal{G},\mathcal{S})}(a_i|par_i^{\mathcal{G}})$$

where $a_i@A_i$ and $par_i^{\mathcal{G}}@Par_i^{\mathcal{G}}$ are consistent with $v@V$,

$$= \prod_{i=1}^{n} p_{(\mathcal{F},\mathcal{R})}(a_i|par_i^{\mathcal{G}})$$

since $(\mathcal{F}, \mathcal{R})$ is a causal supernet of $(\mathcal{G}, \mathcal{S})$,

$$= \prod_{i=1}^{n} p_{(\mathcal{F},\mathcal{R})}(a_i|a_1, \ldots, a_{i-1}) = p_{(\mathcal{F},\mathcal{R})}(v),$$

where it is supposed that the variables $A_1, \ldots, A_n$ in V are ordered $\mathcal{G}$-ancestrally, i.e. no descendants of A_i in $\mathcal{G}$ occur before A_i in the order. This last step

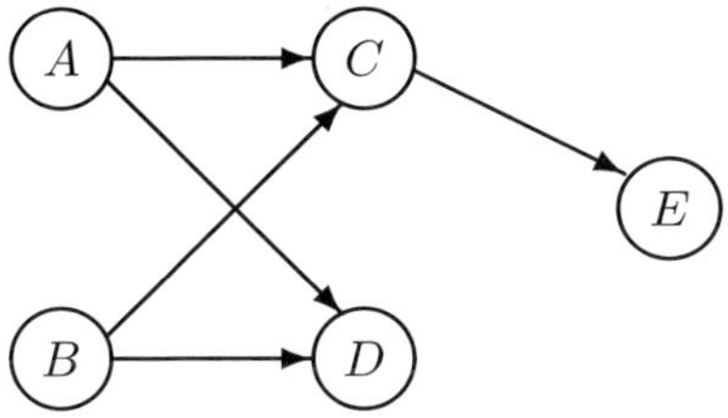

FIG. 10.19. Graph $\mathcal{G}_1$.

follows because $A_i \perp\!\!\!\perp_{\mathcal{G}} A_1, \ldots, A_{i-1} \mid Par_i^{\mathcal{G}}$ implies $A_i \perp\!\!\!\perp_{\mathcal{F}} A_1, \ldots, A_{i-1} \mid Par_i^{\mathcal{G}}$ by Markov consistency.

Similarly $(\mathcal{H}, \mathcal{T})$ and $(\mathcal{F}, \mathcal{R})$ determine the same probability function over the variables of $(\mathcal{H}, \mathcal{T})$. Hence $(\mathcal{G}, \mathcal{S})$ and $(\mathcal{H}, \mathcal{T})$ determine the same probability function over variables they share. ■

Because Theorem 10.3 is a desirable property in itself we shall adopt closure under closest common causes as a consistency condition. We shall say that two non-recursive nets are *consistent* if they are causally and probabilistically consistent, and cccc. By Theorem 10.1 consistency implies Markov consistency.

Having elucidated concepts of consistency for non-recursive nets, we can now say what it means for a recursive net to be consistent.

An assignment v of values to variables in V, the domain of a recursive causal net, assigns values to all simple variables and network variables that occur in V. Take for instance the recursive causal net of Fig. 10.9: here $V = \{B, L, A, F, S\}$ and $b^0l^1a^0f^1s^0$ is an example of an assignment to V. (Note that the level 0 variable B only has one possible assignment b^0.) Consider the assignments v gives to network variables in V. In our example, the network variables are B and A and these have assignments b^0 and a^0 respectively. Each assigned value is itself a recursive causal net, and when simplified induces a non-recursive causal net. Let $\underline{v}$ denote the set of recursive Bayesian nets induced by v (i.e. the set of values v assigns to network variables of V) and let $\underline{v}'$ denote the set of non-recursive Bayesian nets formed by simplifying the nets in $\underline{v}$.

Assignment v is *consistent* if each pair of nets in $\underline{v}'$ is consistent (i.e. if each pair of values of network variables is consistent, when these values are interpreted non-recursively). A recursive causal net is *consistent* if it has some consistent assignment v of values to V. A consistent assignment of values to the variables in a network can be thought of as a model or possible world, in which case consistency corresponds to satisfiability by a model.

In sum, if a recursive causal net is not to be self-contradictory there must be some assignment under which all pairs of network variables satisfy three regularity conditions: causal consistency, probabilistic consistency, and closure under closest common causes.

Note that it is easy to turn a recursive network into one that is causally

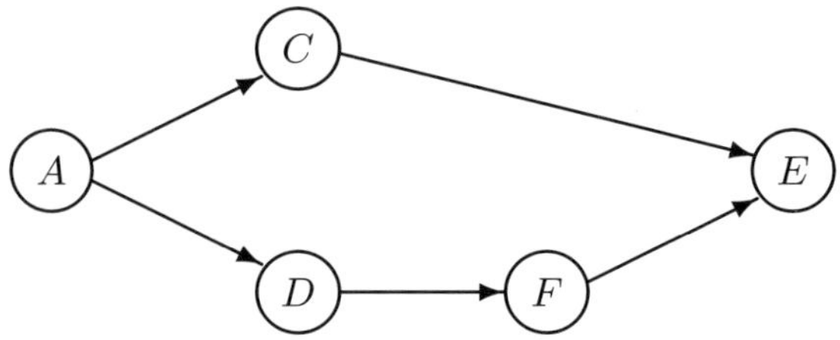

FIG. 10.20. Graph $\mathcal{G}_2$.

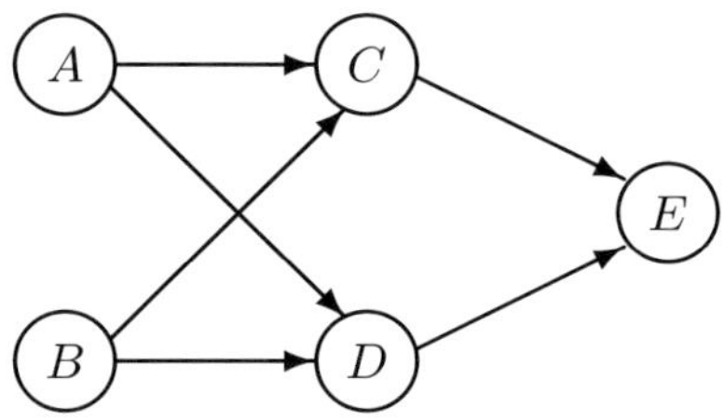

FIG. 10.21. Graph $\mathcal{H}_1$.

consistent, by ensuring that causal chains correspond for some assignment, and then cccc (and so Markov consistent), by ensuring that shared nodes of pairs of graphs also share closest common causes, for some assignment. For example, in order to make $\mathcal{G}_2$ in Fig. 10.20 causally consistent with graph $\mathcal{G}_1$ of Fig. 10.19, we need to introduce a chain that corresponds to the chain $D \longrightarrow F \longrightarrow E$ in $\mathcal{G}_2$, by adding an arrow from D to E in $\mathcal{G}_1$. In order to make $\mathcal{G}_2$ and $\mathcal{G}_1$ cccc (and so Markov consistent) we need to add B to $\mathcal{G}_2$ as a closest common cause of C and D. The modified graphs are depicted in Figs 10.21 and 10.22.

Similarly in practice one would not expect each probability specification to be provided independently and then to have the problem of checking consistency—one would expect to use conditional distributions in one specification to determine distributions in others. For example, a probability specification on $\mathcal{H}_2$ in Fig. 10.22 would completely determine a probability specification on $\mathcal{H}_1$ in Fig. 10.21.

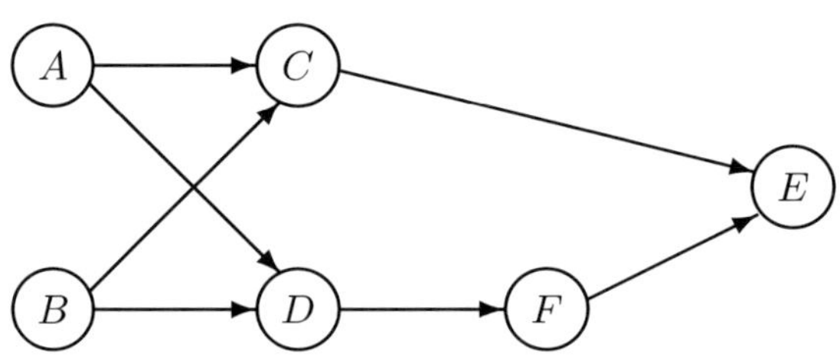

FIG. 10.22. Graph $\mathcal{H}_2$.

10.5 Joint Distributions

Any non-recursive causal net on V is subject to the Causal Markov Condition and accordingly it determines a probability function or joint distribution over V. We shall suppose that a recursive causal net on V is also subject to the Causal Markov Condition, so that it determines a probability function p_a, for each assignment a to a network variable A, defined on the set V_a of variables that occur in the net that a assigns to A. (By Theorem 10.3 the probability functions determined by networks in $\underline{v}'$ will agree on shared variables, for each consistent assignment v to V.) Standard Bayesian net algorithms can be used to perform inference in a recursive causal net, and a wide range of causal-probabilistic questions can be addressed. For example one can answer questions like 'what is the probability of a subsidy given farming?' (see Fig. 10.7) and 'what is the probability of lobbying given agricultural policy a^0?' (see Fig. 10.9).

Certain questions remain unanswered however. We cannot as yet determine the probability of one node conditional on another if the nodes only occur at different levels of the network. For example, we cannot answer the question 'what is the probability of subsidy given lobbying?' While we have a hierarchy of marginal distributions p_a on $V_a \subseteq V$, we have not yet specified a single joint distribution over the domain V of the recursive network as a whole.

In fact as we shall see, a recursive network does determine such an over-arching joint distribution if we make an extra independence assumption, called the *Recursive Markov Condition*: each variable is probabilistically independent of those other variables that are neither its inferiors nor its peers, conditional on its direct superiors.

A precise explication of the Causal Markov Condition and Recursive Markov Condition will be given shortly.

Given a recursive causal net on domain $V = \{A_1, \ldots, A_n\}$ and a consistent assignment v of values to V, we construct a non-recursive Bayesian net, the *flattening*, $v^{\downarrow}$, of v as follows. The domain of $v^{\downarrow}$ is V itself. The graph $\mathcal{G}^{\downarrow}$ of $v^{\downarrow}$ has variables in V as nodes, each variable occurring only once in the graph. Add an arrow from A_i to A_j in $\mathcal{G}^{\downarrow}$ if

- A_i is a parent of A_j in v (i.e. there is an arrow from A_i to A_j in the graph of some value of v) or
- A_i is a direct superior of A_j in v (i.e. A_j occurs in the graph of the value that v assigns to A_i).

We will describe the probability specification $\mathcal{S}^{\downarrow}$ of $v^{\downarrow}$ in due course. First to some properties of the graph $\mathcal{G}^{\downarrow}$.

$\mathcal{G}^{\downarrow}$ may or may not be acyclic. In the farming example $V = \{B, L, A, F, S\}$ of §10.3 the graph of the flattening $(b^0 l^0 a^1 f^1 s^1)^{\downarrow}$ is depicted in Fig. 10.23 and is acyclic. But the graph of the flattening of assignment $b^0 c^1 d^1 e^1$ to $\{B, C, D, E\}$, where B is the level 0 network variable whose value b^0 has graph $C \longrightarrow D$, C and E are simple variables and D is a network variable whose assigned value d^1 has the graph $E \longrightarrow C$, is cyclic. The graph in a non-recursive Bayesian

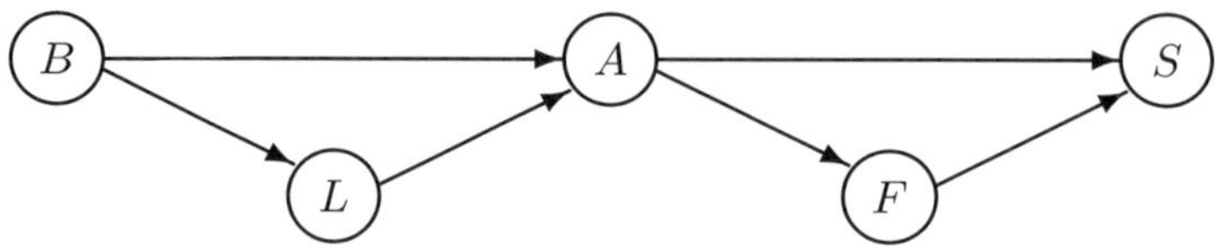

FIG. 10.23. A flattening.

net must be acyclic in order to apply standard Bayesian net algorithms, and this requirement extends to recursive Bayesian nets: we will focus on consistent *acyclic* assignments to the domain of a recursive causal net, those consistent assignments v that lead to an acyclic graph in the flattening $v^{\downarrow}$.[278]

By focussing on consistent acyclic assignments v, the following explications of the two independence conditions become plausible. Given a consistent acyclic assignment v, let PND_i^v be the set of variables that are peers but not descendants of A_i in v, NIP_i^v be the variables that are neither inferiors nor peers of A_i, and $DSup_i^v$ be the direct superiors of A_i. As before, Par_i^v are the parents of A_i and ND_i^v are the non-descendants of A_i. None of these sets are taken to include A_i itself.

Causal Markov Condition (CMC) For each $i = 1, \ldots, n$ and $DSup_i^v \subseteq X \subseteq NIP_i^v$, $A_i \perp\!\!\!\perp PND_i^v \mid Par_i^v, X$.

Recursive Markov Condition (RMC) For each $i = 1, \ldots, n$ and $Par_i^v \subseteq X \subseteq PND_i^v$, $A_i \perp\!\!\!\perp NIP_i^v \mid DSup_i^v, X$.

Then the graph of the flattening has the following property:

Theorem 10.4 *Suppose v is a consistent acyclic assignment to the domain V of a recursive causal net. Then the probabilistic independencies implied by v via CMC and RMC are just those implied by the graph $\mathcal{G}^{\downarrow}$ of the flattening $v^{\downarrow}$ via the usual Markov Condition.*

Proof: Order the variables in V ancestrally with respect to $\mathcal{G}^{\downarrow}$, i.e. no descendants of A_i in $\mathcal{G}^{\downarrow}$ occur before A_i in the ordering—this is always possible because $\mathcal{G}^{\downarrow}$ is acyclic.

First we shall show that CMC and RMC for v imply the Markov Condition for $\mathcal{G}^{\downarrow}$. By Corollary 3.5 it suffices to show that $A_i \perp\!\!\!\perp A_1, \ldots, A_{i-1} \mid Par_i^{\mathcal{G}^{\downarrow}}$ for any $A_i \in V$. By CMC, $A_i \perp\!\!\!\perp PND_i^v \mid Par_i^v, DSup_i^v$, and by RMC, $A_i \perp\!\!\!\perp NIP_i^v \mid DSup_i^v, PND_i^v$. Applying Contraction (§3.2),

$$A_i \perp\!\!\!\perp PND_i^v \cup NIP_i^v \mid Par_i^v, DSup_i^v.$$

Now $\{A_1, \ldots, A_{i-1}\} \subseteq PND_i^v \cup NIP_i^v$ since the variables are ordered ancestrally and v is acyclic, and the parents of A_i in $\mathcal{G}^{\downarrow}$ are just the parents and direct superiors of A_i in v, $Par_i^{\mathcal{G}^{\downarrow}} = Par_i^v \cup DSup_i^v$, so $A_i \perp\!\!\!\perp A_1, \ldots, A_{i-1} \mid Par_i^{\mathcal{G}^{\downarrow}}$ as required.

[278] Cyclic Bayesian nets have been studied to some extent, but are less tractable than the acyclic case: see Spirtes (1995) and Neal (2000).

Next we shall see that the Markov Condition for $\mathcal{G}^\downarrow$ implies CMC and RMC for v. In fact this follows straightforwardly by D-separation. $Par_i^v \cup X$ D-separates A_i and PND_i^v in $\mathcal{G}^\downarrow$ for any $DSup_i^v \subseteq X \subseteq NIP_i^v$, since $Par_i^v \cup X$ includes the parents of A_i in $\mathcal{G}^\downarrow$ and (by acyclicity of v) PND_i^v are non-descendants of A_i in $\mathcal{G}^\downarrow$, so CMC holds. $DSup_i^v \cup X$ D-separates A_i and NIP_i^v in $\mathcal{G}^\downarrow$ for any $Par_i^v \subseteq X \subseteq PND_i^v$, since $DSup_i^v \cup X$ includes the parents of A_i in $\mathcal{G}^\downarrow$ and (by acyclicity of v) NIP_i^v are non-descendants of A_i in $\mathcal{G}^\downarrow$, so RMC holds. ■

Having defined the graph $\mathcal{G}^\downarrow$ in the flattening $v^\downarrow$ of v, and examined its properties, we shall move on to define the probability specification $\mathcal{S}^\downarrow$ of $v^\downarrow$. In the specification $\mathcal{S}^\downarrow$ we need to provide a value for $p(a_i|par_i^{\mathcal{G}^\downarrow})$ for each assignment a_i to A_i and assignment $par_i^{\mathcal{G}^\downarrow}$ to the parents $Par_i^{\mathcal{G}^\downarrow}$ of A_i in $\mathcal{G}^\downarrow$. If A_i only occurs once in $\underline{v}'$ then we can define

$$p(a_i|par_i^{\mathcal{G}^\downarrow}) = p(a_i|dsup_i^v par_i^v) = p_{dsup_i^v}(a_i|par_i^v),$$

which is provided in the specification of the value of A_i's direct superior in v. If A_i occurs more than once in $\underline{v}'$ then the specifications of $\underline{v}'$ contain $p_{dsup_i^{\mathcal{G}}}(a_i|par_i^{\mathcal{G}})$ for each graph $\mathcal{G}$ in $\underline{v}'$ in which A_i occurs. Then $DSup_i^v = \bigcup_{\mathcal{G}} DSup_i^{\mathcal{G}}$ and $Par_i^v = \bigcup_{\mathcal{G}} Par_i^{\mathcal{G}}$, with the unions taken over all such $\mathcal{G}$. Now the specifiers $p_{dsup_i^{\mathcal{G}}}(a_i|par_i^{\mathcal{G}})$ constrain the value of $p_{dsup_i^v}(a_i|par_i^v)$ but may not determine it completely. These are linear constraints, though, and if v is consistent then the constraints are consistent. Thus there is a unique value for $p_{dsup_i^v}(a_i|par_i^v)$ which maximises entropy subject to the constraints holding—this can be taken as its optimal value, and $p(a_i|par_i^{\mathcal{G}^\downarrow})$ can be set to this value.

Having fully defined the flattening $v^\downarrow = (\mathcal{G}^\downarrow, \mathcal{S}^\downarrow)$ and shown that the Markov Condition holds, we have a (non-recursive) Bayesian net,[279] which can be used to determine a joint probability function over V:

Theorem 10.5 *A recursive causal net determines a unique joint distribution over consistent acyclic assignments v of values to its domain, defined by*

$$p(v) = \prod_{i=1}^{n} p(a_i|par_i^{\mathcal{G}^\downarrow}),$$

where $\mathcal{G}^\downarrow$ is the graph in the flattening $v^\downarrow$ of v and $p(a_i|par_i^{\mathcal{G}^\downarrow})$ is the value in the specification $\mathcal{S}^\downarrow$ of $v^\downarrow$. (As usual a_i is the value v assigns to A_i and $par_i^{\mathcal{G}^\downarrow}$ is the assignment v gives to the parents of A_i according to $\mathcal{G}^\downarrow$.)[280]

[279]Note that this Bayesian net is not causally interpreted, since arrows from superiors to direct inferiors are not causal arrows.

[280]Here the domain of p is the set of assignments to V, and p is unique over consistent acyclic assignments. If one wants to take just the set of consistent acyclic assignments as domain of p (equivalently, to award probability 0 to inconsistent or cyclic assignments) then one must renormalise, i.e. divide $p(v)$ by $\sum p(v)$ where the sum is taken over all consistent acyclic assignments.

While a flattening is a useful concept to explain how a joint distribution is defined, there is no need to actually construct flattenings when performing calculations with recursive nets—indeed that would be most undesirable, given that there are exponentially many assignments and thus exponentially many flattenings which would need to be constructed and stored. By Theorem 10.5, only the probabilities $p(a_i|par_i^v dsup_i^v)$ need to be determined, and in many cases (i.e. when A_i occurs only once in the recursive net) these are already stored in the net.

The concept of flattening, in which a mapping is created between a recursive net and a corresponding non-recursive net, also helps us understand how standard inference algorithms for non-recursive Bayesian nets can be directly applied to recursive nets. For example, message-passing propagation algorithms[281] can be directly applied to recursive networks, as long as messages are passed between direct superior and direct inferior as well as between parent and child. Moreover, recursive Bayesian nets can be used to reason about interventions just as can non-recursive networks: when one intervenes to fix the value of a variable one must treat that variable as a root node in the network, ignoring any connections between the node and its parents or direct superiors.[282] In effect, tools for handling non-recursive Bayesian nets can be easily mapped to recursive nets.

A word on the plausibility of the Recursive Markov Condition. It was shown in Chapters 5 and 6 that the Causal Markov Condition can be justified as follows: suppose an agent's background knowledge consists of the components of a causally interpreted Bayesian net—knowledge of causal relationships embodied by the causal graph and knowledge of probabilities encapsulated in the corresponding probability specification—then the agent's degrees of belief ought to satisfy the Causal Markov Condition. This justification rests on the acceptance of the Maximum Entropy Principle and Causal Irrelevance (if an agent learns of the existence of new variables which are not causes of any of the old variables, then her degrees of belief concerning the old variables should not change). An analogous justification can be provided for the Recursive Markov Condition. Plausibly, learning of new variables that are not superiors (or causes) of old variables should not lead to any change in degrees of belief over the old domain.[283] Now if an agent's background knowledge takes the form of the components of a recursive causal net then the maximum entropy function, and thus the agent's degrees of belief, will satisfy the Recursive Markov Condition as well as the Causal Markov Condition. Thus a justification can be given for both the Causal Markov Condition and the Recursive Markov Condition.

[281] See Pearl (1988); Neapolitan (1990).

[282] (Pearl, 2000, §1.3.1)

[283] In the terminology of §11.4, superiority is an influence relation.

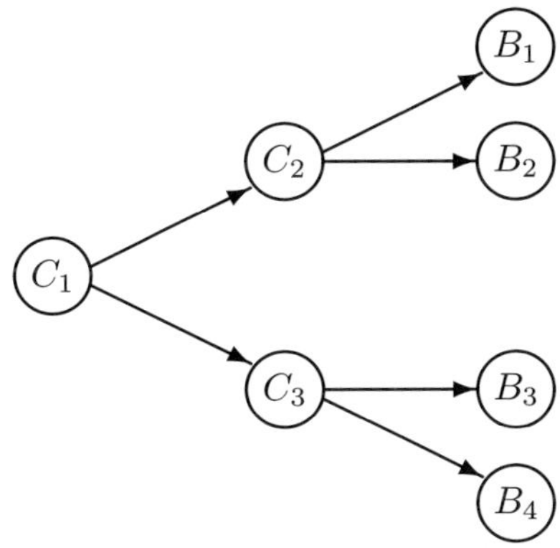

FIG. 10.24. A recursive Bayesian multinet.

10.6 Related Proposals

Bayesian nets have been extended in a variety of ways, and some of these are loosely connected with the recursive Bayesian nets introduced above.

Recursive Bayesian multinets generalise Bayesian nets along the following lines.[284] First, Bayesian nets are generalised to *Bayesian multinets* which represent context-specific independence relationships by a set of Bayesian nets, each of which represents the conditional independencies which operate in a fixed context. By creating a variable C whose assignments yield different contexts, a Bayesian multinet may be represented by decision tree whose root is C and whose leaves are the Bayesian nets. The idea behind recursive Bayesian multinets is to extend the depth of such decision trees. Leaf nodes are still Bayesian nets, but there may be several decision nodes. For example, Fig. 10.24 depicts a recursive Bayesian multinet in which there are three decision nodes, C_1, C_2 and C_3, and four Bayesian nets B_1, B_2, B_3, B_4. Node C_1 has two possible contexts as values; under the first node C_2 comes into operation; this has two possible contexts as values; under the first Bayesian net B_1 describes the domain; under the second B_2 applies, and so on. Figure 10.24 is recursive in the sense that depending on the value of C_1, a different multinet is brought into play—the multinet on C_2, B_1, B_2 or that on C_3, B_3, B_4. Thus recursive Bayesian multinets are rather different to our recursive Bayesian nets: they are applicable to context-specific causality where the contexts need to be described by multiple variables,[285] not to general instances of recursive causality, and consequently they are structurally different, being decision trees whose leaves are Bayesian nets rather than Bayesian nets whose nodes take Bayesian nets as values.

Recursive relational Bayesian nets generalise the expressive power of the

[284] (Peña *et al.*, 2002)

[285] The particular application that motivated their introduction was data clustering—see Peña *et al.* (2002).

domain over which Bayesian nets are defined.[286] Bayesian nets are essentially propositional in the sense that they are defined on variables, and the assignment of a value to a variable can be thought of as a proposition which is true if the assignment holds and false otherwise. *Relational Bayesian nets* generalise Bayesian nets by enabling them to represent probability distributions over more fine-grained linguistic structures, in particular certain sub-languages of first-order logical languages. Recursive relational Bayesian nets generalise further by allowing more complex probabilistic constraints to operate, and by allowing the probability of an atom that instantiates a node to depend recursively on other instantiations as well as the node's parents.[287] Thus in the transition from relational Bayesian nets to recursive relational Bayesian nets the Markovian property of a node being dependent just on its parents (not further non-descendants) is lost. Therefore recursive relational Bayesian nets and recursive Bayesian nets differ fundamentally with respect to both motivating applications and formal properties.

Object-oriented Bayesian nets were developed as a formalism for representing large-scale Bayesian nets efficiently.[288] Object-oriented Bayesian nets are defined over *objects*, of which a variable is but one example. Such networks are in principle very general, and recursive Bayesian nets are instances of object-oriented Bayesian nets in as much as recursive Bayesian nets can be formulated as objects in the object-oriented programming sense. Moreover in practice object-oriented Bayesian nets often look much like recursive Bayesian nets, in that such a network may contain several Bayesian nets as nodes, each of which contains further Bayesian nets as nodes and so on.[289] However, there is an important difference between the semantics of such object-oriented Bayesian nets and that of recursive Bayesian nets, and this difference is dictated by their motivating applications. Object-oriented Bayesian nets tend to be used to organise information contained in several Bayesian nets: each such Bayesian net is viewed as a single object node in order to hide much of its information that is not relevant to computations being carried out in the containing network. Hence when there is an arrow from one Bayesian net B_1 to another B_2 in the containing network, this arrow hides a number of arrows from output variables (which are often leaf variables) of B_1 to input variables (often root variables) of B_2. So by expanding each Bayesian net node, an object-oriented Bayesian net can be expanded into one single non-recursive, non-object-oriented Bayesian net. In contrast, in a recursive Bayesian net, recursive Bayesian nets occur as *values* of nodes not as nodes themselves, and when one recursive Bayesian net causes another in a containing recursive Bayesian net, it is not output variables of the former that cause input variables of the latter net, it is the former net *as a whole* that causes the latter net *as*

[286](Jaeger, 2001)

[287]See Jaeger (2001) for the details.

[288](Koller and Pfeffer, 1997)

[289]See, e.g. Neil *et al.* (2000).

a whole. Correspondingly, there is no straightforward mapping of a recursive Bayesian net on V to a Bayesian net on V: mappings (flattenings) are relative to assignment v to V. Thus while object-oriented Bayesian nets are in principle very general, in practice they are often used to represent very large Bayesian nets more compactly by reducing sub-networks into single nodes. In such cases the arrows between nodes in an object-oriented Bayesian net are interpreted very differently to arrows between nodes in a recursive Bayesian net, and issues such as causal, Markov and probabilistic consistency do not arise in object-oriented Bayesian nets.

Hierarchical Bayesian nets (HBNs) were developed as a way to allow nodes in a Bayesian net to contain arbitrary lower-level structure.[290] Thus recursive Bayesian nets can be viewed as one kind of HBN, in which lower-level structures are of the same type as higher-level structures, namely Bayesian net structures. In fact, HBNs were developed along quite similar lines to recursive Bayesian nets, and even have a concept of flattening. However, there are a number of important differences. As mentioned, HBNs are rather more general in that they allow arbitrary structure. It is questionable whether this extra generality can be motivated by causal considerations: certainly HBNs seem to have been developed in order to achieve extra generality, while recursive Bayesian nets were created in order to model an important class of causal claims. HBNs have been developed in most detail in the case considered in this chapter, namely where lower-level structure corresponds to causal connections. However, the lower-level structures are not exactly Bayesian nets in HBNs: one must specify the probability of each variable conditional on its parents in its local graph *and all variables higher up the hierarchy*. Thus HBNs have much larger size complexity than recursive Bayesian nets. HBNs do not adopt the Recursive Markov Condition—they only assume that a variable is probabilistically independent of all nodes that are not its descendants conditional on its parents and *all higher-level variables*. This has its advantages and its disadvantages: on the one hand it is a weaker assumption and thus less open to question, on the other it leads to the larger size of HBNs. Finally, variables can only appear once in a HBN, but they can appear more than once in a recursive Bayesian net—we would argue that repeated variables are well-motivated in terms of recursive causality (§10.2). Thus HBNs are more restrictive than recursive Bayesian nets in one respect, and more general in another, and have quite different probabilistic structure. However, they share common ground too, and where one formalism is inappropriate, the other might well be applicable.

10.7 Structural Equation Models

Of course, a causal net is not the only type of causal model, and the extension of causal nets to recursive causal nets can be paralleled in other types of causal model.

[290] (Gyftodimos and Flach, 2002)

Recall that a structural equation model contains a causal graph together with a 'pseudo-deterministic' equation determining the value of each effect as a function of the values of its direct causes and an error variable:

$$A_i = f_i(Par_i, E_i),$$

for $i = 1, \ldots, n$ and where each error variable E_i is independently distributed (this assumption allows one to derive the Causal Markov Condition). If we specify the probability distribution of each root variable (the variables which have no causes) and the distributions of the error variables then we have a causal net, since a structural equation determines the probability distribution of each non-root variable conditional on its parents in the causal graph. A causal net does not determine pseudo-deterministic functional relationships however, and so a structural equation model is a stronger kind of causal model than a causal net.

Structural equation models can be extended to model recursive causality as follows. A *recursive structural equation model* takes not only simple variables as members of its domain, but also *SEM-variables* which take structural equation models as values (including a level 0 variable which takes as its only value the top-level model).[291] As with recursive causal nets we can impose natural consistency conditions on a recursive structural equation model: causal consistency and consistency of functional equations. Given an assignment to the domain, we can create a corresponding, non-recursive structural equation model, its *flattening*, and define a pseudo-deterministic functional model over the whole domain by constructing an equation for each variable as a function of its direct superiors as well as its direct causes (and an error variable).

We see, then, that the move from an ordinary causal net to a recursive causal net can be mirrored in other types of causal model. But recursive Bayesian nets also have interesting non-causal applications, as we shall see next.

10.8 Argumentation Networks

Recursive networks are not just useful for reasoning with causal relationships—they can also be used to reason with other relationships that behave analogously to causality. In this section, we shall briefly consider the relation of support between arguments.

In an *argumentation framework*, one considers arguments as relata and attacking as a relation between arguments.[292] Consider the following example.[293] Hal is a diabetic who loses his insulin; he proceeds to the house of another diabetic, Carla, enters the house and uses some of her insulin. Was Hal justified? The argument (A_1) 'Hal was justified since his life being in danger allowed warranted

[291] Warning: in the past, acyclic structural equation models have occasionally been called 'recursive structural equation models'—clearly 'recursive' is being used in a different sense here.

[292] (Dung, 1995)

[293] Due to Coleman (1992) and discussed in Bench-Capon (2003, §7).

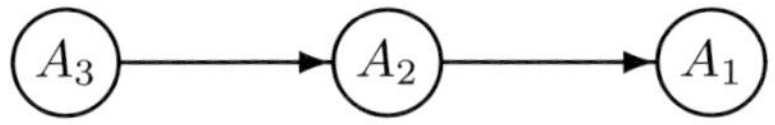

FIG. 10.25. Hal–Carla argumentation framework.

his drastic measures' is attacked by (A_2) 'it is wrong to break in to another's property' which is in turn attacked by (A_3) 'Hal's subsequently compensating Carla warrants the intrusion'. This argument framework is typically represented by the picture of Fig. 10.25.[294]

One can represent the interplay of arguments at a more fine-grained level by (i) considering propositions as the primary objects of interest, and (ii) taking into account the notion of support as well as that of attack. By taking propositions as nodes and including an arrow from one proposition to another if the former supports or attacks the latter, we can represent an argument graphically. In our example, let C represent Hal compensates Carla', B 'Hal breaks in to Carla's House', W 'Breaking in to a house is wrong' and D 'Hal's life is in danger'. Then we can represent the argument by $[C \longrightarrow^{+} B] \longrightarrow^{-} [W \longrightarrow^{-} B] \longrightarrow^{-} [D \longrightarrow^{+} B]$ (here a plus indicates support and a minus indicates attack). In general the fine structure of an argument is most naturally represented recursively as a network of arguments and propositions. This kind of representation may be called a *recursive argumentation network*.

If a quantitative representation is required, recursive Bayesian nets can be directly applied here. The nodes or variables in the network are either *simple arguments*, i.e. propositions, taking values true or false, or *network arguments*, which take recursive Bayesian nets as values. In our example, C is a simple argument with values *true* or *false* while A_2 is a network argument with values $(W \longrightarrow B, \{p(w), p(b|w)\})$ or $(WB, \{p(w), p(b)\})$. Instead of interpreting the arrows as causal relationships, indicating causation or prevention, we interpret them as support relationships, indicating support or attack. The probability $p(a_i|par_i)$ of an assignment a_i to a variable conditional on an assignment par_i to its parents is interpreted as the probability that a_i is *acceptable* given that par_i is *acceptable*. Thus instead of representing support or attack by pluses and minuses, degree of support is represented by conditional probability distributions. If consistency and acyclicity conditions are satisfied, non-local degrees of support can be gleaned from the joint probability distribution defined over all variables.

Note that Bench-Capon argues that the evaluation of an argument may depend on accepted values.[295] In our example, the evaluation of the argument depends on whether health is valued more than property, in which case property argument A_2 may not defeat health argument A_1, or vice versa. These value propositions can be modelled explicitly in the network, so that, e.g. A_1 depends on value proposition 'health is valued over property' as well as argument A_2.

[294](Bench-Capon, 2003)

[295](Bench-Capon, 2003, §5)

In sum, relations of support behave analogously to causal relations and arguments are recursive structures; these two observations motivate the use of recursive Bayesian nets to model arguments. In §11.5 we shall see that this type of system can be implemented in the framework of propositional logic.

11

LOGIC

11.1 Overview

In §4.2 we saw that a range of relationships between variables induce probabilistic dependencies. While causal relationships give rise to dependencies, so do logical, semantic, mathematical, and non-causal physical relationships. A comprehensive picture of an agent's epistemic state would need to show how knowledge of these relationships bear on degrees of belief and how probabilistic knowledge constrains beliefs about these relationships. We have already made a start by tackling the causal case via Causal to Probabilistic Transfer and Probabilistic to Causal Transfer. The next step is to integrate logical knowledge and beliefs into our framework.

After introducing the basics of propositional logic in §11.2, in §11.3 and subsequent sections we shall identify analogies between causal and logical influence. We shall see that the Bayesian net formalism can be applied to reasoning about logical implications, just as it can be applied to reasoning about causal relations. Finally §11.9 and the remainder of the chapter shows how the resulting formalism can be used to provide a framework for probabilistic logic.

11.2 Propositional Logic

A variable A is a *propositional variable* if it takes possible values *true* or *false*. The assignment $A = true$ may be denoted by a^1 and $A = false$ by a^0. A domain V of propositional variables is often called a *language*—it represents an agent's conceptual framework, the entities about which an agent can hold beliefs and knowledge. An assignment $v@V$ is sometimes called a *valuation*.

The *sentences* S_V of the language V are built up recursively:

- $V \subseteq S_V$,
- if $\theta \in S_V$ then its *negation*, *not* θ, written $\neg\theta$, is in S_V,
- if $\theta, \phi \in S_V$ then the *implication*, θ *implies* ϕ, written $\theta \to \phi$, is in S_V.

Connectives other than negation and implication are often used to abbreviate expressions involving negation and implication: the *conjunction* $\theta\phi$ (meaning θ *and* ϕ and sometimes written $\theta \wedge \phi$ or $\theta \& \phi$) stands for $\neg(\theta \to \neg\phi)$, the *disjunction* $\theta \vee \phi$ (meaning θ *or* ϕ) stands for $\neg\theta \to \phi$; the *equivalence* $\theta \leftrightarrow \phi$ (meaning θ *if and only if* ϕ) stands for $(\theta \to \phi)(\phi \to \theta)$. The *literals* of variable $A \in V$ are the sentences $A, \neg A$; an arbitrary literal is sometimes written $\pm A$. A *state* of a set $U = \{A_{i_1}, \ldots, A_{i_k}\} \subseteq V$ of variables is a conjunction $\pm A_{i_1} \cdots \pm A_{i_k}$ containing one literal of each variable. A state of V is sometimes called an *atomic state* or *state description*; clearly the atomic states correspond to the assignments to V.

An assignment v *models* or *interprets* a sentence θ, written $v \models \theta$, if θ is true under v:

- $v \models A$ for $A \in V$ if $a^v = a^1$, i.e. if v assigns the value *true* to A,
- $v \models \neg\theta$ if $v \not\models \theta$,
- $v \models \theta \rightarrow \phi$ if $v \models \neg\theta$ or $v \models \phi$.

A set of sentences Δ is said to *logically imply* a sentence θ, written $\Delta \models \theta$, if each assignment v that models all the sentences in Δ models θ. For example if $V = \{A, B, C\}$ then $\{A, \neg B\} \models B \rightarrow C$ since the valuations that model $\{A, \neg B\}$ are $a^1b^0c^1$ and $a^1b^0c^0$ and these both model $B \rightarrow C$.

The set of sentences S_V of V can itself be thought of as a domain of propositional variables that extends V. A sentence θ is a repeatably instantiatable variable, instantiated by assignments to V, and taking value *true* or *false* depending on whether or not $v \models \theta$. While S_V itself is infinite, a probability function can be defined on a finite subset T of S_V by specifying probabilities of assignments to T, as in §2.2.

A *proof* of a sentence θ from a set Δ of sentences is a list of sentences terminating with θ, each of which is in Δ or is an *axiom* of propositional logic or follows from previous sentences in the list by a *rule of inference* of propositional logic. There are various systematisations of the axioms and rules of inference; one example proceeds as follows.[296] The axioms are (for any sentences θ, ϕ, ψ):

A1: $\theta \rightarrow (\phi \rightarrow \theta)$

A2: $(\theta \rightarrow (\phi \rightarrow \psi)) \rightarrow ((\theta \rightarrow \phi) \rightarrow (\theta \rightarrow \psi))$

A3: $(\neg\phi \rightarrow \neg\theta) \rightarrow ((\neg\phi \rightarrow \theta) \rightarrow \phi)$,

There is one rule of inference, *modus ponens*:

MP: ϕ follows from θ and $\theta \rightarrow \phi$.

We say Δ *proves* θ, written $\Delta \vdash \theta$, if there is a proof of θ from Δ. The above axiom system has the desirable property that $\Delta \vdash \theta$ if and only if $\Delta \models \theta$.

11.3 Bayesian Nets for Logical Reasoning

Despite the fact that propositional logic is primarily concerned with sentences that are (depending on the valuation) certainly true or certainly false, logical reasoning takes place in a context of very little certainty. In fact the very search for a proof of a proposition is usually a search for certainty: one is unsure about the proposition and wants to become sure by finding a proof or a refutation. Even the search for a *better* proof takes place under uncertainty: one is sure of the conclusion but not of the alternative premises or lemmas.

Uncertainty is rife in mathematics, for instance. A good mathematician is one who can assess which conjectures are likely to be true, and from where a proof of a conjecture is likely to emerge—which hypotheses, intermediary steps and proof techniques are likely to be required and are most plausible in themselves.

[296](Mendelson, 1964, §1.4)

Mathematics is not a list of theorems but a web of beliefs, and mathematical propositions are constantly being evaluated on the basis of the mathematical and physical evidence available at the time.[297]

Of course logical reasoning has many other applications, notably throughout the field of artificial intelligence. Planning a decision, parsing a sentence, querying a database, checking a computer program, maintaining consistency of a knowledge base and deriving predictions from a model are only few of the tasks that can be considered theorem-proving problems. Finding a proof is rarely an easy matter, thus automated theorem proving and automated proof planning are important areas of active research.[298] However, current systems do not tackle uncertainty in any fundamental way.

We shall see that Bayesian nets are particularly suited as a formalism for logical reasoning under uncertainty, just as they are for causal reasoning under uncertainty, their more usual domain of application.

The plan is first to describe influence relations in §11.4. Influence relations are important because they permit the application of Bayesian nets: e.g. the fact that causality is an influence relation explains why Bayesian nets can be applied to causal reasoning. We will see that logical implication also generates an influence relation, and so Bayesian nets can also be applied to logical reasoning. In fact it is rather natural to use recursive Bayesian nets for logical reasoning (§11.5). Section 11.6 highlights further analogies between logical and causal Bayesian nets, the presence of which ensure that Bayesian nets offer an *efficient* representation for logical, as well as causal, reasoning. Section 11.7 will show how logical nets can be used to represent probability distributions over clauses in logic programs. Then in §11.8 we shall see how probabilistic knowledge can be used to generate a web of logical beliefs.

11.4 Influence Relations

The objective Bayesian justification for using Bayesian nets to reason about causal relationships (summarised in §6.1) depends crucially on the Causal Irrelevance principle, which says roughly that learning of non-causes of current variables should not change degrees of belief about the current variables (see §5.8).

We shall generalise and call a relation R an *influence relation* if, whenever an agent learns of new variables which do not R the current variables, her degrees of belief over the current variables ought not change.

More formally, we proceed as in §5.8. Suppose the agent has some knowledge ρ of the relation R. For example, for $V = \{A_1, A_2, A_3, A_4\}$ and relation R of Fig. 11.1 the agent might know $\rho = \{A_1RA_2, \neg(A_3RA_2), \neg(A_3RA_4), R \text{ is transitive}\}$. A set of variables $U \subseteq V$ is a *ancestral* with respect to ρ, or ρ-*ancestral*, if it is closed under R as determined by ρ: if variable $A_i \in U$ then

[297]This point is made very compellingly by Corfield (2001).

[298](Bundy, 1999, 2002; Melis, 1998; Richardson and Bundy, 1999)

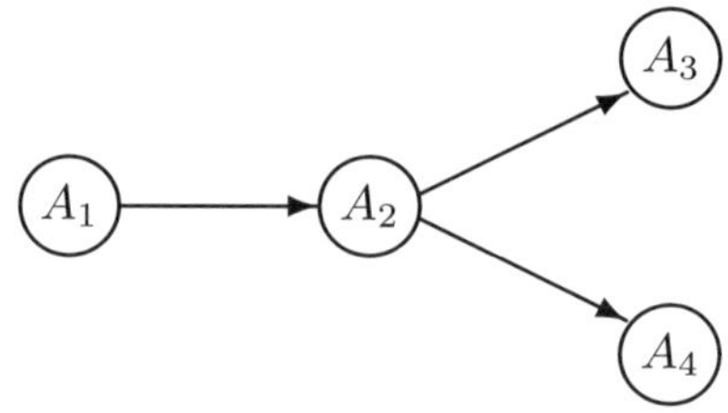

FIG. 11.1. Relation R.

any variable A_j that might RA_i (i.e. A_jRA_i is not ruled out by ρ) is in U. For example $U = \{A_1, A_2, A_4\}$ is ρ-ancestral with respect to the above ρ (note that $\neg(A_3RA_1)$ for otherwise by transitivity A_3RA_2 contradicting ρ). The irrelevance condition then says:

Irrelevance If U is ρ-ancestral and π is compatible on U then $V\backslash U$ is irrelevant to U, i.e. $p_{\rho,\pi\downharpoonright U} = p^U_{\rho_U,\pi_U}$.

In our example, if $\pi = \pi_U = \{p(a_1^1 a_2^0) = 0.9\}$ then $p_{\rho,\pi\downharpoonright\{A_1,A_2,A_4\}}$ is the belief function π on U determined by $\rho_U = \rho = \{A_1RA_2, R \text{ is transitive}\}$ and π.

The irrelevance condition allows a Transfer principle as in §5.8:

***R* to Probabilistic Transfer** Let $U_1, \ldots, U_k$ be the relevance sets (i.e. the ρ-ancestral sets on which π is compatible). Then $p_{\rho,\pi} = p_{\pi',\pi}$, the probability function p satisfying constraints in $\pi' = \{p_{\downharpoonright U_i} = p^{U_i}_{\rho_{U_i},\pi_{U_i}} : i = 1, \ldots, k\}$ and π.

In particular if ρ contains complete knowledge of an acyclic relation R on V and π contains probabilities of variables conditional on their R-parents then $p_{\rho,\pi}$ is represented by a Bayesian net on the graph of R.

The causal relation is an influence relation, and we may speak of a variable being a *causal influence* of its effects. But there are other influence relations apart from causality—logical implication generates an influence relation as we shall now see. A propositional variable A is a *logical influence* of variable B if there is a set of variables D, a literal α of A, a literal β of B and a state δ of D such that $\alpha\delta$ logically implies β, $\alpha\delta \models \beta$, but δ does not logically imply β on its own (α is a necessary part of a set of sufficient conditions for β). A is a *positive logical influence* of B if α is A and β is B or α is $\neg A$ and β is $\neg B$, otherwise it is a *negative logical influence* of B.

In order for logical influence to be a genuine influence relation, learning of a new variable that does not logically influence any of the other variables should not change beliefs over the other variables—the new variable must be irrelevant to the old. But this is rather plausible, for a similar reason to the causal case. Consider an example from number theory involving Fermat's Equation $x^n + y^n = z^n$ for non-zero integers x, y, z, n. Suppose an agent who knows very little about number theory is presented with two propositional variables. E stands for the elliptic curve conjecture of Frey, proved by Ribet, which says that if there is a solution to Fermat's equation for $n \geq 2$ then there is a non-modular elliptic curve with rational coefficients (the details of what these are do not matter for our purposes). T stands for the Taniyama–Shimura Conjecture that all elliptic curves with rational coefficients are modular. The agent knows of no relationship of logical influence between them. She might have beliefs $p(e^1) = 0.5$ and $p(t^1) = 0.5 = p(t^1|e^1) = p(t^1|e^0)$. Later she learns of a new variable, F, signifying Fermat's Last Theorem which says that Fermat's equation has no solution for $n \geq 2$. The agent realises E and T logically imply F, but neither logically implies F on its own, so E and T logically influence F. This new information ought not change the agent's degrees of belief in the original two variables: there would be no reason to give a new value to $p(e^1)$, nor to $p(t^1)$, nor to render the two nodes dependent in any way.[299] (On the other hand, if the agent were to learn that a new variable logically influences both E and T then she may well find reason to change her original degrees of belief. She might render the two original variables more dependent, e.g. by reasoning that if one were true then this might be because the common logical influence is true, which would render the other more likely.)

Thus logical influence does determine an influence relation. A graph in which arrows are interpreted as direct logical influence will be called a *logical graph*. A logical graph is *complete* if some state of the parents of each variable logically imply a literal of the variable, otherwise—if some logical influences are missing—it is *incomplete*. A logical graph need not be acyclic, but if it is it can feature in a Bayesian net—a Bayesian net whose graph is a logical graph will be called a *logical Bayesian net* or simply a *logical net*. If an acyclic logical graph represents an agent's knowledge of logical influences and the agent also knows the probability distribution of each variable conditional on its parents then the probability function that the agent ought to adopt as her belief function is represented by the logical net involving the logical graph and conditional distributions. This provides a justification of the *Logical Markov Condition*, which is just the Markov Condition applied to a logical net.

Causal influence and logical influence are both influence relations, but they are not the only influence relations.[300] In §10.5 we suggested that superiority in a recursive causal net is an influence relation. Subsumption of meaning provides another example: *A semantically influences B* if a B is a type of A. These influence relations are different relations in part because they are normally construed as relations over different types of domains: causality relates physical events, logical influence relates sentences, superiority relates causal relations, and semantic influence relates concepts. Because variables can signify a variety of entities,

[299]It is important to note that the agent learns only of the new variable F and that the two original variables logically influence it—she does not also learn of the truth or falsity of F, which would provide such a reason.

[300]Some terminology: when we are dealing with an influence relation a child of an influence may be called an *effluence* (generalising the causal notion of effect), a common effluence of two influences is a *confluence* (generalising common effect), and a common influence of two effluences is a *disfluence* (generalising common cause).

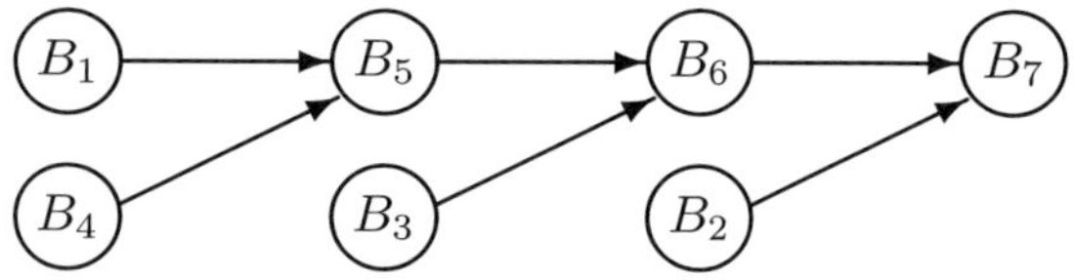

FIG. 11.2. A logical graph.

including events, sentences, relations, and concepts, a set of variables can be related by several influence relations. We will consider interactions between influence relations in §11.8. For now we shall explore logical influence in more detail.

11.5 Recursive Logical Nets

As pointed out in §11.2, a logical proof of a sentence takes the form of a list of sentences. Consider propositional sentences $\theta, \phi, \psi, \ldots$ and the following proof of $\theta \rightarrow \psi$ from $\{\theta \rightarrow \phi, \phi \rightarrow \psi\}$:

1. $\phi \rightarrow \psi$ [hypothesis]
2. $\theta \rightarrow \phi$ [hypothesis]
3. $(\theta \rightarrow (\phi \rightarrow \psi)) \rightarrow ((\theta \rightarrow \phi) \rightarrow (\theta \rightarrow \psi))$ [axiom]
4. $(\phi \rightarrow \psi) \rightarrow (\theta \rightarrow (\phi \rightarrow \psi))$ [axiom]
5. $\theta \rightarrow (\phi \rightarrow \psi)$ [by 1, 4]
6. $(\theta \rightarrow \phi) \rightarrow (\theta \rightarrow \psi)$ [3, 5]
7. $\theta \rightarrow \psi$ [2, 6]

The important thing to note is that the ordering in a proof defines a directed acyclic graph. If we let B_i be the propositional variable signifying the sentence on line i, for $i = 1, \ldots, 7$, and deem B_i to be a parent of B_j if B_i is required for modus ponens in the step leading to B_j, then we get the directed acyclic graph in Fig. 11.2. This is a logical graph because the parents of a node logically imply the node: applying modus ponens to B_i and $B_i \rightarrow B_j$ corresponds to a proof for $B_i, B_i \rightarrow B_j \vdash B_j$, which in turn corresponds to the logical implication $B_i, B_i \rightarrow B_j \models B_j$.

By specifying probabilities of assignments to root variables and conditional probabilities of assignments to other variables given assignments to their parents, we have the components of a logical net. These probabilities will depend on the meaning of the sentences rather than simply their syntactic structure—in our example a specification might start like this: $\mathcal{S} = \{p(b_1^1) = \frac{3}{4}, p(b_2^1) = \frac{1}{3}, p(b_3^1) = 1, p(b_4^1) = 1, p(b_5^1|b_1^1 b_4^1) = 1, p(b_5^1|b_1^0 b_4^1) = \frac{1}{2}, \ldots\}$. In this example assignments to the logical axioms have probability 1, but not so assignments to the hypotheses.

Viewing the lines of the proof as simple variables $B_1, \ldots, B_7$ ignores their logical structure. This structure can be recaptured if we view these sentences as network variables in which case the network as a whole becomes a *recursive logical net*. B_1, for instance, can be construed as a network variable to which b_1^1 assigns a logical net with graph $\phi \longrightarrow \psi$ and b_1^0 assigns a logical net with discrete graph on

ϕ and ψ. Now ϕ and ψ are sentences and have logical structure of their own—if this is known then they can be construed as network variables themselves. Thanks to the recursive definition of a sentence, this procedure will continue until the original propositional variables $A_1, \ldots, A_n$ are retrieved, generating a well-founded recursive Bayesian net as defined in Chapter 10. Note that arrows in this net correspond to the implication connective $\rightarrow$ as well as applications of modus ponens. But each such implication itself corresponds to a logical influence so we still have a logical net: if sentence $\theta \rightarrow \phi$ occurs as one line of a proof from Δ then $\Delta \vdash \theta \rightarrow \phi$; by taking this proof and applying modus ponens to θ and $\theta \rightarrow \phi$ one can show that $\Delta, \theta \vdash \phi$ in which case $\Delta, \theta \models \phi$ and θ is a logical influence of ϕ.

Thus the recursive definition of a sentence leads naturally to the use of recursive logical nets.

Note that a logical graph need not be isomorphic to a logical proof. First, not every logical step need be included in a logical graph. One may only have a sketch of the key steps of a proof, yet one may be able to form a logical graph. Just as a causal graph may represent causality on the macro-scale as well as the micro-scale, so too a logical graph may represent an argument involving large logical steps. In this case the logical graph is still complete—some state of parents still logically implies some literal of their child—but the parents need not be one rule of inference away from their child. Second, one may not be aware even of all the key steps in the proof, and some of the logical influences on which the proof depends may be left out. Here it may no longer be true that a parent state logically implies a child literal. All that can be said is that each parent is involved in a derivation of its child: it is a logical influence of its child.

11.6 The Effectiveness of Logical Nets

We saw in §11.4 that the methodology of Bayesian nets may be applied to logical influence because, like causal influence, logical influence is an influence relation. This offers the opportunity of an efficient representation of an agent's belief function. But two further considerations make a logical net representation particularly effective: there is little redundancy in a logical net and logical nets are often sparse.

A causal net offers an efficient representation of a probability function in the sense that it contains little redundant information. Redundancy occurs if independencies other than those implied by the causal net obtain and a smaller net would suffice to represent the same probability function. However, such redundancy is rare if, as we have argued, Causal Dependence holds much of the time. As explained in §4.3, if Causal Dependence holds and a causal net is complete (in the sense that if the graph includes one cause of a variable then it includes all its causes) then every arrow in a causal net corresponds to a conditional probabilistic dependency and no arrow can be removed if the Causal Markov Condition is still to hold. Thus the fact that causality satisfies Causal Dependence explains why the arrows in a causal net (and the corresponding probability specifiers) are not redundant.

We have seen that logical influence is analogous to causal influence because they are both influence relations, and that this fact can be used to justify the Markov Condition. But the analogy extends further because an analogue of Causal Dependence also carries over to logical influence. Consider a logical influence A of variable B in a complete logical graph. There must be some literal α of A and state δ of $D = Par_B \backslash A$ such that $\alpha\delta$ logically implies some literal β of B. Assuming this logical implication is known to the agent, A and B are likely to be conditionally probabilistically dependent, as follows. Since $\alpha\delta \models \beta$ is known, we have that $p(b|ad) = 1$ for some $a@A, b@B, d@D$. If $p(b|a'd) = 1$ too, where a' is the other assignment to A, then this must be so because the agent's background knowledge constrains $p(b|a'd)$ to be 1 (maximising entropy will never yield extreme probabilities 0 or 1 unless forced to by constraints). This cannot be because $(\neg\alpha)\delta \models \beta$, for otherwise A is redundant in the implication of β and is not a logical influence of B at all. So $p(b|a'd) = 1$ must be a constraint imposed by non-logical knowledge—observed frequencies perhaps. Assuming that such an observation is rare, it will rarely be the case that $p(b|a'd) = 1 = p(b|ad)$ and the conditional dependence $A \rightleftharpoons B|D$ will be the norm. Thus the arrow from A to B in the logical graph is unlikely to be redundant and we have the following principle:

Logical Dependence If A is a logical influence of B then normally $A \rightleftharpoons B|D$, where D is the set of influences which together with A logically imply B.

While Logical Dependence explains why information in a logical net is normally not redundant, we require more, namely that logical nets be computationally tractable.

Recall that both the space complexity of a Bayesian net representation and the time complexity of propagation algorithms depend on the structure of the graph in the Bayesian net. Sparse graphs lead to lower complexity in the sense that, roughly speaking, fewer parents lead to lower space complexity and fewer connections between nodes lead to lower time complexity. Bayesian nets are thought to be useful for causal reasoning just because, it is thought, causal graphs are normally sparse.

But logical graphs are often sparse too, especially if they are derived from proofs as in §11.5. In this case, the maximum number of parents is dictated by the maximum number of premises utilised by a rule of inference of the logic in question, and this is usually small. For example, in the propositional logic of §11.2 the only rule of inference is modus ponens, which accepts two premises, and so a node in such a logical graph will either have no parents (if it is an axiom or hypothesis) or two parents (if it is the result of applying modus ponens). Likewise, the connectivity in such a logical graph tends to be low. A graph will be multiply connected only to the extent that a sentence is used more than once in the derivation of another sentence. This may happen, but occasionally rather

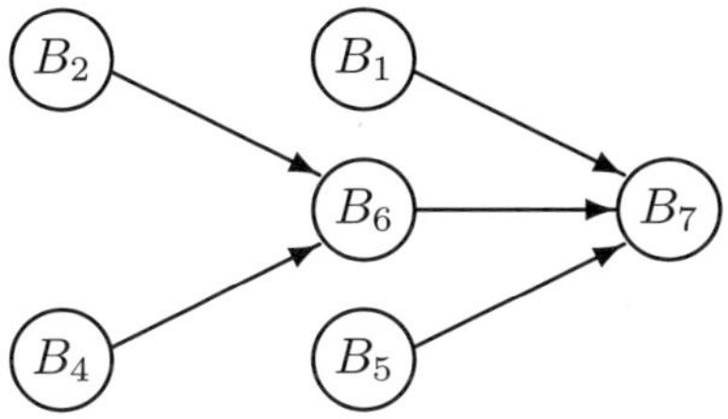

FIG. 11.3. Logical graph from a proof in a logic program.

than pathologically.[301]

In sum, while the fact that logical influence is an influence relation explains why Bayesian nets are applicable at all in this context, Logical Dependence and the sparsity of proofs explain why Bayesian nets provide an efficient formalism for logical reasoning under uncertainty.

11.7 Logic Programming and Logical Nets

Logic programming offers one domain of application. A *definite logic program* contains a set of *definite clauses* which may be positive literals or implications of the form $A_1, \ldots, A_k \rightarrow B$, normally written backwards as B `<-` $A_1, \ldots, A_k$. Logic programs extend propositional logic in that clauses may contain predicates, constants that name individuals, and variables that range over individuals. The computer program Prolog can be used to automatically generate proofs of literals that are queried by the user.[302]

A logical net can be used to represent a probability distribution over clauses in a logic program: the graph in the net can be constructed from proof trees involving the clauses of interest,[303] and one then specifies the probability of each clause conditional on each assignment to its logical influences. By way of example, consider the following definite logic program:[304]

B_1 `proud(X) <- parent(X,Y), newborn(Y).`

B_2 `parent(X,Y) <- father(X,Y).`

B_3 `parent(X,Y) <- mother(X,Y).`

B_4 `father(adam,mary).`

B_5 `newborn(mary).`

[301]One can of course contest this claim by dreaming up a single-axiom logic which requires an application of the axiom for each inference: this logic will yield highly connected graphs. In the same way one can dream up awkward highly connected causal scenarios which will not be amenable to Bayesian net treatment. Thus the pathological cases can occur, but there is no indication that they are anything but rare in practice.

[302]See Nilsson and Maluszyński (1990).

[303]Nilsson and Maluszyński (1990, §9.2) show how to collect proof trees in Prolog.

[304]This is the example of Nilsson and Maluszyński (1990, §3.1).

If we give Prolog the query `<- proud(Z)`, which asks whether the goal `proud(Z)` is false for some instantiation of Z, and use Prolog to find a refutation (a refutation of the falsity of the goal is of course a proof of its truth) we get the chain of reasoning depicted in Fig. 11.3, where B_6 and B_7 are the sentences `parent(adam,mary)` and `proud(adam)` respectively. By adding a probability specification we can form a logical net and use this net to calculate probabilities of interest, such as $p(b_6^1|b_7^1b_5^0)$, the probability that Adam is a parent of Mary given that he is proud but Mary is not newborn.

Thus given a set of sentences that can be written in clausal form, one can construct a logic program representing those sentences and use Prolog to construct a logical graph on the original sentences: logic programming can be used as a general tool for finding proof graphs for logical nets.

On the other hand logic programming can also be used in the absence of an initial set of sentences. Inductive Logic Programming (ILP) techniques can induce a logic program from a database of observed relations.[305] Prolog can then be used to construct a logical graph and this can be augmented with frequencies gleaned from the database to give a logical net. Thus the construction of a logical net from a database can be fully automated.

Applications might even arise within Prolog: one might want to replace the negation-as-failure of Prolog (where the negation of a literal is considered proved if no proof of the literal itself can be found) by a notion of negation-as-low-probability (where one accepts the negation of a literal if its probability is sufficiently low).

Stochastic Logic Programming (SLP) also uses proofs of clauses to define a probability distribution over clauses in a logic program,[306] but does so in a rather different way. SLP works by assigning probabilistic labels to the arcs in the proof tree for a goal, multiplying these together to obtain the probability of each derivation in the proof tree, and then summing the probabilities of successful derivations to define the probability of the goal itself being instantiated. The probability of a particular instantiation of the goal is the sum of the probabilities of derivations that yield that instantiation divided by the probability of the goal being instantiated. Thus SLP can be used to define probability distributions that can be broken down as a sum of products (log-linear distributions). Logical nets, on the other hand, ascribe probabilities directly to clauses, and only use proof trees to determine the logical relations among the clauses and hence the graphical structure of the net. In SLP the probability of an atom is the proportion of derivations of a more general goal that yield that atom as its instantiation,[307] whereas in a logical net the probability of a clause is the probability that it is true, as a universally quantified sentence. SLP represents a Bayesian net *within* the logic, by means of clauses which describe the graphical structure and probability

[305](Muggleton and de Raedt, 1994)

[306](Muggleton, 1996; Cussens, 2001, §2.2)

[307](Cussens, 2001, §2.4)

specification of the corresponding Markov net (formed by linking parents of each node, replacing arrows with undirected arcs, triangulating this graph, and then specifying the marginal probability distributions over cliques in the resulting graph).[308] In contrast a logical Bayesian net over the clauses in a logic program is *external* to the logic program which forms its domain: the probabilities are not part of the logic, in the sense that they are not integrated into the logic program as with SLP.

11.8 Logical Constraints and Logical Beliefs

Just as one is often uncertain as to what causes what, one may not have a perfect idea of what logically implies what. In some situations logic programming can help find a proof which in turn can be used to construct a logical graph, but this is not always possible (if the sentences of interest cannot be written in clausal form) or successful (if the chains of reasoning are too long to be executed in available time, or if the logic programming system fails to find all the required connections). It would be useful to be able to appeal directly to probabilistic considerations to help find a logical graph—such a graph could be used as a guide to planning a proof for example. In this section, we shall sketch how one might construct a logical graph when faced with uncertainty about logical structure.

In §11.4 we saw that logical influence plays a role analogous to causal influence in an agent's epistemic state, and thus knowledge of logical influence can be used to determine an agent's rational belief function p. Thus if an agent has logical constraints λ (i.e. partial knowledge of logical influence relationships among variables V) and probabilistic constraints π, we can apply a *Logical to Probabilistic Transfer* principle to generate a new set π' of probabilistic constraints. Using the techniques of §5.8 one can then find a Bayesian net representation of the belief function $p_{\lambda,\pi} = p_{\pi',\pi}$ that the agent ought to adopt. (Note that if λ contains knowledge of logical implications as well as knowledge of logical influences then this knowledge can be transferred to probabilistic constraints too: if $\alpha\delta \models \beta$ is in λ then π' should contain $p(b|ad) = 1$ for assignments a, b, d corresponding to α, β, δ.)

On the other hand, probabilistic and logical knowledge can also be used to determine a logical belief graph $\mathcal{L}_{\lambda,\pi}$, representing the beliefs about logical influence the agent ought to adopt given her background knowledge. As long as logical relations dominate on the domain—i.e. as long as dependencies are attributable by default to logical influences, rather than causal or semantic influences for instance—we can construct a *Probabilistic to Logical Transfer* principle which transfers π to λ' containing an arrow for each strategic dependency consistent with λ, as in §9.5. Then $\mathcal{L}_{\lambda,\pi} = \mathcal{L}_{\lambda,\lambda'}$ is a graph out of all those that satisfy λ, λ' with fewest arrows. (This approach might even form the basis of an epistemic philosophy of logic, which would proceed analogously to epistemic causality.)

[308](Cussens, 2001, §2.3)

More generally, we may suppose that an agent has causal constraints κ, logical constraints λ, and probabilistic constraints π. To determine $p_{\kappa,\lambda,\pi}$ both Causal to Probabilistic Transfer and Logical to Probabilistic Transfer can be applied and we can set $p_{\kappa,\lambda,\pi} = p_{\pi',\pi'',\pi}$ where π' is the set of transferred causal constraints and π'' is the set of transferred logical constraints. To determine $\mathcal{C}_{\kappa,\lambda,\pi}$ a new Transfer principle is required. If causal relations dominate we can base the principle on the intuition that $\mathcal{C}_{\kappa,\lambda,\pi}$ ought to account for any strategic dependencies in $p_{\kappa,\lambda,\pi}$ that are not already fully accounted for by λ.

Probabilistic to Causal Transfer Directed acyclic graph $\mathcal{C}$ satisfies κ, λ, and π if and only if $\mathcal{C}$ satisfies κ and κ' where probabilistic constraints π are transferred to causal constraints $\kappa' = \{A \longrightarrow B : I_{p_{\kappa,\lambda,\pi}}(A, B|D_B\backslash A, C_A) > I_{p_{\kappa,\lambda,\emptyset}}(A, B|D_B\backslash A, C_A)$, and $A \longrightarrow B$ is consistent with $\kappa\}$. (As before D_B is the set of direct causes of B according to $\mathcal{C}$, and $D_A \subseteq C_A \subseteq NE_A$.)

On the other hand if logical relations dominate then causal beliefs should not account for unexplained dependencies, and $\mathcal{C}_{\kappa,\lambda,\pi} = \mathcal{C}_\kappa$. To determine $\mathcal{L}_{\kappa,\lambda,\pi}$ we can proceed similarly: if logical relations dominate then logical beliefs ought to account for any dependencies that are not already accounted for by κ.

Probabilistic to Logical Transfer Directed acyclic graph $\mathcal{L}$ satisfies κ, λ, and π if and only if $\mathcal{L}$ satisfies λ and λ' where probabilistic constraints π are transferred to logical constraints $\lambda' = \{A \longrightarrow B : I_{p_{\kappa,\lambda,\pi}}(A, B|D_B\backslash A, C_A) > I_{p_{\kappa,\lambda,\emptyset}}(A, B|D_B\backslash A, C_A)$, and $A \longrightarrow B$ is consistent with $\lambda\}$. (Now D_B is the set of direct logical influences of B according to $\mathcal{C}$, and NE_A is the set of variables that are not logical effluents of A in $\mathcal{C}$.)

(As in the causal case $\mathcal{L}_{\lambda,\lambda'}$ is a smallest graph that satisfies λ and λ', though unlike the causal case a logical graph need not be acyclic.) Otherwise if causal relations dominate then $\mathcal{L}_{\kappa,\lambda,\pi} = \mathcal{L}_\lambda$.

One limitation of this analysis is its rather simplistic concept of dominance: either causal relations dominate and unexplained dependencies are to be accounted for causally, or logical relations dominate and unexplained dependencies are to be accounted for logically. A more refined concept would allow some dependencies to be accounted for by causal influences and others to be accounted for by logical influences—perhaps according to knowledge of the entities involved, so that dependencies between physical events would by default be explained causally while dependencies between logically complex sentences would by default be explained logically.

Note that other influence relations can be treated analogously—for instance an agent might have some knowledge of semantic influences, represented by constraints σ, in which case further Transfer principles are needed to determine $p_{\kappa,\lambda,\pi,\sigma}, \mathcal{C}_{\kappa,\lambda,\pi,\sigma}, \mathcal{L}_{\kappa,\lambda,\pi,\sigma}$ and semantic beliefs $\mathcal{S}_{\kappa,\lambda,\pi,\sigma}$.

11.9 Probability Logic

In the remainder of this chapter we shall investigate an interesting application to probability logic. A probability logic is an extension of logic to incorporate probabilities.

We saw in §11.2 that sentences can be construed as variables and that a probability function can be defined on assignments to a finite domain T of sentences by specifying probabilities of assignments to T. This definition is fine when there is a fixed finite set T of sentences of interest. However, if there is no such set T then we may need to define probabilities over the infinite set S_V of sentences. The following construction is normally used. A probability function p defined on (assignments to) domain V of propositional variables induces a function on S_V by defining

$$p(\theta) = \sum_{v@V, v \models \theta} p(v) \tag{11.1}$$

for each sentence $\theta \in S_V$.

Given finite $T = \{\theta_1, \ldots, \theta_k\} \subseteq S_V$, for $t@T$ let $p^T(t) = p(\pm\theta_1 \cdots \pm\theta_k)$ where $\pm\theta_1 \cdots \pm\theta_k$ is the state of T corresponding to t. Then p^T is a probability function on T because

$$\sum_{t@T} p^T(t) = \sum_{\pm\theta_1 \cdots \pm\theta_k} p(\pm\theta_1 \cdots \pm\theta_k) = \sum_{\pm\theta_1 \cdots \pm\theta_k} \sum_{v \models \pm\theta_1 \cdots \pm\theta_k} p(v) = 1.$$

Thus we can think of p as a probability function over S_V. This function can be extended to finite sets $\Delta = \{\theta_1, \ldots, \theta_k\}$ of sentences treating the set as a conjunction of its elements, i.e. by letting $p(\Delta) = p(\theta_1 \cdots \theta_k)$.[309]

Note that eqn 11.1 endows p with a special property, namely that $p(\phi|\Delta) = 1$ whenever $\Delta \models \phi$. When p is given a Bayesian interpretation and this property holds then the agent is said to be *logically omniscient*: the agent must know of all logical implication relationships in order to satisfy this property. Logical omniscience is clearly an inappropriate condition to impose if as in §11.8 one is interested in modelling an agent's uncertainty about logical relationships. However, in our discussion of probability logic we shall be specifically interested in agents that satisfy this idealisation.[310]

In §11.10 we shall discuss a very simple probability logic, based around the notion of partial entailment. Objective Bayesianism is used in §11.11 to provide semantics for this logic, and Bayesian nets are then applied in §11.12 to the problem of finding out about partial entailment relations.

11.10 Partial Entailment

Perhaps the simplest type of probability logic is a propositional logic in which the logical implication relation $\models$ is generalised to *partial entailment* $\models_y$, where

[309] See Paris (1994) for a thorough introduction to probabilistic reasoning over propositional languages.

[310] If necessary logical omniscience can be relaxed at the expense of some simplicity by insisting only that $p(\phi|\Delta) = 1$ if the constraint $\Delta \models \phi$ is in the agent's logical background knowledge λ.

y is a probability. A set $\Delta = \{\theta_1, \ldots, \theta_k\}$ of sentences partially entails sentence ϕ to degree y if and only if ϕ has probability y conditional on Δ:

$$\Delta \models_y \phi \Leftrightarrow p(\phi|\Delta) = y. \tag{11.2}$$

Thanks to logical omniscience, logical implication in propositional logic (also called *propositional entailment*) implies maximal partial entailment, $\Delta \models \phi$ implies $\Delta \models_1 \phi$. If Δ is empty we get a concept of degree of partial truth which corresponds to unconditional probability.

The relationship between probability and partial entailment expressed by eqn 11.2 can be thought of in one of two ways: (i) partial entailment is defined in terms of probability (this is a *probabilistic semantics* for probability logic), or (ii) probability is to be defined in terms of partial entailment (this is a *logical interpretation of probability*). While we will follow the former route in §11.11, there have been some influential proponents of the latter path, as we shall see now.

Jan Lukasiewicz distinguished subjective and physical probability but found both interpretations unsatisfactory: subjective probability because it is too psychologistic, too subjective, and beliefs are unmeasurable (this was before the betting set-up had been introduced), and physical probability because determinism renders it redundant (this was before quantum mechanics) and because the principle of the excluded middle states that a proposition is objectively true or false at every time, precluding physical partial truth. Instead, Lukasiewicz interpreted probability in terms of logic as follows. Rather than defining probability over sentences of propositional logic as we did in §11.9, Lukasiewicz defined probability over *indefinite propositions*, formulae which contain free variables that range over individuals, in terms of the partial truth of the proposition, which is understood thus:

> *By the truth value of an indefinite proposition I mean the ratio between the number of values of the variables for which the proposition yields true judgements and the total number of values of the variables.*[311]

This leads to a new interpretation of probability:

> The interpretation of the essence of probability presented here might be called the *logical* theory of probability. According to this viewpoint, probability is only a property of propositions, i.e., of logical entities, and its explanation requires neither psychic processes nor the assumption of objective possibility.[312]

Interestingly Lukasiewicz seems to have had an epistemic interpretation of logic in mind:

> *Probability, as a purely logical concept, is a creative construction of the human mind, an instrument invented for the purpose of mastering those*

[311] (Lukasiewicz, 1913, p. 17)

[312] (Lukasiewicz, 1913, p. 38)

> *facts which cannot be interpreted by universally true judgements (laws of nature).*[313]

John Maynard Keynes was another key player in the partial entailment tradition. He argued that probability generalises logic, measuring the degree to which an argument is conclusive.[314] Harold Jeffreys also thought of probability as a generalisation of deductive logic, expressing support for an inference given data.[315] In this respect his probability theory was a formalisation of inductive logic.[316]

Carl Hempel closely studied this inductive relationship between evidence and hypothesis, deriving a qualitative logic of confirmation with a well-defined syntax and semantics: 'Confirmation as here conceived is a logical relationship between sentences, just as logical consequence is.'[317] Rudolf Carnap rendered Hempel's theory quantitative by bringing probability into the logic. For Carnap probability was degree of confirmation. This was not cached out in terms of frequency (which he thought to be a valuable concept but quite different) or subjective degrees of belief (which he argued are too psychologistic), but given a distinct logical interpretation. The issue of confirmation is

> a logical question because, once a hypothesis is formulated by h and any possible evidence by e ..., the problem whether and how much h is confirmed by e is to be answered by a logical analysis of h and e and their relations. This question is not a question of facts in the sense that factual knowledge is required to find the answer.[318]

The chief difficulty for the logical interpretation of probability is the lack of any viable epistemology. While Keynes argued that one could ascertain probabilities by perceiving degrees of partial entailment, Frank Ramsey demolished his view thus:

> But let us now return to a more fundamental criticism of Mr. Keynes' views, which is the obvious one that there really do not seem to be any such things as the probability relations he describes. He supposes that, at any rate in certain cases, they can be perceived; but speaking for myself I feel confident that this is not true. I do not perceive them, and if I am to be persuaded that they exist it must be by argument; moreover I shrewdly suspect that others do not perceive them either, because they are able to come to so very little agreement as to which of them relates any two given propositions.[319]

Thus Keynes had the cart before the horse. Rather than understand probability in terms of logic, Ramsey argued that one should understand probability in terms of degree of belief and the betting set-up, and then understand partial

[313] (Lukasiewicz, 1913, p. 38)
[314] (Keynes, 1921)
[315] (Jeffreys, 1931, §2.0)
[316] (Jeffreys, 1939, §1.2)
[317] (Hempel, 1945, p. 24)
[318] (Carnap, 1950, p. 20)
[319] (Ramsey, 1926, p. 27)

entailment in terms of probability. This leads to a probabilistic semantics for probability logic rather than a logical interpretation of probability.

Note that proponents of a logical interpretation of probability either rejected the degree of belief interpretation of probability or regarded it as subsidiary. Lukasiewicz:

> Although probability does not exist objectively [i.e. is not physical], the probability calculus is not a science of subjective processes and has a thoroughly objective nature. Hence the essence of probability must be sought not in a relationship between propositions and psychic states, but in a relationship between propositions and objective facts.[320]

Keynes considered the degree of belief interpretation unnecessary because the logical interpretation leaves no room for subjectivity.[321] Jeffreys was of a similar opinion: the degree of belief interpretation is an optional extra. As he says, 'If we like there is no harm in saying that a probability expresses a degree of reasonable belief.'[322] Carnap also realised that if rational degree of belief is uniquely determined then the mental element is gratuitous and can be omitted.[323] He puts it thus:

> The characterisation of logic in terms of correct or rational or justified belief is just as right but not more enlightening than to say mineralogy tells us how to think correctly about minerals. The reference to thinking may just as well be dropped in both cases. Then we say simply: mineralogy makes statements about minerals, and logic makes statements about logical relations. The activity in any field of knowledge involves, of course, thinking. But this does not mean that thinking belongs to the subject matter of all fields. It belongs to the subject matter of psychology but not to that of logic any more than to that of mineralogy.[324]

Ramsey toppled this view by showing that the degree of belief interpretation provides a more natural foundation for probability and its measurement; it is the logic that is subsidiary. Then even if (as with the objective Bayesian position) probability turns out to be objective, to ignore the mental nature of probability is to commit an instance of what Jaynes called the mind projection fallacy. The mental aspect of probability tends to be accepted by recent advocates of logical viewpoints. Thus Colin Howson, who stresses the analogies between probability and logic but argues that one should consider *consistency* rather than entailment as the logical notion of primary interest, gives a degree-of-belief interpretation of probability and defines a notion of consistency using the betting set-up.[325]

In sum, the logical interpretation of probability faces apparently insurmountable epistemological difficulties: the epistemic route to partial entailment pro-

[320](Lukasiewicz, 1913, p. 37)
[321](Keynes, 1921, §1.2)
[322](Jeffreys, 1931, p. 22)
[323](Carnap, 1950, §2.11)
[324](Carnap, 1950, pp. 41–42)
[325](Howson, 2003)

ceeds via probability itself. This leads to a probabilistic semantics for probability logic.

11.11 Semantics for Probability Logic

If one decides to provide a probabilistic semantics for probabilistic logic rather than a logical interpretation of probability, more work must be done to explain what probability function or functions appear as p on the right-hand side of eqn 11.2.

According to the *standard probabilistic semantics*, $\Delta \models_y \phi$ if and only if $p(\phi|\Delta) = y$ for every probability function p.

The motivation behind this semantics becomes clearer if we generalise the partial entailment relation further. If $\theta_1, \ldots, \theta_k, \phi$ are sentences and $x_1, \ldots, x_k, y$ are probabilities we can write $\theta_1 : x_1, \ldots, \theta_k : x_k \models \phi : y$ to mean 'θ_1 with probability x_1 and ... and θ_k with probability x_k entail ϕ with probability y'. The relation $\models$ here is called *probabilistic entailment*—although the same symbol is used, it is not the same relation as propositional entailment (the logical implication relation of propositional logic). If $\Delta = \{\theta_1, \ldots, \theta_k\}$ then the original partial entailment $\Delta \models_y \phi$ becomes the special case of probabilistic entailment $\theta_1 : 1, \ldots, \theta_k : 1 \models \phi : y$.

The standard probabilistic semantics for probabilistic entailment defines $\theta_1 : x_1, \ldots, \theta_k : x_k \models \phi : y$ if and only if, for all probability functions p such that $p(\theta_1) = x_1, \ldots, p(\theta_k) = x_k$ we also have that $p(\phi) = y$. This is a very close analogue of propositional entailment if we view a probability function as a model: p *models* or *interprets* $\theta : x$, written $p \models \theta : x$, if $p(\theta) = x$; then $\theta_1 : x_1, \ldots, \theta_k : x_k \models \phi : y$ if and only if every model of $\theta_1 : x_1, \ldots, \theta_k : x_k$ is a model of $\phi : y$.[326]

The problem with the standard probabilistic semantics is that it yields rather a weak logic, in the sense that it is rare that any conclusions can be drawn at all. Models of $\theta_1 : x_1, \ldots, \theta_k : x_k$ will often differ as to the probability they give to ϕ; then there will be no probabilistic entailment $\theta_1 : x_1, \ldots, \theta_k : x_k \models \phi : y$ for any y. In the case of partial entailment $\Delta \models_y \phi$ if and only if $y = 0$ and $\Delta \models \neg\phi$, or $y = 1$ and $\Delta \models \phi$. Such a notion of partial entailment adds essentially nothing to propositional entailment.

To get a stronger logic we can appeal to the methods outlined in this book. According to the *objective Bayesian semantics*, a conclusion follows from premisses if and only if, whenever an agent's degrees of belief satisfy the constraints imposed by the premisses, they also satisfy the conclusion.[327]

In the case of partial entailment, $\Delta \models_y \phi$ if and only if $p_\Delta(\phi) = y$. Note that the constraints imposed by background knowledge $\Delta = \{\theta_1, \ldots, \theta_k\}$ are equivalent to those imposed by probabilistic constraints $\pi = \{\sum_{v@V, v\models\theta_i} p(v) = 1 : i = 1, \ldots, n\}$.

[326]This is essentially the approach taken by Howson (2001), though there logic is described using the notion of consistency rather than entailment.

[327]This type of semantics is adopted in Nilsson (1986).

For probabilistic entailment, $\theta_1 : x_1, \ldots, \theta_k : x_k \models \phi : y$ if and only if $p_\pi(\phi) = y$, where $\pi = \{\sum_{v@V, v\models\theta_i} p(v) = x_i : i = 1, \ldots, n\}$.

This logic is stronger for the simple reason that π is a set of linear constraints, so the premisses constrain p to lie in a closed convex set of probability functions and there is a unique entropy maximiser. Thus given $\theta_1, \ldots, \theta_k, \phi, x_1, \ldots, x_k$, there is a unique value y such that $\theta_1 : x_1, \ldots, \theta_k : x_k \models \phi : y$.

11.12 Deciding Probabilistic Entailment

In order to decide whether a probabilistic entailment (with the objective Bayesian semantics) holds, we can use the techniques of Chapter 5 to construct a Bayesian net representation of p_π and then use this net to calculate $p_\pi(\phi)$, comparing the result to y. Here the constraint sets C_i are the sets of propositional variables that occur in θ_i. If few variables occur in each θ_i in comparison with n as n becomes large then the constraint sets will be small relative to n, the induced Bayesian net correspondingly sparse, and the querying for $p_\pi(\phi)$ correspondingly quick. Note that $p_\pi(\phi) = \sum_{u\models\phi} p_\pi(u)$, where the u are assignments to the set U_ϕ of variables that occur in ϕ. Thus by querying the Bayesian network to find these $p_\pi(u)$ one can determine the correct value for $p_\pi(\phi)$. These calculations can be performed efficiently if the graph is sparse and ϕ involves few propositional variables relative to the size of the domain.

Consider an example. Suppose $V = \{A_1, A_2, A_3, A_4, A_5\}$ and we need to decide whether

$$A_1\neg A_2 : 0.9, (A_4A_3) \rightarrow A_2 : 0.2, A_5 \vee \neg A_3 : 0.3, A_4 : 0.7 \models A_5 \rightarrow A_1 : 0.6$$

First we construct an undirected constraint graph by linking propositional variables that occur in the same constraint. This yields the graph of Fig. 5.1. Next we transform this graph into a directed constraint graph (Fig. 5.2). Then we form a Bayesian net by determining the parameters $p(a_i|par_i)$ that maximise entropy. Thus we need to determine $p(a_1), p(a_2|a_1), p(a_3|a_2), p(a_4|a_3a_2)$ and $p(a_5|a_3)$ for all $a_i@A_i$. This can be done by reparameterising the entropy equation in terms of these conditional probabilities and then using Lagrange multiplier methods or numerical optimisation techniques. Finally, we can simplify ϕ into a disjunction of mutually exclusive assignments to the set U_ϕ of variables that occur in it and calculate $p(\phi) = \sum_{u@U_\phi, u\models\phi} p(u)$ by using standard Bayesian net algorithms to determine the marginals $p(u)$.

In our example,

$$\begin{aligned} p(A_5 \rightarrow A_1) &= p(a_5^0 a_1^1) + p(a_5^1 a_1^1) + p(a_5^0 a_1^0) \\ &= p(a_5^0|a_1^1)p(a_1^1) + p(a_5^1|a_1^1)p(a_1^1) + p(a_5^0|a_1^0)p(a_1^0) \\ &= p(a_1^1) + p(a_5^0|a_1^0)(1 - p(a_1^1)). \end{aligned}$$

We thus require only two Bayesian net calculations to determine $p(a_1^1)$ and $p(a_5^0|a_1^0)$.

Note that this method gives a procedure for deciding probabilistic entailment without giving a traditional proof theory involving axioms and rules of inference. It is an open question as to whether there is a proof theory for deciding probabilistic entailment.[328] (In propositional logic the method of truth tables gives a non-proof-theoretic way of deciding whether a propositional entailment holds.)[329]

[328]Paris and Vencovská (1990) made a start at a traditional proof theory but expressed some scepticism as to whether such a goal can be achieved. Halpern (2003) put forward a number of traditional proof procedures for the standard probabilistic semantics.

[329](Mendelson, 1964, §1.1)

12

LANGUAGE CHANGE

12.1 Two Problems of Belief Change

Thus far probability has been defined on the set of sentences of a fixed propositional language or on the set of assignments to a fixed domain of variables. But in practice an agent's language or domain is susceptible to change, and the question naturally arises as to how degrees of belief should change as language changes. In this chapter, we shall explore a response to the language change question.

The problem was identified by Imre Lakatos in his critical analysis of inductive logic:

> What is wrong with 'Bayesian conditionalisation'? Not only that it is '*atheoretical*' but that it is *acritical*. There is no way to discard the Initial Creative Act: the learning process is strictly confined to the initial prison of the language. Explanations that break languages and criticisms that break languages are impossible in this set-up.[330]

Colin Howson concurs:

> An objection, which in my opinion is a considerable one, to this procedure of representing his changes of belief is that it involves, as I remarked, the specification within a fixed language of his total possible future experience, and it commits him for all subsequent times to the way at some initial time he considered this range of possibilities as bearing on the set of events upon whose occurrence he will bet. This seems to me, as it has done to others, unrealistic.[331]

These passages relate to two quite distinct problems that beset Bayesianism. First, Bayesian conditionalisation requires that an agent always remain consistent with a prior probability function: $p_{t+1}(v) = p_t(v|u_{t+1}) = \cdots = p_0(v|u_1 \cdots u_{t+1})$, where u_i is the information received between times $i-1$ and i. However, the agent may decide that her prior p_0 did not adequately assess u_{i+1} or v or the relationship between the two, perhaps because she did not take sufficient notice of background knowledge concerning such far-off outcomes.[332] Thus there may be good reasons to break out of the constraints imposed by a strict adherence to Bayesian conditionalisation.

The second problem is that Bayesian probability is normally defined on a fixed language V. Given this fixed framework, Bayesianism gives advice as to what

[330](Lakatos, 1968, p. 347)

[331](Howson, 1976, p. 296)

[332]Earman (1992, p. 196) argues that belief changes that do not conform to Bayesian conditionalisation may be appropriate when the assumption of logical omniscience fails.

degrees of belief to award sentences or assignments: having fixed a prior one should fix future degrees of belief by Bayesian conditionalisation. But in practice an agent's language often changes over time. There may be new sentences or variables which were not even considered when formulating a prior, in which case Bayesian conditionalisation cannot be applied and Bayesianism fails to offer any guidance as to what degrees of belief to ascribe.

There are various possible solutions to the first problem. One strategy is denial: if the agent is a good objective Bayesian then her prior must have taken all her background knowledge into account and the problem does not arise. A second strategy is to play down the role of Bayesian conditionalisation. One can accept that there are situations in which Bayesian conditionalisation is inappropriate, and allow other ways of updating beliefs.[333] Another strategy is to play down the role of the prior. As noted in §2.8, strict subjectivists often hold that prior beliefs are *washed out*, that is, as agents with different priors conditionalise on the same new evidence their belief functions converge, and consequently their priors have less of a bearing on their current beliefs. Hence, for strict subjectivists the problem of having to remain consistent with a prior becomes less of an issue as time progresses.

The second problem—that of language change—has received less attention and deserves detailed consideration.

The problem of language change is particularly relevant today. This is because Bayesianism is increasingly applied to artificial intelligence,[334] and within AI the automated learning of new linguistic terms is an increasingly important task.[335] The question now arises: how should the degrees of belief of an artificial agent change as its language changes?

Another key application of Bayesianism is within the philosophy of science, to confirmation theory.[336] In this context, the problem of language change is crucial: competing scientific theories are often formulated in different scientific languages, and one must somehow bridge these languages in order to decide which theory is most confirmed by available evidence. Scientific theorising is often viewed as a special case of abductive reasoning, which is the problem of

[333]This line is followed by Jaynes and Earman who advocate a reassessment of priors. Howson claims that Bayesian conditionalisation should not be universally adopted because it can lead to inconsistencies (Howson, 1997, 2001). Howson and Urbach (1989, §13.e) argue, as we have done in Chapter 5, that beliefs may be updated by setting them to frequencies where they are known.

[334]See Pearl (1988).

[335]There are various recent lines of development here. Concept learning is progressing at pace within statistical learning theory: see Vapnik (1995); Cristianini and Shawe-Taylor (2000). New causes and effects are now automatically learned to improve the reliability of causal nets: see Kwoh and Gillies (1996); Binder *et al.* (1997). Multi-agent systems now evolve their own languages in order to communicate to solve problems: Jim and Giles (2000). In the near future linguistic learning may also prove to be important in abductive logic programming (Kakas *et al.*, 1998), Inductive Logic Programming (Muggleton and de Raedt, 1994), and computational linguistics (Hausser, 1999).

[336](Howson and Urbach, 1989; Earman, 1992)

formulating a plausible explanation of some given data.[337] Often one needs to change one's language in order to formulate a plausible explanation, either by adding new theoretical terms or by more radical reconceptualisations, and one needs to evaluate the explanation in the light of the data which prompted it. Bayesianism is an important evaluatory framework—the most plausible hypothesis is usually considered to be that with maximum probability conditional on the data—hence Bayesianism must be extended to cope with changing language if it is to play a role in the abductive process, and scientific theorising in particular.[338]

These applications to artificial intelligence and the philosophy of science pull Bayesianism in opposite directions. Artificial intelligence requires a formalism that is computationally practical and this usually leads to a simple framework and strong assumptions—these characteristics are plain to see in the formalism of causal nets, for instance. But the philosophy of science often aims to be true to science as it is practised and this leads to an expressive linguistic formalism without restrictive assumptions: here probability is often used informally over natural language statements[339] and may even be qualitative rather than quantitative.[340] But despite this methodological divergence the two disciplines are mutually supportive: the philosophy of science often motivates developments in artificial intelligence and assesses AI assumptions, while AI systems can be used to empirically test philosophical accounts of scientific reasoning.[341] Consequently we shall pursue an integrated approach here. We shall first, in §§12.2–12.8, make some rather general comments on the problem of language change, arguing that an agent's choice of language expresses factual knowledge. This will motivate a more formal solution to the problem in §§12.9–12.13, where we shall look at the consequences of several assumptions within the restrictive linguistic framework of the propositional calculus.

12.2 Language Contains Implicit Knowledge

The problem of language change has rarely been discussed in the philosophy of science literature. But where it has been discussed, it has usually been in the context of an appeal to *language invariance*.[342] This is the claim that any de-

[337] See Williamson (2003*a*).

[338] Note that in order to apply Bayesianism to science, one must also apply it to the mathematical theories on which the science depends—see Corfield (2001)—and the comparison of mathematical theories in different mathematical languages is a significant problem in its own right (Kvasz, 2000).

[339] (Howson and Urbach, 1989; Earman, 1992)

[340] (Pólya, 1954*b*, chapter XV)

[341] See Thagard (1988); Gillies (1996); Williamson (2004*b*).

[342] See Carnap (1950, §G of the preface to the second edition); Carnap (1971, §§2.A.2–4, 6.T6–1); Rosenkrantz (1977, §3.6); Forster (1995, §5); Halpern and Koller (1995); Jaynes (2003). Paris (1994); Paris and Vencovská (1997) adopt a notion of language invariance that is weaker than that considered here; the 'Representation independence' of Paris and Vencovská (1997) corresponds more closely to the concept of language invariance in this chapter.

termination of prior probability should only depend on an agent's background knowledge, not on the underlying language. Or in the context of the current problem: an agent's probability function should not change when her language changes, unless she learns new facts at the same time.[343] I shall argue, however, that *language contains implicit knowledge*. This creates a problem for the principle of language invariance: it never applies. For whenever an agent's language changes she will simultaneously gain new knowledge, in which case language invariance offers no constraint on her new probability function. The best way to capture intuitions behind language invariance is to advocate a *conservativity principle* in its stead: when an agent's language changes her new degrees of belief should be as close as possible to her old degrees of belief, given her new knowledge. However, justifications of conservativity are at best pragmatic (§12.7). To apply this new principle we will need to choose an appropriate notion of closeness, make the implicit linguistic knowledge explicit, and specify how that knowledge constrains belief change. The formalities will be dealt with in §12.9 and subsequent sections. For now we shall focus on the claim that language invariance cannot be applied naively.

There are two main ways that language represents knowledge. The choice of predicates in the language says something about those predicates themselves (§12.3) and about how the predicates relate to each other (§§12.4, 12.5).

12.3 Goodman's New Problem of Induction

Nelson Goodman's new problem of induction shows us one way in which inductive inference is not language invariant. Goodman pointed out that some predicates (like 'green') are amenable to inductive generalisation[344] while others (such as 'grue': green before time t and blue after t) are not.[345] Predicates of the former variety are called *projectible* and often refer to what are called *natural kinds*. We tend to include projectible predicates in our natural and scientific languages in order to facilitate inductive reasoning. Hence a natural or scientific language implies certain facts about what the natural kinds are, and a change in language implies a corresponding change in background knowledge.

If languages get better at latching on to natural kinds as they evolve, then there is good reason to reject any straightforward application of the language invariance principle. For example suppose that an agent's current language contains predicates 'grue' and 'bleen' rather than 'green' and 'blue'. The agent believes 'all emeralds are grue' to degree 0.99 (the changeover time t is some time

[343] Strictly speaking, if the domain of the agent's probability function changes then her probability function changes. Thus a precise formulation of the language invariance principle must say something like: the probability of any sentence of the new language should be the same as the probability given to its translation into the old language, if such a translation exists, and if no new factual knowledge is gained in the transition between languages.

[344] Inductive generalisation is the process of producing generalisations like 'all emeralds are green' on the basis of a finite number of observations of green emeralds.

[345] (Goodman, 1954, §3.4)

in the future). But then her language changes, with 'green' and 'blue' replacing 'grue' and 'bleen'. If, as I maintain, this change implies that the new predicates latch on to natural kinds better than the old predicates, then the change alone may warrant giving a lower value than 0.99 to 'all emeralds are green before t and blue after t', the translation of the old sentence into the new language. On the other hand, the previous belief may be enough to warrant a value of 0.99 given to 'all emeralds are green', even though the sentence in the old language 'all emeralds are grue before t and bleen after t' may have had a much lower value.

The lesson to be learned here is that the principle of language invariance can only be applied if there is no change in knowledge as language changes. The principle should take *all* background knowledge into account, even implicit knowledge betokened by choice of language, such as that of natural kinds. This clearly limits the applicability of the principle.

I should mention that Howson and Urbach have cast Goodman's example in a different light.[346] They argue that the new problem of induction is a case of underdetermination of theory by evidence: for future t 'all emeralds are green' and 'all emeralds are grue' have the same empirical consequences up to the present, so there is no evidence (up to the present) that can decide between these two hypotheses. Howson and Urbach claim that it is the choice of prior that distinguishes the confirmation given to these two hypotheses: an agent may have given a higher prior probability to 'all emeralds are green' in which case she will still believe that hypothesis to a greater degree after evidence is collected. None of this is incompatible with what I have said. However, there does appear to be a fact of the matter about which predicates are projectible—this is not just a subjective issue—and so an agent who has evidence that 'green' is projectible while 'grue' is not, will surely be *irrational* to give a higher prior probability to 'all emeralds are grue'. Bayesianism should reflect this: perhaps by invoking a constraint on priors to the effect that projectible concepts are awarded higher prior probability than non-projectible concepts. Now at first sight it appears that no agent can have evidence before t that 'green' is projectible but 'grue' is not. It seems at first sight that no constraint on priors which appeals to the syntax of expressions will be able to differentiate between 'all emeralds are green' and 'all emeralds are grue'. But, I claim, language evolves to latch on to projectible predicates, and so if one and not the other of the predicates 'green' and 'grue' occurs as a primitive predicate of the language, then that alone is evidence of its projectibility. I claim that there is a sortal division in the language between projectible and non-projectible concepts: predicates in the language are likely to be projectible, while ad hoc concepts like 'green before t and blue after t' constructed from primitive linguistic predicates are unlikely to be projectible. This gives a syntactic basis on which a prior constraint could operate, and it is clear

[346](Howson and Urbach, 1989, §7.k)

that language invariance is wildly inappropriate given such a prior constraint.[347]

12.4 The Principle of Indifference

Howson formulates a version of the Principle of Indifference whereby each model (up to isomorphism) of a formal language is given equal probability, and the probability of a sentence is the number of models satisfying that sentence multiplied by the probability of a model.[348] This formulation is not in general language invariant and Howson takes this fact as ground to reject the principle of indifference. But there is another way of looking at this. We can accept that choice of language conveys knowledge about which partition of models the principle of indifference should be applied to, in which case we should not expect applications of the Principle of Indifference to be language invariant. If we accept that reasoning by indifference is a mode of reasoning analogous to inductive generalisation then it will be the evolution of language, in the face of selective constraints generated by the quality of our decision-making, that decides the partition of indifference. In many cases where the principle of indifference can be applied in conflicting ways, there is one way which seems intuitively correct, or leads to better predictions.[349] In such cases there is a fact of the matter as to which language leads to better inferences. In other cases different languages may lead to different belief assignments but the ensuing decisions may be of the same quality. In these cases it does not matter that the Principle of Indifference can be applied in different ways: agents with the same explicit background knowledge but different languages may adopt different belief functions yet remain equally rational.

One possible objection to this view is that *internal* application of the principle of indifference remains problematic. The problem is that within a language there may be two partitions of sentences over which we can apply the principle of indifference but which give conflicting conclusions. The answer is not to apply the Principle of Indifference over partitions of sentences within a language, but to stick to *external* applications, exemplified by Howson's partition of models of the language. There is a grue-some analogy. Our language may have predicates 'green' and 'blue', but we may construct within our language the predicate 'grue', by defining it in terms of green and blue. However, an application of inductive generalisation to both 'grue' and 'green' will give conflicting conclusions. If we

[347] In other cases of underdetermination, simplicity is an issue. The problem is that given any hypothesis one can gerrymander a more complicated hypothesis with the same empirical consequences. Some Bayesians maintain that simpler hypotheses should be given higher priors or that they receive higher likelihoods—e.g. Rosenkrantz (1977, chapter 5) and Howson and Urbach (1989, §15.i.2); see also Sober (1975); Forster and Sober (1994); Forster (1995)—and some notions of simplicity may be amenable to syntactic definition. But simplicity may itself be language-relative. Such constraints may also depend on the makeup of the agent under consideration: what is simple for a human agent is sometimes complicated for an artificial agent and vice versa.

[348] (Howson, 2001, p. 145)

[349] (Jaynes, 1973)

accept that it is the language itself that contains the facts about projectibility then the solution is to avoid inductive generalisations on predicates constructed within the language.

12.5 Indirect Evidence

Choice of language can also imply the existence of relationships and connections among the referents of the linguistic terms. Lakatos argued that a language is a part of any scientific theory, since it implies connections:

> *The choice of a language for science implies a conjecture as to what is relevant for what, or what is connected, by natural necessity, with what.* For instance, in a language separating celestial from terrestrial phenomena, data about terrestrial projectiles may seem irrelevant to hypotheses about planetary motion. In the language of Newtonian dynamics they become relevant and change our betting quotients for planetary predictions.[350]

This is especially true of artificial languages, which are often constructed with a single application in mind. In an expert system for liver diagnosis, for instance, most of the variables will be causally connected. One would expect connections even if the causal structure is uncertain or unknown: identifying a suitable set of variables that may be causally related is a crucial first step to identifying the causal connections that actually pertain, and if those variables are chosen carefully the likelihood of causal connections will be high. If new variables are added to the language of the expert system it is because they are causally related, or are likely to be causally related, to the variables already present.

This observation can be used to motivate the techniques of §9.5 for inferring causal beliefs from probabilistic dependencies. In many applications one would expect the set of variables to be chosen in such a way that they are likely to be causally related, in which case probabilistic dependencies will by default indicate causal connections. If on the other hand variables were chosen randomly then V would be diverse enough to combine variables such as British bread price and the Venetian sea level, and probabilistic dependencies in data would be by default attributable to accidental correlations rather than causal connections.

Lakatos also observed that introducing new variables into a language may change degrees of beliefs involving the old terms:

> the problem of 'indirect evidence' (I call '*indirect evidence relative to L in L^**' an event which does not raise the probability of another event when both are described in L, but does so if they are expressed in a language L^*). ... Indirect evidence—a common phenomenon in the growth of knowledge—makes the degree of confirmation a function of L which, in turn changes as science progresses. Although growth of evidence *within* a fixed theoretical framework (the language L) leaves the chosen c-function [i.e. confirmation function] unaltered, growth of the theoretical framework (introduction of a *new* language L^*) may change it radically.[351]

[350] (Lakatos, 1968, p. 362)

[351] (Lakatos, 1968, p. 363)

In general when language changes there is often implicit knowledge which both guides the ascription of degrees of belief over the new terms, and warrants a change in the beliefs over the old terms. We see this when we examine the ways in which language can change.

12.6 Types of Language Change

Perhaps the simplest form of language change occurs when the language expands to provide a richer means of describing the world. A propositional language expands by the addition of new propositional variables; more complex logical languages expand by the addition of new constants, predicates, relations, or functions; natural languages expand in much more diverse ways, including the addition of new adverbs, slang and intonation. Typically the inadequacies of language are realised during abductive reasoning, i.e. the search for an explanation or hypothesis. For instance, when Mendeleev developed the periodic classification of the elements, a theory was hypothesised which posited elements corresponding to each atomic weight—the referents of these new linguistic constants were only gradually discovered in the world. Similarly one may search for some causal explanation of a set of symptoms, find none in the current language, and so invent a syndrome which refers to the particular combination of symptoms, and invent a new causal term to signify whatever actually causes the syndrome. Further investigation then yields a clearer idea as to the properties of the new hypothesised cause. Note that new variables are often likely to be relevant to, and even indirect evidence for, old variables: on discovering a common cause of two symptoms, e.g. one may judge the symptoms more dependent than previously thought.

Languages also contract. Non-referring or redundant terms are often eliminated: a new cause may be invoked to explain a syndrome, but then a cause in the old language may be found, leading to elimination of the new term. Alternatively a new cause may be found to refer, but to be irrelevant to the variables under consideration in the old language. Thus a variable may be eliminated if it is *not* indirect evidence. Similarly, if a relation is found always or never to obtain then it may be considered uninteresting and removed.

Of course language change can be more complicated. Languages may amalgamate, for instance. Alternatively there may be a non-trivial embedding of the old language into the new language. For example, with the introduction of a distinction a propositional variable A may be replaced by B and C and the transition from old to new language will be accompanied by the knowledge that $A \leftrightarrow (B \vee C)$. One interesting case occurs when the syntax of the language remains the same, but the meaning of some of the terms changes. As Thomas Kuhn noted,

> The need to change the meaning of established and familiar concepts is central to the revolutionary impact of Einstein's theory. Though subtler than the changes from geocentrism to heliocentrism, from phlogiston to oxygen, or from corpuscles to waves, the resulting conceptual transformation is no less decisively destructive of a previously established paradigm.

> We may even come to see it as a prototype for revolutionary reorientation in the sciences. Just because it did not involve the introduction of additional objects or concepts, the transition from Newtonian to Einsteinian mechanics illustrates with particular clarity the scientific revolution as a displacement of the conceptual network through which scientists view the world.[352]

Standard formulations of logic do not take into account the change in meaning of terms; thus a logical reconstruction of such cases may demand a change of syntax when meaning changes, so that, instead of a single mass term m being reinterpreted, Newtonian mass m^N is replaced by Einsteinian mass m^E.

According to Kuhn, two scientific theories may be incommensurable and it may be difficult to find grounds to prefer one over the other. Part of the problem is that it may be difficult for a proponent of one theory to translate the other theory into her own language.[353] This is a genuine problem for Bayesianism: how can an agent evaluate another theory if she cannot formulate that theory in her own language? Perhaps the only solution is to expand her language to formulate the new theory and update her beliefs on the basis of those links between the two languages of which she is aware. Thus if our agent has a belief function over the language of Newtonian mechanics and wants to evaluate special relativity, she could extend her language to include the language in which special relativity theory is formulated, and extend her belief function to this bridge language in the light of any constraints imposed by her knowledge of connections between the terms of the two languages.[354]

12.7 Conservativity

The language invariance principle says that in the absence of any change in factual knowledge, an agent's belief function should not change as her language changes. I have argued that a change in language is accompanied by a corresponding implicit change in factual knowledge. This renders the language invariance principle inapplicable.

The *conservativity principle* is more practical. This says that when an agent's language changes her new degrees of belief should be as close as possible to her old degrees of belief, given her new knowledge. A precise formulation of such a principle will be postponed to §12.10. In this section, we shall examine the rationale behind conservativity from a general perspective.

As explained in §2.7, probability as degree of belief is usually justified by appealing to betting considerations. An agent's degree of belief in a sentence θ

[352] (Kuhn, 1962, p. 102)

[353] (Kuhn, 1962, postscript, pp. 202–204)

[354] One can interpret Kuhn's incommensurability thesis as the stronger claim that there is no common bridge language into which two theories can be translated. However, as pointed out by Earman (1992, §8.2), there is little evidence for this thesis and in examples from the history of science it does always seem to be possible to contrive a (perhaps rather unnatural) overarching language.

is interpreted as the betting quotient q she would give, were she to lose $(q - \tau(\theta))S$, where truth function $\tau = 1$ if θ is true and 0 if θ is false, and where S is an unknown stake which may be positive or negative. In order to avoid the possibility that stakes may be chosen that lead to loss whatever the true situation turns out to be, the agent's betting quotients must satisfy the axioms of probability. Conservativity can be justified along similar lines. Suppose the agent first adopts betting quotient q, and later changes her mind, adopting betting quotient r. Her loss function is then $(q - \tau(\theta))S_1 + (r - \tau(\theta))S_2$. Now it is possible to choose new stake S_2 so that the agent loses money whatever happens: if $S_2 > \max\{-q/rS_1, -(1-q)/(1-r)S_1\}$ then the loss will be positive, whatever the value of $\tau(\theta)$. This fact may be used to justify the claim that an agent should not change her degrees of belief unless she has good reason to. But suppose she does have good reason: she discovers that she will be irrational unless she chooses $r \in R$, where R is a closed subset of $[0, 1]$ such that $q \notin R$. The agent's expected loss will be $r[(q - 1)S_1 + (r - 1)S_2] + (1 - r)[qS_1 + rS_2] = (q - r)S_1$, which is clearly minimised if r is chosen to be the value in R closest to q. Thus in order to minimise expected loss, the agent's new degree of belief must be as close as possible to her old degree of belief, subject to the constraints imposed by new knowledge. This gives a simple justification for conservativity.[355]

There is little doubt that humans are by nature conservative with respect to belief change.[356] As William James observed,

> The individual has a stock of old opinions already, but he meets a new experience that puts them to a strain. Somebody contradicts them; or in a reflective moment he discovers that they contradict each other; or he hears of facts with which they are incompatible; or desires arise in him which they cease to satisfy. The result is an inward trouble to which his mind till then had been a stranger, and from which he seeks to escape by modifying his previous mass of opinions. He saves as much of it as he can, for in this matter of belief we are all extreme conservatives. ...
>
> New truth is always a go-between, a smoother over of transitions. It marries old opinion to new fact so as ever to show a minimum of jolt, a maximum of continuity.[357]

Conservativity has mainly been discussed in the context of propositional beliefs, where an agent's belief state may be represented qualitatively as a set of sentences. However, much that has been said carries over to the Bayesian context of numerical degrees of belief, and it will be useful to examine the main positions.

[355]Note that this justification assumes that minimisation of expected loss is an important goal—this may be disputed, especially considering the fact that expected loss is minimised just when expected gain (where gain is negative loss) is minimised. Note also that the situation becomes more complicated when we generalise from single degrees of belief to belief functions—see §12.10, where pointers to more comprehensive justifications are provided.

[356]In fact it appears we are often too conservative, holding on to beliefs even when we know them to be discredited—see Ross and Anderson (1982).

[357](James, 1907, pp. 148–149)

There are a couple of blind alleys to be wary of. The first picks up on the fact that conservativity allows the possibility of two agents with the same evidence holding different beliefs but being equally rational. In the context of propositional beliefs this has been considered counter-intuitive.[358] But consider the same point in the context of numerical degrees of belief. Two agents start off with priors $p(\theta) = 1/4$ and $q(\theta) = 3/4$ respectively. They then both discover evidence that constrains rational degree of belief in θ to lie in $[1/3, 2/3]$. Changing their degrees of belief conservatively they arrive at the new values $p(\theta) = 1/3$ and $q(\theta) = 2/3$. These degrees are significantly different, yet based on the same evidence. However, there should be nothing counter-intuitive here for a subjective Bayesian. Subjective Bayesianism is built on the premise that different agents can hold different priors, and therefore different posteriors given the same evidence, yet both remain rational. Under objective Bayesianism this case simply does not arise: two agents with the same background knowledge have the same degrees of belief.

The second blind alley is the empirical justification of conservativity.[359] Conservativity might be justified inductively if it could be shown that in the past minimal changes led more often to true theories than did extravagant changes of belief. This is a difficult line to take, however, in view of the fact that we almost invariably change beliefs conservatively,[360] and in view of the fact that our scientific theories tend to be proved wrong eventually.[361]

The more promising justifications of conservativity are typically pragmatic: it is a waste of time, energy, and resources to continually change our beliefs for no reason, or to change them more than the minimum amount. William Lycan put the point thus:

> Mother Nature would not want us to change our minds capriciously and for no reason. Any change of belief, like any change in social or political institution, exacts a price, by drawing on energy and resources. A habit of changing one's mind on a whim or otherwise gratuitously, like a habit of unrestrained social experimentation or a national disposition toward political coups or other sudden power and real estate grabs, would be inefficient and confusing; the instability it would create would be poorly suited to a creature whose need for cognitive organization in aid of sudden and streamlined action is great. (My wife points out that it does help, in the morning, not to have to reason your way to the bathroom.)[362]

Thus conservativity is only justified in as much as it offers pragmatic advantage.

[358] See Goldstick (1971). Sklar (1975); Lycan (1988) hold a contrary view.

[359] (Sklar, 1975, pp. 387–388)

[360] Note that an agent does not always need to retain old beliefs in order to satisfy conservativity. Scientific revolutions may be considered to be instances of conservative belief change, where the minimal change in beliefs that is feasible in the light of new evidence is a revolutionary change.

[361] (Laudan, 1981)

[362] (Lycan, 1988, p. 161)

Willard Van Orman Quine claimed that we need to be conservative in order to explain new or unexpected phenomena within an existing framework:

> Familiarity of principle is what we are after when we contrive to "explain" new matters by old laws; e.g., when we devise a molecular hypothesis in order to bring the phenomena of heat, capillary attraction, and surface tension under the familiar old laws of mechanics. Familiarity of principle also figures when "unexpected observations" (i.e., ultimately, some undesirable conflict between sensory conditionings as mediated by the interanimation of sentences) prompt us to revise an old theory; the way in which familiarity of principle then figures is in favoring minimum revision.
>
> The helpfulness of familiarity of principle for the continuing activity of the creative imagination is a sort of paradox. Conservatism, a favoring of the inherited or invented conceptual scheme of one's own previous work, is at one the counsel of laziness and a strategy of discovery.[363]

Keith Lehrer took the opposite view. He argued that conservativity inhibits discovery.

> The primary problem with this proposal is simply that it is a principle of epistemic conservatism, a precept to conserve accepted opinion. On some occasions, such a precept may provide good counsel, but often it will not. The overthrow of accepted opinion and the dictates of common sense are often essential to epistemic advance. Moreover, an epistemic adventurer may arrive at beliefs that are not only new and revelatory, but also better *justified* than those more comfortably held by others. The principle of the conservation of accepted opinion is a roadblock to inquiry, and, consequently, it must be removed.[364]

Of course, epistemic advances often require the overthrow of accepted opinion. But these advances occur because evidence in favour of new theories often renders old theories untenable for epistemic adventurers and conservatives alike. Lehrer's point misses the mark here for two reasons. The first is that he reads conservativity to entail that one should hold beliefs as close as possible to those of other people. This type of intersubjective agreement is only justifiable in special cases.[365] Indeed it seems quite plausible to hold that epistemic advances might be encouraged in the sciences if research councils fund individuals, each of whom are conservative with respect to their own beliefs, but who as a group hold a broad spectrum of incompatible beliefs. The second confusion in the above passage arises with the thought that the epistemic adventurer may be more justified than the conservative. No one argues that an agent should be conservative in the sense that she ought to stick to her old beliefs in the face of evidence that justifies incompatible beliefs. The agent should change her beliefs to accommodate the new information, but change them only as much as is necessary. Thus

[363] (Quine, 1960, p. 20)
[364] (Lehrer, 1974, p. 184)
[365] (Gillies, 1991)

Lehrer's arguments only succeed against notions of conservativity that few would be willing to uphold, and not the notion of conservativity that we are considering here.

It is wrong to think of conservativity in terms of justification. There is very little motivation for the assertion that a minimal change in beliefs is more justified than a large change in beliefs.[366] Justification has already done its work: given new knowledge certain belief states are justified; from those belief states (which are *all* justified) conservativity advocates adopting the belief state which differs least from one's previous belief state. There is clearly no hope in claiming that justification determines that one should adopt that particular belief state. At best one can claim that the minimal change is most *pragmatic* rather than most *justified*.[367]

Gilbert Harman discusses conservativity from the point of view of belief revision (the updating of qualitative, propositional beliefs). Harman distinguishes between *foundational* belief revision, where an agent keeps track of all the justifications of her beliefs and revises her beliefs according to this stock of knowledge, and *coherence* revision, where one forgets past justifications and assigns new beliefs on the basis of new information and the coherence of new beliefs with old beliefs.[368] Conservativity is then an important constraint for the coherence revision strategies: it allows one to choose a new belief state on the basis of the current state.

While Harman discusses belief revision in the context of propositional beliefs, the same distinction can be applied to numerical degrees of belief. Bayesian belief change is most naturally viewed as a coherence-based approach: e.g. Bayesian conditionalisation determines a new belief function from new evidence and the old function. Agents do not need to keep track of their justifications, and indeed it is of pragmatic advantage that they do not. Harman claims that a foundational approach to Bayesian belief change would require large amounts of space to store a database of all past evidence and justifications, and large amounts of time to maintain consistency of this database and to calculate a most rational belief function consistent with the database. Thus coherence-based Bayesian updating offers what Harman calls 'clutter avoidance': the ability to avoid cluttering the

[366]As Lehrer points out, 'the principle that, what is, is justified, is not a better principle of epistemology than of politics or morals' (Lehrer, 1978, p. 358). Christensen (2000) makes a similar point. Christensen puts forward the principle of *epistemic impartiality*, which says that an agent is not justified in adopting beliefs solely on the basis of their belonging to the agent's present belief state.

[367]It is for this reason that conservativity cannot help with the problem of underdetermination of theory by evidence. Sklar (1975, §3) argues that conservativity can be used to pick one among several equally justified hypotheses. But while conservativity can tell us what to do when we face underdetermination, the application of conservativity depends on there being underdetermination—if only one hypothesis is justified then we do not need conservativity to tell us what to do. Thus conservativity can in no way be thought of as a solution to the problem of underdetermination.

[368](Harman, 1986, chapter 4)

mind with unimportant things.[369] It is no small matter to ensure that Bayesian degrees of belief can be stored efficiently or that Bayesian updating can be performed efficiently, and we shall need to investigate whether or not a coherence approach surpasses a foundational approach in this respect.[370]

12.8 Prospects for a Solution

Lakatos again:

> Carnap tried his best to avoid any 'language-dependence' of inductive logic. But he always assumed that the growth of science is in a sense cumulative: he held that one could stipulate that once the degree of confirmation of h given e has been established in a suitable 'minimal language', no further argument can ever alter this value. But scientific change frequently implies change of language and change of language implies change in the corresponding c-values.
>
> This simple argument shows that Carnap's (implicit) 'principle of minimal language' does not work. This principle of gradual construction of the c-function was meant to save the fascinating ideal of an eternal, absolutely valid, *a priori* inductive logic, the ideal of an inductive machine that, once programmed, may need an *extension of the original programming* but *no reprogramming*. Yet this ideal breaks down. The growth of science may destroy any particular confirmation theory: the inductive machine may have to be reprogrammed with each new major theoretical advance.
>
> Carnapians may retort that the revolutionary growth of science will produce a revolutionary growth of inductive logic. But how can inductive logic grow? How can we change our whole betting policy with respect to hypotheses expressed in a language L whenever a new theory couched in a new language L^* is proposed?[371]

Lakatos' questions at the end of this passage remain as important today as they were in 1968: we still do not know how degrees of belief should change as language changes.

Earman maintains that there is no formal procedure for transforming the belief function in such circumstances:

> Indeed, the problem of the transition from Pr to Pr' can be thought of as no more and no less than the familiar Bayesian problem of assigning initial probabilities, only now with a new initial situation involving a new set of possibilities and a new information basis. But the problem we are now facing is quite unlike those allegedly solved by classical principles of indifference or modern variants thereof, such as E.T. Jaynes's maximum entropy principle, where it is assumed that we know nothing or very little

[369](Harman, 1986, p. 41)

[370]Gärdenfors (1990, §3) picks up on the computational advantages that a coherence approach offers propositional belief revision. Indeed the AGM theory of belief revision that Gardenfors defends is a coherence theory. See also Rott (1999) on this point.

[371](Lakatos, 1968, pp. 363–364)

> about the possibilities in question. In typical cases the scientific community will possess a vast store of relevant experimental and theoretical information. Using that information to inform the redistribution of probabilities over the competing theories on the occasion of the introduction of the new theory or theories is a process that is, in the strict sense of the term, *a*rational: it cannot be accomplished by some neat formal rules or, to use Kuhn's term, by an algorithm. On the other hand, the process is far from being *ir*rational, since it is informed by reasons. But the reasons, as Kuhn has emphasized, come in the form of persuasions rather than proof. In Bayesian terms, the reasons are marshalled in the guise of plausibility arguments. The deployment of plausibility arguments is an art form for which there currently exists no taxonomy. And in view of the limitless variety of such arguments, it is unlikely that anything more than a superficial taxonomy can be developed.[372]

We shall see, contra Earman, that inroads can be made on the problem of language change, at least in the restrictive formal setting of propositional logic. Indeed maximum entropy techniques can help us here. However, there are cautionary lessons to be learned from the analysis so far. Language invariance will not help us because an agent's language contains implicit factual knowledge. This has two repercussions. First, if we are to save intuitions behind language invariance, we will have to generalise it to some form of conservativity principle. Second, this transitional knowledge will have to be made explicit before the more general conservativity rule can be formally applied. Making the transitional knowledge explicit will in general be no mean feat—it is at this stage that insight and an awareness of subtleties of the particular domain come into play—but will clearly be a prerequisite of any formal analysis. Further, Kuhn's problem of incommensurability should lead us to look for a bridge language that encompasses the old and new languages. The relationships between the old and new terms in the bridge language may again be subtle and difficult to ascertain fully, but if knowledge of these relationships can be rendered explicit then the resulting formalisation will have normative value.

12.9 Language Change Update Strategies

We shall now look at the problem of language change from a more formal perspective.

Consider an agent whose initial background knowledge $\beta_0 = (\kappa_0, \lambda_0, \pi_0, \ldots)$ consists of causal constraints κ_0, logical constraints λ_0, probabilistic constraints π_0, and so on. The agent's rational belief function is $p_0 = p_{\beta_0}$, a probability function on propositional language V_0 that is rational given β_0. (As we saw in §11.9 this induces a probability function on the sentences S_{V_0} of V_0.) Suppose the agent's language changes to V_1 and τ is an explicit formulation of *all* the agent's new knowledge gained in the transition from V_0 to V_1, including knowl-

[372] (Earman, 1992, p. 197)

edge implied by choice of the new language. The key task is to define a new rational belief function p_1 over V_1 (and thereby over S_{V_1}).

A *knowledge revision strategy* is a function $\star$ for producing new constraints $\beta = \beta_0 \star \tau$ from initial knowledge β_0 and transitional knowledge τ. A knowledge revision strategy is *maximally forgetful* if $\beta_0 \star \tau = \tau$ for all β_0 and τ; it is *maximally retentive* if $\beta_0 \star \tau = \beta_0 \cup \tau$ whenever τ is consistent with β_0. We shall suppose here that a fixed knowledge revision strategy has been chosen and that $\beta = \beta_0 \star \tau$ represents all the constraints imposed by background knowledge that are operational after the transition to new language. We shall also suppose that these constraints can be transferred to a set of purely probabilistic constraints π_β using the transfer principles outlined in §§5.8 and 11.4.

We shall call $V = V_0 \cup V_1$ the *bridge language*, and $V_+ = V \backslash V_0 = V_1 \backslash V_0$ the *additional language*. Note that if any of the variables in V_0 change meaning in the transition to V_1 (as in the case of the move from Newtonian to Einsteinian mass mentioned in §12.6) then the syntax should reflect this change by introducing new variables to correspond to the new meanings (thus the bridge language would contain a distinct variable for each type of mass). This framework allows us to achieve our key task by defining a rational belief function p on V, given V_0, p_0 and β, and then setting $p_1 = p_{\downharpoonright V_1}$, the restriction of p to V_1.

Unfortunately Bayesian conditionalisation does not help us much here. The principle of Bayesian conditionalisation says that when the agent learns θ she should set her new degrees of belief to her old degrees conditional on θ, $p_1(\phi) = p_0(\phi|\theta)$, for each sentence ϕ of V_1. This rule is fine when the agent's language does not change, but is only helpful in our context if the transitional knowledge takes the form of set of sentences or sentence $\theta \subseteq S_{V_0}$ and $\phi \in S_{V_0}$, since p_0 is only defined on the sentences of V_0. Thus we require a more general way of determining the agent's new belief function.

Let $\mathbb{P}, \mathbb{P}_0$ signify the sets of probability functions defined on V, V_0 respectively. Let $\mathbb{P}_\beta \subseteq \mathbb{P}$ be the set of probability functions on V that satisfy β (equivalently, that satisfy the probabilistic constraints π_β that are the result of transferring constraints in β). What we require is a way of transforming $p_0 \in \mathbb{P}_0$ into some suitably rational $p \in \mathbb{P}_\beta$. Define a *language change update strategy* (or just *update strategy* for short) on V given p_0 and β, to be a function $\Upsilon(V, p_0, \beta)$ that selects a rational belief function $p \in \mathbb{P}_\beta$, given rational $p_0 \in \mathbb{P}_0$ and constraints β.

What form should Υ take? What makes a particular belief function $p \in \mathbb{P}$ rational, given p_0 and β? This is the key issue we now face. Two approaches stand out. The maximin update strategy (§12.10) fits well with intuitions about conservativity and can be implemented using Bayesian nets (§12.11). However, it does not handle indirect evidence properly (§12.5) and should be rejected, I argue, in favour of the maxent update strategy (§12.13).

12.10 The Maximin Update Strategy

In §§12.7 and 12.8 it was pointed out that intuitions behind language invariance could be salvaged to some extent if we assume that rational belief should change as little as possible as language and knowledge changes.

An update strategy Υ is *conservative* if, for each p_0 and β, $\Upsilon(V, p_0, \beta)$ is a function $p \in \mathbb{P}_\beta$ that is closest to p_0 according to the cross entropy measure of distance:

$$d_{V_0}(p, p_0) = \sum_{v_0 @ V_0} p(v_0) \log \frac{p(v_0)}{p_0(v_0)}.$$

There are several well-known arguments to the effect that a new belief function should minimise cross entropy relative to the old function, subject to constraints imposed by β.[373] These arguments can be construed both as reason to employ conservative update strategies in general and as reason to explicate the notion of conservativity via minimum cross entropy. Since minimum cross entropy updating generalises Bayesian conditionalisation,[374] the resulting conservative update strategy will too.

However, minimising cross entropy will only constrain the new belief function p over V_0. Ensuring that $d_{V_0}(p, p_0)$ is minimised may fix the restriction $p_{\downharpoonright V_0}$ of p to V_0, but it will tell us nothing about p on V_+. Thus we must look for a further constraint to choose an appropriate function p from all those functions equally close to p_0 on V_0.

From the objective Bayesian point of view the rational thing to do is to apply the Maximum Entropy Principle and choose a function in $\mathbb{P}_\beta$ that maximises the entropy

$$H_V(p) = -\sum_{v @ V} p(v) \log p(v).$$

We thus have the following recipe for determining p on V given p_0 and β: choose a function from $\{p \in \mathbb{P}_\beta : p \text{ minimises } d_{V_0}(p, p_0)\}$ that maximises entropy $H_V(p)$. We shall call this the *maximin update strategy*, Υ_{Mm}. If we let $\mathbb{DP}_\beta = \{p \in \mathbb{P}_\beta : p \text{ minimises } d_{V_0}(p, p_0)\}$ and $\mathbb{HP}_\beta = \{p \in \mathbb{P}_\beta : p \text{ maximises } H_V(p)\}$ then $\Upsilon_{Mm}(V, p_0, \beta) \in \mathbb{HDP}_\beta$.

An important case occurs when $\mathbb{P}_\beta$ is a convex and closed set, for then minimising cross entropy fixes p uniquely over V_0, and maximising entropy fixes p uniquely over V. Thus the maximin update strategy fixes a unique rational belief function in this case. If the constraints in π_β are linear, i.e. of the form $\sum_{i=1}^r a_i p(\theta_i) = b$ for $\theta_i \in S_V, i = 1, \ldots r$, then closure and convexity are guaranteed.[375] Closure and convexity will be the norm if the arguments of §5.4 are accepted.

Minimising cross entropy is equivalent to maximising

$$-d_{V_0}(p, p_0) = -\sum_{v_0} p(v_0) \log \frac{p(v_0)}{p_0(v_0)}$$

[373] These are detailed in Paris (1994, pp. 120–126).

[374] (Williams, 1980)

[375] (Paris, 1994, Proposition 6.1)

$$= -\sum_{v_0} p(v_0) \log p(v_0) + \sum_{v_0} p(v_0) \log p_0(v_0)$$
$$= H_{V_0}(p) + E \log p_0$$

over probability functions in $\mathbb{P}_\beta$, where E is the expectation with respect to p. Since $\log x$ is strictly increasing in x for $0 < x \leq 1$, the expectation of $\log x$ is maximised just when the expectation of x, judged according to future belief function p, is maximised. Thus minimising cross entropy can be thought of as a balance between maximising the entropy over V_0 and maximising the expectation of current beliefs.

The next step, maximising entropy, requires maximising

$$H_V(p) = -\sum_{v_0, v_+} p(v_+|v_0)p(v_0) \log p(v_+|v_0)p(v_0)$$
$$= -\sum_{v_0, v_+} p(v_+|v_0)p(v_0) \log p(v_+|v_0) - \sum_{v_0} p(v_0) \log p(v_0)$$
$$= H_{V_+|V_0}(p) + H_{V_0}(p)$$

over probability functions in $\mathbb{P}_\beta$, where $v_+ @ V_+ = V \backslash V_0$. Now if $\mathbb{P}_\beta$ is convex and closed then the terms $p(v_0)$ are fixed by the cross entropy minimisation, and so entropy is maximised by maximising $-\sum_{v_0, v_+} p(v_+|v_0)p(v_0) \log p(v_+|v_0)$ with respect to the parameters $p(v_+|v_0)$.

We have seen in Chapter 5 how a Bayesian net can be constructed to efficiently represent a probability function that maximises entropy. In §12.11 we shall digress to outline a similar approach for minimising cross entropy efficiently. The two techniques can be combined to implement the maximin update strategy using Bayesian nets.

12.11 Cross Entropy Updating of Bayesian Nets

Current techniques for updating Bayesian nets tend to implement Bayesian conditionalisation: an observation is made which takes the form of an assignment u to a subset U of the variables V in the net, and then the probability specifiers of the net are updated from $p(a_i|par_i)$ to $p(a_i|upar_i)$ so that the net represents probability function $p(v|u)$, the Bayesian conditionalisation update of the original function $p(v)$.[376] There are methods for updating network parameters using Jeffrey conditionalisation (a generalisation of Bayesian conditionalisation)[377] and for updating network structure in the light of new statistical data,[378] but no general implementation of cross entropy updating. In this section, we shall redress the balance by showing how the minimum cross entropy update of a Bayesian net can be calculated.

[376] (Pearl, 1988, chapter 4; Neapolitan, 1990, chapters 6–7; Lauritzen and Spiegelhalter, 1988)

[377] (Valtorta *et al.*, 2002)

[378] (Buntine, 1991; Lam and Bacchus, 1994*b*; Friedman and Goldszmidt, 1997; Tong and Koller, 2001)

The problem is this. Given a domain of variables $V = \{A_1, \ldots, A_n\}$, a Bayesian net $(\mathcal{H}_0, \mathcal{S}_0)$ on V representing an initial probability function p_0, and a set $\pi = \{\pi_1, \ldots, \pi_m\}$ of new probabilistic constraints of the form $f_i(z_i) \geqq 0$ for $i = 1, \ldots, m$, how can one construct a Bayesian net $(\mathcal{H}, \mathcal{S})$ on V representing a probability function p that is closest to p_0, out of all the functions that satisfy π?

The procedure for solving this problem is a modification of the procedure of §§5.5, 5.6, and 5.7 for constructing a Bayesian net that represents the entropy maximiser. Instead of maximising entropy we are minimising cross entropy

$$\begin{aligned} d(p, p_0) &= \sum_{v@V} p(v) \log \frac{p(v)}{p_0(v)} \\ &= \sum_{v@V} x^v \log \frac{x^v}{p_0(v)} \end{aligned}$$

with respect to the x-parameters $x^v = p(v)$.

The first step is to construct an undirected graph $\mathcal{G}$ representing probabilistic independencies satisfied by p. To do this first we take an undirected graph $\mathcal{G}_0$ with respect to which p_0 factorises. This might be the undirected constraint graph used in the construction of $\mathcal{H}_0$, or if that is not available one can instead take a triangulation $(\mathcal{H}_0^m)^T$ of the undirected *moral graph* $\mathcal{H}_0^m$, formed by taking the variables of $\mathcal{H}_0$ and adding edges between variables with a common child in $\mathcal{H}_0$ and between variables which are directly connected by an arrow in $\mathcal{H}_0$ (any separation in $\mathcal{H}_0^m$ corresponds to a D-separation in $\mathcal{H}_0$,[379] though the converse is not true in general).[380] Then we add edges between any two variables that occur in the same constraint in π. (Thus the graph $\mathcal{G}$ can be constructed as the union of the undirected constraint graph for p_0 and the undirected constraint graph for π.) We then have an analogue of Theorem 5.1:

Theorem 12.1 *If Z separates X from Y in $\mathcal{G}$ then $X \perp\!\!\!\perp_p Y \mid Z$ for a minimum cross entropy update p.*

Proof: The proof is analogous to that of Theorem 5.1. If $x \in \mathbb{P}_\pi$ is a local minimum of d then there are constant Lagrange multipliers $\mu, \lambda_1, \ldots, \lambda_m \in \mathbb{R}$ such that

$$\frac{\partial d}{\partial x^v} + \mu + \sum_{i=1}^{m} \lambda_i \frac{\partial f_i}{\partial x^v} = 0 \qquad (12.1)$$

for each assignment $v@V$, where μ is the multiplier corresponding to the additivity constraint $\sum_{v@V} x^v = 1$, and where $\lambda_i = 0$ for each inequality constraint which is not effective at x (i.e. for each inequality constraint π_i such that $f_i(x) > 0$).

[379] (Lauritzen, 1996, Lemma 3.21)

[380] Because $(\mathcal{H}_0^m)^T$ represents independencies in p_0 and is triangulated, p_0 factorises according to $(\mathcal{H}_0^m)^T$—see Lauritzen (1996), Propositions 2.5 and 3.19.

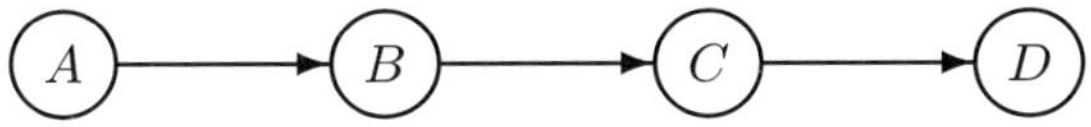

FIG. 12.1. $\mathcal{H}_0$.

FIG. 12.2. $\mathcal{G}_0$.

Now

$$\frac{\partial f_i}{\partial x^v} = \frac{\partial f_i}{\partial z_i^{c_i}}$$

where c_i is the assignment to C_i that is consistent with v. Furthermore,

$$\frac{\partial d}{\partial x^v} = 1 + \log \frac{x^v}{p_0(v)},$$

so eqn 12.1 can be written

$$\log x^v = \log p_0(v) - 1 - \mu - \sum_{i=1}^{m} \lambda_i \frac{\partial f_i}{\partial z_i^{c_i}},$$

where each $c_i \sim v$.

$\mathcal{G} = \mathcal{G}_0 \cup \mathcal{G}_\pi$ is the union of an undirected graph $\mathcal{G}_0$ with respect to which p_0 factorises and the undirected constraint graph $\mathcal{G}_\pi$ for π. That p_0 factorises according to $\mathcal{G}_0$ means that $p_0(v) = \prod_{j=1}^{l} g_j(w_j)$ for some functions $g_1, \ldots, g_l$, where $v \sim w_j@W_j$ and $W_1, \ldots, W_l$ are the cliques of $\mathcal{G}_0$.

So,

$$x^v = e^{-\mu-1} \prod_{j=1}^{l} g_j(w_j) \prod_{i=1}^{m} e^{-\lambda_i (\partial f_i / \partial z_i^{c_i})}. \tag{12.2}$$

Thus p factorises according to complete subsets of $\mathcal{G}$ and so factorises according to $\mathcal{G}$ itself.[381] The Global Markov Condition follows: if Z separates X from Y in $\mathcal{G}$ then $X \perp\!\!\!\perp_p Y \mid Z$.[382] Hence the theorem holds for local minima p, and in particular for global minima p. ■

Next we can construct a directed graph $\mathcal{H}$ that represents independencies of p using the algorithm outlined at the beginning of §5.7. For example, suppose $\mathcal{H}_0$ is Fig. 12.1 and π contains one constraint involving A, B, and D. Then p_0 factorises with respect to the undirected graph Fig. 12.2, and Fig. 12.3 is

[381] (Lauritzen, 1996, pp. 34–35)

[382] (Lauritzen, 1996, Proposition 3.8)

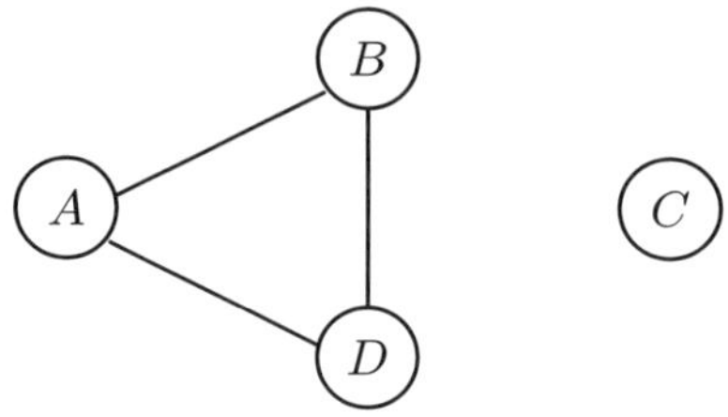

FIG. 12.3. $\mathcal{G}_\pi$.

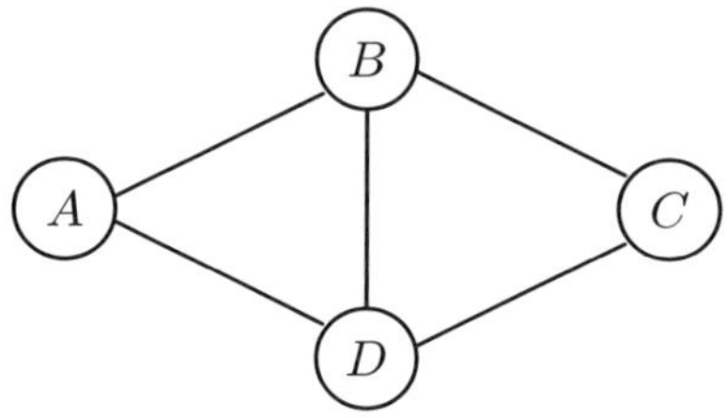

FIG. 12.4. $\mathcal{G}$.

the undirected constraint graph, so Fig. 12.4 is their union $\mathcal{G}$ representing independencies in p. The graph yielded by the construction method of §5.7 with a maximum cardinality search ordering of A, B, D, C is Fig. 12.5.[383]

The final step is to determine corresponding probability specifiers $\mathcal{S}$ in order to yield a Bayesian net. By reparameterising cross entropy in terms of $y_i^u = p(a_i^u | par_i^u)$ we get

$$d(p, p_0) = \sum_{v@V} x^v \log \frac{x^v}{p_0(v)}$$

[383]The example shows that while following this procedure will ensure that $\mathcal{H}$ efficiently represents the independencies of p, it will not necessarily lead to a graph $\mathcal{H}$ that extends $\mathcal{G}_0$. If the arrow from C to D is induced by a causal constraint and it is important to retain this arrow in the new graph $\mathcal{G}$ then the constraint itself (or rather its transferred version) must be retained in π.

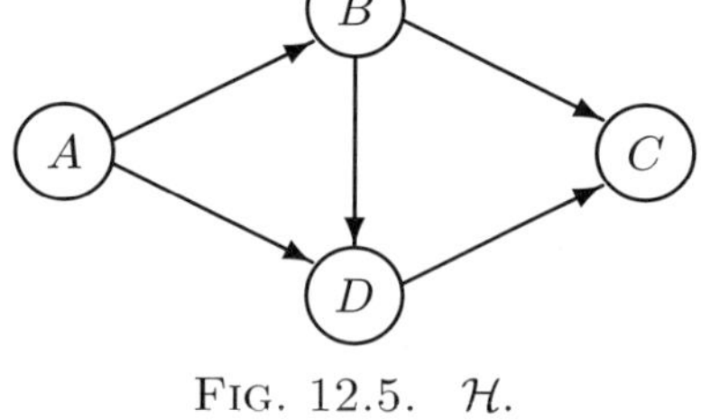

FIG. 12.5. $\mathcal{H}$.

$$= \sum_{v@V} \left(\prod_{j=1}^{n} y_j^v \right) \log \prod_{i=1}^{n} \frac{y_i^v}{p_0(v)}$$

$$= \sum_{v@V} \left(\prod_{j=1}^{n} y_j^v \right) \sum_{i=1}^{n} [\log y_i^v - \log p_0(v)]$$

$$= \sum_{i=1}^{n} \sum_{v@V} \left(\prod_{j=1}^{n} y_j^v \right) \log \frac{y_i^v}{p_0(v)}$$

$$= \sum_{i=1}^{n} \sum_{v@V} \left(\prod_{A_j \in Anc_i'} y_j^v \right) \log \frac{y_i^v}{p_0(v)},$$

where $Anc_i' = \{A_i\} \cup Anc_i$ consists of A_i and its ancestors in $\mathcal{H}$.

One can use numerical or Lagrange multiplier methods to find values of the y-parameters that minimise d. The latter approach involves solving the equation

$$\frac{\partial d}{\partial y_i^v} + \mu_i^v + \sum_{i=1}^{m} \lambda_i \frac{\partial f_i}{\partial y_i^v} = 0$$

with

$$\frac{\partial d}{\partial y_i^v} = \sum_{A_k : A_i \in Anc_k'} \sum_{u@V, u \sim_i v} \left(\prod_{A_j \in Anc_k', j \neq i} y_j^u \right) \left[\log \frac{y_k^u}{p_0(u)} + I_{k=i} \right]$$

where $I_{k=i} = 1$ if $k = i$ and 0 otherwise, $u \sim_i v$ if u is consistent with v on A_i and its parents, and $\lambda_i = 0$ for each inequality constraint π_i which is not effective at y_i^v.

Note that the following result (which can be proved using Lagrange multiplier methods or by analysis of the properties of cross entropy)[384] can be used to simplify the calculation of y-parameters of unconstrained variables:

Proposition 12.2 *Let $C \subseteq V$ be the variables occurring in π and $B = V \backslash C$. Then $p(b|c) = p_0(b|c)$ for all assignments b and c to B and C respectively.*

Note also that the methods of §§5.5, 5.6, and 5.7 for maximising entropy can be derived as a special case of the above procedure for minimising cross entropy. The entropy maximiser in $\mathbb{P}_\pi$ is the function in $\mathbb{P}_\pi$ that is closest to the entropy maximiser in the whole space $\mathbb{P}$, which is the function q that gives the same probability $q(v) = 1/||V||$ to each assignment. To see that H is maximised when $d(p,q)$ is minimised, simply write

$$d(p,q) = \sum_{v} p(v) \log p(v) - \log \frac{1}{||V||} \sum_{v} p(v) = -H(p) + \log ||V||.$$

[384](Williamson, 2003*b*, §§14, 16)

Now the function q is represented by a Bayesian net involving a discrete graph (i.e. no arrows) and specification $\{q(a_i) = 1/||A_i|| : a_i@A_i, i = 1, \ldots, n\}$. If we set p_0 to this function and apply the above procedure for minimising cross entropy then the undirected graph $\mathcal{G}$ is just the undirected constraint graph $\mathcal{G}$ of §5.6, the directed graph $\mathcal{H}$ is the directed constraint graph $\mathcal{H}$ of §5.7 and the equations of this section for determining y-parameters are equivalent to those of §5.7.

Returning now to the language change problem, we can combine the methods of this section for minimising cross entropy with those of §§5.5, 5.6, and 5.7 for maximising entropy to implement the maximin update strategy:

Min: Minimise cross entropy on V_0: form the union $\mathcal{G}^{V_0} = \mathcal{G}_0 \cup \mathcal{G}_\beta^{V_0}$ of the undirected constraint graph for p_0 with an undirected constraint graph for β on V_0,[385] transform this graph into a directed acyclic graph and determine probability specifiers.

Max: Maximise entropy on V, subject to the constraint that p over V_0 is fixed. First form an undirected constraint graph $\mathcal{G}$. While the constraint set for the constraint that p over V_0 is fixed is V_0 itself, the undirected graph $\mathcal{G}^{V_0}$ that represents the independencies of $p_{\lfloor V_0}$, produced in the previous step, can be substituted for the complete graph on V_0, so $\mathcal{G} = \mathcal{G}^{V_0} \cup \mathcal{G}_\beta = \mathcal{G}_0 \cup \mathcal{G}_\beta$. Next transform this graph into a directed constraint graph and determine probability specifiers with the help of the net produced at the previous step.

12.12 Compatibility and Indirect Evidence

There is an important problem with conservative update strategies and the maximin strategy in particular: they do not take indirect evidence into account. If a new variable is indirect evidence for old variables then there may be reason to change degrees of belief in the old variables. However, unless the new evidence strictly contradicts the old degrees of belief, a conservative update strategy will not permit any changes of degrees of belief on the old language.

Recall that β is compatible with p_0 defined on V_0 if there is some p defined on V which extends p_0 and satisfies β. Now if β is compatible with p_0 then any probability function in $\mathbb{P}_\beta$ that is closest to p_0 on V_0 extends p_0 itself—degrees of belief on V_0 do not change. But compatibility is rather a weak consistency notion. Transitional knowledge may be compatible with p_0 yet still count as indirect evidence. But then for a conservative update strategy, indirect evidence that is compatible can never change degrees of belief over V_0.

[385] Note that $\mathcal{G}_\beta$, the undirected constraint graph of β, is a graph on the whole of V but we need a graph on V_0. If β is compatible on V_0 we can just take the undirected constraint graph of β_{V_0}. Otherwise form an undirected graph on V_0 by connecting two variables with an edge if they are directly connected in $\mathcal{G}_\beta$ or if there is a path from one to the other in $\mathcal{G}_\beta$ whose interior involves variables not in V_0.

Take for instance the example of §5.8 involving smoking S, lung cancer L, bronchitis B and chest pains C (see Fig. 5.5). In this example the original language is $V_0 = \{L, B\}$ and p_0, say, renders L and B independent. The agent then learns of a common cause S of L and B, and that there is a positive dependency between S and its effects, with transitional knowledge consisting of κ as in Fig. 5.4 and $\pi = \{p(l^1|s^1) = 0.2, p(l^1|s^0) = 0.01, p(b^1|s^1) = 0.3, p(b^1|s^0) = 0.05\}$. In this case it seems plausible that L and B ought to be rendered more dependent than they originally were. But the new knowledge is compatible with original belief function p_0. Thus a conservative update strategy would yield a new probability function identical to p_0 on $\mathcal{L}_0$; the fact that the new knowledge is indirect evidence has not been taken into account.

12.13 The Maxent Update Strategy

Section 12.7 introduced the distinction between coherence and foundational approaches to belief change. The maximin update strategy is conservative and thus coherence-based. But foundational update strategies are also possible. The *maxent update strategy* $\Upsilon_M(V, p_0, \beta) = p_\beta \in \mathbb{HP}_\beta$ just involves adopting a belief function that maximises entropy, from all those that satisfy constraints β. This update strategy is not conservative at all: the prior degrees of belief p_0 are ignored when it comes to choosing p.

The maxent update strategy resolves the problem of indirect evidence. A maximum entropy probability function will by default render lung cancer and bronchitis dependent when presented with smoking as indirect evidence. Indeed the maximum entropy techniques of §5.8 were devised to deal with just this sort of case and the justification of Causal Irrelevance in §5.8 was even couched in terms of learning new variables, i.e. language change.

The procedure for maximising entropy under language change is a straightforward application of the techniques of §§5.5, 5.6, 5.7, 5.8, and 11.4. Transfer all non-probabilistic constraints into probabilistic constraints (§§5.8, 11.4), and recursively construct a Bayesian net by building undirected constraint graphs (§5.6) and transforming them into Bayesian nets (§5.7).

There is a pragmatic argument against the maxent strategy based on Harman's argument given at the end of §12.7. While from a formal point of view choice of background knowledge revision strategy is independent of the choice of belief function update strategy, some combinations are more plausible than others. Because the maximin strategy takes p_0 into account and this function encapsulates previous knowledge β_0, one can couple the maximin belief update strategy with a maximally forgetful background knowledge revision strategy—past knowledge β_0 will still guide the setting of new degrees of belief. On the other hand the maxent strategy ignores p_0, so in order to ensure that β_0 influences new degrees of belief it makes most sense to couple maxent with a maximally retentive background knowledge revision strategy. Now there are pragmatic reasons for preferring a forgetful knowledge revision strategy over a retentive strategy: a forgetful strategy offers 'clutter avoidance'. Because of the natural pairing of a forgetful knowledge strategy with a conservative belief strategy, we then have a pragmatic reason to be conservative. Thus the maximin update strategy is to be preferred over the maxent update strategy for pragmatic reasons.

There are two problems with this argument. First, it should be rationality considerations, not pragmatic considerations, that decide between background knowledge revision strategies. There seems to be little question that a maximally forgetful agent will fare less well than one who remembers past constraints and revises them in the light of new information. Second, even if a maximally retentive knowledge revision strategy were adopted, it is far from clear that the agent would be significantly worse off. While introducing new probabilistic constraints can increase the size of constraint sets and thereby increase the complexity of the entropy maximisation task, the size n of the language increases at the same time and it may well be that increase in complexity is small as a function of n. Moreover, as pointed out in §5.8, extra causal constraints can simplify the entropy maximisation task; the same is the case with knowledge of other influence relations.

In sum then, while conservativity might appear to be a pragmatic way to salvage intuitions behind language invariance, it leads (at least when explicated using cross-entropy distance) to obstinate agents who are unable to change degrees of belief in the face of indirect evidence. A foundational approach based on maximising entropy seems to be much more plausible from a normative point of view, and can be implemented using the Bayesian net techniques developed in this book.

REFERENCES

Andersson, Steen A., Madigan, David, and Perlman, Michael D. (1997). A characterisation of Markov equivalence classes for acyclic digraphs. *Annals of Statistics*, **25**, 505–541.

Armstrong, Helen and Korb, Kevin B. (2003). Minimal I-map dags: necessary and sufficient conditions. Technical Report 2003/132, School of Computer Science and Software Engineering, Monash University, Melbourne.

Arntzenius, Frank (1992). The common cause principle. *Philosophy of Science Association*, **1992(2)**, 227–237.

Bacon, Francis (1620). *The New Organon*. Cambridge University Press (2000), Cambridge. Ed. Lisa Jardine and Michael Silverthorne.

Benacerraf, Paul (1973). Mathematical truth. In *Philosophy of mathematics: selected readings* (Second (1983) edn) (ed. P. Benacerraf and H. Putnam), pp. 403–420. Cambridge University Press, Cambridge.

Bench-Capon, T.J.M. (2003). Persuasion in practical argument using value based argumentation frameworks. *Journal of Logic and Computation*, **13(3)**, 429–448.

Bender, E.A., Richmond, L.B., Robinson, R.W., and Wormald, N.C. (1986). The asymptotic number of acyclic digraphs 1. *Combinatorica*, **6(1)**, 15–22.

Bernoulli, Jakob (1713). *Ars Conjectandi*. cerebro.xu.edu/math/Sources/JakobBernoulli/ars_sung/ars_sung.html. Trans. Bing Sung.

Billingsley, Patrick (1979). *Probability and measure* (Third (1995) edn). John Wiley and Sons, New York.

Binder, John, Koller, Daphne, Russell, Stuart, and Kanazawa, Keiji (1997). Adaptive probabilistic networks with hidden variables. *Machine Learning*, **29**, 213–244.

Blake, C. L. and Merz, C. J. (1998). UCI repository of machine learning databases. http://www.ics.uci.edu/~mlearn/MLRepository.html. University of California, Irvine, Dept. of Information and Computer Sciences.

Bundy, Alan (1999). A survey of automated deduction. In *Artificial intelligence today: recent trends and developments* (ed. M. Wooldridge and M. M. Veloso), Volume 1600 of *Lecture Notes in Computer Science*, pp. 153–174. Springer, Berlin.

Bundy, Alan (2002). A critique of proof planning. In *Computational logic: logic programming and beyond, essays in honour of Robert A. Kowalski* (ed. A. C. Kakas and F. Sadri), Volume 2407 of *Lecture Notes in Computer Science*, pp. 160–177. Springer, Berlin.

Buntine, Wray (1991). Theory refinement on Bayesian networks. In *Proceedings of the 7th Annual Conference on Uncertainty in Artificial Intelligence* (ed. B. D. D'Ambrosio, P. Smets, and P. P. Bonissone), pp. 52–60. Morgan

Kaufmann.

Butterfield, Jeremy (1992). Bell's theorem: what it takes. *British Journal for the Philosophy of Science*, **43**, 41–83.

Carnap, Rudolf (1950). *Logical foundations of probability.* Routledge and Kegan Paul, London.

Carnap, Rudolf (1971). A basic system of inductive logic part 1. In *Studies in inductive logic and probability* (ed. R. Carnap and R. C. Jeffrey), Volume 1, pp. 33–165. University of California Press, Berkeley CA.

Cartwright, Nancy (1983). *How the laws of physics lie.* Clarendon Press, Oxford.

Cartwright, Nancy (1989). *Nature's capacities and their measurement.* Clarendon Press, Oxford.

Cartwright, Nancy (1997). What is a causal structure? In *Causality in crisis? Statistical methods and the search for causal knowledge in the social sciences* (ed. V. R. McKim and S. Turner), pp. 343–357. University of Notre Dame Press, Notre Dame.

Cartwright, Nancy (1999). Causality: independence and determinism. In *Causal models and intelligent data management* (ed. A. Gammerman), pp. 51–63. Springer, Berlin.

Cartwright, Nancy (2001). What is wrong with Bayes nets? *The Monist*, **84(2)**, 242–264.

Cheeseman, Peter (1983). A method of computing generalised Bayesian probability values for expert systems. In *Proceedings of the 6th International Joint Conference on Artificial Intelligence*, pp. 198–202.

Chickering, David (1996). Learning Bayesian networks is NP-complete. In *Learning from data* (ed. D. Lenz and H. Fisher), Volume 112 of *Lecture Notes in Statistics*, pp. 121–130. Springer-Verlag.

Chow, C. K. and Liu, C. N. (1968). Approximating discrete probability distributions with dependence trees. *IEEE Transactions on Information Theory*, **IT-14**, 462–467.

Christensen, David (2000). Diachronic coherence versus epistemic impartiality. *The Philosophical Review*, **109(3)**, 349–371.

Church, Alonzo (1936). An unsolvable problem of elementary number theory. *American Journal of Mathematics*, **58**, 345–363.

Coleman, J. (1992). *Risks and wrongs.* Cambridge University Press, Cambridge.

Cooper, G. F. (1990). The computational complexity of probabilistic inference using Bayesian belief networks. *Artificial Intelligence*, **42**, 393–405.

Cooper, Gregory F. (1999). An overview of the representation and discovery of causal relationships using Bayesian networks. In *Computation, causation, and discovery* (ed. C. Glymour and G. F. Cooper), pp. 3–62. MIT Press, Cambridge MA.

Cooper, Gregory F. (2000). A Bayesian method for causal modelling and discovery under selection. In *Proceedings of the 16th Conference on Uncertainty in Artificial Intelligence* (ed. C. Boutilier and M. Goldszmidt), pp. 98–106. Morgan Kaufmann.

Cooper, Gregory F. and Herskovits, Edward (1992). A Bayesian method for the induction of probabilistic networks from data. *Machine Learning*, **9**, 309–347.

Corfield, David (2001). Bayesianism in mathematics. In *Foundations of Bayesianism* (ed. D. Corfield and J. Williamson), pp. 175–201. Kluwer, Dordrecht.

Cover, Thomas M. and Thomas, Joy A. (1991). *Elements of information theory.* John Wiley and Sons, New York.

Cowell, Robert G., Dawid, A. Philip, Lauritzen, Steffen L., and Spiegelhalter, David J. (1999). *Probabilistic networks and expert systems.* Springer-Verlag, Berlin.

Cristianini, Nello and Shawe-Taylor, John (2000). *Support vector machines and other kernel-based learning methods.* Cambridge University Press, Cambridge.

Csiszár, I. (1991). Why least squares and maximum entropy? An axiomatic approach to inference. *Annals of Statistics*, **19(4)**, 2032–2067.

Cussens, James (2001). Integrating probabilistic and logical reasoning. In *Foundations of Bayesianism* (ed. D. Corfield and J. Williamson), pp. 241–260. Kluwer, Dordrecht.

Dagum, Paul and Luby, Michael (1993). Approximating probabilistic inference in Bayesian belief networks is NP-hard. *Artificial Intelligence*, **60**, 141–153.

Dagum, Paul and Luby, Michael (1997). An optimal approximation algorithm for Bayesian inference. *Artificial Intelligence*, **93**, 1–27.

Dai, Honghua, Korb, Kevin, Wallace, Chris, and Wu, Xindong (1997). A study of causal discovery with weak links and small samples. In *Proceedings of the 15th International Joint Conference on Artificial Intelligence (IJCAI-97).* Nagoya, Japan, August 23-29.

Dash, Denver and Druzdzel, Marek (1999). *A fundamental inconsistency between causal discovery and causal reasoning.* Proceedings of the Joint Workshop on Conditional Independence Structures and the Workshop on Causal Interpretation of Graphical Models. The Fields Institute for Research in Mathematical Sciences, Toronto, Canada.

Dawid, A. P. (1982). The well-calibrated Bayesian. *Journal of the American Statistical Association*, **77**, 604–613. With discussion.

Dawid, A. P. (2001). Causal inference without counterfactuals. In *Foundations of Bayesianism* (ed. D. Corfield and J. Williamson), pp. 37–74. Kluwer, Dordrecht.

de Finetti, Bruno (1937). Foresight. its logical laws, its subjective sources. In *Studies in subjective probability* (Second (1980) edn) (ed. H. E. Kyburg and H. E. Smokler), pp. 53–118. Robert E. Krieger Publishing Company, Huntington, New York.

Dowe, Phil (1993). On the reduction of process causality to statistical relations. *British Journal for the Philosophy of Science*, **44**, 325–327.

Dowe, Phil (1996). Backwards causation and the direction of causal processes. *Mind*, **105**, 227–248.

Dowe, Phil (1999). The conserved quantity theory of causation and chance raising. *Philosophy of Science (Proceedings)*, **66**, S486–S501.

Dowe, Phil (2000*a*). Causality and explanation: review of Salmon. *British Journal for the Philosophy of Science*, **51**, 165–174.

Dowe, Phil (2000*b*). *Physical causation.* Cambridge University Press, Cambridge.

Drake, R., Reddy, S., and Davies, J. (1998). Nutrient intake during pregnancy and pregnancy outcome of lacto-ovo-vegetarians, fish-eaters and non-vegetarians. *Vegetarian Nutrition*, **2(2)**, 45–52.

Dung, Phan Minh (1995). On the acceptability of arguments and its fundamental role in nonmonotonic reasoning, logic programming and n-person games. *Artificial Intelligence*, **77**, 321–357.

Earman, John (1992). *Bayes or bust?* MIT Press, Cambridge MA.

Eells, Ellery (1991). *Probabilistic causality.* Cambridge University Press, Cambridge.

Fetzer, James H. (1982). Probabilistic explanations. *Philosophy of Science Association*, **2**, 194–207.

Forster, Malcolm and Sober, Elliott (1994). How to tell when simpler, more unified, or less *ad hoc* theories will provide more accurate predictions. *British Journal for the Philosophy of Science*, **45**, 1–35.

Forster, Malcolm R. (1995). Bayes and bust: simplicity as a problem for a probabilist's approach to confirmation. *British Journal for the Philosophy of Science*, **46**, 399–324.

Franklin, James (2001). Resurrecting logical probability. *Erkenntnis*, **55**, 277–305.

Freedman, David and Humphreys, Paul (1999). Are there algorithms that discover causal structure? *Synthese*, **121**, 29–54.

Friedman, Nir and Goldszmidt, Moises (1997). Sequential update of Bayesian network structure. In *Proceedings of the 13th Conference on Uncertainty in Artificial Intelligence'*, pp. 165–174.

Gaifman, H. and Snir, M. (1982). Probabilities over rich languages. *Journal of Symbolic Logic*, **47(3)**, 495–548.

Gärdenfors, Peter (1990). The dynamics of belief systems: foundations vs. coherence theories. *Revue Internationale de Philosophie*, **44**, 24–46.

Garside, G. R., Holmes, D. E., and Rhodes, P. C. (1998). Using maximum entropy to estimate missing information in tree-like causal networks. In *Proceedings of the 7th International Conference on Information Processing and Management of Uncertainty in Knowledge-Based Systems*, pp. 359–366. La Sorbonne, Paris.

Garside, G. R., Holmes, D. E., and Rhodes, P. C. (2000). Using maximum entropy to estimate missing information in tree-like causal networks. In *Advances in Fuzzy Systems—Application and Theory 20* (ed. B. Bouchon-Meunier, R. R. Yager, and L. A. Zadeh), pp. 174–184. World Scientific.

Garside, Gerald R. and Rhodes, Paul C. (1996). Computing marginal probabilities in causal multiway trees given incomplete information. *Knowledge-Based*

Systems, **9**, 315–327.

Gillies, Donald (1991). Intersubjective probability and confirmation theory. *British Journal for the Philosophy of Science*, **42**, 513–533.

Gillies, Donald (1996). *Artificial intelligence and scientific method.* Oxford University Press, Oxford.

Gillies, Donald (2000). *Philosophical theories of probability.* Routledge, London and New York.

Gillies, Donald (2002). Causality, propensity, and Bayesian networks. *Synthese*, **132**, 63–88.

Gillies, Donald (2003). Handling uncertainty in artificial intelligence, and the Bayesian controversy. In *Induction and deduction in the sciences* (ed. F. Stadler). Kluwer, Dordrecht.

Gillies, Donald (2004). Hempelian and Kuhnian approaches in the philosophy of medicine. *Studies in History and Philosophy of Biological and Biomedical Sciences*. To appear.

Gillispie, Steven B. and Perlman, Michael D. (2002). The size distribution for Markov equivalence classes of acyclic digraph models. *Artificial Intelligence*, **141**, 137–155.

Glymour, Clark (1997). A review of recent work on the foundations of causal inference. In *Causality in crisis? Statistical methods and the search for causal knowledge in the social sciences* (ed. V. R. McKim and S. Turner), pp. 201–248. University of Notre Dame Press, Notre Dame.

Glymour, Clark (2001). *The Mind's Arrows: Bayes nets and graphical causal models in psychology.* MIT Press, Cambridge MA.

Glymour, Clark (2003). Learning, prediction and causal Bayes nets. *Trends in Cognitive Sciences*, **7(1)**, 43–48.

Glymour, Clark and Cooper, Gregory F. (ed.) (1999). *Computation, causation, and discovery.* MIT Press, Cambridge MA.

Goldstick, Daniel (1971). Methodological conservatism. *American Philosophical Quarterly*, **8**, 186–191.

Goodman, Nelson (1954). *Fact, fiction and forecast* (Fourth (1983) edn). Harvard University Press.

Gopnik, Alison, Glymour, Clark, Sobel, David M., Schulz, Laura E., Kushnir, Tamar, and Danks, David (2004). A theory of causal learning in children: causal maps and Bayes nets. *Psychological Review*, **111(1)**, 3–32.

Gyftodimos, Elias and Flach, Peter (2002). Hierarchical Bayesian networks: a probabilistic reasoning model for structured domains. In *Proceedings of the ICML-2002 Workshop on Development of Representations* (ed. E. de Jong and T. Oates), pp. 23–30. University of New South Wales.

Hacking, Ian (1975). *The emergence of probability.* Cambridge University Press, Cambridge.

Hagmayer, York and Waldmann, Michael R. (2002). A constraint satisfaction model of causal learning and reasoning. In *Proceedings of the 24th Annual Conference of the Cognitive Science Society.* Erlbaum, Mahwah, NJ.

Halpern, Joseph Y. (2003). *Reasoning about uncertainty.* MIT Press, Cambridge MA.

Halpern, Joseph Y. and Koller, Daphne (1995). Representation dependence in probabilistic inference. In *Proceedings of the 14th International Joint Conference on Artificial Intelligence (IJCAI 95)* (ed. C. S. Mellish), pp. 1853–1860. Morgan Kaufmann, San Francisco CA.

Harman, Gilbert (1986). *Change in view: principles of reasoning.* MIT Press, Cambridge MA.

Hausman, Daniel M. (1999). The mathematical theory of causation: review of 'causality in crisis? statistical methods and the search for causal knowledge in the social sciences' edited by vaughn r. mckim and stephen turner'. *British Journal for the Philosophy of Science*, **50**, 151–162.

Hausman, Daniel M. and Woodward, James (1999). Independence, invariance and the causal Markov condition. *British Journal for the Philosophy of Science*, **50**, 521–583.

Hausser, R. (1999). *Foundations of computational linguistics.* Springer, Berlin.

Healey, Richard (1991). Review of Paul Horwich's 'Asymmetries in time'. *Philosophical Reviews*, **100**, 125–130.

Heckerman, David, Meek, Christopher, and Cooper, Gregory (1999). A Bayesian approach to causal discovery. In *Computation, causation, and discovery* (ed. C. Glymour and G. F. Cooper), pp. 141–165. MIT Press, Cambridge MA.

Hempel, Carl G. (1945). Studies in the logic of confirmation. In *Aspects of scientific explanation and other essays in the philosophy of science*, pp. 3–51. The Free Press (1970), New York.

Hempel, Carl G. and Oppenheim, Paul (1948). Studies in the logic of explanation. In *Theories of explanation* (ed. J. C. Pitt), pp. 9–50. Oxford University Press (1988), Oxford. With postscript.

Hesslow, Germund (1976). Discussion: two notes on the probabilistic approach to causality. *Philosophy of Science*, **43**, 290–292.

Hitchcock, Christopher Read (1993). A generalised probabilistic theory of causal relevance. *Synthese*, **97**, 335–364.

Holmes, D. E. (1999). Efficient estimation of missing information in multivalued singly connected networks using maximum entropy. In *Maximum entropy and Bayesian methods* (ed. W. von der Linden et al.), pp. 289–300. Kluwer, Dordrecht.

Holmes, D. E. and Rhodes, P. C. (1998). Reasoning with incomplete information in a multivalued multiway causal tree using the maximum entropy formalism. *International Journal of Intelligent Systems*, **13**, 841–858.

Holmes, D. E., Rhodes, P. C., and Garside, G. R. (1999). Efficient computation of marginal probabilities in multivalued causal inverted multiway trees given incomplete information. *International Journal of Intelligent Systems*, **12**, 101–111.

Howson, Colin (1976). The development of logical probability. In *Essays in memory of Imre Lakatos* (ed. R. S. Cohen, P. K. Feyerabend, and M. W. Wartofsky), Volume 39 of *Boston Studies in the Philosophy of Science*, pp. 277–298. Reidel, Dordrecht.

Howson, Colin (1997). Bayesian rules of updating. *Erkenntnis*, **45**, 195–208.

Howson, Colin (2001). The logic of Bayesian probability. In *Foundations of Bayesianism* (ed. D. Corfield and J. Williamson), pp. 137–159. Kluwer, Dordrecht.

Howson, Colin (2003). Probability and logic. *Journal of Applied Logic*, **1(3-4)**, 151–165.

Howson, Colin and Urbach, Peter (1989). *Scientific reasoning: the Bayesian approach* (Second (1993) edn). Open Court, Chicago IL.

Hume, David (1748). Enquiry into the human understanding. In *Enquiries concerning human understanding and concerning the principles of morals* (Third (1975) edn). Clarendon Press, Oxford.

Humphreys, Paul (1989). *The chances of explanation: causal explanation in the social, medical, and physical sciences.* Princeton University Press, Princeton NJ.

Humphreys, Paul (1997). A critical appraisal of causal discovery algorithms. In *Causality in crisis? Statistical methods and the search for causal knowledge in the social sciences* (ed. V. R. McKim and S. Turner), pp. 249–263. University of Notre Dame Press, Notre Dame.

Humphreys, Paul and Freedman, David (1996). The grand leap. *British Journal for the Philosophy of Science*, **47**, 113–123.

Hunter, Daniel (1989). Causality and maximum entropy updating. *International Journal in Approximate Reasoning*, **3**, 87–114.

Ide, J. S. and Cozman, F. G. (2002). Generating random Bayesian networks. In *Proceedings of the 16th Brazilian Symposium on Artificial Intelligence (SBIA 2002)*, pp. 366–375. Springer-Verlag, Berlin. Advances in Artificial Intelligence.

Jaeger, Manfred (2001). Complex probabilistic modeling with recursive relational Bayesian networks. *Annals of Mathematics and Artificial Intelligence*, **32(1-4)**, 179–220.

James, William (1907). What pragmatism means. In *Essays in pragmatism by William James* (ed. A. Castell), pp. 141–158. Hafner (1948), New York.

Jaynes, E. T. (1957). Information theory and statistical mechanics. *The Physical Review*, **106(4)**, 620–630.

Jaynes, E. T. (1973). The well-posed problem. *Foundations of Physics*, **3**, 477–492.

Jaynes, E. T. (2003). *Probability theory: the logic of science.* Cambridge University Press, Cambridge.

Jeffreys, Harold (1931). *Scientific inference* (Second (1957) edn). Cambridge University Press, Cambridge.

Jeffreys, Harold (1939). *Theory of Probability* (Third (1961) edn). Clarendon Press, Oxford.

Jim, Kam-Chuen and Giles, C. Lee (2000). Talking helps: evolving communicating agents for the predator-prey pursuit problem. *Artificial Life*, **6(3)**, 237–254.

Jordan, Michael I. (ed.) (1998). *Learning in Graphical Models.* MIT Press (1999), Cambridge MA.

Kakas, Antonis C., Kowalski, Robert, and Toni, Francesca (1998). The role of abduction in logic programming. In *Handbook of logic in artificial intelligence and logic programming* (ed. D. M. Gabbay, C. J. Hogger, and J. A. Robinson), Volume 5, pp. 235–324. Oxford University Press, Oxford.

Kant, Immanuel (1781). *Critique of pure reason* (Second (1787) edn). Macmillan (1929). Trans. Norman Kemp Smith.

Karimi, Kamran and Hamilton, Howard J. (2000). Finding temporal relations: causal Bayesian networks vs. C4.5. In *Proceedings of the 12th International Symposium on Methodologies for Intelligent System (ISMIS2000).*

Karimi, Kamran and Hamilton, Howard J. (2001). Learning causal rules. Technical Report CS-2001-03, Department of Computer Science, University of Regina, Saskatchewan, Canada.

Keynes, John Maynard (1921). *A treatise on probability.* Macmillan (1948), London.

Koller, Daphne and Pfeffer, Avi (1997). Object-oriented Bayesian networks. In *Proceedings of the 13th Annual Conference on Uncertainty in Artificial Intelligence*, pp. 302–313.

Kolmogorov, A. N. (1933). *The foundations of the theory of probability.* Chelsea Publishing Company (1950), New York.

Korb, Kevin B. (1999). Probabilistic causal structure. In *Causation and laws of nature* (ed. H. Sankey), pp. 265–311. Kluwer, Dordrecht.

Korb, Kevin B., Hope, Lucas R., and Hughes, Michelle J. (2001). The evaluation of predictive learners: some theoretical and empirical results. In *Proceedings of the 12th European Conference on Machine Learning* (ed. L. D. Raedt and P. Flach), Volume 2167 of *Lecture Notes in Computer Science*, pp. 276–287. Springer, Berlin.

Korb, Kevin B. and Nicholson, Ann E. (2003). *Bayesian artificial intelligence.* Chapman and Hall / CRC Press, London.

Kuhn, Thomas S. (1962). *The structure of scientific revolutions* (Second (1970) edn). University of Chicago Press, Chicago IL.

Kvasz, Ladislav (2000). Changes of language in the development of mathematics. *Philosophia Mathematica*, **8(3)**, 47–83.

Kwoh, Chee-Keong and Gillies, Duncan F. (1996). Using hidden nodes in Bayesian networks. *Artificial Intelligence*, **88**, 1–38.

Lad, Frank (1999). Assessing the foundation for Bayesian networks: a challenge to the principles and the practice. *Soft Computing*, **3(3)**, 174–180.

Lagnado, David A. and Sloman, Steven (2004). The advantage of timely intervention. *Journal of Experimental Psychology: Learning, Memory and Cognition*, **30(4)**. To appear.

Lakatos, Imre (1968). Changes in the problem of inductive logic. In *The prob-*

lem of inductive logic: Proceedings of the International Colloquium in the Philosophy of Science (London 1965) (ed. I. Lakatos), Volume 2, pp. 315–417. North-Holland, Amsterdam.

Lam, Wai and Bacchus, Fahiem (1994*a*). Learning Bayesian belief networks: an approach based on the MDL principle. *Computational Intelligence*, **10(4)**, 269–293.

Lam, Wai and Bacchus, Fahiem (1994*b*). Using new data to refine a Bayesian network. In *Proceedings of the 10th Conference on Uncertainty in Artificial Intelligence*, pp. 383–390.

Laplace, Pierre Simon marquis de (1814). *A philosophical essay on probabilities.* Dover (1951), New York.

Laudan, Larry (1981). A confutation of convergent realism. *Philosophy of Science*, **48(1)**, 19–48.

Lauritzen, Steffen L. (1996). *Graphical models.* Clarendon Press, Oxford.

Lauritzen, S. L. and Spiegelhalter, D. J. (1988). Local computation with probabilities in graphical structures and their applications to expert systems. *Journal of the Royal Statistical Society Series B*, **50(2)**, 157–254. With discussion.

Lehrer, Keith (1974). *Knowledge.* Clarendon Press, Oxford.

Lehrer, Keith (1978). Why not scepticism? In *Essays on knowledge and justification* (ed. G. Pappas and M. Swain), pp. 346–363. Cornell University Press, Ithaca NY.

Lemmer, John F. (1996). The causal Markov condition, fact or artifact? *SIGART Bulletin*, **7(3)**, 3–16.

Lewis, David K. (1973). Causation. In *Philosophical papers*, Volume 2, pp. 159–213. Oxford University Press (1986), Oxford.

Lewis, David K. (1980). A subjectivist's guide to objective chance. In *Philosophical papers*, Volume 2, pp. 83–132. Oxford University Press (1986), Oxford.

Lewis, David K. (1986). Causal explanation. In *Philosophical papers*, Volume 2, pp. 214–240. Oxford University Press (1986), Oxford.

Lewis, David K. (2000). Causation as influence. *Journal of Philosophy*, **97(4)**, 182–197.

Lukasiewicz, Jan (1913). Logical foundations of probability theory. In *Jan Lukasiewicz' selected works* (ed. L. Borkowski), pp. 16–63. North-Holland (1970), Amsterdam.

Lukasiewicz, Thomas (2000). Credal networks under maximum entropy. In *Proceedings of the 16th Annual Conference in Uncertainty in Artificial Intelligence* (ed. C. Boutilier and M. Goldszmidt), pp. 363–370. Morgan Kaufmann, San Francisco CA.

Lycan, William G. (1988). *Judgement and justification.* Cambridge University Press, Cambridge.

Mani, Subramani and Cooper, Gregory F. (1999). A study in causal discovery from population-based infant birth and death records. In *Proceedings of the AMIA Annual Fall Symposium*, pp. 315–319. Hanley and Belfus Publishers, Philadelphia PA.

Mani, Subramani and Cooper, Gregory F. (2000). Causal discovery from medical textual data. In *Proceedings of the AMIA Annual Fall Symposium*, pp. 542–546. Hanley and Belfus Publishers, Philadelphia PA.

Mani, Subramani and Cooper, Gregory F. (2001). Simulation study of three related causal data mining algorithms. In *Proceedings of the International Workshop on Artificial Intelligence and Statistics*, pp. 73–80. Morgan Kaufmann, San Francisco CA.

Markham, M. J. and Rhodes, P. C. (1999). Maximising entropy to deduce an initial probability distribution for a causal network. *International Journal of Uncertainty, Fuzzyness and Knowledge-Based Systems*, **7(1)**, 63–68.

McKim, Vaughn R. and Turner, Stephen (1997). *Causality in crisis? Statistical methods and the search for causal knowledge in the social sciences.* University of Notre Dame Press, Notre Dame.

Melancon, G., Dutour, I., and Bousquet-Melou, M. (2000). Random generation of dags for graph drawing. Technical Report INS-R0005, Centrum voor Wiskunde en Informatica.

Melis, Erica (1998). AI techniques in proof planning. In *Proceedings of the 13th European Conference on Artificial Intelligence* (ed. H. Prade), pp. 494–498. John Wiley, Chichester.

Mellor, D. H. (1988). On raising the chances of effects. In *Probability and causality: essays in honour of Wesley C. Salmon* (ed. J. Fetzer). Reidel, Dordrecht.

Mellor, D. H. (1995). *The facts of causation.* Routledge, London and New York.

Mendelson, Elliott (1964). *Introduction to mathematical logic* (Fourth (1997) edn). Chapman and Hall, London.

Menzies, Peter (1996). Probabilistic causation and the pre-emption problem. *Mind*, **105**, 85–117.

Menzies, Peter (2003). Is causation a genuine relation? In *Real metaphysics: festschrift for D. H. Mellor* (ed. G. Rodriguez-Pereyra and H. Lillehammer). Routledge, London.

Menzies, Peter and Price, Huw (1993). Causation as a secondary quality. *British Journal for the Philosophy of Science*, **44**, 187–203.

Mill, John Stuart (1843). *A system of logic, ratiocinative and inductive: being a connected view of the principles of evidence and the methods of scientific investigation* (Eighth (1874) edn). Harper and Brothers, New York.

Miller, David (1994). *Critical rationalism: a restatement and defence.* Open Court, Chicago IL.

Muggleton, Stephen (1996). Stochastic logic programs. In *Advances in inductive logic programming* (ed. L. D. Raedt), pp. 254–264. IOS Press, Amsterdam.

Muggleton, Stephen and de Raedt, Luc (1994). Inductive logic programming: theory and methods. *Journal of Logic Programming*, **19–20**, 629–679.

Neal, Radford M. (2000). On deducing conditional independence from d-separation in causal graphs with feedback. *Journal of Artificial Intelligence Research*, **12**, 87–91.

Neapolitan, Richard E. (1990). *Probabilistic reasoning in expert systems: theory and algorithms.* Wiley, New York.

Neapolitan, Richard E. (2003). *Learning Bayesian networks.* Pearson / Prentice Hall, Upper Saddle River NJ.

Neil, Martin, Fenton, Norman, and Neilsen, Lars (2000). Building large-scale Bayesian networks. *The Knowledge Engineering Review*, **15(3)**, 257–284.

Nilsson, Nils J. (1986). Probabilistic logic. *Artificial Intelligence*, **28**, 71–87.

Nilsson, Ulf and Maluszyński, Jan (1990). *Logic, programming and prolog.* John Wiley and Sons, Chichester.

Noordhof, Paul (1998). Causation, probability and chance, review of 'The facts of causation' by D. H. Mellor. *Mind*, **107(428)**, 855–875.

Papadimitriou, Christos H. (1994). *Computational complexity.* Addison Wesley, Reading MA.

Papineau, David (1994). The virtues of randomisation. *British Journal for the Philosophy of Science*, **45**, 437–450.

Paris, J. B. (1994). *The uncertain reasoner's companion.* Cambridge University Press, Cambridge.

Paris, J. B. and Vencovská, A. (1990). A note on the inevitability of maximum entropy. *International Journal of Approximate Reasoning*, **4**, 181–223.

Paris, J. B. and Vencovská, A. (1997). In defence of the maximum entropy inference process. *International Journal of Approximate Reasoning*, **17**, 77–103.

Paris, J. B. and Vencovská, A. (2001). Common sense and stochastic independence. In *Foundations of Bayesianism* (ed. D. Corfield and J. Williamson), pp. 203–240. Kluwer, Dordrecht.

Pearl, Judea (1988). *Probabilistic reasoning in intelligent systems: networks of plausible inference.* Morgan Kaufmann, San Mateo CA.

Pearl, Judea (1999). Graphs, structural models, and causality. In *Computation, causation, and discovery* (ed. C. Glymour and G. F. Cooper), pp. 95–138. MIT Press, Cambridge MA.

Pearl, Judea (2000). *Causality: models, reasoning, and inference.* Cambridge University Press, Cambridge.

Pearl, Judea, Geiger, Dan, and Verma, Thomas (1990). The logic of influence diagrams. In *Influence diagrams, belief nets and decision analysis* (ed. R. M. Oliver and J. Q. Smith), pp. 67–87. Wiley, Chichester.

Peña, J. M., Lozano, J. A., and Larrañaga, P. (2002). Learning recursive Bayesian multinets for clustering by means of constructive induction. *Machine Learning*, **47(1)**, 63–90.

Pólya, George (1945). *How to solve it* (Second edn). Penguin (1990).

Pólya, George (1954*a*). *Induction and analogy in mathematics*, Volume 1 of *Mathematics and plausible reasoning.* Princeton University Press, Princeton NJ.

Pólya, George (1954*b*). *Patterns of plausible inference*, Volume 2 of *Mathematics and plausible reasoning.* Princeton University Press, Princeton NJ.

Popper, Karl R. (1934). *The Logic of Scientific Discovery.* Routledge (1999), London. With new appendices of 1959.

Popper, Karl R. (1959). The propensity interpretation of probability. *British Journal for the Philosophy of Science*, **10**, 25–42.

Popper, Karl R. (1983). *Realism and the aim of science.* Hutchinson, London.

Popper, Karl R. (1990). *A world of propensities.* Thoemmes, Bristol.

Price, Huw (1991). Agency and probabilistic causality. *British Journal for the Philosophy of Science*, **42**, 157–176.

Price, Huw (1992*a*). Agency and causal asymmetry. *Mind*, **101**, 501–520.

Price, Huw (1992*b*). The direction of causation: Ramsey's ultimate contingency. *Philosophy of Science Association*, **1992(2)**, 253–267.

Quine, Willard Van Orman (1960). *Word and object.* MIT Press and John Wiley, Cambridge MA.

Railton, Peter (1978). A deductive-nomological model of probabilistic explanation. In *Theories of explanation* (ed. J. C. Pitt), pp. 119–135. Oxford University Press (1988), Oxford.

Ramsey, Frank Plumpton (1926). Truth and probability. In *Studies in subjective probability* (Second (1980) edn) (ed. H. E. Kyburg and H. E. Smokler), pp. 23–52. Robert E. Krieger Publishing Company, Huntington, New York.

Ramsey, Frank Plumpton (1929). General propositions and causality. In *F. P. Ramsey: philosophical papers* (ed. D. H. Mellor), pp. 145–163. Cambridge University Press (1990), Cambridge.

Reichenbach, Hans (1935). *The theory of probability: an inquiry into the logical and mathematical foundations of the calculus of probability.* University of California Press (1949), Berkeley and Los Angeles. Trans. Ernest H. Hutten and Maria Reichenbach.

Reichenbach, Hans (1956). *The direction of time.* University of California Press (1971), Berkeley and Los Angeles.

Rhodes, P. C. and Garside, G. R. (1995). Using maximum entropy to compute marginal probabilities in a causal binary tree need not take exponential time. In *Proceedings of ECSQARU'95: Symbolic and Quantitative Approaches to Reasoning and Uncertainty* (ed. C. Froidevaux and J. Kohlas), pp. 352–363. Springer, Berlin.

Rhodes, P. C. and Garside, G. R. (1998). Computing marginal probabilities in causal inverted binary trees given incomplete information. *Knowledge-Based Systems*, **10**, 213–224.

Richardson, Julian and Bundy, Alan (1999). Proof planning methods as schemas. Technical Report 949, Informatics Department, University of Edinburgh.

Rissanen, Jorma (1978). Modeling by shortest data description. *Automatica*, **14**, 465–471.

Rosenkrantz, Roger D. (1977). *Inference, method and decision: towards a Bayesian philosophy of science.* Reidel, Dordrecht.

Ross, L. and Anderson, C. A. (1982). Shortcoming in the attribution process: on the origins and maintenance of erroneous social assessments. In *Judgements under uncertainty: heuristics and biases* (ed. D. Kahneman, P. Slovic, and A. Tversky), pp. 129–152. Cambridge University Press, Cambridge.

Rott, Hans (1999). Coherence and conservatism in the dynamics of belief. *Erkenntnis*, **50**, 387–412.

Russell, Bertrand (1913). On the notion of cause. *Proceedings of the Aristotelian Society*, **13**, 1–26.

Salmon, Wesley C. (1971). Statistical explanation. In *Statistical explanation and statistical relevance*, pp. 29–88. University of Pittsburgh Press, Pittsburgh PA.

Salmon, Wesley C. (1980*a*). Causality: production and propagation. In *Causation* (ed. E. Sosa and M. Tooley). Oxford University Press, Oxford.

Salmon, Wesley C. (1980*b*). Probabilistic causality. In *Causality and explanation*, pp. 208–232. Oxford University Press (1988), Oxford.

Salmon, Wesley C. (1984). *Scientific explanation and the causal structure of the world.* Princeton University Press, Princeton NJ.

Salmon, Wesley C. (1997). Causality and explanation: a reply to two critiques. *Philosophy of Science*, **64(3)**, 461–477.

Salmon, Wesley C. (1998). *Causality and explanation.* Oxford University Press, Oxford.

Savitt, Steven F. (1996). The direction of time. *British Journal for the Philosophy of Science*, **47**, 347–370.

Scheines, Richard (1997). An introduction to causal inference. In *Causality in crisis? Statistical methods and the search for causal knowledge in the social sciences* (ed. V. R. McKim and S. Turner), pp. 185–199. University of Notre Dame Press, Notre Dame.

Schramm, Manfred and Fronhöfer, Bertram (2002). Completing incomplete Bayesian networks. In *Proceedings of the Workshop on Conditionals, Information and Inference*, pp. 231–244. FernUniversität 13–15 May.

Seidenfeld, Teddy (1979). Why I am not an objective Bayesian. *Theory and Decision*, **11**, 413–440.

Shafer, Glenn (1996). *The art of causal conjecture.* MIT Press, Cambridge MA.

Shafer, Glenn (1999). Causal conjecture. In *Causal models and intelligent data management* (ed. A. Gammerman), pp. 17–32. Springer, Berlin.

Shannon, Claude (1948). A mathematical theory of communication. *The Bell System Technical Journal*, **27**, 379–423 and 623–656.

Shannon, Claude and Weaver, Warren (1949). *The mathematical theory of communication.* University of Illinois Press (1964), Urbana.

Shimony, Solomon E. and Domshlak, Carmel (2003). Complexity of probabilistic reasoning in directed-path singly-connected Bayes networks. *Artificial Intelligence*, **151**, 213–225.

Shore, J. E. and Johnson, R. W. (1980). Axiomatic derivation of the principle of maximum entropy and the principle of minimum cross-entropy. *IEEE Transactions on Information Theory*, **IT-26**, 26–37.

Sklar, Lawrence (1975). Methodological conservatism. *Philosophical Review*, **84**, 374–400.

Skyrms, Brian (1980). *Causal necessity: a pragmatic investigation of the necessity of laws.* Yale University Press, New Haven.

Smith, J. W., Everhart, J. E., Dickson, W. C., Knowler, W. C., , and Johannes, R. S. (1988). Using the ADAP learning algorithm to forecast the onset of diabetes mellitus. In *Proceedings of the Symposium on Computer Applications and Medical Care*, pp. 261–265. IEEE Computer Society Press.

Sober, Elliott (1975). *Simplicity.* Oxford University Press, Oxford.

Sober, Elliott (1988). The principle of the common cause. In *Probability and causality: essays in honour of Wesley C. Salmon* (ed. J. H. Fetzer), pp. 211–228. Reidel, Dordrecht.

Sober, Elliott (2001). Venetian sea levels, British bread prices, and the principle of the common cause. *British Journal for the Philosophy of Science*, **52**, 331–346.

Sosa, Ernest and Tooley, Michael (ed.) (1993). *Causation.* Oxford University Press, Oxford.

Spirtes, Peter (1995). Directed cyclic graphical representation of feedback models. In *Proceedings of the 11th Annual Conference on Uncertainty in Artificial Intelligence*, pp. 491–498. Morgan Kaufmann, Montreal.

Spirtes, Peter, Glymour, Clark, and Scheines, Richard (1993). *Causation, Prediction, and Search* (Second (2000) edn). MIT Press, Cambridge MA.

Sucar, L. Enrique and Gillies, Duncan F. (1994). Probabilistic reasoning in high-level vision. *Image and Vision Computing*, **12(1)**, 42–60.

Sucar, L. Enrique, Gillies, Duncan F., and Gillies, Donald A. (1993). Objective probabilities in expert systems. *Artificial Intelligence*, **61**, 187–208.

Sundaram, Rangarajan K (1996). *A first course in optimisation theory.* Cambridge University Press, Cambridge.

Suppes, Patrick (1970). *A probabilistic theory of causality.* North-Holland, Amsterdam.

Tenenbaum, Joshua B. and Griffiths, Thomas L. (2001). Structure learning in human causal induction. In *Advances in Neural Information Processing Systems* (ed. T. Leen, T. Dietterich, and V. Tresp), Volume 13, pp. 59–65. MIT Press, Cambridge MA.

Thagard, Paul (1988). *Computational Philosophy of Science.* MIT Press / Bradford Books, Cambridge MA.

Tikochinsky, Y., Tishby, N. Z., and Levine, R. D. (1984). Consistent inference of probabilities for reproducible experiments. *Physical Review Letters*, **52**, 1357–1360.

Tong, Simon and Koller, Daphne (2001). Active learning for structure in Bayesian networks. In *Proceedings of the 17th International Joint Conference on Artificial Intelligence* (ed. B. Nebel), pp. 863–869. Morgan Kaufmann, San Francisco CA.

Tooley, M. (1987). *Causation: a realist approach.* Clarendon Press, Oxford.

Tversky, Amos and Kahneman, Daniel (1977). Causal thinking in judgement under uncertainty. In *Basic problems in methodology and linguistics* (ed. R. Butts and J. Hintikka), pp. 167–190. Reidel, Dordrecht.

Uffink, Jos (1995). Can the maximum entropy principle be explained as a consistency requirement? *Studies in History and Philosophy of Modern Physics*, **26B**, 223–261.

Uffink, Jos (1996). The constraint rule of the maximum entropy principle. *Studies in History and Philosophy of Modern Physics*, **27**, 47–79.

Valtorta, Marco, Kim, Young-Gyun, and Vomlel, Jiri (2002). Soft evidential update for probabilistic multiagent systems. *International Journal of Approximate Reasoning*, **29**, 71–106.

van Fraassen, Bas C. (1980). *The scientific image.* Clarendon Press, Oxford.

Vapnik, Vladimir N. (1995). *The nature of statistical learning theory* (Second (2000) edn). Springer-Verlag, Berlin.

Venn, John (1866). *Logic of chance: an essay on the foundations and province of the theory of probability.* Macmillan, London.

Verma, T. and Pearl, J. (1988). Causal networks: semantics and expressiveness. In *Proceedings of the 4th Annual Conference on Uncertainty in Artificial Intelligence* (ed. R. D. Shachter, T. S. Levitt, L. N. Kanal, and J. F. Lemmer), pp. 69–78. North-Holland (1990), Amsterdam.

Verma, T. and Pearl, J. (1990). Equivalence and synthesis of causal models. In *Proceedings of the 6th Annual Conference on Uncertainty in Artificial Intelligence* (ed. P. P. Bonissone, M. Henrion, L. N. Kanal, and J. F. Lemmer), pp. 255–268. North-Holland, Amsterdam.

von Mises, Richard (1928). *Probability, statistics and truth* (Second (1957) edn). Allen and Unwin, London.

von Mises, Richard (1964). *Mathematical theory of probability and statistics.* Academic Press, New York.

Waldmann, Michael R. (2001). Predictive versus diagnostic causal learning: evidence from an overshadowing paradigm. *Psychonomic Bulletin and Review*, **8**, 600–608.

Waldmann, Michael R. and Martignon, Laura (1998). A Bayesian network model of causal learning. In *Proceedings of the 20th Annual Conference of the Cognitive Science Society* (ed. M. A. Gernsbacher and S. J. Derry), pp. 1102–1107. Erlbaum, Mahwah NJ.

Wallace, C. S. and Boulton, D. L. (1968). An information measure for classification. *The Computer Journal*, **11**, 185–194.

Wallace, Chris S. and Korb, Kevin B. (1999). Learning linear causal models by MML sampling. In *Causal models and intelligent data management* (ed. A. Gammerman), pp. 88–111. Springer, Berlin.

Wendelken, Carter and Shastri, Lokendra (2000). Probabilistic inference and learning in a connectionist causal network. In *Proceedings of the Second International Symposium on Neural Computation.* Berlin, May.

Williams, Peter M. (1980). Bayesian conditionalisation and the principle of minimum information. *British Journal for the Philosophy of Science*, **31**,

131–144.

Williamson, Jon (1999). Countable additivity and subjective probability. *British Journal for the Philosophy of Science*, **50(3)**, 401–416.

Williamson, Jon (2000*a*). Approximating discrete probability distributions with Bayesian networks. In *Proceedings of the International Conference on Artificial Intelligence in Science and Technology*, pp. 106–114. Hobart Tasmania, 16–20 December.

Williamson, Jon (2000*b*). A probabilistic approach to diagnosis. In *Proceedings of the 11th International Workshop on Principles of Diagnosis (DX-00)*. Morelia, Michoacen, Mexico, 8–11 June.

Williamson, Jon (2001*a*). Bayesian networks for logical reasoning. In *Proceedings of the AAAI Fall Symposium on Using Uncertainty within Computation* (ed. C. Gomes and T. Walsh), pp. 136–143. AAAI Press.

Williamson, Jon (2001*b*). Foundations for Bayesian networks. In *Foundations of Bayesianism* (ed. D. Corfield and J. Williamson), pp. 75–115. Kluwer, Dordrecht.

Williamson, Jon (2002*a*). Maximising entropy efficiently. *Electronic Transactions in Artificial Intelligence Journal*, **6**. www.etaij.org.

Williamson, Jon (2002*b*). Probability logic. In *Handbook of the logic of argument and inference: the turn toward the practical* (ed. D. Gabbay, R. Johnson, H. J. Ohlbach, and J. Woods), pp. 397–424. Elsevier, Amsterdam.

Williamson, Jon (2003*a*). Abduction and its distinctions: review of 'Abduction, reason, and science: processes of discovery' by Lorenzo Magnani. *British Journal for the Philosophy of Science*, **54(2)**, 353–358.

Williamson, Jon (2003*b*). Bayesianism and language change. *Journal of Logic, Language and Information*, **12(1)**, 53–97.

Williamson, Jon (2004*a*). Causality. In *Handbook of Philosophical Logic* (ed. D. Gabbay and F. Guenthner), Volume 13. Kluwer, Dordrecht. To appear.

Williamson, Jon (2004*b*). A dynamic interaction between machine learning and the philosophy of science. *Minds and Machines*. To appear.

Williamson, Jon and Gabbay, Dov (2004). Recursive causality in Bayesian networks and self-fibring networks. In *Laws and models in the sciences* (ed. D. Gillies). King's College Publications, London.

Woodward, James (1997). Causal models, probabilities, and invariance. In *Causality in crisis? Statistical methods and the search for causal knowledge in the social sciences* (ed. V. R. McKim and S. Turner), pp. 265–315. University of Notre Dame Press, Notre Dame.

Yoo, Changwon, Thorsson, V., and Cooper, G. (2002). Discovery of causal relationships in a gene-regulation pathway from a mixture of experimental and observational DNA microarray data. In *Proceedings of the Pacific Symposium on Biocomputing*, pp. 498–509. World Scientific, New Jersey.

Yule, G. Udny (1926). Why do we sometimes get nonsense-correlations between time series? A study in sampling and the nature of time-series. *Journal of the Royal Statistical Society*, **89(1)**, 1–63.

INDEX